Group
Development
in Practice

Group Development in Practice

Guidance for
Clinicians and Researchers
on Stages and Dynamics of Change

Virginia Brabender and April Fallon

American Psychological Association
Washington, DC

Published by
American Psychological Association
750 First Street, NE
Washington, DC 20002
www.apa.org

To order
APA Order Department
P.O. Box 92984
Washington, DC 20090-2984
Tel: (800) 374-2721; Direct: (202) 336-5510
Fax: (202) 336-5502; TDD/TTY: (202) 336-6123
Online: www.apa.org/books/
E-mail: order@apa.org

In the U.K., Europe, Africa, and the Middle East, copies may be ordered from
American Psychological Association
3 Henrietta Street
Covent Garden, London
WC2E 8LU England

Typeset in Goudy by Steve McDougal, Mechanicsville, MD

Printer: Book-Mart Press, Inc., North Bergen, NJ
Cover Designer: Naylor Design, Washington, DC
Technical/Production Editor: Harriet Kaplan

The opinions and statements published are the responsibility of the authors, and such opinions and statements do not necessarily represent the policies of the American Psychological Association.

Library of Congress Cataloging-in-Publication Data

Brabender, Virginia.
  Group development in practice : guidance for clinicians and researchers on stages and dynamics of change / Virginia Brabender and April Fallon. — 1st ed.
      p. ; cm.
  Includes bibliographical references and index.
  ISBN-13: 978-1-4338-0408-3
  ISBN-10: 1-4338-0408-5
  1. Group psychotherapy. I. Fallon, April. II. American Psychological Association. III. Title.
  [DNLM: 1. Psychotherapy, Group—methods. 2. Group Processes. 3. Models, Psychological. 4. Psychoanalytic Theory. WM 430 B795g 2009]
  RC488.B725 2009
  616.89'152—dc22   2008021015

British Library Cataloguing-in-Publication Data
A CIP record is available from the British Library.

Printed in the United States of America
First Edition

To my Dad, Richard F. Brabender. Dad, I have been proud of you all of my life, but never more so than in the past 5 years in which you have dealt with Mom's illness in such a selfless way.

—*Virginia Brabender*

To important male figures who have mentored me in my personal and professional life—my father, Theodore James Fallon; my thesis advisor, Paul Rozin; and my undergraduate advisor and teacher, Herbert Klions.

—*April Fallon*

CONTENTS

ACKNOWLEDGMENTS

We thank the patients, staff, and administration of Friends Hospital, Philadelphia, Pennsylvania, where 25 years ago we were given the opportunity to work in an environment that both valued group psychotherapy and was committed to the continuing training of those who provided it. Our current affiliations—Widener University, Chester, Pennsylvania (Virginia Brabender) and Fielding Graduate University, Santa Barbara, California (April Fallon)—are ones that provide the intellectual climates for scholarly growth. We acknowledge the wise and careful editorial input of Dennis Debiak, Annie Yocum, Amanda Swartz, and Grace Jacobsen as well as the generous and cheerfully offered secretarial support of Carol Bricklin and Jeanne Nolan. We thank the very helpful assistance of the American Psychological Association Books editorial staff, including Tyler Aune, Harriet Kaplan, Susan Reynolds, Margaret Sullivan, and Debbie Felder. Much appreciation goes to Yvonne Agazarian, who helped us capture the essence of systems-centered theory. Our families—a delightfully blended group of eight—nurtured us not only with their love for us but also with their fondness for one another.

Group
Development
in Practice

1

INTRODUCTION TO STAGE DEVELOPMENT IN PSYCHOTHERAPY GROUPS

The idea that groups follow a series of phases or stages is not, relatively speaking, new. What is new is that researchers and clinicians are becoming more aware of the benefits of a progressive stage or developmental approach to group psychotherapy and are beginning to refine their methods of studying and applying group developmental models in practice. Our own empirical and clinical work over a combined period of 50 years has led us to develop a five-stage model of group development that we present in this book. We believe that this model has practical value to group psychotherapists and heuristic value to theorists and researchers alike.

As our clinical experience and our review of the extant theory and research on group development attest, group psychotherapy is a more effective treatment when the therapist considers group developmental issues in concert with the contextual variables articulated in the empirical literature. We believe that this is true not only for traditional unstructured long-term groups but also for more focused or time-limited groups, such as cognitive–behavioral groups for specific disorders. Group development has implications for how therapists introduce groups to their members, how they structure (or do not structure) group sessions, how they lead groups through the various phases or stages of development, and ultimately how successful groups are in achieving the goals of their members.

Our book is written for experienced group psychotherapists, for therapists who are relatively new to group psychotherapy, and for graduate students and others in training, all of whom may come from various clinical disciplines. These disciplines include clinical and counseling psychology, clinical social work, psychiatry, couples and family therapy, and pastoral counseling, to name a few. We include in this audience therapists who conduct traditional long-term unstructured groups as well as those who lead, or plan to lead, focused time-limited groups in inpatient and outpatient settings as well as in the newly developing world of cybergroups. This book is also written for researchers and those interested in developing or refining theoretical approaches to group psychotherapy.

Our primary goal is to provide readers with in-depth coverage of group development, historically and contemporaneously, focusing on theory; research; and, of course, practice. We review the empirical and theoretical literature, describe others' models of group development, and present the five-stage model of group development that has evolved for us as we have integrated theory, research, and practice over the years. We conclude by identifying significant gaps in theory and research to provide direction for future work in these areas. Although we describe the literature on child and adolescent groups that bears on our topic, this book is primarily about group development as it pertains to adult psychotherapy groups.

BENEFITS OF A PROGRESSIVE STAGE APPROACH FOR GROUP PSYCHOTHERAPISTS

We believe that a progressive stage or developmental approach to group psychotherapy has many benefits and can be applied by group therapists operating from very different theoretical perspectives. Although textbooks and other books on group psychotherapy or counseling typically include a chapter on development as it occurs in groups, we believe that the topic is too important for such a brief treatment.

Even at this later stage of our careers, we have found that the study of group development enriches our thinking about our work in groups in a variety of ways. Each of these will be mentioned briefly here and then described more fully in chapter 2. A developmental perspective on group psychotherapy

- helps the therapist make stronger links between group process and outcome;
- focuses the therapist's attention on the role of time in the psychological lives of group members and the group as a whole;

- stimulates the therapist's awareness of the parallels (or lack thereof) between individual and group development, individual psychology, and group psychology;
- allows the therapist a way to identify and understand all parts composing the group systemically: the individual, the group leader, the group as a whole, subgroups, the context in which the group takes place, and the larger context for both members and leaders (e.g., family, culture);
- draws attention to the contribution of various theoretical perspectives that can aid therapists in working with the type of groups they lead; and
- contributes to the growth of the group psychotherapist, a process that can be further enhanced by the use of supervision, psychotherapy, or both.

In addition, a stage or developmental perspective can be applied not only to traditional unstructured groups but also to more focused groups (e.g., behavioral groups for social phobia) and to groups emerging from postmodern frameworks (e.g., social constructionism, narrative psychology). Furthermore, this perspective is compatible with contemporary intellectual paradigms such as chaos theory and complexity theory and is congruent with a positive psychology perspective.

In terms of training, developmental approaches to group psychotherapy are extremely helpful in that they assist students in placing the bewildering arrays of information in context and provide a framework for organizing and using this information. For all of these reasons, group psychotherapists, regardless of their theoretical orientation or experience level, can benefit from obtaining knowledge of how groups develop and from learning the skills needed to effect changes from a developmental point of view.

ORIGINS OF OUR FIVE-STAGE APPROACH TO GROUP DEVELOPMENT

Group development captivated us early in our practice of group psychotherapy. Virginia Brabender was a newly minted clinician working in a private psychiatric hospital and was soon joined by April Fallon, who was in her clinical psychology internship. Like so many beginning group psychotherapists at the time (see Butler & Fuhriman, 1986), little formal academic training underpinned our initial group experiences.

Didactic training during clinical psychology internships exposed both of us to the writings of Turquet (1975), Le Bon (1895/1960), Ezriel (1952), Whitaker (1958), and Bion (1961), whose work we explore in depth in chapters 3 and 4 of this volume. These writers outlined group level dynamics that they did not see at the time as having a developmental aspect. That is, for these writers, particularly Bion, groups move from one dynamic pattern to another without exhibiting any particular type of progression. Their descriptions accorded with some of our experiences and did not capture others.

The type of group we conducted in this inpatient setting was limited to eight sessions. A cohort of members entered shortly after admittance and remained in the group for 2 weeks, four sessions per week, with sessions lasting 90 minutes. Seeing one group follow another, all with the same structural features in regard to time and place, facilitated our discernment of patterns across the groups.

Reflecting on our continued study of group therapy, initially we were awestruck to witness firsthand the aptness of the descriptions provided by writers who focused on the group as a whole. For example, Bion's dependency and fight–flight basic assumptions came alive in the groups we led. However, another set of phenomena seemed equally compelling: The 2-week groups, one after another, seemed to manifest various patterns over the life of the group in an orderly way.

In the beginning of these co-led time-limited groups, members showed an almost exaggerated politeness toward one another. They also retreated from immediate issues while continually entreating the therapist to provide guidance and succor. This set of behaviors appeared to correspond closely to Bion's dependent basic assumption group (further described in chaps. 3 and 4). We came to realize that this period in the life of the group was simply that—a phase the group was going through.

Following this rather staid, nonconfrontational but enthusiastic era was another in which members were increasingly testy with one another and eventually dissatisfied with us. Although we had the intellectual satisfaction of seeing Bion's fight–flight assumption group in action, we worried whether it was possible for members to derive benefit from a therapeutic experience that had turned so sour. Our apprehensions were not borne out. Our groups moved into a different period characterized by more intensive psychological work, heightened self-disclosure, and a greater balance between positive and negative feelings. For some groups, the ending of the group appeared to be a focal point of the last sessions; for others, it merely continued in this serious work mode.

Seeing a pattern appear where neither of us expected one was mysterious and exciting. Yet, amidst this orderliness in how the groups seemed to change, variation was present. Each group had its own style of handling issues and its own way of diffusing tensions. Some of the features that differentiated our groups appeared to have significance for what the group could accomplish over its life. That is, a group's way of pursuing a given theme in one period seemed to affect the depth of its engagement with other successive themes. For example, groups showed some differences in how they pursued the fight–flight period. Some groups reached a pitch of hostility against us, and when they did, they seemed to move into a more productive work period thereafter. Other groups showed a more desultory hostility, lacking vibrancy and direction, and were less able to enter assiduously into a work period.

When we began to immerse ourselves more deeply in the group development literature, we were both chagrined and gratified to discover that we were less trailblazing than we had imagined. In fact, many had observed the patterns that we noticed, and these observers of group life worked in a variety of different settings—inpatient units, outpatient clinics, private practices, academia, training groups, and organizations. We learned that a number of well-articulated models of group development existed (described in depth in chap. 3, this volume), some of which went far beyond our own construction of stages and their relationship to one another. Others had also observed that despite an orderly progression, significant variation exists from group to group, even in the same setting.

Later in our careers, we both conducted outpatient psychotherapy groups. Our groups were long term, with some members remaining in the group for a number of years. The opportunities to compare these groups with our short-term group experiences as well as to garner the developmental observations of group psychotherapists attending our workshops and presentations over the years have provided a foundation for the five-stage model presented in this text. Within the group developmental literature, the terms *phase* and *stage* are used, sometimes interchangeably. In our earlier writings, we have used both terms. However, for the purposes of our current model, we use the term *stage* because it captures certain properties of each developmental period more completely. Whereas *phase* typically implies a cyclic process, *stage* connotes the notion of progression and the idea that what is occurring in the present is influenced by a group's history. It also leads more directly to the examination of process–outcome relationships (e.g., Does a higher level of group maturity bring a greater capacity to accomplish group and individual goals? Is passage through particular stages associated with the achievement of particular goals?).

These three elements—the compelling appearance of group development in our fledgling group psychotherapy days, our subsequent discovery of the at least seeming ubiquity of group development phenomena across a vast range of types of groups, and the individuality of groups despite their developmental commonalities—have supported our interest in group development that has now spanned several decades and has resulted in this book.

ORGANIZATION OF THE BOOK

This book is divided into three parts. Part I comprises three chapters, each of which provides the necessary background to understand, evaluate, and apply our five-stage model of group development that is presented in Part II.

In chapter 2, we describe in more depth the benefits of thinking about groups from a developmental perspective and illustrate our discussion with clinical vignettes. In chapter 3, we provide a history of the thinking on group development, a rich narrative that is finely interwoven with the history of group psychotherapy itself. We describe both the earliest and most contemporary theories about group development. In chapter 4, we review the research literature on group development. We focus most particularly on the evidence for the existence of developmental stages in groups and on how group development affects outcome.

Part II begins with chapter 5, which is devoted to our five-stage model of group development. After reviewing each stage, we provide a clinical vignette from a long-term psychotherapy group to illustrate the characteristic behavior of group members at that stage. This theoretical orientation of the group's therapist is psychodynamic, but as is illustrated in chapter 7, stage development need not be limited to either long-term or unstructured groups. It is applicable to a number of short-term and more structured approaches. In chapter 6, the role of the group psychotherapist in facilitating group development in the five stages is the central focus, although there is, of course, some overlap with the dynamics described in the previous chapter (e.g., subgroup development and challenges to the therapist's authority).

Chapters 7 and 8 form a pair in that they each introduce new theoretical applications of developmental thinking. Chapter 7 applies our five-stage model to short-term and structured groups, such as cognitive–behavioral, behavioral, interpersonal problem solving, social skills, and psychoeducational groups. Chapter 8 features postmodern approaches to psychotherapy (e.g., social constructionism, intersubjective and narrative therapies) that hold promise of enhancing and being enhanced by developmental concepts. In each of these two chapters, we use vignettes from groups to illustrate our ideas.

In Part III, we return to some of the theorists and researchers described in chapters 3 and 4 as well as to our own five-stage theory of group development. Specifically, in chapter 9, we look at contextual variables as they influence group development. These include, but are not limited to, research on member characteristics (e.g., gender, status, ethnicity), time, leadership structure, and the various settings in which groups are conducted. In chapter 10, we take stock of the status of the field of group development as it pertains specifically to psychotherapy groups from empirical, theoretical, and practical points of view. We provide a final clinical vignette that integrates much of what we have presented previously in this book

In summary, this book provides the experienced clinician, the therapist who may be new to group psychotherapy, and the graduate student or trainee with the knowledge base that, in conjunction with skill development, can enable all to partake of the benefits of using a developmental perspective in groups.

I

GROUP DEVELOPMENT: BENEFITS, THEORY, AND RESEARCH

2

ADVANTAGES OF A DEVELOPMENTAL APPROACH TO GROUP PSYCHOTHERAPY

Many benefits, both professional and personal, accrue from group psychotherapists' adoption of a developmental perspective. The trainee or the senior practitioner; the group psychotherapist conducting groups in inpatient settings, prisons, private practices, and community mental health centers; and the group working together for a 2-week period or a 2-year period—all of these can realize the benefits of a developmental approach. Awareness of these advantages may enhance the practitioner's potential to capitalize on them. In this chapter, we delineate these benefits, focusing first on those consequences that are likely to affect favorably a therapist's effectiveness within the group and subsequently on those outcomes that also extend to the therapist's activities outside of the group. For example, some benefits are realized in the practice not only of group psychotherapy but also in modalities other than group psychotherapy. Other salubrious effects may occur in the therapist's personal as well as professional life.

BENEFITS WITHIN THE PSYCHOTHERAPY GROUP

In at least seven important ways, a developmental approach is likely to render a group psychotherapist's work more effective.

Training the Group Psychotherapist

For many trainees, fledgling experiences as group therapists are confusing and overwhelming events. Tracking individual members, interactions between and among members and between members and the therapist in what can be a very fast-paced session is typically quite daunting. Some trainees simplify the task by taking an individual therapy approach within the group. In this format, the therapist moves from member to member, interacting with each member for a segment of time on an individual basis. When such an approach is used, the trainee deprives him- or herself of the unique properties of the group that give it potency. Indeed, meta-analytic studies of group-level approaches have generally shown that group psychotherapy fares better in relation to individual psychotherapy when the former focuses on the group rather than on the individual members and their histories (Fuhriman & Burlingame, 1994). We suggest that developmental thinking provides an antidote to perplexity. The developmental model offers "a road map to follow and provide a sense of what [the therapist] can generally expect at different times in the life of the group" (Brossart, Patton, & Wood, 1998, p. 5).

Consider the case of two trainees who co-led a group in an AIDS treatment facility:

> The trainees had been surprised that despite their inexperience as group leaders, their first 3 sessions of a 10-session group had gone well. Members took turns telling the stories of their illness and offering one another compassion over their suffering, physical and psychological. In Session 4, however, members seemed to be sniping at one another. Some members took the position that the solution to difficulties lay in each member's willingness to take responsibility. Other members complained about individuals in their lives who impeded them from happiness and productivity. For example, one woman spoke about her work supervisor, who seemed irritated at the amount of time she was absent from work. Whereas some members argued that she should strive to avoid absences even when not feeling well, others placed the blame for her difficulties on the supervisor's shoulders. Some wondered whether she was demanding too much from herself in working at all; a few members offered her tips on finding a new position; other members sulkily sat in silence.
>
> The trainees were disturbed to note that the atmosphere of the group was contentious. Interventions to encourage members to respond to one another with greater kindness and warmth were to no avail. After the session ended, the trainees wondered whether the session could have "made some members worse." They could not understand why the group

had changed so much from one session to the next and why members seemed to be going off in so many directions. They were glad they were meeting with their supervisor later in the day.

The supervisor helped the trainees see that the appearance of agreement in the initial sessions was likely at the cost of acknowledgment of differences. Hence what seemed to the trainees to be manifestations of deterioration in the group were actually evidence of progress: Members were feeling sufficiently secure to share reactions that could (and did) increase tension. The relief in this realization enabled the trainees to use their resources to understand what themes united members' seemingly disparate offerings. The supervisor helped the trainees appreciate that members were grappling with the question of how to deal with their conflicting longings to be taken care of and to assume responsibility for their own lives. The supervisor suggested that this conflict has universality and must be addressed within every life. Although different members were representing different sides of the conflict, the supervisor noted, the conflict existed not only within each member but also within the group as a whole. In the supervision session, the trainees went on to explore the emotional reactions they had within the session.

Without the trainees' gaining some understanding of the phenomena emerging in the group session, a number of negative consequences could ensue. The trainees could have shifted their style of intervening within the group. From such a shift, the almost inevitable inference for members to draw would be that the expression of disagreement is unacceptable to authority. Members' ensuing interactions would be ostensibly affable but superficial. The trainees might also have developed a wariness of group process, a worrisome conclusion given the evidence that approaches emphasizing group process have more favorable outcomes (Fuhriman & Burlingame, 1994). Finally, the trainees could easily have lost confidence in their ability to develop as group psychotherapists, an unwarranted conclusion given members' behavior in the session, which any experienced group psychotherapist would anticipate.

A full use of a developmental perspective would also help the trainees work together more effectively as a team. Over time, relationships between cotherapists vary in tenor. At times, the cotherapists may work together in synchrony and at other times be at loggerheads; at times, they may be mutually supportive and at other times, competitive. Greene, Rosencrantz, and Muth (1985) demonstrated that the dynamics between a cotherapy pair is affected in part by the dynamics of the group itself. For example, the trainees in our illustration may have noticed themselves becoming fractious in their attitude toward one another, and this feature relates back to the tensions among the members. By recognizing that at any time the cotherapy relationship becomes permeated with the developmental phenomena within the group, therapists benefit from reflecting on their own interactions.

A developmental perspective not only helps the therapist understand the group better but also provides direction as to potentially useful interventions at different points in group life. These intervention implications are described in chapter 6.

Using Time Therapeutically

Group developmental thinking helps the group psychotherapist acknowledge the role of time in the psychological lives of members. As Arrow, Poole, Henry, Wheelan, and Moreland (2004) observed, "How group members think about time and collective group norms about the meaning of time shape the way a group handles temporal matters" (p. 76). Any particular time span—be it eight sessions, 3 months, or into perpetuity—provides both opportunities and challenges. Groups aware of a distinct time limit, particularly if that time limit is brief, have a special pressure to make progress. This pressure can lead the group to be courageous in tackling work that otherwise might be put off. Additionally, as MacKenzie (1994a) noted, "The member must deal with the necessity of accepting that not enough therapy will be experienced" (p. 257).

Conversely, the pressure may limit the breadth and depth of work. Members may be less inclined to pursue the tributaries of their troubles; they could thereby fail to discover psychological elements residing in those tributaries that may have more importance to the their central difficulties than was evident initially. When time is at least putatively unlimited, members can be more expansive in the goals they are willing to set. The standard of relevance becomes less despotic. However, members may have a diminished incentive to delve into painful matters given that they can console themselves with the availability of future sessions for such work.

How members relate to time provides a portal to their relationships with time outside of the group, and for many group members, such as Alanna, the mismanagement of time is a factor that hinders the maintenance of stable relationships:

> The group, in its 7th of 12 sessions, had been underway for 15 minutes when Alanna entered the room. As she sat down, she said with some measure of charm, "Oh, I'm so sorry. I'm just hopeless when it comes to being where I need to be when I need to be there." She giggled lightly and then said, "Well, what have we been talking about?"
>
> Imani began to recount the exchanges that had taken place, but Tony interrupted, saying that he resented having to proceed through this weekly exercise. The group was silent for a moment, and members shifted uncomfortably in their seats.
>
> Imani said, "Alanna has shared with us all the work pressures on her. I think we are here to be understanding of one another."

Tony retorted, "Yes, but her lateness is affecting the rest of us. Every time she comes in late—and I think she was on time only for the first session—we have to start over. We never really recapture where we were."

Laurie added, "We have only five sessions after today. We can't afford to be having replays of sessions during the sessions. I don't feel I've made nearly enough progress to be able to leave."

Alanna responded, "Imani, thank you for defending me, and I do have a lot of pressures at work, but the truth is, I am always late for everything. It doesn't matter if I have pressure or not. I am late for meetings at work, and in fact, it is legendary. I have been written up for this problem. But I keep repeating it and I am probably more frustrated by it than anyone in this room."

Members then showed curiosity about Alanna's lateness and briefly questioned her about the experiences that evening that led to the lateness. She revealed that she thought of leaving earlier for the session but had a picture of herself arriving early and having to sit with the therapist. Other members shared that they had this same apprehension and that some waited in the hall to avoid this possibility. Members laughed as they shared fantasies about the awkward conversations they might have with the therapist during the delay.

The therapist wondered aloud what it was that led members to challenge Alanna in this session as opposed to earlier sessions. Members talked about how its being the seventh session had special significance—less than half of the time in the group remained. Members talked about their goals for the group and the disparity between where they were now and where they hoped to be on leaving the group. Being reminded of members' presenting problems, members indicated that they would be more able to assist one another to find opportunities to address these issues within the group. In Alanna's case, the issue was a sense of never being able to marshal her talents effectively to have a career rather than merely a job. Tony said he believed that her sense of stagnating was connected to the chronic lateness, and he hoped they could figure out how. Alanna agreed that such an investigation held promise for helping her in relation to the frustration that brought her into the group.

In the seventh session of a long-term group, a member such as Tony might well have confronted Alanna. However, particularly in the early phases of group life, the members may have lacked sufficient impetus to tolerate the discomfort of conflict and rally around his challenge. In the present group, members' worry about the passing of time emboldened them to support Tony's effort to discourage breeches of the temporal boundaries of the group.

In a long-term group, for example, Alanna may discover that her fear of being alone with the therapist masks a wish to have the therapist's exclusive attention. She may gain recognition of a sense of deprivation that is tied to this longing. Whether any given member can develop such awareness in either a short- or long-term group depends on a great variety of factors, including personality characteristics such as psychological mindedness (Piper,

Rosie, Joyce, & Azim, 1996). Nonetheless, all factors being equal, more thoroughgoing explorations and insights are likely to be accomplished to the extent that members have time to engage in them.

Using Context Therapeutically

An emphasis on group development is conducive to the therapist's acknowledging the context of psychological work. The Western focus on individuality has resulted in an insufficient recognition and exploration of how an individual's context affects his or her experience and behavior and vice versa. A group developmental vantage inherently entails an examination of culture in several respects. A group's current patterns of interactions can be explored in the context of both its past and its aspirations for its future. An individual member's experience and behavior are contextually understood in relation to the operative group dynamic as well as that member's own cultural background and intrapsychic, interpersonal, and relational present, history, and aspirations for the future. Consider Sal's behavior in a psychotherapy group:

> Sal came to the group bearing holiday presents for members of a 9-month-old group. As he distributed them, members' manifestations of pleasure and gratitude seemed strained and restrained. Although the members opened their gifts, the therapist kept her gift unwrapped in front of her. The therapist asked Sal how he felt about the group's reaction to his presents. He said he thought he had surprised them.
>
> Another member observed, "Sal, I think you may be disappointed in our response. I hope you know if we seem uncomfortable, it's not a rejection of you but we're not sure if it is all right for us to be accepting presents in here."
>
> Tasmia said, "Susan [the therapist] hasn't opened her gift. I'm not sure I should have opened mine."
>
> Franklin said, "I think we're just getting neurotic over this. Everyone gives gifts at the holidays and that's what Sal did."
>
> Tasmia rejoined, "Yes, but these relationships we have are not everyday kinds of relationships. Don't get me wrong: I think Sal's bringing us all presents is very sweet. However, if we do in here what we do out in the world, then this loses its specialness. We were told in the beginning that we should try to put our feelings and urges into words so we can understand them. That means, to me, that if we want to give a gift, we should talk about how we want to do it and not do it."
>
> Sal responded, "Well, I'm really sorry. I didn't mean to violate any rule. It's just I can't imagine having the kind of important relationship that I do with each of you and not giving the person a present. It just doesn't compute for me. If you want, you can give the gifts back. Maybe I was naive about something I should have understood better."

Clearly, Sal's gesture poses a problem for the group in that the members and the therapist want on the one hand to protect the verbalization norm that has been established in the group and on the other hand to safeguard Sal's self-esteem. In this circumstance, the group's and the therapist's analysis of context can provide insights contributing to the conflict's resolution. The group's history is one contextual feature. Earlier in the group, the members may have partaken in a barometric event in which the group revolted against the therapist in an expression that contained both verbal and nonverbal components. An example of a nonverbal expression would be members' conspiring to arrive late to a given session or to configure themselves in some nonstandard seating arrangement.[1] The group's recognition of its own strides would create a reluctance to return to a mode associated with an earlier era in its life. At the same time, some members of the group are likely to feel sympathetic toward Sal's joining efforts and wary of a more Spartan posture toward one another.

Insight into Sal's and other members' cultural backgrounds may provide a source of information concerning the different modes of relating to which members are drawn. For example, the group may learn that Sal's cultural background requires gifts as regular accompaniments of holidays such that for Sal to fail to provide a gift at a holiday is to declare that person as insignificant to him. For other members, gift giving may carry a different implication—for example, it may signify that a relationship of intimacy exists, and some members may find disturbing the notion that their 9-month-old relationships with the other members are intimate. For still others, as in the case of Tasmia, gifts represent the conventional and the mundane and as such, signify a trivialization of members' relationships with one another.

In the same way that a child's maturation is studied in terms of his or her family environment, developmentalists investigate the group in terms of the forces impinging on it (such as boundary intrusions that create instabilities in the group, limiting its development) and how the group and its transpirings affect the broader environment. Often these group–environment relationships are seen with particular salience when treatment takes place in a broader treatment context, such as a residential treatment center or day hospital:

> Three of the eight group members were denied passes to leave the unit because of behavior that was disrespectful to the staff and other residents (loud swearing in the hall). The members of the group were split between those who felt that the punishment was deserved and those involved in the transgression who saw staff members as overreacting. In the session, members responded in a testy manner toward one another. The therapist acknowledged members' differences but wondered aloud

---

[1] An example of such a nonverbal expression in one author's experience was to arrive in the group session only to find all members sitting on the floor rather than in their chairs.

whether there was not something that all of the members shared: their annoyance in the last session at the therapist for not responding to a direct question that would signify the therapist's support of one faction of the group or another. One member, agreeing that she had been exasperated on leaving the session, indicated that the events of the group had contributed to her yelling in the hall. She was roundly supported in this claim by the other members who had engaged in the sanctioned behavior. One member said, "I'm not saying it's your [the therapist's] fault, but I do think you had a big role." Other members doubted whether the group events could have been of sufficient importance to create that outcome but, in a milder way, did question whether the therapist's reticence was prudent. The therapist said he thought that the group did indeed take their frustration with him out into the unit and that the loud swearing may have been the kind of expressiveness they would have liked to have achieved in the group but felt they could not. This comment was followed by a discussion of members' perception of themselves as being far more contained in the group and in other modalities than outside and a sense of artificiality associated with that containment. Even the quieter members talked about feeling relieved in hearing the loud swearing—that finally, some residents were expressing themselves in a way that seemed real.

As we discuss in chapter 5 of this volume, the members were grappling with a developmental concern that comes predictably in the early but not earliest life of the group: that conflicts that are activated—in this case the conflict between open expression of hostility toward authority and fears of the consequences of such an expression—are ones members take into the world with them. When the context is sufficiently contained such that the therapist can take stock of it, then that context becomes a valuable source of information and illustration for the therapist to use to move the group along its developmental journey.

Comprehensive Accounting of Group Phenomena

The life of the group can be understood from the vantage of different levels of analysis. One level is the individual member and his or her behaviors, reactions, conflicts, fantasies, and so on. The interaction between members, and between each member and the therapist, constitutes another level. Members also can form into subgroups in which a set with similar but not identical positions in relation to an issue becomes a working unit. Finally, the group as a whole—its atmosphere, themes, interactional patterns— offers another tier of analysis.

The different levels of analysis are like different lenses on a camera— each level offers a potentially useful perspective on the group phenomena. As such, each level is a resource. Some approaches focus exclusively on a given level of analysis. For example, an interpersonal approach gives great attention to dyadic interactional patterns but little focus on group, subgroup and group-as-a-whole levels. When the interpersonal therapist focuses exclusively on interactions to the neglect of broader themes, the therapist will be denying him- or herself and the group a resource. He or she will be ignoring data on the big picture into which individual interactions fit. A particular advantage of a group developmental view is that it encompasses consideration of all units of analysis in the system of the group. As the following vignette and its discussion suggest, a developmental focus allows for a great deal of flexibility in the level at which both analysis and intervention occur:

> Dennis ambled into a morning group session late, saying he was tired from watching a TV show the night before. One member asked what the show was, and Dennis mentioned a common espionage show that all of the members recognized—yet, only Iona and Sheldon expressed enthusiasm for it. These three members began a lively discussion for 5 minutes when another member, Fatima, interrupted them and said, "I don't think the show is a reason for being late, and I don't think talking about it is a good use of the group's time."
>
> Dennis gave an exaggerated look of being taken aback and said, "Aren't we hoity-toity?" Sheldon laughed.
>
> Marion, glaring at both Sheldon and Dennis, replied, "I don't appreciate your tone of mockery, and I think Fatima is absolutely correct. When someone's late, we just lose our focus. I think it's rude to the therapist and inconsiderate, and your celebrating it with this frivolous conversation makes it that much worse."
>
> Iona added, "You know—that's what gets on my nerves about the group. If we're not serious every second, it's worthless. Couldn't there be something good about our sharing our interests outside of this group? Isn't there something good about not talking about our problems every second but taking a moment to talk about what brings us joy?"
>
> Dennis said, "Yeah, and besides, she [the therapist] said we were supposed to communicate openly. To me, that means talking about . . . whatever."
>
> Fatima responded, "Very clever . . . using the therapist's own words to break the rule of showing up on time and wasting time." Lewis said, "For once I was enjoying our conversation, but you're ruining it. He was late by only a few minutes, and talking about the show was fun."

The therapist experiencing this segment of group life could respond on a range of levels. The therapist could focus at the level of the individual member such as Fatima and ponder how her reaction fits into her own psychology. Why was she the one to interrupt the conversation? Might this behavior, particularly her insistence on adherence to group rules, represent a strong identification with authority? If so, what are the social consequences of this identification? As Iona suggested, does Fatima (along with others) have a constricted capacity for play, and if so, what toll does it take on the forging of intimate connections? The therapist could focus on Fatima's trajectory through the group and help her to create a narrative that allows for varied options in responding to peers.

Alternatively, the therapist could focus at the subgroup level. If the reader were asked what alliances had formed in the group, certainly the connections between the subgroup of Dennis, Iona, and possibly Sheldon and Lewis and that of Fatima and Marion would be salient. The therapist might consider how each member in these subgroups could find comfort in being in the group but use that comfort to understand his or her unique position in relation to the issue at hand. For example, Fatima may realize that for her, the importance of observing rules is paramount, whereas for Marion, protecting the leader against any challenge is key. Ultimately this greater awareness of how members differ from one another could facilitate members' identifying with individuals who are in other subgroups, and these broadened identifications might help participants achieve an expanded, more robust sense of self. Hence the subgroup-oriented therapist actively promotes the formation of subgroups and guides them to maximize members' learning (Agazarian, 1997).

The group psychotherapist also could focus at the level of the group as a whole. This therapist would ask, "How do the actions and reactions of this individual member (or subset of members) function as voices of trends within the group as a whole?" The therapist might wonder how Dennis's tardiness and the poverty of his excuse reveal a psychological element that is shared by all members (even if not consciously accessible). The therapist might speculate that Dennis was serving as a bellwether for a burgeoning restlessness with the rules of the group.

The flexibility of the unit of analysis within a developmental conceptualization broadens the range of clinical situations in which it can be applied. For example, certain populations may require a more individual focus. A group of individuals who are being seen immediately following a trauma may require the comfort of individual attention, particularly in the earliest stage of development. A group of sex offenders may find an individual focus too evocative of shame, the burden of which is more distributed (and hence manageable) when the group psychotherapist intervenes at the level of the subgroup and the group as a whole. Also, certain therapists may have a level of intervention more compatible with their personality styles. An individual unit of analysis is likely to be associated with a more behaviorally active therapist. Time frame also may affect the level of analysis that is optimal. For example, in short-term psychotherapy, the therapist may require the efficiency of subgroup- and group-level interventions.

Process and Outcome Relationships

Thinking about group development draws the therapist's attention to links between process and outcome. That is, by understanding the workings of a group, the therapist can more fully tap the potential of the group to benefit its members (Wheelan, 1999). Research (e.g., see McRoberts, Burlingame, & Hoag, 1998; Toseland & Siporin, 1986) provides a strong indication of the benefits of group psychotherapy. Yet, to maximize the potential benefits of group, knowledge of how those benefits are achieved is needed. Research on specific factors is useful in helping the therapist to negotiate the moment-to-moment events that constitute a session:

> Soledad had been reticent throughout the seven sessions of an eight-session day hospital group. Her occasional comments seemed less on topic than those of other members and were typically met with an awkward silence. In the last session, members were giving one another summative feedback. Soledad interrupted as members were providing feedback to another member, saying, "I want to know what you all think of me. Now don't hold back. I want to know everything."

This open-ended invitation provided the therapist with a dilemma. Knowing that Soledad would be likely to receive feedback that would highlight her relational insufficiencies, the therapist could either support this process, structure it so that it had a particular character, or prevent the feedback to Soledad altogether.

Here the therapist's knowledge of process–outcome relationships could come to her rescue. On the one hand, the finding that members who receive more feedback have more favorable outcomes (Flowers & Booraem, 1990) might compel the therapist to encourage members to offer feedback to Soledad. On the other hand, research has shown that constructive or negative feedback is rarely experienced as helpful when it is offered in the absence of positive feedback. Furthermore, positive feedback should generally precede negative feedback (see Brabender, 2006). These findings argue in favor of the therapist's structuring the feedback. For example, she might ask members what strengths they have noted in how Soledad participated in the group. If the therapist anticipated that members would not be forthcoming with positive feedback, she might offer her own feedback to Soledad. Investigators (e.g., Tschuschke & Dies, 1994) have observed that critical feedback is less helpful when it is given at the end of the group, especially when members have not been receiving it throughout the group. This finding suggests that the therapist should be chary of Soledad's reception of negative feedback at the end of the group.

Group developmental models account not only for what processes are important but also for how those processes are activated and how they depend on one another. For example, it is not enough to know that feedback is helpful to members' achievement of a more adaptive interpersonal style. What is necessary for members to use feedback? Group developmental theory points to members' engagement with one another, an engagement that occurs very early in the life of the group. The therapist, cognizant of the relationship between engagement and feedback, can from the group's inception work vigorously to promote each member's active involvement with the other members of the group. In our example, the therapist, noting Soledad's reticence, might have worked energetically from the beginning of the group to ensure that Soledad would be thoroughly engaged with the other members. Hence, ultimately, the knowledge of the interrelationship of processes over time and their relationship with outcome provides a blueprint for intervention.

Relationships Between Psychotherapy Groups and Other Types of Groups

A focus on group development allows for an appreciation of the interconnections among different types of groups. One of the unfortunate aspects of the history of group psychotherapy is the divide that has existed between efforts to understand group phenomena as they come into being in a therapeutic setting and such phenomena in other types of contexts such as work settings. Historically, there has been less of this compartmentalization in group development research. Prominent group developmental writers such as Tuckman (1965) have given attention to the differences and similarities among therapy groups, groups devoted to personal enhancement, and task groups. Probably the most prominent similarity is that developmental potential, the capacity of a group to grow, exists among all types of groups.

In this book, we attempt to continue this integrative tradition within group developmental theory and research through our effort to weave the insights that can be obtained from social psychology and the study of work or task groups into developmental applications of the psychotherapy group. Contemporary psychotherapy groups take many forms. Indeed, some structured applications, such as cognitive and behavioral groups, may be closer to task groups in employment settings than to process-oriented groups. Accordingly, the vast literature on developmental aspects of task groups could offer possibilities of how developmental concepts could be used in those structured models in which they have not historically been accessed by practitioners.

Compatibility of Group Development Theory With Emerging Paradigms

Group developmental thinking is potentially compatible with emerging intellectual paradigms, a compatibility that ensures that group developmental theory can be continually updated by new theoretical and empirical discoveries. These discoveries at times have made new techniques available to the group psychotherapist.

This notion of compatibility among particular paradigms is one that we develop much further in this book, but several examples are in order here. First, group developmental thinking has been integrated with complexity theory by many writers (e.g., Brabender, 1997; Wheelan & Williams, 2003). Furthermore, preliminary research studies such as those by Wheelan and Williams (2003) demonstrated that progressive stage models and complexity theory each account for different aspects of how groups change. Together, they provide a more adequate picture of the predictable transformations that occur in groups over time. Second, group developmental approaches have been successfully integrated with new narrative approaches as we show in detail in chapter 5 of this volume. The group creates its own story over time, with each developmental stage providing a segment of the plot. Narrative approaches enable the group psychotherapist to make optimal use of the group's and each member's individual stories. Third, group developmental approaches have been integrated with change models describing change in phasic terms.

In chapter 3 of this volume, we outline the history of thinking on change in groups. As we discuss, some theoreticians see the group as *phasic*, that is, alternating between states such as work states and basic assumption states. These approaches, although different from the progressive stage models to be explored in this text, have descriptive value in capturing certain aspects of group life. MacKenzie's (1990) model shows how phasic and stage elements can be integrated into a single model.

PERSONAL AND PROFESSIONAL BENEFITS

The benefits of developmental thinking to the therapist's personal life and professional life beyond conducting psychotherapy groups are discussed in the two sections that follow.

Using Groups to Pursue Goals Beyond the Alleviation of Suffering

A group developmental focus has compatibility with a positive psychology perspective. The stages of development do not merely characterize the maturation of persons with psychopathology; the stages, at least as they are construed in most major theories, are universal and describe the ways in which humans reckon with progressively more complex issues. Although groups with a developmental focus can be conducted to lessen suffering, they may also be used to enable individuals to grow—to achieve greater happiness in life and to be more successful in meeting goals. Accordingly, the skills the therapist cultivates in conducting psychotherapy groups from a developmental perspective, with some adaptation, can be transferred to other types of groups such as wellness-oriented groups.

For example, Ellen Daniell (2006) wrote about a group of female scientists who met every other Thursday in a problem-solving group to explore the challenges of having an academic career. Daniell wrote about the group's achievement of cohesion, the members' developing self-knowledge, and the members' ability to function more effectively in their careers. Yet, in this type of group, members' knowledge of group developmental stages (and indeed, the members of this group could tacitly or explicitly have had such knowledge) could be useful at points at which such a group hits a snag. For example, were members to feel irritated with one another, they could explore the hypothesis that the irritation was specific to some group-level developmental tension, such as the restiveness of early Stage 2 of our five-stage model of group development (see chap. 4, this volume), when members are beginning to recognize differences with one another.

During the many years in which Virginia Brabender presented the developmental stages in her introductory group psychotherapy course, the students were invariably astonished at how well the stages described the history of their own interactions. At the time the students took the course, they were in the fall semester of their 3rd year of training in a 5-year program. They had gone through the first 2 years as a cohort, spending approximately 18 hours together each week. In the 1st year of training, the students were sanguine and nurtured idealized views of the program, the faculty, and one another. Typically in the 2nd year of training, the students experienced some dissatisfaction and disillusionment, and students showed irritation with one another and resentment of program requirements. By the 3rd year, students showed a new seriousness of purpose, and relationships with one another achieved a new level of constructiveness. Hearing about the stages of group development in the introductory class provided students with a sense of coherence and reasonableness to their changing reactions to the interpersonal dimensions of their academic experience.

Development of the Person of the Group Psychotherapist

Awareness of group development is conducive to the growth of the group psychotherapist. To do effective work within a given stage, the group psychotherapist must be aware of what affects and yearnings are stimulated by the conflicts and tasks of the stage. Developmentally based self-focusing, particularly when abetted by supervision or exploration with a cotherapist, enables the therapist to gain greater access to and insight into psychological elements than he or she may have achieved earlier in his or her development. In this way, the therapist is given an opportunity to complete developmental tasks more thoroughly and resolve conflicts more satisfactorily than may have been done previously. In this regard, consider the following illustration:

> Two mental health professionals had begun a psychotherapy group; one of them, Dr. Kerry, had had a great deal of experience, and the other, Ms. Storr, had a very limited fund of group work. Ms. Storr was participating in the group to gain greater experience and to learn from Dr. Kerry. During the most recent sessions, Ms. Storr had been a focus of the group as

members devalued her for her junior status and other perceived deficiencies. Dr. Kerry had been quite impressed with Ms. Storr's robustness and resilience in the face of this attack. The group moved from Ms. Storr to Dr. Kerry, whom they decried for a different set of weaknesses pertaining more to negligence (in holding back her knowledge) rather than inadequacy.

After the group had expressed a good deal of dissatisfaction, it entered a period in which members showed a benign but more indifferent stance toward the therapists. They lightheartedly talked about the possibility of one member having an affair as a means of coping with her marital difficulties. During these sessions, Dr. Kerry had noticed that Ms. Storr appeared limp and melancholy. In their regular debriefing, Dr. Kerry asked Ms. Storr if she felt that she [Ms. Storr] was having any particular reaction to the transpirings in the group. Ms. Storr said that she found recent sessions to be boring, not nearly as stimulating as those in which the members were expressing their disappointment with the cotherapists. Dr. Kerry wondered whether Ms. Storr found it gratifying to be in the spotlight, even if the attention received was negative. Ms. Storr initially expressed some amusement at this possibility but then ruefully added that she wanted to discuss the matter with her therapist.

Ms. Storr followed through with her plan to explore with her individual therapist the psychological underpinnings of her ennui, precipitated by the members' appearing less interested in her. She discovered that being in the limelight, for good or ill, secured her mother's attention at a very early age. Her prodigious verbal abilities as a toddler and then a young child enabled her to garner the amazement of all adults in her surroundings. Her mother responded to their reaction as a great personal triumph and showed Ms. Storr abundant affection. However, when circumstances did not allow her mother to obtain this vicarious affirmation, Ms. Storr wilted in the same way that she did in the session. Ms. Storr came to associate loss with any sequence of events that placed her out of the spotlight. This aspect of her interpersonal relationships and its roots had not appeared with the same clarity earlier in treatment. Ms. Storr's ability to access the hurt underlying her seeming uninterest enabled her not only to show more consistent vitality in the group but also to more clearly understand her reactions to events in her personal life involving the same or similar social stimuli.

In our example, Ms. Storr used both supervision and personal therapy as means of learning from her group experience. For seasoned therapists, it is often possible to engage in self-exploration by using the internal and external data from the sessions to do productive personal work.

CONCLUSIONS

The benefits of a group developmental approach are manifold. This perspective is highly useful for new group psychotherapists who are attempting to understand what might otherwise be a chaotic array of events that unfold in any session. Group developmental theory also helps the trainee understand how his or her reactions and interactions with the cotherapist fit into a broader group dynamic. This understanding is one that integrates observations and research findings from both psychotherapy groups and groups conducted outside of a therapeutic context. This elucidating role of developmental theory is a feature that should characterize any good theory. For example, any model, be it cognitive–behavioral theory or interpersonal theory, can serve this function: It can tell the group therapist what he or she is seeing and why. However, group developmental theory distinguishes itself from many other approaches in that its constructs do not sacrifice the complexity and richness of group phenomena. It provides a structure into which events can fit at both micro- and macrolevels. A related benefit of group developmental theory is that it fosters an appreciation of the context of group events. Group developmental theory not only permits an analysis of different levels of specificity in the group but also provides the theoretical equipment to see how these units are related to one another. As such, it is both aesthetically and intellectually satisfying.

Satisfactions notwithstanding, the purpose of group psychotherapy is to effect the amelioration of psychological difficulties, and group developmental theory provides the means to do so. Specifically, group developmental theory offers the means to characterize group process. It enables the investigator to study how variations in process mediate outcome. In chapter 3 of this volume, we provide evidence for the links between developmental processes and a range of outcomes. For the present, suffice it to say that a developmental perspective serves the cardinal goal of helping the therapist conduct the group more effectively.

Group developmental thinking assists the therapist in work outside of the group. The contextual understanding required for group developmental work provides a deepened understanding of how an individual's context affects his or her internal life and behavior. It also provides the therapist with the tools to participate as leader or member in groups that aim to enhance functioning.

Finally, the group developmental approach potentially contributes to the maturation of the group psychotherapist as a person. This potential is likely to be realized most fully if insights garnered from the group receive further analysis in therapy or supervision.

3

THEORETICAL HISTORY OF GROUP DEVELOPMENT IN ITS APPLICATION TO PSYCHOTHERAPY GROUPS

The history of thinking on group development is a complicated and fragmented one because both research and theory construction occurred in two distinctly different intellectual traditions: academic and clinical. These traditions were at times independent and at other times mutually influential. One originated in the group dynamics academic arena and often entailed the study of work groups occurring in both natural and laboratory settings. Social psychology took the lead in this effort, later followed by education and political science (MacKenzie, 1994a). The second major tradition was clinical; it involved a focus on the psychotherapy group and was connected to disciplines that address psychological difficulties such as clinical psychology, psychiatry, and social work. Certain group explorations borrowed from both branches. For example, the sensitivity group movement, which sprung up in the 1960s, drew on elements of both group dynamics and psychotherapy groups (Yalom, 1995). In this chapter we describe the history of scholarly thinking on group development, a history that serves as a foundation for examining the developmental characteristics of psychotherapy groups.

First, we look at the forerunners of the group as a construct and system. Second, we describe how later theorists characterized change processes occurring during group life, which led to the early group developmental models. Many of these models, which were termed *progressive*, came to be applied to psychotherapy groups in the late 1950s and culminated in Tuckman's (1965) seminal article that first captured the interactional patterns and themes of the stages as they unfolded in therapy groups. These continue to dominate the literature to this day, albeit with refinements and individual variation depending on variables such as the setting of the group.

We describe how models of group development are similar and how they are different in ways that include number of stages, units of analysis, the role of leadership, and tasks versus conflict emphasis, to name a few. We conclude the chapter by reviewing new paradigms for considering group development, such as complexity and chaos theory, the punctuated equilibrium approach, and the social entrainment model.

THE GROUP AS A CONSTRUCT: THEORETICAL FORERUNNERS

The roots of scholarly writings on group development go back to antiquity. Greek and Roman philosophers introduced into their works elements that presaged contemporary group development theory. For example, the Greek scholar Heraclitus's works contained three principles (described by Durant, 1939) that were the intellectual forerunners to contemporary group developmental thinking. The first principle is the ubiquity of change, the idea that whatever exists within the universe is in a constant state of transformation; inherent in the notion of group development is the notion that such transformations occur over time and group developmental theory attempts to describe their character. The second principle is that within all of the seeming fragments of existence, a force unifies all phenomena, a notion that antedated the idea of the group as a whole. The third principle was the coexistence of opposites, the view that no pole of a continuum can exist without its opposite also being present, although possibly less apparently so. Heraclitus saw the tension between these opposites as creating a matrix for change. In fact, the existence of opposites has been regarded as a major mechanism catapulting a group from one phase of development to the next (e.g., Bennis & Shepard, 1956).

THE ORIGINS OF THE GROUP AS A CONCEPT

Between antiquity and modern times, many philosophers have touched on ideas that achieved full flowering in the 20th century. However, not until the early 1900s did the sociocultural events unfold that led scholars to articulate views on group life that foreran group developmental theory. The sociocultural events were those international conflicts that escalated to World War I. The anticipation and ultimate outbreak of war was on a scale that was unprecedented because of not only the multiplicity of peoples and nations clashing but also the large-scale lethality of the weapons made possible by the industrial revolution. As the power of the group became evident to the intellectual community (Anthony, 1972), a group of writers attempted to characterize the psychological features of group life.[1] Members of the intellectual community through the phenomena of war could clearly see that groups could exhibit properties that were other than what could be observed by members considered individually. These writers posited features compatible with groups having the necessary power to perform acts of large-scale human annihilation.

Contributions of Le Bon

One scholar who secured attention to group phenomena primarily because of the radical character of his conception of group life was the sociologist Gustave Le Bon. Writing about exceedingly large groups such as those formed during the French Revolution, Le Bon (1895/1960) posited the existence of a group mind, which had all of the behavioral features of an undisciplined child. Thought processes activated by the large group situation were seen by Le Bon as those characteristic of early childhood. Individuals operating under the influence of the group mind experience a "sentiment of invincible power" that leads them to be selfish, uncontrolled, wrathful, and interested in the unbridled pursuit of pleasure.

Governing the behavior of group members is the phenomenon of *contagion* wherein group members show a hypnotic level of submissiveness to the direction of others and put the welfare of the group before their own. For example, why are so many individuals willing to fight in wars? As part of their membership in the large group, Le Bon (1895/1960) answered, individuals forfeit their ability to reason the merits of such an action to their individual lives and simply submit to the direction of authority figures for the sake of a group goal they uncritically embrace.

Contributions of McDougall

McDougall (1920, 1923), like Le Bon, saw the activities of individuals formed as an unorganized crowd as "excessively emotional, impulsive, violent, fickle, inconsistent, irresolute and extreme in action," and at its worst, the crowd's behavior was "like that of a wild beast" (McDougall, 1923, p. 64).

---

[1]Wheelan (2005) pointed out that recent terrorist events have renewed scholarly interest in the distinctive and sometimes malignant features of group life.

He too gave as an example of such a crowd some of the activities of large groups of people during the French Revolution. Yet, he also recognized that groups, even exceedingly large groups, can achieve a higher level of organization in which they are not driven by their impulses and are capable of greater productivity than could be achieved by individuals acting independently. Although McDougall had a good deal to say about groups, pertinent to our purpose is his asseveration that the primary feature that leads a group to a more sophisticated form of "collective life" is "continuity of existence" (1923, p. 69). In other words, no group, regardless of its composition or other structural features, can realize its potential for constructive action if it has not had the opportunity to develop over time.

Contributions of Freud

In *Group Psychology and the Analysis of the Ego*, Freud (1921/1955) argued that although Le Bon's description of the group mind was "brilliantly executed" (p. 13), particularly in its assertion that the group mind is ruled largely by unconscious mental activity, his formulation was limited insofar as it was based on groups (such as revolutionary groups) that appear quickly and last briefly. Somewhat different, Freud believed, are the dynamics pertaining to groups that have a more stable existence. Here Freud introduced the notion, important for our purposes, that the factor of time in a group makes a difference in how a group can operate. A group, he noted, becomes established as an entity through members' development of emotional ties with one another through a process of identification. The basis of members' identification with one another is their common relationship to the leader. In this regard, he wrote,

> The uncanny and coercive characteristics of group formations . . . may therefore with justice be traced back to the fact of their origin from the primal horde. The leader of the group is still the dreaded primal father; the group still wishes to be governed with unrestricted force; it has an extreme passion for authority . . . in Le Bon's phrase, it has a thirst for obedience. (Freud, 1921/1955, p. 59)

Freud's view that groups form through members' shared relationship to the leader as a parental figure has been resident in most contemporary group developmental theories: They hold that members can address their relationships with one another only once they have addressed their thoughts, feelings, and impulses in relation to the leader. Freud also emphasized empathy as a vehicle by which members forge connections with other members; the role of empathy, too, came to figure prominently in members' work in groups that have gone beyond the formative stages, that is, mature groups.

In their writings, Le Bon, McDougall, and Freud made clear their belief in the existence of group level phenomena. However, it was Triggant Burrow

(1927) who actually introduced the term *group as a whole*, conveying that this layer of group life has properties related to but separable from individual phenomena, and emphasized that it is worthy of exploration.

Opposition to Group-as-a-Whole Thinking

The early decades of the 20th century also saw the contributions of thinkers such as Floyd Allport (1924, 1961) who argued a different point of view. They held that group phenomena consist of the activities of individual group members and nothing more.[2] They maintained that neither a transcendent group as a whole nor a set of group dynamics occur beyond the summed behaviors of individual group members. For such writers, although individuals in the group may develop, the group does not develop. The critique of both group-as-a-whole and group developmental thinking continues to this day and, as O'Leary and Wright (2005) noted, supports the notion of the human mind as an encapsulated, separate entity. O'Leary and Wright attributed the relative emphasis of individual therapy over group and family therapy in many training settings to be a manifestation of the persuasiveness of this critique.

Contributions of Lewin

Despite the critiques, thinking about the group as a whole or as a system continued to advance. Among the pioneers on group life, no one played a more significant role than the social scientist Kurt Lewin (1948, 1951). Lewin posited that individual behavior can only be understood through a grasp of his or her psychological field or life space, which "consists of the person and the psychological environment as it exists for him" (Lewin, 1951, p. xi). Groups too have life spaces, which encompass the group itself and the environment in which it resides. To understand either the behavior of the members of the group or the group as a whole, one must achieve cognizance of the distribution forces across the social field, a distribution that will drive or inhibit any given individual or group behavior. The driving and inhibiting forces create conflict that propels development. As the distribution of forces changes, the social field (the group, its subgroups, individual members, and the group's context) is altered. In characterizing these forces, Lewin (1951) wrote,

> The concept of the psychological field as a determinant of behavior implies that everything which affects behavior at a given time should be

---

[2]Another type of criticism of group-as-a-whole thinking has been of its utility. As group historian Scheidlinger (2006) noted, in a follow-up study (Malan, Balfour, Hood, & Shooter, 1976) on a group that was conducted according to Bion's and Ezriel's theoretical frameworks, group members reported that the group experience was extremely unhelpful. They indicated that the therapist appeared indifferent to their well-being. This well-publicized study dampened enthusiasm for the group-as-a-whole approach to treatment. Yet, theory development within this framework continued.

represented in the field existing at that time, and that only those facts can affect behavior which are part of the present field. (p. 241)

This principle of contemporaneity departed sharply from Freud's emphasis on motives rooted in early experience.

The second principle Lewin emphasized, interdependence, established the reciprocal influence of all elements of the life space. Hence, changes in the group beget changes in its members. Changes in individual members influence other members and the group as a whole. Embedded in this principle of interdependence is a conceptual framework for understanding the relationship of the individual to the group; it provides an explanation for how it can be that individuals in a psychotherapy group may benefit from the developmental changes in the group as a whole. The emphasis on contemporaneous determinants of experience, the interdependence of properties, the importance of the group in relation to its context, and conflict as a basis of change are all notions that have achieved residency in developmental approaches.

Another paradigm emerging from the physical sciences that has had a profound effect on developmental approaches was general systems theory (GST), a framework proposed by von Bertalanffy (1950) that accounts for the interrelationships among systems and their subsystems. Like field theory, GST entails the view that to understand a system, one must grasp not merely the working of its parts but also the dynamics of the whole. von Bertalanffy identified a property of all systems and subsystems that reside within a hierarchy of systems, the property of isomorphy. *Isomorphism* is the repetition of structural and functional features within a system and subsystems in a hierarchy of systems. This feature suggests that those tensions manifesting at the level of the group also exist at the level of the individual member. The GST paradigm is developmentally focused in that it recognizes that development is an inherent aspect of open systems, that is, systems whose boundaries are permeable to the environment. GST shaped the writings of the Durkins (H. E. Durkin, 1964; J. E. Durkin, 1981), who drew the implications of systems thinking for the psychotherapy group. GST later influenced the conceptualizations of Agazarian and colleagues (Agazarian, 1997; Agazarian & Gantt, 2005), who proposed the theory of living human systems, a developmental approach integrating many of the theoretical ideas of GST with Lewinian concepts of group life.

EARLY CONCEPTIONS OF GROUP LIFE

The theoreticians we have considered established the group as an entity separate from its individual members. However, it was for later theorists to provide a more detailed conception of change processes occurring during group life. Prominent among those theorists who had a particularly great influence on group developmental theory are Bales, Bion, Ezriel, and Foulkes. Although none of these theorists sought to characterize comprehensively the changes that a group undergoes across its life span, each theorist addressed the issue of how groups change. Whereas Bales's contributions were in the group dynamics tradition, the conceptualizations of Bion, Ezriel, and Foulkes were based at least in part on their work with psychotherapy group.

Bales

Robert Bales and colleagues (Bales, 1950; Bales & Strodtbeck, 1951) studied problem-solving groups to understand the processes activated as members work on a problem. Their research suggested that two different types of processes are engaged as members work together. The first is a set of *task functions* that pertain to the specifics of the problem at hand. Examples of behaviors associated with these functions are asking questions and giving opinions. The second set of functions is *socioemotional* and concerns the regulation of group tension. A natural rhythm of group life, Bales and colleagues observed, is that as a group works on a problem, tension builds. Continued progress requires the release of tension so that the group can achieve equilibrium. Groups vary in terms of how the socioemotional functions are performed. For some, it may be joking with one another, for others complaining, and for still others, focusing on irrelevant topics. Bales saw change in the group as the alternation between a task focus and a socioemotional focus, between an increasing disequilibrium and a return of equilibrium.

Bales viewed the ability of a group to undergo changes leading to the restoration of equilibrium as contingent on the leadership of the group. Bales believed that a group requires individuals with expertise in the socioemotional and task functions and that often this expertise does not reside within the same individual. The notion of distributed leadership, leadership that is shared across various members and dependent for deployment on the dynamic needs of the group, came to be a familiar one among group developmental thinkers.

Bion

Wilfred Bion (1959, 1962) was a military psychiatrist responsible for establishing programs of care in a military hospital in London. He recognized that the psychotherapy group provided a means of efficient treatment and conducted groups in London's Tavistock Clinic. On the basis of these experiences seen through the lens of Melanie Klein's (1948) psychoanalytic thinking, Bion described group life as being constituted of two contrasting psychological frameworks: basic assumption and work group. Within the basic assumption framework, three assumption states occur: basic dependency, fight–flight, and pairing. The *basic assumption* state is an archaic or primitive mode of relating in which group members attenuate the anxiety stimulated by group membership by creating a fantasy about it. The group behaves as if an imaginary construction of the group were indeed true.

The basic assumption *dependency* group is one in which members share a fantasy that their needs will be gratified magically and completely by an omniscient, omnipotent leader. The hallmark of the basic assumption *fight–flight* group is members' shared belief that their survival as a group is in jeopardy. Their group preservation, they believe, can only be met by being led in fight by a powerful figure or by fleeing. The basic assumption *pairing* group is a framework in which members act as if they believe that the union of a pair of members will bring about salvation for all members of the group.

When groups are operating within any of these basic assumption frameworks, cognition is childlike, impulses and urges press for discharge, and affects are intense. Bion contrasted the basic assumption modes with the work group mode. In the work group, members manifest a dramatically greater ability to maintain a task focus. This ability entails the capacities to use mature thinking and to harness impulses and feelings. Whereas in the basic assumption modes, the individual who gains leadership is the person who enables the group to maintain the fantasy associated with the particular basic assumption state, in the work group, the leader will be the one who is best qualified to help the group perform its task. Bion also accounted for individual members' relationships with the group through the notion of *valency*. He believed that different members resonated to the themes of the moment at different levels of intensity based on their own history, personality proclivities, and so on.

Bion's model of group change was, like Bales's model, cyclical: He believed that groups oscillated between the basic assumption modes and the work group modes. Despite the nondevelopmental character of the psychological states that Bion saw as characterizing group life, his thinking was highly influential on later theory in that the patterns he identified provided the rudiments of the developmental stages of those models that depicted groups as progressing. Bion, like Bales, also contributed the notion that leadership in a group is a function that changes depending on the psychological state of the group. Who will become leader rests on the group needs within the moment. Later developmental theorists such as Ariadne Beck (1974) proposed models that built on this notion of dynamic leadership.

Ezriel

H. Ezriel was also a group-as-a-whole object relationist who integrated the group as a whole with the intrapsychic life of the individual group member (Horwitz, 1993). Ezriel saw the group situation as inviting unconscious wishes and longings to press for fulfillment in members' interactions with one another and the therapist. For example, members may each aspire to have all of the therapist's love, attention, and aid. Yet, Ezriel also saw that these wishes were associated, unconsciously, with fantasies of calamitous events that would occur if such wishes were gratified ("If I am the exclusive beneficiary of the therapist's resources, then I will be killed by the other members").

According to Ezriel, the group-as-a-whole conflict between the wish and the fear of the calamity gives rise to a common group tension. To keep these wishes repressed, a repression needed by the danger attached to them, members enter into a required relationship, which by its very structure prevents the wish from directly asserting itself. Each member may satisfy the requirement to keep the wishes at bay in a different fashion. One member may intellectualize, another may complain incessantly, and still another may simply withdraw. All of these maneuvers limit the satisfaction members can derive from their relationships with one other and with people outside the group. The task of the therapist then is to interpret both the conflict giving rise to the common group tension and each member's individual way of responding to the conflict. Ezriel's emphasis on the individual in the context of the group as a whole provides a clear view of how members can have their treatment needs addressed even as the therapist maintains a focus on the dynamics of the group as a whole.

Foulkes

The British analyst S. H. Foulkes (1964) contributed the concept of the *group matrix* to describe the communication network a group builds as members interact; the matrix captures the history of the group (Pines & Hutchinson, 1993). Foulkes provided a bridge between the group-as-a-whole perspective, developmental thinking, and psychopathology as he described how the group matrix changes over time. According to Foulkes, early in group life, communications are not direct: Members communicate through symptoms rather than through the direct expression of thoughts and feelings. Yet, the matrix develops, and as it does, members identify blocks to clear communications with one another. With the removal of such blocks, members' reliance on symptoms to reveal themselves to the social world diminishes. An interpersonal shift can be observed as well: Whereas members begin the group with a primary focus on the leader, they gradually emancipate themselves from this dependent tie through a movement that Foulkes (1964) referred to as a crescendo of the group's authority and a decrescendo of the leader's (or therapist's)[3] authority. Foulkes identified the mechanism of mirroring as one critical to the group's maturation. Mirroring occurs when members recognize different facets of themselves in the other members. Through mirroring,

---

[3]Foulkes did not use the terms *leader* or *therapist* but rather *conductor* to emphasize the nondirectiveness of this role and the importance of the group leading itself.

members build the matrix that increasingly gains in complexity and coherency and provides individual members the environment for growth.

Scheidlinger

Significant contributions to group-as-a-whole theory continue to be made and, as they are, provide enrichment for group developmental models. We mention here two especially important contributions. Scheidlinger (1982) proposed the concept of the "mother group" to describe members' perception of the group as a nurturing supportive entity. Scheidlinger's work is significant for group developmentalists because it entails a shift from a father-oriented characterization of early group life to one in which the mother is the central figure in members' thoughts and feelings. He also captured the phenomenology of members' internal lives in the early phases of the group.

Harkening back to some of Le Bon's and McDowell's conceptions of the destructive potential of group life, Nitsun (1996) identified the phenomenon of the *antigroup*, in which members by their behavior attempt to ensure the group's destruction. This position is starkly at odds with Foulkes's view of the group continually moving to more mature levels of developmental organization (Schermer, 2005). Nitsun's conceptions are important for developmental theorists because they suggest that groups can, at times, operate in a way that is at odds with the developmental needs of its members and hence can exert a pathogenic influence on their well-being.

EARLY GROUP DEVELOPMENTAL MODELS

Understanding current group developmental thinking requires a knowledge of the contributions of the following seminal thinkers.

Bennis and Shepard

After Bion (1961) outlined the basic assumption states and the work group mode, the question of when these different formations appear was an inevitable one. Bennis and Shepard (1956) answered it by proposing a model of development in which the basic assumptions represent different levels of maturity of group life. They wrote, "The very word development implies not only movement through time but also a definite order of progression" (p. 426). They saw the group as moving through phases during each of which the group is confronted with a series of conflicts. Resolving conflicts entails removing obstacles to clear communication. Hence, like Foulkes, Bennis and Shepard saw group development as a progression toward increasingly direct communication. The chief obstacles to direct communication, they held, lay in members' orientations toward authority and intimacy.

On the basis of their observations of experiential groups that they led over a 5-year period for graduate students, Bennis and Shepard (1956) posited that two broad phases characterize group life, with the first phase entailing members' engagement with authority issues and the second, their pursuit of conflicts related to the establishment of intimacy. Each phase involves three subphases, characterized by its own distinctive themes. Because of the historical importance of the Bennis and Shepard model, the phases and subphases are described in some detail in this chapter.

Dependence Phase

During the *dependence* phase, the group grapples with its conflictual stances toward authority figures. In the *dependence–flight* subphase, members confront the ambiguity of early group life; uncertainties abound. For example, members often become preoccupied with the issue of what should be their common goal. Yet, no uncertainty is more salient or important than uncertainty about the leader. On the one hand, members expect that this individual possesses the omnipotent capacity to care for their needs completely. Given his or her power, following the leader's directives and securing the leader's approval are crucial to members. On the other hand, the leader appears to withhold his or her talents and gifts. Members show two trends in relation to this predicament. They engage in the behaviors that in the past have led to authority figures' approbation. However, even more conspicuously, they engage in a repertoire of flight behaviors, including focusing on issues external to the group. Members flee from the ambiguity of the situation, their sense of helplessness in relation to the leader, their worries about the future of the group, and other aspects of their immediate experience.

The group shifts into the *counterdependence–fight* subphase as dissatisfaction with the leader foments. For a period, members sustain the hope that the leader is simply waiting to summon his or her magic on behalf of the group. As it becomes increasingly apparent that the stance the leader has adopted is not going to change, members more openly express their anger toward the leader. Members respond to the ineffectual leader problem by developing two subgroups. One subgroup attempts to fill the void established by the leader by engaging in the activities that are attributed to leaders (e.g., setting agendas). Another subgroup takes on the task of interfering with any new structure that others seek to construct. This group adopts a more clearly antiauthority position in which opposition is given to any authority figure who emerges whether that authority is manifested by the designated leader or another member or subgroup of members. Within this subphase, members' fearfulness prevents them from having anything more than a covert expression of discontent with the leader. However, their manifestations of disagreement with one another will be much more direct.

In the *resolution–catharsis* subphase, the independents, or members who have been identified with neither of the emerging subgroups, come to the forefront in helping the members to approach more directly their feelings toward the leader. That is, in a matter-of-fact way they help the group to realize that the question of whether the group actually needs the leader must be addressed. As members allow themselves to recognize directly the depth of their questioning of the leader's contribution, they proceed to the *barometric event*, a symbolic gesture in which one or more members representing the group challenges the therapist's authority. Through this challenge, members shift to a view of the group that is not reliant on the presumed magical powers of the leader to satisfy their needs. As they lessen their reliance on the leader to obtain benefits from group participation, they increasingly assume responsibility for their own progress. Bennis and Shepard also described the jubilation and triumph that accompanies this emancipation from members' perceived subjugation by the leader.

Interdependence Phase

The resolution–catharsis subphase tends to move quickly into the first subphase of the second phase of group development, the phase of *interdependence*. The name of this phase conveys that members now recognize their dependency on one another for their forward movement in the group. During this phase, members address the range of their reactions to establishing intimate relations with other members. The onset of the first subphase of this period, labeled *enchantment–flight*, is distinguishable by a very noticeable emotional tone in the sessions. As Bennis and Shepard (1956) noted, "The group is happy, cohesive, relaxed" (p. 429). In establishing this blissful atmosphere, members are responding to both their success in challenging the leader and their eagerness to distance themselves from the acrimony of the preceding subphase. A hallmark of this subphase is members' insistence on having total agreement among themselves. Of course, the achievement of genuine and constant unanimity is impossible, so this criterion can be met only by denying differences. However, because the evidence for differences among members will build, the group's use of denial cannot sustain itself; members increasingly chafe at the pressure to be in accord with one another. Consequently, this subphase typically is short lived.

In the *disenchantment–fight* subphase, the members bifurcate into subgroups representing two stances toward intimacy. The members who were most in harmony with the ethos of the last subphase, the *overpersonals*, band together to defend the preceding subphase's spirit of unity. Those who had felt the greatest internal tension in being called on to deny their differences from other members, the *counterpersonals*, organize into a subgroup. This subgroup's position is, "We each are autonomous beings whose right to be individuals is under siege by other group members." Bennis and Shepard (1956) noted that both subgroups see intimacy as fraught with danger. For the overpersonals, unless all differences among members are eliminated, the self-esteem of each member is imperiled because attunement to differences invites rejection. For the counterpersonals, the sheer act of committing to a group ravages one's personal identity and the self-esteem derived from it.

Bennis and Shepard (1956) saw the specter of the group ending as ushering in the final subphase, *consensual validation*. Because Bennis and Shepard were working within the framework of a course, the ending coincides with the need for an evaluation. They observed that both the counterpersonals and overpersonals resist evaluation because for the former, it means a violation of privacy and for the latter, the acknowledgment of differences among members. Once again, however, the independents, the individuals unfettered by conflicts about intimacy, are able to assist others in tolerating the anxiety associated with this task. The work of the independents can take various forms (e.g., an independent may ask the group for an evaluation of him- or herself), but the consequence of their interventions is that the group can seriously pursue the task of taking stock. As Bennis and Shepard noted, the group's capacity to do this work entails the group's acceptance of a set of values:

> 1. Members can accept one another's differences without associating "good" and "bad" with the differences. 2. Conflict exists but is over substantive issues rather than emotional issues. 3. Consensus is reached as a result of rational discussion rather than through a compulsive attempt at unanimity. 4. Members are aware of their own involvement, and of other aspects of group process, without being overwhelmed or alarmed. 5. Through the evaluation process, members take on greater personal meaning to each other. (p. 433)

Members' achievement of these values enables a directness of communication that has not been possible at any earlier point in the group. Bennis and Shepard saw this achievement as well as the continued work in the evaluation task as creating, for at least some members (depending on their level of participation in the group's development), the potential for "valid communication" (p. 435) and diminished autism in relationships outside of the group.

Rather than seeing this kind of progression as being in any way guaranteed, Bennis and Shepard (1956) recognized that a range of factors affects the group's ability to progress. Events external to the group can affect group development as can group composition. The presence of independents can be critical to the group's ability to move to the next subphase. Traumatic events can lead the group not only to fail to progress but also to regress to an earlier point of development.

Group development from Bennis and Shepard's (1956) perspective has elements of both conflict resolution and task accomplishment. Within each broad phase, the group addresses and resolves conflicts related to authority and intimacy. However, the group must also accomplish a series of tasks to engage in conflict resolution. For example, individuals must achieve a diminishment in their felt helplessness by becoming ensconced in the supportive structure of a subgroup. The greater confidence that this affiliation brings enables members to become more courageous in their communications. Later developmental models emphasize the conflict aspect, task aspect, or both.

Schutz

In the same period in which Bennis and Shepard (1956) were writing, Schutz (1958) provided an alternative to the progressive model: He posited that groups, even two-person groups, cycle through three stages emphasizing themes of inclusion, control, and affection, successively. Individual members, he qualified, may be so consumed with an alternate theme that they may not resonate to the current group theme. Schutz believed that a group's recycling through the phases is a common phenomenon:

> When a person changes a tire and replaces the wheel, he first sets the wheel in place and secures it by sequentially tightening each bolt, but just enough to keep the wheel in place and make the next step possible. Then the bolts are tightened farther, usually in the same sequence, until the wheel is firmly in place. And, finally, the bolt is gone over separately to secure it fast. In a way similar to the bolts, the need areas are worked on until they are handled satisfactorily enough to continue with the work at hand. Later on they are returned to and worked over to a more satisfactory degree. (pp. 171–172)

This recycling allowed for individual differences in members' abilities to work within the developmental phases: What any member did not achieve in the first go-around could be remedied later (Schutz, 1958).

Mann

A variation on the cycle model is one that postulates some progression among the various periods of group life but also specifies a final deteriorative period that is akin to dying and death in the lives of individuals. An example of the life cycle model is that of Mann and colleagues (Mann, 1966; Mann, Gibbard, & Hartman, 1967), who studied groups of students over 32 meetings. *Appraisal*, the initial stage, is characterized by a high level of flight and apprehension. In the second stage, *confrontation*, members challenge authority. *Internationalization*, the third stage, involves a diminishment of resistance and a greater investment in work and cooperative relations. In the *separation* stage, the group returns to the avoidant mode of functioning seen in the initial stage, although members continue to be engaged with one another. Only a subset of the models that propose a termination stage are life cycle models. A life cycle model is one in which the dissolutive character of the final stage is its central feature. For example, in Mann's model, the group is unable to maintain its higher level of functioning achieved in prior stages.

THE APPLICATION OF PROGRESSIVE DEVELOPMENTAL
MODELS TO THERAPY GROUPS

Shortly after Bennis and Shepard (1956) proposed their model, clinicians began to consider the relevance of developmental concepts to group treatment situations. In the next several decades, psychologists (e.g., Caple, 1978; Garland, Jones, & Kolodny, 1965; Mann, 1966; E. A. Martin & Hill, 1957; Yalom, 1970) constructed a plethora of models that in some way took account of group development in how the process of the group was conceptualized. Each stage was regarded as a set of opportunities for members to complete a significant piece of psychological work related to the difficulties that brought the individual into treatment. For example, some members may have had difficulty achieving intimacy in long-term relationships. Within most models, a stage occurs in the relatively mature group in which conflicts related to intimacy become manifest. Members are thereby afforded the chance to address these conflicts anew and potentially in a more successful way.

Over the decades, the models of group development were many and were constructed with different clinical venues, age groups, and clinical problems in mind. Developmental models were devised not only for groups focused on verbal exchanges but also for activity-oriented groups (e.g., see Garland's [1992] description of children's groups).

Tuckman

Progressive development models of the 1960s and 1970s tend to share a number of characteristics, many of which were captured by Tuckman (1965) in his seminal and summative article (MacKenzie, 1994a)[4] discussing the developmental literature on psychotherapy groups, human relations training groups (*T-groups*), and natural groups versus laboratory groups.

Tuckman (1965) depicted psychotherapy group development as being characterized by a series of stages that have a predictable set of themes, with each subsequent set of themes building on those of the prior stage. In keeping with Bales's (1950) division of socioemotional and task functions, he characterized each stage with a description of the interpersonal realm and the task realm. In Stage 1, *forming*, the group experience is launched by a period in which members transform themselves from a collection of individuals to a bona fide group. During this period, members shift from seeing themselves as a mere collection of individuals to a view of themselves as a group. They orient themselves to the rules and processes of the group and begin to engage with one another. Yet, members see the therapist as the primary change agent

---

[4]MacKenzie (1994a) saw the Tuckman (1965) article as the capstone of all of the theory and research that had occurred on group development since theoreticians and researchers began addressing it; as such, its historical significance is inestimable.

and await the therapist's ministrations. In Stage 2, *storming*, the group structure is plagued with intragroup conflict, defensiveness, ambivalence, and competition. Polarization in relation to issues of dependency and leadership results in conflict. The task aspect features emotional expression by members as a form of resistance to disclosure, joining, and task requirements. In Stage 3, *norming*, the group becomes a cohesive unit with common goals and group spirit; members function as a team. Conflict recedes as the task of exploring and discussing individual group members and their problems and experiences becomes paramount. Members express feelings constructively as the cohesive structure of the group enables the discovery of personal relations. A final stage, *performing*, is described by Tuckman (1965) as follows:

> This is a stage of mutual task interaction with a minimum of emotional interference made possible by the fact that the group as a social entity has developed to the point where it can support rather than hinder task processes through the use of function-oriented roles. (p. 390)

Rogers (1970), describing this same period, noted that members at this juncture see the group as truly their own and know that they are responsible for making those self-revelations that will allow them to derive significant benefit from the group.

In a later article, Tuckman and Jensen (1977) posited the existence of a stage related specifically to the ending of the group for those groups in which members have a shared ending point. Although they did not provide an elaborate discussion of this period, they did note that this stage, which they called *adjourning*, involves members' focus on separation issues.

COMMON FEATURES OF PROGRESSIVE STAGE MODELS

Since the early 1970s, models that have developed within the stage progression paradigm have shared with Tuckman's (1965) model the general sequence of themes that he described. However, other similarities among these models also exist. First, most models incorporate the important notion of invariance or the concept that groups must proceed through the stages in a fixed way. Later developmental requirements demand that earlier ones have been satisfied.

Second, the progressive models assume that a variety of features distinguish each stage from the other stages. They hold that each stage possesses a characteristic set of themes or issues that can be inferred from members' comments and behaviors. For example, in the earliest stage, as noted previously, the theme of trust asserts itself more prominently than other potential themes. Each stage also has a characteristic pattern of interaction. In the early life of the group, for instance, members show by their nonverbal behavior that their communications are being directed toward the therapist rather than toward one another. As Caple (1978) observed, "As a member speaks to the group, he or she may watch the facilitator/leader for signs of acceptance and support" (p. 471). Later, members show more attunement to one another. Each stage has a particular set of norms or implicit rules about what behaviors are or are not acceptable to members. For example, Rutan and Stone (2001) noted that whereas a particular disruptive activity (such as loudly chewing gum) may be tolerated by the group in the earliest stage of development, once the group achieves maturity, it is regarded as unacceptable and therefore results in a confrontation of the offender. Still later, although this activity may not be seen as desirable, it is regarded as having meaning and being worthy of exploration. Finally, at each stage the group has a set of competencies that qualify it to perform certain tasks and not others. For example, early in group life, members show some capacity to identify with one another's experience but not an ability to engage in a sophisticated decision-making process that takes into account different positions in the group.

Third, most models also posit the potential of groups to proceed through stages at different rates, to become fixated or locked within a given stage, or to undergo regression in which they return to an earlier stage. As in individual development, not all groups achieve the level of maturity that others do (Kuypers, Davies, & Hazewinkel, 1986; Wheelan, 2005). Although most group theorists agree that groups have regressive potential, questions remain about the character of the reaction. Does a group that regresses to a stage act in a manner identical to a group newly proceeding through the same stage? Is the regression of a group different from that of an individual? Weinberg (2006) noted that groups may be restrained in depth of regression by the resources for reality testing available in the group. The collective resources of the group enable regressive reversals (i.e., movement out of a regressive episode) to occur more commonly in group psychotherapy than in individual therapy.

A group's progression, fixation, or regression as well as its rate of progress through a given stage are generally understood as being determined by a variety of factors internal and external to the group. Internal events that are often cited include membership change (Corder, Whiteside, Koehne, & Hortman, 1981), absences (Garland, 1992), violations in confidentiality (Roback, Ochoa, Bock, & Purdon, 1992), impending termination (Slater, 1966; Wheelan, 2005), and any other event that quickly or drastically raises the threat level for members.

External factors include the philosophy, values, and attitudes of the broader treatment environment in which the group is embedded; the support the broader group environment offers in allowing the group to maintain stable boundaries between it and its context; and the socioeconomic pressures placed on the group's operations (Brabender & Fallon, 1993). An example of the last factor is a third-party payer's agreement to pay for the number of sessions necessary for a member to accomplish a particular set of goals in the group. Some models allow for the possibility of the group being at one stage and an individual member being at another. For example, Garland (1992) noted that when a new member enters, although the group regresses, it can return to the preregressive point quickly. However, that new member will most likely have to do work characteristic of stages earlier than that in which the group is residing.

A fourth common feature of progressive stage models is that as groups mature, they become more effective (Chidambaram & Bostrom, 1996). For example, the presumption is made that as groups proceed through the developmental stages, they become better able to perform therapeutic tasks and fulfill the goals established on their launching. This notion is one that has been subjected to considerable empirical scrutiny and is discussed further in chapters 4 and 10 of this volume.

DIFFERENCES AMONG PROGRESSIVE STAGE MODELS

The progressive stage models differ from one another in a variety of ways. Differences among group models are due to variability in the type, length, composition, and context of the group on which a model is based as well as the broader theoretical orientation that the model builder brought to the enterprise of running a group. The relationship between these factors and group development is discussed in chapters 7, 8, and 9 of this volume. For the present, we discuss five particularly notable factors accounting for variability among developmental approaches: (a) the role attributed to group development in promoting favorable outcomes, (b) the primary organizational level at which developmental phenomena are described, (c) the number of stages, (d) the importance of leaders or other members in fostering group development, and (e) the task-versus-conflict emphasis. Each of these areas is discussed in turn.

The Role of Group Development in the Fulfillment of Treatment Goals

Models vary on the extent to which they see positive outcomes of group participation as a direct or indirect consequence of the operation of developmental processes. For some models, group development is the warp and woof, the sine qua non, of how group treatment works. Each developmental period provides members with the opportunity to redress challenges that characterize their own individual development. In meeting the challenges in the group more satisfactorily than they have done individually, members advance their own intrapsychic and interpersonal well-being. Examples of approaches that use group development as primary therapeutic tools are the object relations (Kibel, 2005) and systems-centered approaches (Agazarian, 1997).

For other models, a certain level of maturity must occur in the group to enable members' use of a particular set of processes critical to the goals of the group and the individual members. For example, the interpersonal approach emphasizes interpersonal learning wherein members receive and offer one another feedback within an atmosphere of affective engagement. Only with group maturity do members come to trust and care about one another at a deep level, and until they can do so, their ability to either provide or accept feedback is extremely limited. Members benefit from proceeding through the initial stages of group development because work in these stages enables members' full involvement in interpersonal learning.

Primary Organizational Level at Which Group Phenomena Are Described

Theoretical approaches differ in whether functioning of the individual, subgroup, or group as a whole is emphasized in the description of the model. Some models, such as Kutter's (1995), emphasize the dynamics of the individual member, whereas others, such as Yalom's (1995), focus on dyadic activity and thematic concerns over the course of the group.

To provide a more in-depth discussion of the relationship between the level of a system on which a model focuses and the interventions characteristic of that model, we feature Agazarian's (1997, 2004) developmental approach, called *systems centered therapy* (SCT). SCT was derived from Agazarian's "theory of living human systems" (TLHS; Agazarian, 1997). TLHS rectifies the problem of the historical use of two sets of concepts and terms to account for individual versus group dynamics. It provides a unified and coherent description of the dynamics of human living systems, regardless of whether the system is an individual, a couple, a family, a group, or an organization. Within this framework, systems are defined as *isomorphic*: Every system in a defined hierarchy is similar in structure and function. Thus, determining structural or functional variables from any one system will generalize to all systems in the hierarchy. This permits discovery of the equivalence in the system variables in individuals, groups, and organizations and solves an important problem in research into these apparently different phenomena.

All of the systems within a hierarchy exhibit three properties: They organize their energy, move in the direction of goals, and correct their courses based on ongoing feedback. Central to TLHS is the postulate that human systems function, survive, and develop toward greater complexity by discriminating and integrating differences. The SCT method, which elicits discrimination of differences in the apparently similar and similarities in the apparently different, is called *functional subgrouping* to distinguish it from the spontaneous or stereotype subgrouping that is characteristic of all groups. Agazarian recognized that subgrouping has been perceived by group psychotherapists (e.g., see discussion of subgrouping in Yalom, 1995) as a pernicious force, often leading to negative outcomes and stunting group development. The basis of this perception is that subgroups can form along stereotypic lines or some shared external designation and can be characterized by impermeability. For example, a group may separate into subgroups according to gender. Members of each gender may have stereotypic perceptions of the members of the alternate subgroup (e.g., the subgrouped men may see the women in the group as stereotypically feminine), and they may fail to revise their notions about the other members regardless of incoming data (impermeability).

In contrast to such a subgroup structure, Agazarian recognized the potential for members to subgroup in a functional way, that is, in a way that would serve the group's survival, growth, and movement toward its goals. In systems-centered groups, members are required to come together around similarities rather than splitting around differences, thus reducing system tendencies to scapegoat differences rather than integrate them. As members form into a subgroup based on their recognition of a common position, they begin to recognize that indeed they are not identical to one another vis-à-vis the issue at hand. That is, they begin to discriminate differences. At the same time, they are perceptually alive to the unfolding of subgroups other than their own and increasingly see that members of those subgroups, who at first seemed entirely different, are in certain respects similar to them. When this occurs, members of the group can integrate what was apparently different into their own experience.

In thinking about developmental phases, Agazarian drew on the Lewinian concept of a force field. Each developmental phase presents to members a set of differences that must be discriminated and integrated at both the individual and subgroup level in order for the group to move on to the next stage. The force field comprises forces that drive the group toward this goal of discriminating and integrating differences or restraining them from doing so. Although Agazarian's (1997) developmental sequence is complex and is not described here in its entirety, an example is given of functional subgrouping within a developmental phase.

Our illustration focuses on an era of group life in which members make the transition from the authority phase into the intimacy phase. Following members' experience of confronting the leader with their projections (particularly the negative projections onto authority figures that are characterized by anger and outrage), they can turn their attention away from the leader to their relationships with each other. In many developmental models, the group psychotherapist approaches the positive and negative poles of members' stances toward intimacy sequentially. That is, members are first supported in exploring their enchantment and then their subsequent disenchantment. The critical shift in Agazarian's thinking was in recognizing that functional subgrouping provides the means by which members can address simultaneously forces propelling them toward both enchantment and disenchantment. According to SCT, the advantage of this simultaneity is not mere efficiency. This feature, by managing both enchantment and alienation simultaneously in functional subgroups, enhances the depth and completeness of exploration into the conflicts around separation and individuation. For example, in the subgroup formed around yearnings for intimacy (i.e., the enchanted subgroup), members reach the awareness that their terror is based on the expectation that all intimacy will be lost if members differ from one another. In turn, members who join the subgroup of despair recognize that in spite of the conviction that they are forever alienated and alone, they are in fact exploring their experience of isolation together (Agazarian, 1997).

In conclusion then, for Agazarian, the basic unit of analysis is the functional subgroup because it is through this method that discrimination and integration of information is supported and the goals of system survival, development, and transformation in all phases of development are more easily met.

Number of Stages

From the early history of group developmental thinking, variability has existed in the number of stages or phases different models include. Tuckman noted in his 1965 review that most extant approaches posited four stages. However, Tuckman also specified that some approaches (e.g., observations of a group of drug addicts by Thorpe & Smith, 1953) built on the experiences of members who had a strong resistance to attaching to others and posited a stage prior to the traditional Stage 1. In this prestage, members overcame their negativity in relation to connection. Some contemporary developmental models such as Kieffer's (2001) psychological model of the self also posit a pregroup phase for persons who have a high vulnerability to annihilation anxiety. Tuckman and Jensen (1977) argued for the inclusion of a fifth stage specifically devoted to termination issues. As noted earlier, progressive models that also include a terminal stage in which the dissolution of the group is the primary focus of the stage are termed *life cycle* models (Munich, 1993). Within such models, group development is seen as recapitulating individual development.

Current approaches to group psychotherapy typically involve either four or five stages, with the fifth stage included when the group has a clear ending. An example of a particularly prominent four-stage model is MacKenzie's (1997), which is especially suitable for short-term group work. MacKenzie's first stage of *engagement* entails members establishment of a sense of cohesion. In the *differentiation* stage, members address first their differences with one another and ultimately their dissatisfaction with the leader. MacKenzie (1997) used the term *differential* rather than the more customary label *conflict* to capture "the importance of self-assertion and self-definition that underlie the process" (p. 279). In the third stage, *interpersonal work*, the group achieves greater intimacy and works intensively on individual concerns and in that work, engages members in a deeper degree of self-reflection. The fourth stage, *termination*, may occur at varying points in the group's life depending on circumstances, such as the departure of a member. Termination activates problems related to grief over loss and self-management, given that members are now called on to function more independently.

Yet, exceptions to the four- or five-stage models exist. Probably the best-established system that goes beyond the traditional four or five stages is that of Ariadne Beck (1974) who, with her colleagues, has proposed a nine-stage model based on the analysis of transcripts from client-centered groups. A distinguishing feature of this system is that Beck examined the role not only of the therapist, the designated leader, but also of the members of the group who take on leadership roles and perform important functions in moving the group forward. Because of the prominence of the model and research it has stimulated, we provide a thumbnail description of each stage in the paragraphs that follow.

In Phase 1[5] (A. P. Beck, 1974) the members forge a commitment to becoming a group that can work on mutually established goals. The *task leader*, the therapist, assists the members in opening up lines of communication among them. The *emotional leader*, in an emerging role, tends to the wide range of affects stimulated by the group's beginning and strives to ameliorate any feelings that may be disturbing to members. The task and emotional leaders begin to develop an especially intimate relationship that is an aid to the group as it moves through the developmental stages.

In Phase 2, the group aims to establish a direction and in this effort, looks to the designated leader of the group, the therapist. However, the members feel an uncertainty about how the group will direct them, an uncertainty with which (they imagine) they cannot confront the powerful therapist. This uncertainty makes members fearful that the group could dissolve into nothingness. This pressure leads members to identify a *scapegoat*, a type of group leader, who serves as the target of their frustrations. Members believe that by ridding the group of the scapegoat, they will divest the group of all that could destroy it. In the group's coming to awareness of this dynamic, the group achieves clarity about its values.

In Phase 3, the group recognizes individual members in their uniqueness. Members disclose personal information and explore different modes of communication. The emotional leader assists members in deepening the communication among themselves by providing a model of personal exploration. The emotional leader draws on the supportive resources of the group to un-

---

[5]The term *phase* is used in this context because A. P. Beck (1974) described her model in terms of phases. In later chapters, we primarily use the word *stage* because it connotes more clearly a progression rather than a succession and, in our view, leads more directly to the examination of process–outcome relationships (i.e., whether a higher level of group maturity brings a greater capacity to accomplish group and individual goals).

dergo growth and thereby demonstrates how the group offers a special environment for achieving structural personality change.

In Phase 4 the group works to achieve greater intimacy, an accomplishment made possible by the achievement of greater cohesion in the prior stage. Members learn more about others' close relationships outside the group, including sexual aspects. Feelings of warmth, caring, and tenderness reign at this time. At this time, the task leader is seen not merely as an authority figure but as a complex being in part because of the task leader's greater sharing. This shift is essential to the entire group's movement toward a new depth of involvement.

In Phase 5, the intensity of members' expressions of affection for and affinity with one another implies a level of commitment that creates apprehension in members. They wonder whether they will be able to meet the needs of other members satisfactorily, whether their own needs will be met, and whether the give and take of mutuality will be achieved. This phase sees the emergence of the *defiant leader*, who provides the clearest and strongest cautionary voice for the perils of closeness and the conformity that seems to attend it. The group agrees to accommodate the special needs of this member for self-protection, an act that sets the stage for the group's responsiveness to each member's individual needs.

In Phase 6, the leadership pattern is reorganized such that a broader sharing of leadership functions takes place and greater flexibility occurs in different members' performing different functions. At the same time, the importance of the emotional leader, whose key functions from this point on "are to act as a low-key coordinator and to be the main support person to the other members including the Designated Leader" (A. P. Beck, 1974, p. 450), is acknowledged. In fact, at this time the emotional leader takes over some of the responsibilities of the task leader with respect to guiding and support functions, and this move is a symbolic expression of the members making the group their own.

In Phase 7, the group is characterized by self-confrontation, in which members examine the issues that brought them into therapy. Members recognize the complexity of each member's personality and the inherent difficulty of psychological change. The mutual respect members have for what each is up against leads to a level of cohesion not achieved previously. The scapegoat leader now achieves some prominence because members' capacity to see the multifaceted character of each individual enables them to recognize that more exists within the scapegoat than what they previously had been able to comprehend.

In Phase 8, members wonder whether they can transfer the learning in the group to the outside to have satisfying, intimate, enduring relationships. This phase entails the group's most intense work facilitated by members' greater sensitivity to subtle interpersonal cues and deepened capacity to see one another as multifaceted beings (A. P. Beck, 1974). A. P. Beck (1974) noted that many groups often fail to reach this level of development, leaving members with some dissatisfaction.

In Phase 9, the final phase, members confront the ending of the group experience. A major aspect of this process is reckoning with the high level of importance members have had for one another. The task and emotional leaders are critical in helping members to give expression to loving feelings for each other, and they thereby enable members to achieve a unity in their rapport with one another despite the imminence of separation.

As the reader may have noticed, a good deal of overlap exists between A. P. Beck's stages and the traditional four- or five-phase models, particularly those derived from the Bennis and Shepard (1956) model. Beck's Phases 1 and 2 resemble the dependant and fight–flight stages quite closely. The features of Beck's Phases 3 and 4 are typically combined into a third stage of development that follows the group's negotiation of the authority crisis. Beck's last stage of development is similar to the termination stage posited by many approaches. However, Phases 5 through 8 are unique to Beck's model. Perhaps, as MacKenzie (1994a, 1997) suggested, Beck was merely subdividing the later phases of development, which have been subjected to less study than earlier phases.

The Contributions of Leaders

Models vary in whether the therapist effects change in the group by working to create a growth-promoting atmosphere within the group or by fostering more specific interpersonal and intrapsychic patterns within members. Models that emphasize the group's potential to develop see the leader's crucial activities as geared toward the cultivation of a growth-promoting atmosphere. Foulkes's (1986) group analysis is consistent with this view: Provided that the therapist or conductor creates a group environment with certain types of stability, the group will move from a therapist-focused (or *conductor-focused* in Foulkes's terminology) to a member-focused mode in which members are able to engage in transformational interpersonal work:

> [The therapist] knows that a good number of therapeutic or anti-therapeutic factors depend on culture he creates and especially on the manner in which he does this. He has made himself into the first servant of the group, into the instrument the group can use, but he has also forged the group, and continues to do so, into the instrument of group-analytic psychotherapy. It is of the greatest importance to realize that in this form of treatment the group itself is the active agency for change. (Foulkes, 1986, p. 107)

According to this approach, the therapist, rather than engineering group development, helps the group address any obstacle to a natural growth process.

Within many other models (e.g., Yalom's [1983] interactional agenda model), the therapist's actions are direct rather than indirect: The therapist affects not merely the atmosphere but also more specific interactional patterns within the group. Within these models, the therapist may make a variety of interventions to catapult the group's development. For example, the object relations therapist (Alonso & Rutan, 1984) interprets symbolic manifestations of displeasure with the therapist to enable members to make more direct expressions toward him or her.

Task Versus Conflict Emphasis

Since Bennis and Shepard (1956) presented their group developmental approach, many therapy group models (e.g., Agazarian, 1997; Brabender & Fallon, 1993) have been constructed that emphasize the resolution of conflicts as the vehicle by which groups progress from one stage to another. The work of the stage is the crystallization of each side of the conflict, often through the formation of subgroups, and the subgroup's movement toward greater tolerance for the position and accompanying psychological contents expressed by the alternate subgroup. These approaches are compatible with a conflict model of psychopathology (Kibel, 1987) wherein psychological difficulties are rooted in the individual's unsatisfactory resolutions of a set of basic conflicts that every human being must successfully negotiate to achieve maturity.

Other models give greater emphasis to the group's performance of certain tasks within each stage. For example, such models see members in the earliest stage of development as needing to develop trust in the group and in one another. Following the completion of this task, members enter a stage in which the task at hand is to learn to manage conflict and differences within the group. Task-oriented approaches are most compatible with a deficit approach to psychopathology (Kibel, 1987), in which psychological problems are rooted in the individual's failure to acquire adaptation-promoting structures in the course of individual development.

In the past 3 decades, developmental models have been applied to a wide range of populations and contextual circumstances. What has characterized the group psychotherapy literature, however, is a tendency to describe the developmental pattern for a group in a given setting without the systematic collection of data on that group or the comparison of that group with those in other settings (including population, time frame, and other structural conditions). In fact, one purpose of the current volume is to inspire more systematic comparative studies of developmental patterns in psychotherapy groups.

Table 3.1 summarizes the progressive stage models we have discussed here.

TABLE 3.1
Models of Group Development

Model	Stages	Orientation emphasis (conflict vs. task)	Type of group	Phase-specific role and behaviors of leader or therapist	Comment

Bennis and Shepard (1956)	1. Dependence
	  • Dependence: flight
	  • Counterdependence: fight
	  • Resolution: catharsis
	2. Interdependence
	  • Enchantment: flight
	  • Disenchantment: fight
	  • Consensual validation
		Conflict	Training	The leader exercises care not to subvert a natural developmental process.	The historical importance of this model is inestimable; the relatively easy transfer of theoretical constructs derived from observations on a group of residents to therapy groups argues against the compartmentalization of findings from different types of groups.

Tuckman (1965); Tuckman and Jensen (1977)	1. Forming 2. Storming 3. Norming 4. Performing 5. Adjourning	Task	Training, experiential, therapy	This model focuses on activities of members separate from the interventions of the designated leader.	This model is important in that it incorporates extant research based on 50 studies, 26 based on therapy groups, 11 on training groups, and 13 on natural or laboratory groups.
Agazarian (1997)	1. Dependence–flight 2. Counterdependence–fight 3. Power–authority 4. Overpersonal enchantment 5. Counterpersonal disenchantment 6. Interdependence–work	Task and conflict	Therapy and training	The therapist helps the members to form into subgroups, engage in differentiation of positions within subgroups, integrate with alternate subgroups, and challenge defenses.	Agazarian has developed a highly specific group process technology for enabling the group to move from stage to stage.

	Stages				
A. P. Beck (1974, 1981a, 1981b)	1. Making a contract 2. Establishment of a group identity and direction 3. The exploration of individuals in the group 4. The establishment of intimacy 5. The exploration of mutuality 6. The achievement of autonomy through reorganization of the group's structure 7. Self-confrontation and the achievement of interdependence 8. Independence, the transfer of learning 9. Termination of group and separation from significant persons	Conflict	Long-term outpatient	The therapist supports the emergence of different types of leaders at different developmental stages.	This model provides the most comprehensive account of how the membership participates in the leadership of the group and does so in varying ways across the developmental phases. This approach provides attention to the mechanisms by which a shift occurs from one phase to another.
MacKenzie (1997)	1. Engagement 2. Differentiation 3. Individuation 4. Intimacy 5. Mutuality 6. Termination	Task and conflict	Short term	There are subtle shifts in therapist bearing from phase to phase.	MacKenzie outlined for each stage the ramifications of maturation for the individual member and the group as a whole. MacKenzie's model is particularly useful for short-term groups.

continues

TABLE 3.1
Continued

Model	Stages	Orientation emphasis (conflict vs. task)	Type of group	Phase-specific role and behaviors of leader or therapist	Comment
Wheelan (2005)	1. Dependency and inclusion 2. Interdependency and fight 3. Trust and Structure 4. Work 5. Termination	Task	Groups conducted in work settings and to a lesser extent therapy and personal growth groups.	The leader has specific goals at each stage of development. Goals vary depending on the type of group being led.	Wheelan's model is distinguished by the rigor with which it has been tested.
Brabender and Fallon (this volume, chaps. 5 and 6)	1. Formation and engagement 2. Conflict and rebellion 3. Unity and intimacy 4. Integration and work 5. Termination	Task and conflict	Inpatient and outpatient psychotherapy	The therapist varies a range of interventions selected with mindfulness of stage. Interventions are directed both toward helping members complete the tasks of the stage as well as assisting members in accessing the resources that will enable them to resolve stage-specific conflicts.	This model specifies a range of interventions within each stage to enable members to complete the tasks and resolve the conflicts of that stage.

ALTERNATIVES TO THE PROGRESSIVE MODEL

Some approaches to group development see the group as continually cycling through a series of developmental stages, even with a stable membership. Although cycling approaches are more prevalent in the organizational psychology literature, an example within the group psychotherapy literature is Schutz's (1958) previously described model in which the group members address and readdress issues pertaining to inclusion, control, and affection. Within the more recent group psychotherapy literature, cyclic approaches often are used to describe the process of very brief psychotherapy groups for which the presumption exists that the groups do not have sufficient longevity to undergo the type of developmental process described by a progressive model.

As MacKenzie (1997) noted, the cyclic and progressive approaches are potentially compatible with and capable of being integrated into a comprehensive theoretical model of group development. For example, Bales's view of groups as moving between task and emotional domains may occur in every stage of development. In other words, certain recurrent cyclic models may capture micropatterns within a broader stage pattern. See Figure 3.1 for MacKenzie's depiction of a conceptualization integrating cyclic and progressive descriptions of change (1997, p. 283).

Yalom and Leszcz (2005), who wrote about the process of interpersonal learning in which members accept and offer feedback, described a two-stage process in which affect is evoked through member exchanges and then members strive to understand the experiences that led to these affects. Many developmental writers incorporate this concept of interpersonal learning into their descriptions of members' work within the developmental stages, particularly the latter stages. As such, they acknowledge the presence of cyclic phenomena within a progressive model.

THE CONTRIBUTION OF THEORY TO THINKING ON THE DEVELOPMENT OF THERAPY GROUPS

Early models of group psychotherapy had their foundation in psychodynamic theory and, most especially, object relations thinking. Bion's articulation of the basic assumption states was rooted in Melanie Klein's paranoid–schizoid and depressive positions (McLeod & Kettner-Polley, 2004). The concept of containment so critical to understanding the role of the therapist was based on Melanie Klein's concept of projective identification. Many approaches such as Agazarian's (1997) systems-centered psychotherapy and MacKenzie's (1990) short-term approach integrated psychodynamic concepts with GST (von Bertalanffy, 1968). The psychodynamic aspect provided a framework for understanding the goals that members should address and the

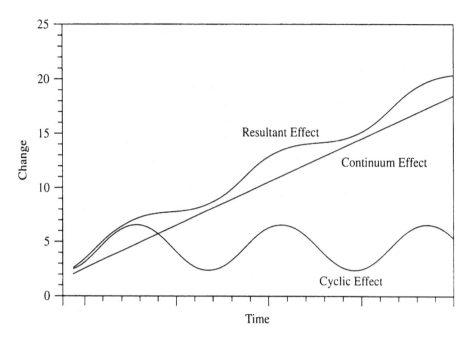

Figure 3.1. From *Handbook of Group Psychotherapy: An Empirical and Clinical Synthesis* (p. 258), by A. Fuhriman and G. M. Burlingame (Eds.), 1994, New York: Wiley. Copyright 1994 by Wiley. Reprinted with permission of John Wiley & Sons, Inc.

sequence of issues that arise in a group. GST has provided a means of conceptualizing the relationships between individual members, subgroups, and the group as a whole. In the past 2 decades, developmental stages have been considered from the vantage of a greater array of theoretical orientations such as self psychology (Kieffer, 2001), constructivism (Brower, 1996), and intersubjective approaches (Cohen, 2000).

NEW PARADIGMS FOR CONSIDERING GROUP DEVELOPMENT

In recent decades, other paradigms for characterizing group development have appeared. These recently emerging approaches were inspired by theoretical developments in the physical and biological sciences that address the role of uncertainty and unpredictability in the changes in complex adaptive systems (Masterpasqua & Perna, 1997; Perna & Masterpasqua, 1997).

Complexity–Chaos Theory

The complexity sciences provide new insights into change in the psychotherapy group. From the standpoint of complexity theory and its subarea of chaos theory (Masterpasqua & Perna, 1997), complex adaptive systems

have certain characteristics that have frequently been ascribed to psychotherapy groups, particularly approaches based on GST (von Bertalanffy, 1968).
As such, the mechanisms that are identified within complexity theory accounting for system change may apply to psychotherapy groups as well.

According to complexity theory, four features characterize complex systems: irreversibility, dissipativeness, nonlinearity, and the capacity to self-
organize. *Irreversibility* refers to the notion that the present status of a system
is a result of the entirety of its history. Group theorists such as Agazarian and
Peters (1981) have noted that within the system of the group, current events
that contrast with past events do not nullify the latter; they merely lead to an
expansion of the group's complexity. For example, if members who have
clashed in an earlier stage are at present on highly amiable terms, the ami-
ability does not eliminate the adversarial dimension; these elements coexist
in a higher order representation of members' experiences of one another.
The *dissipative* aspect of a system pertains to the constant exchange of information in which a system and the broader environment in which it is embedded engage (Prigogine & Stengers, 1984). This feature had long been
recognized by general systems theorists (Durkin, 1982) as a fundamental feature of group life. The group is a system that exchanges information with
other groups; the subgroups of the group and the individual members are
subsystems that also send and receive input.

Nonlinearity is the lack of a direct relationship between a perturbation
(information) to a living system and the reaction to the systems. Nonlinearity
has commonly been observed to characterize the unfolding of group process.
For example, MacKenzie (1983), who examined the relationship between
the dimensions of the climate of the group (engagement, avoidance, and
conflict), and the number of sessions, found a nonlinear function for each of
the three dimensions. Associated with nonlinearity is the principle of sensitivity to initial conditions. Systems that are engaged with the environment
by importing information from the environment and exporting information
into the environment are poised at the "edge of chaos" (Lewin, 1992, p. 51)
or in the transitional space between order and chaos wherein seemingly trivial
bits of information impinging on a system transform that system. As Gould
(1991) wrote, speaking of how an individual's input into a system can alter
that system, "Perturbations, starting as tiny fluctuations wrought by individuals, can accumulate to profound and permanent alterations in much larger
worlds" (p. 505).

The final feature of complex adaptive systems is that they *self-organize*,
possessing the wherewithal to move from chaos to order. That is, systems
have the potential to evolve structures that reduce the group's vulnerability
to being radically altered by minor perturbations. The structures that arise to
order a system are neither predictable on the basis of a knowledge of the units
composing the system nor entirely determined by environmental input.

The recognition of a group's capacity to self-organize is what gave rise to group-as-a-whole and GST depictions of group life. Furthermore, group developmental stage models are descriptions of how a group self-organizes. Were groups unable to self-organize, the issue of how they do so would become moot.

The fact that groups manifest the properties of irreversibility, dissipativeness, nonlinearity, and self-organization raises the possibility that the complexity–chaos theory characterization of changes in living systems may apply to the psychotherapy group. According to the complexity–chaos system account of development, a psychotherapy group poised at the edge of chaos in a state of maximal sensitivity to the environment will follow one of any number of courses. These courses are strange attractors that set parameters for how a group can operate. Yet, within these parameters, infinite variation can be seen in a group's behavior. The reader might envision—as chaos theorists often do (e.g., M. D. Lewis & Junyk, 1997)—the group as a ball that has landed in a basin (the strange attractor). Although the rolls of the ball can show infinite variation that is unpredictable, the variation is within certain limits established by the shape of the basin. Once a group moves in the direction of a strange attractor, a period of order ensues. However, if the group continues to have an active exchange of information with the environment, the group can move close to a chaotic state in which the group once again can be sensitive to system-altering perturbations.

The complexity–chaos description of how change occurs in a group can be understood as a model alternate to group developmental stage–phase models. Stacey (2005) for example, argued that complexity theory accounts for change purely in terms of local action—an idea at odds with the existence and operation of a system. For Stacey, the construct of the group as a whole is epiphenomenal (see Schermer, 2005). The notion of a group as a system or as a whole, it may be argued, is the foundation of group developmental approaches.[6] Group developmental models see the group as a whole or the group system undergoing development with individuals partaking of this system development. Stacey also argued that when individual agents determine the unfolding of events in the group, then each group will necessarily have its own unique "evolutionary path" (Stacey, 2005, p. 194), a notion in direct opposition to the theorem that groups progress through a common set of stages.

Conversely, others (e.g., Brabender, 1997; Gantt & Agazarian, 2004; Wheelan, 2005) who have focused on different aspects of complexity theory

---

[6]Schermer (2005), who was the section editor of the special series in the journal *Group* on group-as-a-whole theory in which Stacey's (2005) article appeared, argued that Stacey, although making many important points, including the danger of unduly reifying the notion of the group as a psychological reality, neglected the role of context provided by the group, a context to which group members are sensitive and that influences their behavior. Schermer saw context as providing theoretical justification for the postulation of the group as a whole.

have noted that these two paradigms are not inherently incompatible. The greatest potential for their integration exists in relation to group developmental stage–phase models that identify the subgroup as the basic unit of analysis in group life because, in this instance, the environment becomes the broader group. Like the basin described earlier, the subgroup is a container for members' adopting a particular solution to a psychological conflict. The explorations of the subgroup are like the trajectories of the ball within the basin. As Gantt and Agazarian (2004) noted, these subgroups must be sufficiently stabilized to do critical exploratory work. The work within a subgroup enables it to become more porous, that is, increase its exchange of information with the environment including alternate subgroups (an exchange that is not invariable in groups). This intensive exchange enables the group to move closer to the edge of chaos in which the subgroups' assimilation of a new strange attractor can be transformational, leading the group to move toward another set of developmental conflicts. Alternatively, however, subgroups may move toward a more regressive position. Finally, subgroups that stay far from chaos are least likely to show progressive or regressive changes; in other words, far-from-chaos groups are most likely to become fixated.

Efforts to apply complexity–chaos theory to group psychotherapy have been largely metaphorical; they have not entailed the mathematical modeling of complexity–chaos theory postulates found in the physical sciences. However, in the next chapter, we discuss research efforts that are underway to examine group process with some of the methods used in the physical science applications of complexity–chaos theory. Such efforts will enable group psychotherapists to determine whether group change is best described by a progressive stage model, a nonlinear model derived from complexity–chaos theory, or some hybrid of the two.

The Punctuated Equilibrium Approach

Although complexity–chaos theory is probably the most common alternative to stage–phase models, other models have been proposed. Gersick (1988) described a punctuated equilibrium approach to change in groups. This approach is important in that experimentally it has been used as a competitive model with the stage–phase progressive model. Gersick observed that groups develop patterns early in their histories and may fail to revise these patterns for extended periods. She likened this early pattern to psychotherapy, in which events in the initial session appear to have a formative effect on the relationship. During the period of stability that follows the group's initial pattern, a diminished sensitivity to the environment is observed. At the midpoint of the group's life, members show a dramatic receptivity to new perspectives; the group's former equilibrium is now punctuated. Gersick (1988) wrote,

> The midpoint appears to work like an alarm clock, heightening members' awareness that their time is limited, stimulating them to compare

where they are with where they need to be and to adjust their progress accordingly: it is "time to roll." (p. 34)

Although the midpoint is a natural time for the group to transition into new modes of behavior, some groups make this shift at other times.

The three conditions that are necessary for the transition to occur are that the group understands the task and has the resources for pursuing it, has some sense of urgency with respect to the task, and believes that sufficient time is available to make progress on the task. During the transition point, the group has a heightened responsiveness to environmental input and takes a more active role in using the resources of the environment.

Although Gersick's (1988) model of group change is seen as a competitor model for progressive stage–phase models, as with complexity–chaos theory, some theorists have argued that a punctuated equilibrium model can be combined with a progressive model. For example, Chang, Bordia, and Duck (2003) argued that each model deals with different aspects of unfolding group phenomena. The punctuated equilibrium model illumines members' sense of the passage of time and pacing in relation to completion of the task. The progressive model describes changes in task and socioemotional aspects of members' experience. Once again, however, a conceptualization of two models' compatibility is insufficient to establish the value of integrating them in accounting for group change; such conceptual accounts should lead to testable hypotheses concerning group changes, applying each model independently and in combination.

Social Entrainment

The social entrainment model proposed by Kelly and McGrath (1988; McGrath, 1991) provides another perspective on how change occurs in a group over time through the concept of entrainment. According to McGrath (1991), entrainment can occur "within individuals, between individuals, and between individuals and their embedded systems" (p. 164). Entrainment may mold physiological processes or social behaviors, with the latter being of greater interest to the group psychotherapist. Social entrainment involves a coordination among group members' behaviors that occurs over time and can be affected by both external and internal factors. That is, when an element within a system moves into a rhythmic pattern, other elements in that system will also move into that pattern. For example, on an inpatient unit, the overall atmosphere of the unit may engender a set of behaviors in the group: If a number of members have been precipitously discharged (an event external to the group), members in the group may exhibit patterns of insecurity. Within the group, as one member engages in interrupting behavior (internal behavior), others follow suit, and eventually interruptions become a normative activity. According to McGrath, social entrainment can affect the abil-

TABLE 3.2
Models of Group Processes

Model type	Description	Group phenomena for which the model accounts
Progressive stage	Development is organized into stages, each of which builds on the other. At each stage, the structural features of the system and the patterns of interaction among the elements of the system change.	This model describes well the qualitatively different patterns of interaction over periods of group life and the influence of events of earlier periods on later phenomena observed in the group.
Cyclical	This model depicts the group cycling and recycling through a limited number of phases.	Group psychotherapists commonly observe that groups return to issues that they had addressed earlier in the life of the group.
Complexity and chaos	Change in complex adaptive systems is characterized by irreversibility, dissipativeness, nonlinearity (including sensitivity to initial. conditions), and self-organization.	Chaos theory accounts for the experience of both therapists and group members that the group moves into periods in which behaviors seem unpredictable and sessions have a fragmented quality and also into periods of organization and relative stability.
Punctuated equilibrium	Long periods of stability are punctuated by environmental upheavals that lead to system changes that are rapid and radical.	The transition from one stage to another is not invariably gradual. For example, once the group proceeds through the barometric event, the group tends to reorganize in a rapid and dramatic fashion.
Robust equilibrium	The robust equilibrium model predicts a brief period of instability followed by a steady state.	The period that precedes the consolidation of a subgrouping structure is often a chaotic one. Once the subgrouping structure is in place, the group tends to use that structure for a relatively protracted period (relative to the chaotic period).
Entrainment	The autonomous processes within a system move toward increasing synchrony with one another.	The group often exhibits a pattern synchronous with the external event; members exhibit patterns synchronous with the group as a whole.
Adaptive contingency	Changes occur based on external and internal contingencies.	Psychotherapy groups have been shown to be affected not only by internal events but also by the climactic features of the system in which the group is embedded (Astrachan, Harrow, & Flynn, 1968).

ity of the group to perform the tasks of various developmental stages. For instance, if the previously mentioned interrupting behavior is consonant with the goals of a given stage, the entrainment may serve to advance the group's development. Table 3.2 summarizes models of group processes we have discussed here.

CONCLUSION

Many writers (e.g., Elfant, 1997; Yalom & Leszcz, 2005) on group psychotherapy have exhorted group therapists not to emphasize developmental stages to such an extent that other group phenomena are missed. Rutan and Stone (2001) wrote, "Thus far no schema describing group development has been able to do justice to the complexity of internal fantasies and behavioral transactions that occur when a small group of individuals organize and begin to work together" (p. 37). The emergence of other approaches such as complexity–chaos theory and punctuated equilibrium models, when examined in concert with progressive stage–phase approaches, holds promise for enabling the group psychotherapist to address more fully the manifold dimensions on which groups change over time.

4

EMPIRICAL INVESTIGATIONS OF GROUP DEVELOPMENT

Scientific interest in groups started in the late 1800s with the burgeoning of the social science disciplines, although scholars had been observing groups for centuries. Pioneering scientists from the fields of economics, political science, anthropology, sociology, and psychology each uniquely incorporated a particular slant of group examination in their study of human behavior and institutions (Forsyth & Burnette, 2005). Their efforts, though, were not without theoretical and methodological controversies. Some felt that the study of group behavior was too ambitious when scientists had such limited understanding of the individual. Understanding of human behavior at the time was centered on stimulus–response learning and conditioning, and scientists had little understanding of the relationship of mental states to nervous system functioning. Others questioned the existence of group-level processes and argued that group behavior could be understood as the sum of its individual components (Cartwright & Zander, 1968). Only after decades of research demonstrated the existence and powerful influence of group-level processes such as norms, leadership, and cohesiveness did respected skeptics such as Floyd Allport rescind their protests (Allport, 1924, 1961). The study of how and why groups change over time is little more than a half century old.

In this chapter, we first discuss methodological issues affecting research in group development. The acquisition of knowledge in the area of group process has followed the typical pattern of other areas of social science and has been intricately intertwined with technological advances. To appreciate the current state of the knowledge base, a brief examination of some of the questions and issues facing group development researchers is essential.

Second, we describe the early research efforts on group development. The work of Bales (1950; Bales & Strodtbeck, 1951) and Bion (1961), who proposed a cyclical model of group process, is contrasted with the work of others who supported a progressive model (Bennis & Shepard, 1956; Stock & Thelen, 1958). Tuckman's (1965; Tuckman & Jensen, 1977) elaboration of a stage model based in part on his empirical review of the literature marked a transition from this early period to the contemporary involvement of a more rigorous empirical methodology.

Third, we present three types of empirical evidence that support a stage theory of development. The study of therapeutic factors looks at how individual group member's perceptions of the importance and presence of these factors change over the life of the group. The examination of leadership patterns involves the centrality of specific types of group leaders and their systematic changes over the course of the group. In a third group of studies, the maturity of the group (number of sessions) is linked to characteristics of the group climate in student and organization groups with evidence for a model of progressive development. This section is followed by the evidence and writing that does not support a progressive stage model.

A progressive stage model is only useful if it has some relationship to the success of the group and its members. In our final question, we tackle the issue of whether outcome, individual or group success, is related to a group that is functioning at a more advanced level of development. We present evidence from inpatient and outpatient groups, process and training groups, and organizational groups. We conclude that there is a resoundingly positive relationship between stage of development and outcome.

THE CONTRIBUTION OF RESEARCH TO THE STUDY OF GROUP DEVELOPMENT

In any field of study, a summary research chapter often is presented simply and elegantly. It rarely captures the uncertainty, tentativeness, and downright messiness on which the scaffolding was built. To do so would mire the reader in too many details of the empirical problems common to all areas of study and prevent researchers from making any meaningful statements about the subject matter as they continuously diluted the strength of their assertions. It is important to know that although researchers in the area of group development have worked hard to advance their knowledge base, they have and are continuing to overcome many obstacles to their study. We briefly discuss the conceptual issues, problems in methodology, technological advances, and interpretation of findings.

Conceptual Issues

Each theory of group development that is presented is a coherent story of how a group changes over time. Take, for instance, this description (with the text references removed) of the second of five stages in a theory of group development:

> The second *stage* is described as a *period* of *counterdependency* and *conflict*. Issues of *power*, *authority*, and *competition* are *debated* at this stage . . . these early *struggles* regarding authority and *status* are prerequisites for *subsequent increases* in *cohesion* and *cooperation*. (Wheelan & Williams, 2003, p. 444; emphasis added)

This description illustrates the difficulties a researcher has in providing empirical support for that statement. Each italicized term requires considerable deliberation.

First, consider the conceptual question highlighted by the use of *stage*. A developmental process has the potential to be continuous or composed of stages or steps. A belief in a discrete change versus a continuous one will determine how one goes about studying the process. Does the group progress through discrete stages (e.g., MacKenzie, 1990), or does it cycle back (e.g., Bales, 1950; Bion, 1961)? If the latter is the case, under what circumstances does that phenomenon occur? If a particular stage is not manifest, what does this absence mean for the group process? Can other stages occur or is the group's growth stunted? Is there a way a group can compensate for a lost stage?

Second, testing the veracity of a theory requires that each term be operationalized, so that it is observable and measurable. The references to time (e.g., "period of counterdependency," "subsequent") require specification of a time frame. Should time be measured in hours or by sessions or purely by stage characteristics? How does one decide when to take the measurements? Is each of the stages approximately equal in time? Terms such as *power*, *authority*, and *competition* can be captured in a measure of thematic content, but they can also refer to an interaction between individuals. How does one measure a power struggle between individuals? How does one decide what a debated issue is or when it is necessary to label such an issue as a struggle for status? Should content or process be measured? Are both counterdependency and conflict needed, or is one enough to label the interaction as Stage 2?

Another important conceptual issue concerns how one defines the purpose of the group (MacKenzie, 1994a). When a laboratory study uses a clearly defined task (e.g., designing a solution to a complex problem), success can be determined by some external measure, such as the time to reach a solution or the number of solutions found. The outcome is a group product. In a psychotherapy group, however, success is based on how many members feel better (e.g., 5 out of 8 patients no longer meet criteria for depression). The outcome is the composite of each member's health, which is basically an individual outcome. Is the same process of development required for successful completion of a group task versus an individual one?

Problems in Methodology

Methods of observation, correlation, and experimental intervention are all integral parts of the empirical method. As discussed in the section later in this chapter, "Early Study of Group Development," early work relied primarily on observation and personal experience for theory construction (e.g., Bennis & Shepard, 1956; Bion, 1961). Authors' findings were impressionistic, subject to personal bias and a priori conceptualization. Later studies tended to use empirical methodology, focusing on more objective measures of the strength of a relationship between two variables. Empirical methodology requires that constructs be operationally defined, and this definitional enterprise may involve tackling important but thorny conceptual issues. For example, can one track group process by looking at individuals only, or must there be some measure of the group climate? Should investigators rely on members' perceptions or require independent behavioral analysis?

Instruments measuring these concepts require creative thought, cross-validation, and proper establishment of psychometric properties (e.g., reliabilities and validities) to enable the professional community to communicate deftly and precisely about the same phenomenon. To bring such an instrument to fruition can take a decade of a researcher's life, as has been the case for Beck's sociometric measure of leadership roles (A. P. Beck, 1974, 1981b). Once the instrument is available, how does one determine when to implement its use? Is it sufficient to administer it once or are several equally spaced administrations necessary? If the data do not yield the hypothesized findings, is it because the theory is incorrect or has the timing of instrument administration been incorrectly determined? The well-standardized instrument often mandates a standardized procedure of data collection. However, the often unacknowledged dark side of any methodological paradigm is that it can only report on the questions it asks and cannot speak to the procedure it does not use or the data that it does not collect, thus potentially limiting what researchers "see."

Studies using a true experimental design are still rare in the area of group development. By far the most common design is to examine an already organized group in progress (Wheelan, Burchill, & Tilin, 2003) created for a purpose other than the pursuit of a scientific question. The lab groups created by Bales (1950) and Kivlighan and colleagues (Kivlighan & Lilly, 1997; Kivlighan & Mullison, 1988; Kivlighan, Multon, & Patton, 2000), enabled a focus on variables of significance.

Technological advances such as the widespread use and acceptance of videotaping have allowed for improved methods of recording data. The use of tapes and other electronic products is less subject to human error than is note-taking. Tapes permit independent review, enable establishment of interrater reliability, and entail less intrusiveness than a group observer who makes notes. Permanent recordings also facilitate the recoding of new variables at some future time. Regardless of the technological advances, group development research is labor intensive; considerable time is consumed identifying units of behavior and categorizing them. For example, in the Wheelan, Davidson, and Tilin study (2003), transcripts from 26 groups were transcribed, and 31,782 units of communication were identified and catalogued into one of eight categories.

Statistical Advances

The widespread use of computers and availability of statistical packages has greatly enhanced researchers' ability to track and analyze a great many more variables than was previously possible when all statistical analyses were calculated by paper and pencil. Bales and Strodtbeck (1951) had little statistical help available to them. Their chi-squares and creative use of transpositions were cumbersome compared with today's more technologically driven methods. They concluded that their groups were not following a random pattern but could only hypothesize judiciously about phases in problem-solving groups. Later multivariate analyses supported the study of a greater number of variables but could only do so if the relationships were linear. These methods limited researchers in tracking complicated systems.

Within the past few years, growth curve analysis has made possible the examination of variable relationships that may be curvilinear in nature (Kivlighan & Lilly, 1997) and enables researchers to track individual members over time (see the methodological discussion by Burlingame, Fuhriman, & Johnson, 2004). Nascent efforts of the application of chaos or complexity theory (see chap. 3, this volume) to the area of group development have allowed investigation of the usefulness of multidimensional visual representations of the group system (Wheelan & Williams, 2003). These new paradigms of analysis have facilitated the greatest amount of growth and knowledge in this area because they have encouraged researchers to consider group change as a much more complex process.

Interpretation of Findings

Thus far, each research team has developed its own model and method-ological paradigm to study group development. In addition, group therapy researchers have been for the most part unaware of their counterparts in social psychology and organizational development (and vice versa). As a result, little cross-fertilization has occurred in terms of theory and empirical work.

Although awareness of others investigating group process has increased, the question still remains as to whether the findings of one set of investigators on one type of group are applicable to another type. Is the development similar in work groups, training groups, therapy groups, and laboratory task groups? Does the length of time allotted for the task affect stage development? Does the number of members in the small group influence the ability of the group to progress through stages? How does leadership impact development? Is group process affected by demographics such as gender, age, intelligence, status, and ethnicity? How does group process affect outcome? With little intergroup exchange, many of these questions remain insufficiently (and in some cases barely) explored. In the remainder of this chapter, we examine what knowledge has been empirically acquired in these areas. We hope that different research groups will begin to recognize the value of each other's contributions.

EARLY STUDY OF GROUP DEVELOPMENT

Robert Bales (1950) is credited with the earliest empirical work in group development. Using single-session laboratory groups run as problem-solving exercises, Bales developed a system to code interaction patterns in small groups. His interactional process analysis was composed of 12 categories of behavior, which collapsed into four broader areas: *attempted answers* (gives suggestion, opinion, or orientation), *questions* (asks for orientation, opinion, or suggestion), *positive reactions* (shows solidarity, shows tension release, or agrees), and *negative reactions* (shows tension, shows antagonism). The attempted answers and questions areas pertain to member activities that are instrumental to the assigned task. Positive and negative reactions areas are expressive functions that regulate emotional tension. Bales observed that as the group attempts to work on the task, tensions build. These tensions begin to interfere with task resolution unless dealt with by emotional activity. Such activity then permits the group to return to the task with renewed energy. Bales identified two leaders in this process: the task and the socioemotional leaders. The instrumental and emotional functions oscillate over time, an observation that led Bales to conclude that there are recurring cyclical patterns in small groups. He felt all groups balanced both task and socioemotional activity. Given the brief span of Bales's groups, MacKenzie (1994a) averred that the cyclical pattern observed by Bales was not two different stages of group development but represented a micropattern that could be expected in all stages of group.

Bales and Strodtbeck (1951) observed 22 single-session problem-solving groups occurring in the natural environment. Using their 12-category system to code interaction, they concluded that "when considered as an aggregate [they] show a significant departure from a random distribution of acts between phases" (p. 494). Their descriptive statistics suggest that orientation statements are highest in the first phase and then progressively drop. Evaluation statements remain quite high throughout the phases. Positive and negative reactions and control statements increase over time with positive statements always remaining proportionately higher than the other two. On the basis of these findings, Bales and Strodtbeck offered a three-phase developmental progression. In the initial stage, members are concerned with orientation and the giving of information. This is followed by a period of information evaluation. A decision is made in a phase that involves control, during which there is support for some opinions and rejection of others. These findings and conclusions form the foundation on which most small group studies rest. MacKenzie (1994a) has indicated the seminal nature of Bales's work.

> Bales's recognition of the importance of the group roles of task and socioemotional leadership links group development to the characteristics of the members. It deepens the understanding of the relationship between the individual and the group that was first identified by Lewin. The two theoretical approaches of group development and group roles have formed the principle axes for understanding group level process. (p. 229)

For the next 2 decades, a number of authors, such as Bennis and Shepard (1956) and Bion (1961), primarily clinicians, wrote of their observations and experiences concerning group development (for a review of their work, see chap. 3, this volume). Thelen and colleagues, using Bales's instrumental and expressive functions, devised observational categories based on Bion's theory (Stock & Thelen, 1958). They rated natural units of group interaction[1] (referred to as the Behavioral Rating System) and collected group members' perceptions of the group and members (Reactions to Group Situations Test). Although their interests were primarily in finding empirical support for some of Bion's concepts, such as valency and basic assumption groups, they concluded that the group balanced its efforts between basic assumption states and work, and they came to believe that as each group assumption state emerged, the group dealt with it in an increasingly mature way (MacKenzie, 1994a, 1994b). In their final published efforts, they did find

---

[1]Units were determined by observers' judgment of a natural break in the content and participation of the members.

preliminary evidence for stages of group development and furthermore provided some evidence to support their view of the interplay between the group-advancing stages and individual and subgroup obstructions (Stock & Thelen, 1958).

In summary, each of these three clinician-scholars provided thoughtful observations about group process. Bennis and Shepard (1956) supported the notion that groups move through successive stages. Bion (1961) appeared to reject this model of developmental progress in favor of one that is more cyclic, underscoring that the group periodically regresses from the task to struggle with socioemotional issues. Stock and Thelen (1958), although initially supporting Bion's approach, did find some support for a stage model.

Tuckman (1965) conceptualized a developmental model of group process by organizing more than 50 articles that dealt with either research data or theory. He separated his review into therapy (26 studies), training (11 studies), and natural and laboratory groups (collapsed because there were too few studies in each) and summarized the literature for each type of group. He identified four stages of development that could be discerned from each of these types of groups. In keeping with Bales's division of socioemotional and task functions, he characterized each stage by a description of the interpersonal or group structure realm and the task realm. These stages—forming, storming, norming, and performing—are described in chapter 3. Although Tuckman's review included therapy, training, and natural and lab groups, the last group is underrepresented, so it is difficult to assert that his postulated stages are characteristic of all types of groups. In addition to the limited number of studies, evaluation of the experimental rigor of those studies included is lacking. Most of those reviewed were observations based on single groups. These observations were more descriptive and subject to the impressionistic biases of the observer, who was usually the therapist. The standards for qualitative studies had not developed to the rigorousness is the case today (Josselson & Lieblich, 2003). Tuckman used the equivalent of the box tallying method of analysis to support his assertions, counting the number of published studies to support his theory. This method gives Bales's seminal work the same weight as therapists' observations of their group. The use of meta-analysis was not to occur for another 15 years. At the time it was written, Tuckman's article was an important summation of a disjointed field, even though by his own admission his conceptual system was merely suggested by the data rather than supported by it.

Although Tuckman is most known for his stage sequencing, he attempted to find commonalities among the different types of groups (laboratory, natural, psychotherapy, and training) and to identify some ways in which these types of groups might manifest differently across the developmental stages. He also discussed the importance of addressing separately the task aspect and the interpersonal aspect (or group structure) for the continuity of development to be recognized. He noted that particularly in the therapy and training groups, this separation is difficult. Tuckman's thoughts in this regard are helpful because they set the stage for an examination of how developmental phases might appear in group process groups versus more structured groups such as cognitive–behavioral groups (for further discussion, see chap. 7, this volume). For example, speaking of the second stage of development, Tuckman wrote, "The task stage will be most evident when the task has as its goal self-understanding and self-change, namely, the therapy- and training-group tasks, and will be considerably less visible in groups working on impersonal, intellectual tasks" (1965, p. 386).

A decade later, Tuckman followed up on his original research review (Tuckman & Jensen, 1977). In his survey of 22 new empirical papers, he found only one that actually attempted to test his theory. Runkel, Lawrence, Oldfield, Rider, and Clark (1971) investigated three groups of 15 to 20 college students. Each group was to decide on a project, collect data, interpret it, and write a final report. Unfortunately, observers were given only descriptions of Tuckman's four stages and were instructed to fit what they observed into one of the stages in the model. Results did support Tuckman's theory of group development. However, rather than being given Tuckman's model and being asked to fit their observations into that system, the observers should have been requested to record their observations independently.

Most of the other studies reviewed supported at least some aspects of Tuckman's theory. Only two studies substantially deviated from the four-stage Tuckman model. One was a 9-month study of two sections of a social relations course. Groups were self-analytic. Using a computer content analysis, Dunphy (1968) identified six stages, three of which could be folded into Tuckman's second phase. The biggest discrepancy was that there was no stage similar to performing. The other study involved psychiatric patients in an 18-session group (Heckel, Holmes, & Rosecrans, 1971; Heckel, Holmes, & Salzberg, 1967). The data pointed to a two-stage group process. However, significant methodological flaws were present, including the attrition of one half of the members. Tuckman concluded that what little empirical work had been published generally supported his proposed model.

CONTEMPORARY EFFORTS TO TEST PROGRESSIVE STAGE MODELS

In the 1980s, additional efforts were made to formulate models of group development (A. P. Beck, 1974; MacKenzie & Livesley, 1983; Wheelan, 2005). Each group, conscientious in its efforts to concretize its models, worked to develop methodology to allow empirical investigation. Each theory predicts particular changes in group process over time, and observations ensconced within that contextual paradigm mark whether these shifts actually occur. These researchers' collective contributions to this effort have resulted in three areas of inquiry that generally provide support for a progressive developmental model of group process. These areas, the study of therapeutic factors, leadership roles, and group climate, are examined in the following sections.

Therapeutic Factors

Although not designed to track stage development, changes in members' perceptions of the importance of various therapeutic factors over the life of the group provides support for group progression.

Measurement of Therapeutic Factors

One empirical approach to tracking changes in groups is through an examination of how member perceptions of their significant experiences may change over time. The first method, referred to as the *direct approach* (Bloch, Reibstein, Crouch, Holroyd, & Themen, 1979), descended from the therapeutic factors devised by Corsini and Rosenberg (1955) to delineate a taxonomy of potential therapeutic processes. The technique was modified and extended to have terminating group members complete a questionnaire or Q sort to determine retrospectively those aspects of the experience perceived as important (Bloch et al., 1979; Yalom, 1995). Yalom's (1970, 1995) Q sort requires the placement of 60 statements representing 12 therapeutic factors into piles from most to least helpful. This procedure allows for the comparison of relative importance among factors. Yalom (1995) proposed that the salience of particular therapeutic factors would vary as a function of developmental stage (i.e., the instillation of hope would be critical at the commencement of a group but less prominent as the group progressed). Procedurally, this is a time-consuming and difficult task for the individual. Yalom has provided little psychometric information, and the research that is available suggests that items sometimes do not statistically correlate highly with their assigned category.

A second approach, the *critical-incident technique*, requires group members to describe the most important or critical event of the session. This more indirect method infers a therapeutic factor from the incident, and then either categories are developed to capture the sample or the incident is placed into a predetermined classificatory scheme. The critical-incident technique is quickly and easily administered, allowing for multiple administrations. It has the potential advantage of examining a change process over time and can accommodate a revision of the classification system as incoming data may support. However, it requires a minimum level of writing skill, engagement in the task, and adequate interrater reliability of critical incident placement into categories, and it assumes that a series of single incidents for each individual will capture the complexity of the group change process (for an excellent review, see DeLucia-Waack & Bridbord, 2004).

A third more recent and promising method of measuring is the Therapeutic Factors Inventory (Lese & MacNair-Semands, 2000). It uses a 7-point Likert scale and has participants rate 99 questions (9 questions for each 11 factors). It has good internal consistency and test–retest psychometrics. Although based on Yalom's theory and factors, the Therapeutic Factors Inventory asks members to rate the presence of a factor rather than to follow Yalom's original instructions to rate the relative helpfulness of a factor.

Evidence of Group Progression

An initial study by Freedman and Hurley (1980) involving 28 undergraduates in a 9-week course (50 hours) used Yalom's Q sort at the initial, middle, and final meeting. They found that with increasing group experience, catharsis and interpersonal output (improving interpersonal skills) were perceived as more helpful. Similarly, a study by Butler and Fuhriman (1983) found that members' interactions deepened with continued group involvement. They used the Curative Factors Questionnaire (variation of the Q sort) to sample a cross section of 23 therapy groups (91 patients), which had been meeting for a minimum of 6 months prior to their study. Members in therapy groups meeting for a longer time were more likely to value acceptance (cohesiveness), self-understanding (insight), and learning from interpersonal actions (interpersonal learning output). Finally, MacNair-Semands and Lese (2000) had members of 15 therapy and support groups complete the Therapeutic Factors Inventory on Sessions 3 through 6 and 8 through 12. All therapeutic factors increased with time in the group; universality, instillation of hope, imparting information, recapitulation of family, cohesiveness, and catharsis increased significantly. Although these studies do not provide specific support for a stage model, they did observe changes consistent with most progressive stage models.

Support for a Stage Model

The Butler and Fuhriman (1983) study assumed that data obtained in a single session from a cross section of groups meeting for varying lengths of time were equivalent to data collected from a single group over time. In an effort to correct for this difficulty, MacKenzie (1987) used a longitudinal design with four outpatient psychotherapy groups. In this study, 34 members completed a critical-incident form at the end of the first 20 sessions. Five sessions equally spaced across that time period were chosen for analysis. Twelve categories of therapeutic factors were collapsed into three groups: *morale* (acceptance, instillation of hope, and universality), *self-revelation* (self-disclosure, catharsis), and *psychological work* (self-understanding, learning from interpersonal actions, and vicarious learning). MacKenzie found psychological work increased and morale decreased with advancing sessions. Self-revelation initially dropped and then increased to its highest levels with more advanced sessions. This pattern was interpreted to mean that the initial self-disclosures, which were likely superficial, dropped, and the later revelations occurred with deeper self-exploration (MacKenzie, 1987). The MacKenzie study was the first to find evidence for a stage model rather than simply a progression as the previously mentioned studies had found. These trends suggest the importance of common factors initially and the growth of deeper self-reflection later (MacKenzie, 1997). However, the patterns were reported in percentage endorsed and were not subject to statistical analysis. The interpretation of the phasic nature of self-disclosure, however, is a demonstration of how this methodology alone is not able to capture the complexities of this phenomenon. Another problem with this study is that interrater reliabilities reached only modest levels even when categories collapsed into three groups (kappa coefficients ranging from .28 to .35).

Using a longitudinal design over 11 sessions, Kivlighan and Mullison (1988) studied three groups (18 students) with the critical-incident technique. They found that universality was an important factor early in the life of the group, and interpersonal learning was more highly valued later in group life. It should be noted that groups were analyzed using a split-half design (Sessions 1 to 5 early, 6 to 11 late) that may have masked sensitive changes in the group climate (MacKenzie, 1994a).

In the previous studies (Butler & Furhiman, 1983; Freedman & Hurley, 1980; Kivlighan & Mullison, 1988; MacKenzie, 1987; MacNair-Semands & Lese, 2000), length of time in therapy is equated with advancing stage of development, which is not necessarily the case. In an attempt to rectify this problem, Kivlighan and Goldfine (1991) used the Critical Incident Questionnaire to study six process groups (36 students completing a group psychotherapy course). Groups met for 1 1/2 hours twice a week for 13 weeks. Six judges using the framework of MacKenzie's model of group development and the Group Climate Questionnaire (GCQ; MacKenzie, 1983) made determinations as to when each group entered each of the first three stages. (The model is described in detail in the section on group climate later in this chapter.) Critical incidents were classified into 1 of 10 therapeutic factors (Bloch et al., 1979). Results provided partial support for the predictions that Yalom (1995) made, derived from a developmental model.

As predicted, groups showed significant decreases in universality and hope, suggesting that feelings of hopefulness and universality are important in early group development but are less so later. Unexpectedly, the importance of guidance increased over the course of development (consistent with Kivlighan & Mullison, 1988). The authors hypothesized that the absolute levels of advice and suggestion (the main constituents of guidance) did not change, but group members recorded them increasingly as critical events when they were articulated in a more personal way (later stage) in contrast to a general, less specific, and personal manner (initial stage). Also as predicted, an increase in catharsis occurred over the first three stages of development. This finding is consistent with the notion that as participants explored more personal issues (a characteristic of a later stage of development), they experienced an affective release. Somewhat contrary to expectation, acceptance was an important factor both at the initial and later phases of group development, with it being less so during the middle phase; acceptance is essential when initially engaging with the group as well as when examining more personal concerns.

In this study, interpersonal learning, self-understanding, vicarious learning, altruism, and self-disclosure were not related to group development. Because these were not therapy groups, it is possible that certain mechanisms did not come into play or that a larger sample would have revealed these differences. In addition, these findings may reflect that individuals with different interpersonal styles may value different aspects of the group experience. The lack of change in interpersonal learning over the duration of the group is especially surprising. The authors explained this latter finding in terms of the possibility that the group did not move into the later stages in which interpersonal learning may be especially strong. The possibility of this outcome, that the group may not progress, shows the difficulty of creating tests for the existence of developmental stages.

The studies using therapeutic factors as the dependent variable to measure changes in groups provide some support for the notion that groups change in definable and measurable ways over the life of the group. However in this context, three limitations exist. The first problem is conceptual. By definition, therapeutic factors measure individuals' perceptions about what is important to them about the group experience. Developmental theory would predict that these perceptions would change in a systematic way; by and large the research supports the theory. At the same time, developmental theory predicts that the processes themselves would change over the life of the group. Unfortunately, the prominence of these processes can be ascertained merely through inference when the only data collected are members' self-reports. Second, members may be influenced by the therapist's view of what is important. The therapist's developmental model may be imposed on members' perceptions (Sandahl, Lindgren, & Herlitz, 2000). The third problem is the lack of methodological rigor and small sample sizes characterizing most of the studies. Only the Kivlighan and Goldfine (1991) study subjects the data to statistical hypothesis testing. Despite these limitations, this collection of studies represents a significant advancement in terms of positive empirical support for the concept of group development when compared with the observational and anecdotal work of the earlier decades.

Leadership Patterns

With underpinnings in general systems theory (J. E. Durkin, 1981), client-centered therapy (Rogers, 1970), and developmental psychology (Piaget, 1960), Ariadne Beck and her collaborators developed and elaborated on a theory of group development spanning several decades beginning in the late 1960s (A. P. Beck, 1974, 1981a, 1981b; Brusa, Stone, Beck, Dugo, & Peters, 1994). This theory was based on both informal observation and participation in groups as well as careful study of small (6 to 9 members), time-limited therapy (15 to 20 sessions), training, and encounter groups (A. P. Beck, 1974). These closed groups were relatively unstructured from the onset, and the client-centered leader intervened at both individual and group levels. This context enabled the evolution of a group-as-a-whole dialectical process over the life of these short-term groups, out of which emerged a consistent, discernible, and invariant sequence of interactional patterns.

Beck hypothesized the potential for nine phases in which certain unique structures, tasks, and leaders emerge, which may aid or thwart individual and interpersonal changes (A. P. Beck & Lewis, 2000c). Beck and colleagues' nine-phase model is described in chapter 3 of this volume. Beck posited that the appearance of the nine phases as well as the patterns within each were necessary for the group to function successfully and achieve its stated goals. In her theory, Beck focused on group level issues, the process, and emerging leadership roles as ways of differentiating each of the phases of development.

Beck articulated four leadership functions, each of which is usually fulfilled by a single individual for the life of the group but in their absence would be taken up by another individual. The *designated* or *task* leader is usually the official leader or senior therapist of the group. He or she must be interpersonally skilled and emotionally supportive. The *emotional* leader, important throughout the life of the group, helps manage the emotional life of the group and is often most ready for significant personal growth. The *scapegoat* leader, often insensitive to the more subtle cues in communication, becomes the target for negative affect from the group. His or her struggle with self-assertion versus group conformity crystallizes for the members their own conflicts in this area and in doing so helps the group clarify norms and goals, particularly during the second phase. His or her style forces the group during other phases to communicate more directly. The *defiant* leader, usually an individual who is experiencing psychological and social alienation in his or her outside life, expresses conflict about dependence versus independence. Demanding to be cared for beyond reasonable limits of the group, he or she is reluctant to be involved in a mutual relationship with peers to satisfy these needs. As noted in chapter 3, different leaders emerge at different phases. For example, the emotional leader emerges in the first phase of development and is critical to members' forging initial connections with one another. In Phase 5, the defiant leader, a member who is threatened by intimacy and dependency, becomes prominent.

This detailed theory is potentially empirically testable with A. P. Beck's (1974) enormous and rich data set of approximately 36 groups. To date, however, only a handful of studies have been published primarily around emerging leadership functions; some of these are demonstrations of how the tenets of her theory could be empirically tested but would not meet the standards of hypothesis testing (A. P. Beck, Eng, & Brusa, 1989; A. P. Beck & Lewis, 2000a, 2000b, 2000c). Her reports have often captured an inside view of the triumphs and disappointments that occur in research. Tenacious, tedious, intensive data analysis has yielded tentative, but promising findings.

Central to Beck and colleagues' theory of group development is the hypothesis that different leadership structures emerge over the nine phases. To test this hypothesis, A. P. Beck and Peters (1981) devised a brief instrument that could differentiate each of the leadership roles. The development of this instrument illustrates the typical manner in which empirical work proceeds in a clinical domain—a maneuvering back and forth between clinical observation and sociometric data occurs. A series of questions using a sociometric technique was compared with clinical judgments of leadership. Using 6 of the original 18 questions, Peters and Beck (1982) could clearly distinguish the designated and emotional leaders from all others, but the defiant and scapegoat leaders could not be differentiated from each other. If Beck was correct that different phases require differentially active roles by the four leaders, then completing these questions only once at the end of the group may have obscured changing perceptions. In an attempt to rectify this problem, A. P. Beck et al. (1989) analyzed the questions by phase. Each group was given 7 to 10 questions once. Of the 36 groups analyzed, the use of 3 questions (rank-order group members according to the pleasure derived from each, in terms of the risks they take, and according to how ambivalent they are about being in group) nicely differentiated each of the leaders over the span of the nine phases proposed by Beck. However, only question means for each leader were graphed by phase because the questions were administered only once per group. This sociometric effort has undergone further development. In a study by Brusa, Stone, Beck, Dugo, and Peters (1994), 273 group members (in 31 psychotherapy groups) answered a subset of the standard 18 questions. Groups were clinically evaluated to be in Phases 2 through 6 and 9. A discriminant function analysis of the four leadership role assignments yielded a 97% hit rate with clinically identified roles. The scapegoat leader was the least accurate with a hit rate of 81% (Brusa et al., 1994). Although promising, this work has not yet been replicated or cross-validated with another sample of group members.

Beck's work not only supports her particular model of group development but also the more general idea that the life of the group is organized into a series of stages.[2] It should also be underscored that Beck's model, in

---

[2]C. M. Lewis and Beck (1983) also explored the use of the Experiencing scale developed by Gendlin (1967). They were interested in the relationship of individual self-exploration and the process of group development. Preliminary findings indicated that the scale reflects changes from one stage to another. For example, turn-taking of self-exploration occurs in Phase 3. Although promising, no further publications have appeared on this project; it is discussed briefly in the "Leadership Patterns" section in this chapter.

terms of the early stages, has considerable overlay with other developmental models such as MacKenzie's (1990).

Group Climate

The therapeutic factors approach asks the question of what individual members have found helpful. Systematic changes in what has been helpful can point to group development. The leadership pattern approach examines the emergence of certain leadership structures at different times in the group. Who fulfills these functions and when this is perceived by its members has been offered as evidence of group development. Examining the atmosphere in a group over time shifts the focus of investigation away from the individual onto the group as a whole.

Three research groups led by A. P. Beck, Kivlighan, and Wheelan, respectively, have attempted to investigate group development by using the concept of group climate. Each group, whose work is explored in some detail, has a slightly different theory of group development, and as needed, these theories are summarized to make the findings understandable.

Studies of Beck's Model

A. P. Beck and her colleagues, whose theory was delineated in the previous section, characterized each of the nine phases by identifying leadership functions, interpersonal processes, and intrapersonal processes and group-as-a-whole processes (A. P. Beck, 1974). Although Beck has not directly attempted to study group climate, one of her goals was to operationalize the phases and transitions between them (A. P. Beck, 1983; C. M. Lewis, Beck, Dugo, & Eng, 2000). However, even demonstrating the transition from one phase to the next is a formidable task. In preparation for analyzing these transitions, the research team needed to articulate behavioral units and validate instruments to measure unfolding processes. The initial focus of the Beck group was on the transition from Phase 2 to Phase 3, which was concretized as three criteria: movement from competitiveness to cooperation (interpersonal); movement from defensive behavior to mutual exploration (intrapersonal); and movement from struggle around organizational and norm development to concentration on personal concern (group as a whole). Measures of interpersonal hostility and support (Hostility/Support scale) and group-as-a-whole transition from norm concerns to personal concerns (Normative–Organizational/Personal Exploration Scale) were developed. The Experiencing Scale (Gendlin, 1967), a measure of intrapsychic exploratory behavior, was adapted (A. P. Beck, 1983; Dugo & Beck, 1984; C. M. Lewis & Beck, 1983). Each of these scales engaged outside raters who required training and acceptable interrater reliability. The laborious process of tape or transcript review then began.

The results to date have been mixed. For the three groups in which this method was applied, two demonstrated clear transition with all criteria met. The third group was reported to have difficulties with development, but the specifics were not presented (A. P. Beck, 1983; C. M. Lewis et al., 2000). Without a larger sample, it is difficult to know whether the criteria of phase transition would be supported. Beck and colleagues have expressed belief that the application of empirically validated instruments will catalyze researchers' understanding and aid in refinement of how group structures are created and evolve. It appears, however, that the labor-intensive nature of the specific instruments used will significantly limit how quickly this research group will be able to share their findings.

Another exciting aspect of what the Beck group has done is to collaborate with those who have other systems of measuring process and demonstrate how each system would analyze the same session (A. P. Beck & Lewis, 2000a, 2000b, 2000c, 2000d; C. M. Lewis & Beck, 2000). This particular demonstration highlights the confluence of various systems to provide layers of information about a single session. However, its application could readily be instituted to explore the development of group process over time.

Studies of the MacKenzie and Livesley Model

On the basis of their observations and data, MacKenzie and Livesley (1983, 1984) articulated a group development theory that includes five stages plus termination. MacKenzie (1983) also developed a methodology to study these group development changes, the GCQ. The short version of this questionnaire (GCQ–S), with 12 items, uses a 7-point Likert scale. This questionnaire contains three factor-analytic subscales—Engaged, Avoiding, and Conflict. The Engaged scale encompasses engagement, support, self-disclosure, challenge, and cognition related to cohesion. The Avoiding scale captures the avoidance of responsibility in the change process. The Conflict scale represents interpersonal conflict and distrust. Its reliability and validity are adequate (MacKenzie, 1983, 1990). It is the most frequently used instrument to measure group process in growth and psychotherapy groups.

Kivlighan and colleagues used the GCQ–S to test the MacKenzie and Livesley model. Kivlighan and Goldfine (1991) studied changes in therapeutic factors with student growth groups. In that study, the GCQ–S was also administered after every session. It was then used by judges to determine the stage of each group as well as the trends of each of its three component factors. For the six groups, 12.3 sessions was the mean for Stage 2, and 17.7 sessions was the mean for Stage 3. Using multivariate analysis, researchers found engagement increased linearly over the three stages; avoidance decreased linearly over the three stages; and conflict, which was initially low to moderate, increased to higher levels and then decreased close to initial levels. No differences among the six groups in these trends were obtained. These findings are consistent with MacKenzie's (1990) description of the first three stages of development.

During Stage 1, scores on the Engagement and Conflict subscales are relatively low, whereas Avoidance is relatively high. During Stage 2, Conflict is high, whereas Engagement and Avoidance are at a moderate level. In Stage 3 in which members begin to explore more personal concerns, Engagement is relatively high, whereas Avoidance and Conflict are relatively low.[3] Although the groups in this study were growth groups composed of college students, an analysis of group climate data revealed no significant differences between this sample and psychotherapy groups reported on by MacKenzie (1983).

In a later study with a similar but larger sample size (83 participants, 14 groups) and format, Kivlighan and Lilly (1997) used growth curve analysis, a more powerful alternative to the earlier multivariate analysis of variance for analyzing repeated measures. Some of their findings were consistent with their earlier study. However, the larger sample size and the ability to take into account therapeutic gain enabled a more sophisticated analysis. Unlike the earlier study, which was not able to distinguish any significant differences in climate patterns among groups, this study found that there were no consistent growth patterns for all groups, although there was high agreement among group members as to their climate. Rather, patterns of engagement, conflict, and avoidance were related to therapeutic gain. Also groups varied in total sessions completed (14 to 26). Number of sessions did not influence group pattern. Rather, within limits, groups of varying lengths followed similar developmental patterns. Other findings in this study are discussed in the next section.

Using an advanced statistical procedure known as *tuckerizing*, Brossart, Patton, and Wood (1998) analyzed a preexisting data set similar to the one used by Kivlighan and Lilly (1997). This method preserves individual input while at the same time allowing for group similarities to emerge. Brossart et al. also attempted to evaluate the degree of congruence between the MacKenzie and Livesley (1983) model and the members' reported experiences. Using four groups of students that met for 28 sessions, investigators had participants complete the GCQ–S after each session and also complete questionnaires addressing their goals and issues. Only the Conflict subscale was analyzed. The results revealed high levels of conflict occurring early in group life and then dropping during the individuation stage. Although the MacKenzie and Livesley theory predicts an increase in conflict, they suggested that it is likely to occur more gradually than was manifested in this study. Inconsistent with the theory, Brossart et al. found high levels of con-

---

[3]One problematic aspect of this methodology was its circularity: It appears that the GCQ–S was used by judges to determine stage of the group, and these stages were the groupings that were then used to determine the relative impact of each of the three factors at each stage.

flict during the later stages of group development (mutuality), which surpassed Stage 2 (differentiation) levels. The use of three different growth curves allowed for the interpretation that only some members may have been experiencing high levels of conflict, whereas others may have reached resolution in the early stages of the group.

Studies Using Wheelan's Model

Wheelan (2005) formulated her own scheme of how groups change and develop across time using Tuckman's (1965; Tuckman & Jensen, 1977) review and her own empirical work with both nonprofit and for-profit organizations. In her five-stage model, Stage 1 deals with issues of inclusion and dependency as members endeavor to recognize behavior acceptable to leader and other members. During Stage 2, identified as the *counterdependency* stage, issues of power, authority, and competition are focused on. Struggles with authority and status are viewed as essential requirements for ensuing increases in cooperation and cohesion. Stage 3 has an atmosphere of trust, in which there is more open and mature negotiation of goals, roles, group structure, and division of labor. In Stage 4, designated as the *work* stage, an increase in task orientation, more open exchange of ideas and feedback, and enhanced goal achievement occur. When a distinct ending to the group is planned, Stage 5 is peppered with disruption and conflict as positive feelings are expressed and issues of separation are explored. Wheelan offered supporting preliminary evidence for the validation of these stages (Verdi & Wheelan, 1992; Wheelan & McKeage, 1993; Wheelan & Verdi, 1992).

Wheelan created the Group Developmental Observation System (GDOS) to code members' verbalizations. Eight categories were derived from the work of Bion, Thelen, and Stock. Each complete articulated statement is placed into one of the categories—dependency statements, counterdependency statements, fight statements, flight statements, pairing statements, counterpairing statements (which are avoidance of intimacy), work statements, and unscorable statements. Agreement between independent coders was 85% to 95%. Wheelan also designed the Group Development Questionnaire (GDQ) to measure group change or development. Consisting of 60 statements, it measures her first four stages of group development. Validation of scale included establishment of retest reliability and internal consistency as well as concurrent, construct, and criterion-related validity (Wheelan & Hochberger, 1996). Higher scales (representing higher stages) are associated with higher productivity and effectiveness ratio. Likewise, a higher productivity and effectiveness ratio is correlated with lower scores on the earlier scales (Wheelan & Tilin, 1999).

Wheelan used these two instruments to study ongoing for-profit and not-for-profit organizational groups in their natural settings. To address the question of whether a relationship exists between members' perceptions of their groups' development and length of time that the groups have been meeting, Wheelan examined a cross section of groups meeting for 1 to 15 months prior to the study (Wheelan et al., 2003). In the first sample, 26 work groups (180 individuals) from 12 organizations completed the GDQ. Two groups were judged to be in Stage 1, two groups in Stage 2, 12 groups in Stage 3 (meeting an average of 5.2 months), and 12 in Stage 4 (meeting an average of 8.5 months). In the second sample of 88 groups (639 participants) meeting for 1 to 7 months prior to the study, each member completed the GDQ at the end of the meeting. Of 88 groups, 27 were judged to be in Stage 1 (meeting an average of 2.6 months), 14 in Stage 2 (meeting an average of 3.7 months), 28 in Stage 3, and 19 in Stage 4. Both Stage 3 and 4 groups had been meeting for more than 4.6 months. The investigators obtained a significant difference in both samples with regard to the age of the group and members' perceptions of group development. Statistically, Stage 1 groups met significantly less time than Stage 3 and 4 groups (Wheelan et al., 2003). The investigators also found that as the size of the group increased, members were more likely to see the group as having the characteristics of the earlier stages of development but that individual factors such as age, gender, education, and length of service were not related to perceptions of group development. The authors had no explanation as to why in the first sample Stage 4 groups had been meeting for an average of 8.5 months whereas in the second sample, Stage 4 groups had been meeting on average 4.6 months.

All 26 groups in the first sample were audiotaped, and their statements were coded using the GDOS. Group stage was determined by members' perceptions (GDQ). Members were also asked how productive they felt that their group was on a scale of 1 to 4. Individual and group level analyses were performed. Results revealed that the age of the group was correlated with the number of dependency, fight, and work statements that individuals made in the group. Groups that met for less time were more likely to have individuals who made more dependency and fight statements and fewer work statements. A group-level analysis produced consistent results. Groups with higher proportions of dependency and fight statements had met for less time. Conversely, groups with higher percentages of work statements tended to have met for more time. Members of older groups also perceived themselves to be more productive than those who had been meeting for less time. Analysis of members' perceptions of the group development revealed similar findings. Members of groups meeting for longer durations tended to see their groups as having fewer Stage 2 characteristics and more Stage 3 and 4 characteristics. Members who saw themselves to be in Stage 3 made more counterdependent and fight statements than members who saw themselves in Stage 4 of group development. The longer a group had been meeting, the greater number of Stage 4 characteristics members perceived in the group and the fewer characteristics of Stage 2 groups.

This study is an important one in that it not only used much larger sample sizes than had earlier studies but it also combined both independent and objective assessments of group members' behavior (verbalizations) and the more subjective measure of members' perceptions of group interaction. The study also expanded the applicability of the notion of group development beyond the clinical or college volunteer population to include functioning adults in a work setting. It provides support for the traditional models of group development, demonstrating that both verbal behaviors and members' perceptions of the group climate change in predicted directions across time.

With a sample similar to that in the previously described groups, Wheelan and Williams (2003) used a promising and exciting new technology for data analysis to examine group development. These investigators used nonlinear methods derived from complexity theory (see chap. 3, this volume) and research to visually map the communication dynamics of groups during a single meeting. A sample of 108 participants involved in 16 ongoing company groups (group age 1 to 30 months) were audiotaped and completed the GDQ. Transcriptions of the audiotapes were coded on the basis of the GDOS. One group was perceived by its members to be in Stage 1, 8 groups in Stage 3, and 7 groups in Stage 4. The coded statements from each group were recorded in sequence into the Chaos Data Analyzer software. A wavelet transform test constructed a color visual representation of the dynamic patterns of each group. The final product was a color image of the verbal exchange sequence that transpired during the group meeting. Using complexity–chaos theory as a model, six individuals inspected the images visually for similarities and differences. Shape, color, overall tone, and visual clarity were compared.

The patterns that emerged could be placed into three tiers. The only characteristic that differentiated Tier 3 groups from the others is that 80% of them had been meeting for 4 months or less. In Tier 1, communication patterns were longer than in the other two tiers. There were also fewer patterns because work and pairing statements composed 93% of the verbalizations. The authors interpreted this finding as "members of these groups were working and supporting each other's ideas and suggestions with regard to the group's task" (Wheelan & Williams, 2003, p. 458). For Tier 2 groups, the overall tone was more active and erratic and less symmetrical than that of Tier 1 groups. Tier 2 groups manifested more communications patterns and a greater number of shifts in those patterns than Tier 1 groups. Work and pairing statements still constituted the vast majority (82%), but they occurred in more attenuated bursts interspersed with brief recurring patterns of flight or focus on members' reactions to the leader. Tier 3 groups have the most erratic patterns. Of their statements, 66% were still work and supportive statements, but they oscillated with frequent patterns of flight and conflict or patterns that emphasized members' reactions to the leader. The researchers saw this pattern as the group's struggle to preserve the direction of the discussion and stay on task. Statistically, significant differences in percentage of work statements between each tier were obtained. Tier 1 and 2 groups also had a lower percentage of fight and flight statements compared with Tier 3 groups. Tier 1 group members had proportionately fewer dependency statements than Tier 3 group members. These objective findings are consistent with members' perceptions of group functioning. Members of Tier 1 groups perceived themselves to be functioning at a higher level of group development than members of Tier 3 groups. This perception speaks to a major assumption of group developmental theory that group-level phenomena exist.

Group development theory predicts that groups occupying different stages of group development would communicate differently; the results of this study support this hypothesis. Although all groups began with a work and pairing or supportive communication configuration, members of Tier 1 groups were able to maintain a work focus for a longer period of time. For Tier 2 groups, pattern shifts were more frequent. Work and pairing were interspersed with periods of flight. Neither the work and pairing patterns nor the flight patterns increased over the life of the session. In Tier 3 groups, pattern changes were frequent. Unlike the other two tiers, work and pairing patterns were disrupted by conflict. Each pattern of fight increased the duration of the successive pattern of flight, thus exacerbating difficulties for group members to return to the task.

Summary

Until recently, analysis of group climate was limited by linear research methods. The Wheelan and Williams study and that of Kivlighan have allowed for the analysis of more complex relationships in the group. Kivlighan used a growth curve analysis that could examine effects at both individual member and overall group levels. This study introduced chaos theory to the study of group development (McGrath, Arrow, & Berdahl, 2000; Wheelan, 1996b). This approach more accurately allows groups to be seen as complex adaptive systems. These constellations are not the result of individuals, but rather they are unique patterns created by their joint interactions. The GDOS system enables the generation of visual representations of group development process, permitting the possibility of using constructs of chaos theory. Early findings seem to suggest that although commonalities exist from group to group with respect to process, each group has its own unique process trajectory as well.

The three lines of evidence (therapeutic factors, leadership, and group climate) provide support for the model of progressive stages. The weakest support is provided by the therapeutic factors studies both because the research findings are inconsistent and because the predictions from the progressive models are not direct and unambiguous. Measures of therapeutic factors were not designed to delineate stages of group development, although future researchers may provide a rationale for the prediction of particular patterns of factors for each stage. The data on leadership patterns hold promise, particularly with support by other research groups using different venues to provide further validation. The group climate studies are especially useful because the methods used (especially the GCQ–S and the GDQ) were devised specifically to examine developmental phenomena. Consequently, predictions of how groups should perform on these measures over time can be made with greater directness than with measures that have evolved outside of a group development framework.

NEGATIVE EVIDENCE FOR PROGRESSIVE DEVELOPMENTAL STAGES

The evidence for progressive developmental stages is not entirely positive. Two lines of research give those supporting a stage theory of group development some pause. The first questions were raised in the classic studies of Bales and Strodtbeck (1951). Seeger (1983), in his review of problem-solving groups, distinguished between the process of problem solving and the group formation process. He argued that problem-solving groups generally did not follow sequential stages unless they had not previously met. He saw phase development as a reflection of formative group process development and not what is required to complete the group's task.

Cissna (1984) reviewed the literature and found that 13 studies failed to find developmental trends. He reviewed each of the studies that he was able to locate and found that in addition to methodological flaws, many of them assumed that particular sessions (often equally spaced) would reveal certain stages. Many also measured aspects of group life that researchers now know may not be revealing of changes in developmental phenomena (e.g., source of communication; relative frequency of speaking; whether the utterance was an assertion, request, or proposal). Cissna concluded that groups have a unique developmental time frame of development and that it is possible that not all groups are successful in proceeding through the identified stages. These conclusions do not discredit a theory of group developmental phenomena.

The second line has led to the development of the punctuated equilibrium theory as an alternative to sequential group development. Gersick (1988) studied eight field teams that were working on short-term projects. Teams met for varying lengths of time from 7 days to 6 months. Every meeting was observed, audiotaped, and transcribed. The transcribed text of the meeting was analyzed using qualitative methodology without preconceived theoretical dimensions. The analysis of the data did not support a progressive stage model and led to an alternative model. Gersick observed that each group has a distinctive approach to its task, which it maintains through a period of inertia that extends to about half the time allotted. Members of the group maintain a "habitual routine," and little is accomplished until external pressures change it. This event is followed by a transition in which goals and objectives of the team are completed. Gersick proposed to call what she saw the punctuated equilibrium model (see chap. 3, this volume). She admitted that her study design may have influenced the process. Team members could have been affected by the project-imposed time constraints, which could modify the normal process of group development.

In a second study, Gersick (1989) observed eight master of business administration student groups as they worked on creative projects. All of the groups generated similar patterns. Each group developed an interactional style, which continued until the midpoint. At the midpoint, each group underwent a transition in which goals and methods were examined and evaluated. This new interactional pattern was maintained until the end, concluding with a high level of activity in the last session. The author interpreted these studies to indicate that the framework in which the group took place, particularly the time context, was a significant factor in molding the group change process and asserted that individual, group, and organizational levels of analysis might have been bridged by this model (Gersick, 1991). Small sample size, narrow participant type, and open-ended observational analysis are possible criticisms of this study. It has also been suggested that level of observation affects whether change is seen as incremental or punctuated (Wollin, 1999). Seers and Woodruff (1997) amplified this distinction of levels of observation. They distinguished between the Tuckman (1965) tradition of sequential development as representing the evolution of psychosocial dynamics and Gersick's studies, which focused on task progress. They contended that Gersick's studies potentially confounded group development and task completion, delineating little about group behavioral patterns. They supported their contentions with two studies that demonstrated that task pacing and group development are distinguishable phenomena, although sometimes they may co-occur; studying groups that are task driven with deadlines may muddle researchers' understanding of group development.

These studies are significant and should give pause to what otherwise appears to be almost an unopposed view. They suggest that in certain contexts alternate models to the progressive stage model may provide a more descriptive account of how groups change over time.

IS PROCESS LINKED TO OUTCOME?
DOES DEVELOPMENT MAKE A DIFFERENCE?

Thus far, we have concentrated our focus on the evidence for a progressive model of development in a group. Our review suggests that although the findings of some studies are at odds with the existence of progressive developmental stages, the preponderance of the evidence supports the descriptive value of this concept. With that point relatively well established, we need to ask whether development will make a difference in members' outcomes. If group development is a major phenomenon in defining the group, then a group's development should have some important linkage to outcomes. Until recently, this question presented a formidable challenge because to examine it directly required a dynamic rather than static analysis (Kivlighan & Lilly, 1997). The only methods previously available were pre–post difference scores or repeated measures of multivariate analysis. The first method estimates amount of change rather than actually measuring the process of change, and the second is plagued by a host of statistical problems (Kivlighan & Lilly, 1997). Now the availability of hierarchical linear modeling allows for one way of appropriately examining the change process in a study using repeated measures. We review the evidence that development is indeed linked to outcome for psychotherapy groups, training and process groups, and organizational groups in their natural setting.

In the review that follows, two types of studies are presented. One type links process variables with outcomes without specifically determining the stages through which the group proceeded. These studies are relevant because the processes studied have developmental implications. If engagement increases, the presumption is that the group is showing greater maturity. However, a linear increase in engagement is actually more consistent with a continuous change model (unless the group has failed to go beyond Stage 1). Hence, a given study may support development–outcome relationships, but not a stage development–outcome model. The second type of study explicitly examines developmental stages in relation to outcome.

Psychotherapy Groups

A series of studies have measured process and outcome relationships (see Table 4.1). Although all fall short of being able to unequivocally demonstrate that a particular sequence influences outcome, they generally support the notion that to the extent that a group develops, members are able to accomplish their goals. The studies ranged in length of time in group, meetings per week, closed versus open membership, theoretical orientation, and the country in which the study took place. We review both inpatient and outpatient group psychotherapy studies.

Inpatient Studies

Groups conducted in inpatient settings are of particular interest because outcomes of members of the group are likely to be affected by many factors and therapeutic involvements that are different from those that affect the outpatient psychotherapy group.

Tschuschke, MacKenzie, and colleagues conducted two studies examining process and outcome relationships in an inpatient setting. MacKenzie and Tschuschke (1993) took process measures of two psychoanalytically ori-

TABLE 4.1
Studies Investigating Developmental Process–Outcome Relationships

Study	Year	Format	Finding
Inpatient therapy			
MacKenzie and Tschuschke	1993	Two psychoanalytic inpatient groups, 93 sessions	Early engagement scores were not related to group outcome.
Tschuschke, MacKenzie, Haaser, and Janke	1996	Used data from MacKenzie and Tschuschke (1993)	At 18-month follow-up, most successful members were involved with early interpersonal work.
Outpatient therapy			
Phipps and Zastowney	1988	Nine community mental health groups, 56 patients	Successful groups showed a pattern consistent with more advanced developmental stages. In unsuccessful groups, members' lack of improvement was associated with groups in which engagement was not higher than avoidance or conflict.
Tschuschke and MacKenzie	1989	Two weekly psychoanalytic groups (Germany)	Positive outcome was associated with pattern of painful disclosures followed by hostility. Poor outcome was associated with being unable to move through differentiation phase.
Sexton	1993	One group, 12 sessions of verbal therapy and exercise (Norway)	Early positive ratings by therapist were associated with later symptom improvement in patients.
Castonguay, Pincus, Agras, and Hines	1998	12 sessions, 65 eating disorders in cognitive–behavioral therapy groups	Pattern of early high engagement followed by high conflict produced favorable outcomes.
Process and training groups			
MacKenzie, Dies, Coché, Rutan, and Stone	1987	53 groups (4 sessions, 4 hours each), 555 group therapists	Successful groups had decreased conflict over time and shifted to deeper psychological exploration.
Kivlighan and Jauquet	1990	Six personal growth groups, 26 sessions	An increase occurred in realistic, here-and-now, and interpersonal dimensions of goals with increasing sessions.
Kivlighan	1997	72 groups, 372 students, 28 sessions	Positive outcome was associated with the leader, early task orientation, and later relationship connection with the leader.

Kivlighan and Lilly	1997	14 groups, 84 students, 14–26 sessions	Positive outcome was associated with stage development as proposed.
Kivlighan and Tarrant	2001	233 adolescents, 8 sessions, 2 hours each	Positive relationship was evident between participant outcome and stage development. Group climate mediated outcome.

Organizational groups

Wheelan, Murphy, Tsumura, and Kline	1998	44 work groups of financial teams	Group productivity was positively related to group development as measured by member perceptions of internal dynamics.
Wheelan and Lisk	2000	263 undergraduate students	Positive correlation was evident between grade point average and stage of group development.
Wheelan, Burchill, and Tilin	2003	17 intensive care units, 394 staff	Perceived higher stage of group development was associated with lower mortality rate of patients.
Wheelan and Kesselring	2005	61 elementary school faculty groups	Faculty perceived higher stage of group development was related to fourth-grade children's greater proficiency in reading, science, and citizenship on standardized tests.

ented inpatient groups that met for 93 sessions over a 6 1/2-month period. The investigators used the GCQ–S subscale Engagement to Measure Group Work, a questionnaire using semantic differential items to tap relatedness, and outcome measures including the Revised Symptom Checklist and target goal ratings. Consistent with developmental theory, the investigators hypothesized that early engagement scores would predict outcome as would overall levels of engagement. However, this hypothesis was not supported at termination, 12-month follow-up, or 18-month follow-up. The authors considered that perhaps group members (consistent with the directions) may have been describing the groups' engagement rather than their own. If a disparity exists between their own engagement and collective engagement, a relationship would not be expected between their perception of collective engagement and their personal outcome. The investigators did find that participants obtaining higher relatedness scores had better outcomes.

A follow-up study (Tschuschke, MacKenzie, Haaser, & Janke, 1996) on these same groups focused on members' actual behaviors. Self-reports and observer process ratings concerning five therapeutic factors (Emotional Relatedness to the Group, Self-Disclosure, Feedback, Interpersonal Learning-Output, and Family Reenactment) were collected. The process ratings were based on videotapes of every second session of the 93 sessions. The outcome measures were the same as in the prior study. There was general concordance of outcome for the patient, the therapist, and an independent observer. The Systematic and Multiple Level Observation of Groups method (Bales & Cohen, 1979) was used to assess feedback subcategories of task versus emotional behavior, dominance versus submission, and positive versus negative behavior as well as self-disclosure. At 18-month follow-up, the most successful members had exhibited higher levels of interpersonal work in the early sessions (first and second quarters of the group) than the least successful members. Although the least successful members performed more interpersonal work in the latter portion of the group, it did not help them (or as Tschuschke et al. [1996] said, "late bloomers do not blossom," p. 43). No pattern was observed between feedback subcategories and outcome. Two groups is a small sample size, and the authors acknowledged that the patterns may have been particular to groups held within a larger therapeutic milieu. Yet, their finding of the importance of early participation is consistent with a larger corpus of research from a variety of settings.

Outpatient Studies

Inpatient studies have difficulty isolating the impact of the group from that of other therapeutic treatments. In contrast, process–outcome relationships of outpatient groups may be somewhat easier to discern. In an early but particularly strong study, Phipps and Zastowny (1988) used outpatient groups meeting 6 to 24 months prior to the commencement of the study. Using a repeated measures design over a 6-month period that assessed patient outcome and level of functioning (Brief Symptom Inventory) and group leadership style (Group Leader Behavior Instrument) and used the GCQ, they found two patterns of group process. The first pattern had highest engagement and then lower conflict and avoidance. Avoidance was higher than conflict and both would periodically increase. These groups appeared to manage conflict with a relatively stable climate of engagement and the best outcomes. In the other pattern, engagement was not invariably higher than others, and there was not a large difference between engagement and conflict and avoidance scores. This latter group pattern appeared unable to master the postdifferentiation phase. This study is perhaps the best demonstration of the relationship between developmental stage progression and outcome.

Tschuschke and MacKenzie (1989) studied two weekly psychoanalytic outpatient groups in Germany using verbal content analysis scales. One group had a successful outcome; the other did not. The verbal content analysis identified group climate. The more successful group (outcomes judged by therapist ratings of individuals) spent prolonged periods first in painful self-disclosure followed by periods of greater hostility directed toward others. The pattern repeated itself and eventually resulted in a lasting state of reduced affect. The second group with poorer outcomes failed to show any consistent pattern and appeared unable to move through the differentiation stage. Although the sample size was small and the outcome measures were weak, the findings are promising (MacKenzie, 1994b).

Sexton (1993) examined a group of Norwegian outpatients who participated in 30 minutes of verbal therapy followed by aerobic exercise, group exercises, and brief discussion. Both therapist and patients completed symptom scales at each session. Although no overall measure of group climate or process was used, changes in patient symptoms and therapist ratings allow for the inference of a change process. The author found that therapists' ratings of the session importance for a patient and positive feelings for the patient in the early sessions were more relevant to outcome then the same ratings in later sessions. This suggests that with successful therapy, there is mutual positive regard and an increase in patient positive alliance and therapist positive feelings; the therapist records some improvement, and some sessions later, the patient reports insight into his or her problems. Likewise, the patient's lack of perceived improvement appears to result in more negative feelings in the therapist toward patient a few sessions later. Of course, because these relationships are correlational, no direction of causation can be determined, only hypothesized.

The most recent study, conducted by Castonguay, Pincus, Agras, and Hines (1998), is especially important because it is unique in studying process–outcome relationships in the context of a structured cognitive–behavioral outpatient group. Symptomatic ratings were taken before and after treatment. Members were asked to complete a group version of the Therapy Session Report (Orlinsky & Howard, 1966). Castonguay et al. found that overall, engagement increased across the sessions, whereas negative affective climate increased, reaching a peak in the middle sessions, and then decreased. The authors noted that these patterns were consistent with progressive stage models such as MacKenzie's (1994b). Process and outcome measures were significantly related. The researchers found that the client's experience of positive affectivity in the beginning of treatment and the perception of a negative group climate in the middle of treatment were predictive of a favorable treatment response. Significant limitations of this study are its correlational nature, the significant attrition of members (10 out of the original 75), and the specificity of the population (binge-eating patients).

In summary, the inpatient and outpatient studies generally showed that group development is a good thing for group members. Future studies would provide a clearer picture of relationships between stages and outcome by taking a broader view of group development as was done in the Phipps and Zastowny (1988) study. Rather than looking merely at individual scores such as the Engagement subscale of the GCQ–S, investigators should consider the overall pattern of scores to determine whether groups that progress beyond the formative stages show outcomes superior to groups that remain within the formative stages. Also, like the Tschuschke et al. (1996) study, future studies should include measures of process beyond the individual member's self-report. Therapy group studies are plagued by human subject concerns, balancing known effective treatments with questions of science and design.

Process and Training Groups

Investigations with process and training situations allow greater potential for more rigorous methodologies, although outcome may assume a different meaning when participants are in therapy versus training groups. Consequently, the studies done on the relationship between process and outcome have offered the clearest view of the relationships between these domains. Five studies using a group format have yielded robust evidence for the existence of a model of group development. Sample sizes were much larger than the psychotherapy groups studied. Although outcome was assessed differently for each study, all but one used the GCQ–S with multiple administrations. Statistical methods were superior, and results were comparable.

MacKenzie, Dies, Coché, Rutan, and Stone (1987) studied 53 psychodynamic and special interest groups (impressively, 555 participants) at the American Group Psychotherapy Association Institute in 1982 who completed the GCQ–S and the Global Outcome Form. A stepwise regression analysis revealed that engagement was highly predictive of outcome for each session, and in the last sessions, conflict was negatively correlated with outcome. Both successful and unsuccessful groups (determined by the Global Outcome Form) began with similar levels of conflict. In the successful groups conflict decreased, suggesting that they mastered intragroup tension and could move on, whereas the less successful ones were unable to move beyond a conflictual process. In the final sessions, the more successful groups shifted to a focus on deeper psychological exploration. All groups increased on the Engaged scale throughout the sessions, but the most successful groups were significantly higher on engagement for all four sessions than the least successful groups. One more finding of interest is that the psychodynamic groups and the special interest groups, which were presumably more structured, did not differ from one another. Perhaps the weakest part of the study was the outcome measure, which was a self-report measure. The authors concluded that the patterns on the GCQ–S supported a group development hypothesis and demonstrated that the greater the progress through the stages, the better the outcome.

Kivlighan and colleagues, in a series of investigations of students involved in personal growth groups, carried out a series of programmatic studies that related group process to outcome. They sought patterns of leadership in relation to outcome with 372 students in 72 groups (Kivlighan, 1997). Outcome was measured by identification of problem areas and the level of distress experienced with these participants before and after group. Members had better outcomes when leaders initially focused on reinforcing therapeutic norms through task-oriented interventions and later emphasized their personal connection with members.

In another study, Kivlighan and Jauquet (1990) had group members complete the GCQ–S and a problem (agenda) card. Three judges rated agendas on realism, here-and-now focus, and emphasis on interpersonal issues. Sessions were grouped into early, middle, and late for comparison. Consistent with the MacKenzie et al. (1987) study, engagement increased over time, whereas avoidance decreased over time. Conflict increased and then decreased. A significant increase in realistic, here-and-now, and interpersonal dimensions of goals occurred over the sessions. In the early sessions, when goals were more realistic, group members engaged in more productive work. In the middle and late sessions, when focusing on interpersonal agendas in the here and now, members were engaged and less avoidant of work. Middle sessions are also a time to deal with conflict and power. The authors suggested that in the early phase of a group, leaders may want to encourage the development of realistic agendas and then shift members to setting agendas with significant interpersonal components and here-and-now dimensions as the sessions progress. Caution should be exercised when applying these findings to a clinical population, as these group members were nonpatient volunteers.

The Kivlighan and Lilly (1997) study is of interest because of the variation in the number of sessions completed (14 to 26). Groups meeting for differing numbers of sessions followed similar developmental patterns with no relationship between number of sessions and group outcome. As in the Kivlighan (1997) study, therapeutic gain is related to a high level of engagement throughout. A low–high–low pattern for conflict correlated with positive outcome. It seems that groups need to begin with little conflict to foster cohesion. Conflict later permits the challenge of defenses and the deepening of intimacy. However, conflict must be resolved by the end to have a good outcome. A quadratic relationship with avoidance was related to therapeutic outcome (high–low–high–low). Although the authors offered no explanation for this variation, it is a relationship that makes sense for progressive group development; avoidance is high at the commencement as group members are getting to know each other, then low when issues of authority are being addressed, high as the group attempts to focus on issues of intimacy, and low during work.

Kivlighan and Tarrant (2001) expanded their study of group development to the adolescent population, using structured group sessions, didactic instruction, and discussion. Leaders with little formal group training were given 16 hours of instruction emphasizing member-to-member interaction. In an additional twist, leaders were given a questionnaire that measured their intentions in the sessions. In addition to the Group Climate Questionnaire, they completed symptom inventories. Findings indicated that adolescents liked their leaders and benefited from the sessions. The relationship between group climate and participant outcome was consistent with previous findings. Increases in active engagement across sessions were related to member benefit. Decreases in conflict with time were related to participants liking their therapist. The adolescents felt more positive about leaders who structured the discussions, solicited elaborations, and gave feedback. They felt more negatively about leaders' attempts to do individual therapy in the group. The relation between leaders' intentions and member outcome was mediated by group climate; efforts to do therapy were negatively related, and intentions to provide a safe environment were positively related to an increasingly active and engaged climate. Even in these semistructured groups, group climate is an important mediator of outcome.

We present a final study by Kivlighan, McGovern, and Corazzini (1984) not because it supports a process–outcome relationship but because it is one of the few examples of an actual experiment that attempts to manipulate (although unsuccessfully) group climate. A small number of students were given sheets on the expression of anger and intimacy either at an appropriate time (anger sheet during storming or intimacy sheet during norming) or an inappropriate time (anger sheet during norming and intimacy sheet during storming) in development. For intimacy, the results were as predicted, but for anger, the sheet helped no matter what the timing. The authors interpreted this result to indicate that expressing anger is generally not comfortable. Aside from the small number of participants, one problem with interpreting the results is that there was no measure of what the therapists might have naturally done in the group to neutralize the incongruous directions.

Groups in Work Settings

Using the GDQ, Wheelan and associates have established a relationship between productivity and stage of group development in many field settings. In one study, financial teams functioning at higher levels of group development were able to earn more income in less time and were rated higher in customer service than teams functioning at lower levels of group development (Wheelan, Murphy, Tsumura, & Kline, 1998). In a second study, undergraduate groups functioning at higher stages of development obtained higher grade point averages than did participants in cohort groups functioning at lower stages of development (Wheelan & Lisk, 2000). These findings are consistent with those from the therapy and process group studies.

With the aforementioned studies, the outcome measure is of the individual in the group. When the outcome affects an individual who is one step removed from group, the power of the group process can be seen as even more impressive. Using the GDQ, Wheelan, Burchill, and Tilin (2003) found that employees of intensive care units (primarily White female nurses, working an average of 12 years in the unit) who perceived themselves to be functioning at higher stages of group development had lower than predicted mortality rates than did other intensive care unit staff who perceived themselves to be functioning at lower levels. Similarly, the students of faculty whose peer groups were functioning at higher levels of development scored higher on a standardized proficiency test in citizenship, reading, and science than the students of faculty groups functioning at lower levels of group development (Wheelan & Kesselring, 2005).

Summary

Strong evidence exists for the link between outcome or productivity and stage of development. Studies with strong experimental design, especially those on work or training groups and organizational task groups, show a substantial connection between group development and productivity. However, using a cross-sectional design does not permit an exploration of the transition of stages. It is possible that successful outcomes could occur in a group that achieves maturation with little time spent in the earlier stages. Process–outcome studies with psychotherapy groups generally have lacked the methodological rigor of studies on work groups. A major problem is the lack of a clear and consistently applied standard for what constitutes group development. These studies rely excessively on self-report measures and are frequently characterized by small sample sizes. Studies of process and training groups consistently support the relationship between stage development, allow for evaluation of individual and group outcome, but sometimes lack the statistical power (because of the number of groups) to explore relationships with moderate effects.[4]

CONCLUSION

Considerable evidence exists that many interpersonal domains change systematically over the life of the group. To date, the model that has been most carefully studied in relation to the psychotherapy group is the progressive stage model, which embraces a number of stages (ranging in number from three to eight). Evidence from group climate, therapeutic factor, and leadership studies supports a stage model. Furthermore, evidence suggests that without this progression, interpersonal and intrapersonal changes are attenuated for its members. Rivaling the progressive stage model is a punctuated equilibrium model, which embraces a two-stage process in which the initial period is characterized by little accomplishment followed by a transition about midway through the duration of the group after which unfolds new productive interactional exchanges. Currently, insufficient empirical

---

[4]If moderate or small effects are predicted, a greater N is required than if the expected effects are large.

work has been conducted directly pitting one model against the other. It is possible that the particular model of development is context and task specific. It is also possible that the level at which observation takes place affects whether the change is viewed as punctuated or of a more continuous nature. Many studies have chosen somewhat arbitrary points at which to measure the phase, and little work has actually attempted to capture the shift in phases. Finally, much more work is needed to determine the extent to which the development of a psychotherapy group is associated with favorable outcomes.

II

A FIVE-STAGE MODEL OF GROUP DEVELOPMENT

5

AN ILLUSTRATION OF A GROUP THROUGH ITS DEVELOPMENT

In this chapter, we present our five-stage model of group development. We developed this model by integrating common themes from the theoretical literature reviewed in chapters 2 and 3, the empirical literature reviewed in chapter 4, and our own experiential learning as female group psychotherapists over a combined period of approximately 50 years.

In presenting our model, we use the term *stage* because it connotes in a more explicit way the notion of a progression. The concept of *phase*, in contrast, suggests a more or less continuous recycling (such as the phases of the moon; La Coursiere, 1980). As noted earlier, our experience and that of other therapists is that the group's past experience informs the present. For example, Agazarian and Peters (1981) noted that groups achieve greater systemic complexity over the course of development. Even if a group regresses to an earlier stage, our observation is that the group contains elements of the stages in which it has previously resided.

Although we have labeled the stages for ease of understanding, the labels fail to capture the multifaceted character of each stage. Each stage represents a set of conflicts; adaptive tasks; and other emotional, cognitive, and motivational elements that differ somewhat according to context. Which aspects of the stage are important in a given group may depend on such factors as the focus of the group, the setting, and so on. Therefore, the reader should view the label as a heuristic and should freely emphasize other aspects of any stage to the extent that they are pertinent to his or her group.

Throughout the chapter, we illustrate each stage within the context of a hypothetical long-term unstructured group. We first present the members of the group. Then we describe, in theoretical terms, the developmental characteristics of each stage, followed by an illustrative vignette from that stage of group development and then an analysis of that vignette retrospectively. Our intent in presenting our five-stage model is to illustrate the natural lines of group development, particularly as we have observed them in a long-term group.

DESCRIPTION OF A HYPOTHETICAL GROUP

The context of this group is a female psychotherapist's private practice. Group members are obtained from her own individual therapy private practice and those of other practitioners. All of the members are in concomitant individual therapy. In selecting members, the therapist limited the range of social and emotional impairment such that all members reside at the high end of psychosocial functioning. The therapist did not accept individuals who had either ongoing severe difficulties in reality testing or impairments in the capacity to think coherently.

The group is composed of eight members, all of whom started at the same time. Membership is diverse with regard to age, ethnicity, race, education, and socioeconomic status. Members entered the group with the understanding that they could remain in the group until their work was complete. Members realized that with the departure of old members, new members would be accepted into the group.

Members are introduced in alphabetical order. This is followed by a description of Stage 1, and then a vignette of the third session of the group is presented.

Group Members

Cassidy is a 23-year-old Hispanic college senior whose college career has been interrupted by bouts of substance abuse and depression. She feels that both problems were caused by bad turns taken in two successive romantic relationships. She is considering returning to school.

Henry is a 71-year-old Caucasian man who is a bagger at a local supermarket; he became depressed after his wife died. He is a very social individual and is active in his church but nonetheless experiences considerable loneliness.

Jade is a 27-year-old African American woman who has been in abusive relationships throughout her young adult life. She is in such a relationship currently but is thinking of obtaining a restraining order for her boyfriend. She works as a nurse in a geriatric facility and in that capacity functions effectively and enjoys positive relationships with her patients, her peers, and her supervisor.

Jeffrey is a single, 31-year-old Caucasian man with posttraumatic stress disorder from witnessing the bombing death of two of his colleagues. This well-educated businessman complains that he wants a long-term committed relationship, but no one he meets is up to his standards.

Lee is a 38-year-old Caucasian woman who does fund-raising and is at times abrasive but also has an ability to lead the group toward its goal. She entered the group after discovering that her husband was having an affair. He complained that her controlling attitude made him want to take a sabbatical from the marriage. As Lee sees it, she has no interest in controlling anyone.

Mark is a 43-year-old Caucasian man who came to the group because of anxiety associated with his need to seek a new job after having lost his former employment 2 months before entering the group. He seems to lack any close relationships but did not identify this area as one of concern.

Mort is a 48-year-old obese Caucasian man who lives with his elderly mother and works in the family delicatessen. For many years, he has harbored an interest in turning his hobby of creating miniature military figures out of plaster or metal into an occupation but has never summoned the courage to do so. His only social life is going to monthly meetings with his modeling club and meeting occasionally with friends who are also interested in modeling artifacts.

Zachariah is a 24-year-old African American man with a history of minor criminal offenses, episodes of depression, and difficulties with anger management in relationships with authority. He does not tend to have long-term intimate relationships but does not see this lack as a problem. Although he has had a somewhat unstable work history, in the past year he has had consistent employment working as a line repairman for the phone company.

Stage 1: Formation and Engagement

The reader can achieve an empathetic grasp of group members' reactions to the event of joining the group by recalling his or her own entrances into new groups, especially groups of strangers who, by virtue of the circumstance, were likely to have great significance for the reader. Moving to a new neighborhood and participating in a welcoming party would be an example. Feelings of unease and longings to be accepted would be natural. Although entrance into a psychotherapy group shares some common ground with this situation, important differences exist as well. The psychotherapy group members' presence, if voluntary, is an acknowledgment of the possession of a psychological problem. Furthermore, participation in the group, it is understood, entails the revelation of the problem to the other members. Except for individuals who have been seasoned by past group experiences or who by virtue of their character styles are unable to summon a self-protective wariness, this demand elicits worries about a negative event such as being humiliated, attacked, or rejected. Also different from the neighborhood welcome party is the fact that the goals of group participation are somewhat more specific and yet the processes are, in members' views, vague. Members enter the group specifically for the alleviation of psychological problems, yet even when members have proceeded through a thoroughgoing preparation in which particular processes are identified as of potential benefit, they feel uncertain as to how activity in the group will lead to the accomplishment of the goals. A third difference is that the group, unlike the neighborhood welcome party, offers a clear authority presence in the person of the therapist. Yet, the therapist is not performing the directorial functions typical of authority figures. This fact creates a disjunction between members' expectations and their experiences.

The ambiguity of the group situation and members' desire to avoid the dangers inherent in this new involvement lead members to engage in a predictable set of behaviors. Typically, members alleviate anxiety by observing those social conventions that in the past have allowed them to successfully navigate unfamiliar social situations. Each member has his or her own understanding of what these conventions are, and this understanding is based on his or her identity, unique history, and cultural background. For some members, the convention may be an effort simply to be polite to the other members and to make small talk that avoids tension-arousing areas. For other members, it may be use of the discourse of past therapeutic experiences, such as referencing the principles and using the terminology of Alcoholics Anonymous (AA). For still others, it may entail the use of a detailed storylike narrative of the psychological problems that brought the member into treatment. Members' stereotypic behaviors provide a route not only to avoid reality but also to control others: By operating within familiar paradigms, members seek to induce others to do the same and thereby foster others' predictability.

The array of conventional behaviors that members use during this initial stage serves to avoid many of the realities of their situation. Members avoid the affect stimulated by their entrance into the group as well as a direct acknowledgment of the risks that the conventional behaviors are designed to avert. They spare themselves a direct confrontation with their uncertainty over whether their goals will be realized by their participation in the group.

Although members' flight behaviors provide them the means to tolerate the precariousness of initial group involvement, more critical to their survival in the group and capacity to benefit from it is, in their perceptions, their relationship with the therapist. Members enter the group with an expectation that any assistance derived from the group will be rendered by the therapist, whose curative capabilities are imagined—at least unconsciously—to be unlimited. The view of the therapist as omnipotent and beneficent derives from the helpless young child's perception of the parent as all-providing, a perception that is summoned in adulthood when that same helplessness is experienced.

Behaviorally, members' felt reliance on the therapist can be seen in diverse ways. Members frequently manifest a highly deferential attitude to the therapist. The therapist's contributions to the discussion—regardless of their importance—are treated as treasures. Members speak with one another but covertly direct their comments to the therapist. For instance, one member may answer another member's question while frequently glancing over to see the therapist's reaction to his or her response. Members may direct questions to the therapist that specifically tap the therapist's expertise.

Stage 1 Vignette (Session 3)

In the first two sessions, all of the members had shared information about their life circumstances and the difficulties that had brought them into the group. However, some members had shared much more than others.

Therapist: I have an announcement to make. Mark will no longer be continuing with us. He called me this morning and indicated he did not want to return. I encouraged him to come in and speak with the group about his decision, but he declined to do so.

Cassidy: What did he say? Did he give a reason?

Therapist: Actually, very little. He didn't want to discuss the matter with me either.

Lee: I can't say that I'm very surprised. He looked so uncomfortable. He was sweating, looking at his watch.

Henry: What do you mean? Are you saying you didn't expect him to be here?

Lee: I didn't expect him to stay for very long. He just didn't seem to be connecting with the rest of us.

Henry: Probably it was my fault that he didn't. I kind of went on and on about my wife's illness and death, and the period that followed. After I left last week, I worried that I monopolized the group's time.

Lee: Absolutely not! Even though I haven't lost a spouse—not yet, anyway—I could relate to what you went through and so could Jade and Cassidy. We all said so. In fact, by your telling your story, you helped the rest of us open up.

Jade: Yeah, I didn't think I would be able to talk about my boyfriend and what he did to me. When I left, I felt better that I did. I had

	kind of been dreading getting into that stuff, so it was a relief that I did. And I didn't feel scared coming here tonight like I did in the other sessions.
Jeffrey:	And I conveyed to all of you some of my feelings about losing my friends in the bombing. I didn't talk at length, but each of us can't talk at length each session. I assume that this is how it is going to work: One of us will go into our problem in depth, and the others will see if they can relate.
Cassidy:	You put it very well, Jeffrey. You have a way of putting things that makes sense. Maybe Mark just couldn't wait for his turn.
Mort:	[to the therapist] Have you ever had a patient who had a bad reaction from antidepressant medication?
Zachariah:	[speaking to Cassidy as if Mort had not spoken] I doubt it! He just looked like he was bored with the rest of us. I mean, how could you not be moved by Henry's story? But he just sat there looking like he was waiting for the session to end.
Jade:	I don't think we really asked him about himself. Maybe we should have made more of an effort to draw him out.
Cassidy:	I think I did ask him a question, and he just answered with a few words . . . like he didn't want to be bothered with talking.
Therapist:	The group is puzzling over who's to blame for Mark's leaving. Is it Mark, or is it the group?

[brief silence; Jade smiles at the therapist]

Lee:	I just think it takes a great deal of courage to make this commitment, and most people just aren't ready for it. I work in a big organization—50 people or so—and I can count on one hand the people who have very few problems. The rest should be here. But are they? I'm not any worse off than the rest of them . . . I'm just willing to make the commitment. We all are . . . all except Mark.
Cassidy:	That's one of the first things I learned in AA. You have to accept that you need help.
Zachariah:	It makes me mad that we're the ones society sees as weak. We're actually the strong ones.
Jade:	I agree with that, Zach, and that's why I respect all of you so much.
Mort:	I think I'm weak. I was born weak.

[silence]

Therapist:	Do others sometimes share Mort's sense of being weak?

Henry:	Yeah, sure. When my wife died, I turned into a tiny, little baby [*shakes his head*]. But . . . but suppose Mark came with a big problem, and I started jawing about losing my wife, and he just never got to talk. He might have said to himself, "This isn't going to work for me here."
Jade:	Yeah, suppose he's shy and couldn't bring up his problem.
Jeffrey:	Perhaps, but I just don't see that we can do anything about it now. He's gone. I think we're wasting our time talking about someone who's now out of our lives.
Mort:	Maybe we could contact him and ask him if he could give us another chance.
Jeffrey:	Remember the rule that we don't contact one another outside of group?
Henry:	I know Mark is gone for good, but it could happen again with someone else . . . and pretty soon, the group could be down to . . . well, just me talking about losing my wife. I suppose she'd [*pointing to the therapist*] have to stay. Hey, Doc, I have a request: If I'm babbling too long, will you let me know?
Jade:	Of course she will!
Lee:	I have just the remedy. We'll begin our session by going around to each member and finding out if each person has something important to share. That way, no one gets neglected.
Zachariah:	Great idea!
Cassidy:	Sounds fine to me, too. We'll start next week.

Characteristic Stage 1 Behaviors Seen in This Vignette. This session shows many of the distinctive features of early group life. Members interact with one another exhibiting a high level of politeness and formality. Conflict is not expressed in direct terms: Members find ways of sidestepping overt disagreement with one another, such as changing the topic. Members also show a lack of purpose. For example, members spend time talking about Mark's departure, but Jeffrey doubts whether it is worthwhile. Mort sees the group as a place to get expert opinion on pharmacologic issues.

Still another feature is members' lack of genuine connection with one another. At times, members may directly respond to another member's point; at others, members act as if a member had not spoken. Later in the life of the group, Mort's question about medication would have been explicitly labeled as off topic. At one point, it might have provoked anger because it constituted an interruption of ongoing dialogue, but at another point, members may have recognized the defensive aspect of such communication. Mort's question also illustrates the kind of testing that Tuckman (1965) described as being highly characteristic of this phase. Mort is testing the boundaries of acceptable behavior in the group: He is seeing whether the therapist and other members will accept his asking for individual assistance from the therapist vis-à-vis his symptoms.

The members borrow liberally from other frameworks, such as Cassidy's use of AA concepts, because the group has not yet evolved its own framework for understanding its experience. Members are interested in discerning and applying the group rules. For example, Jeffrey is quick to remind Mort about the no-socializing rule in relation to Mort's suggestion to contact Mark. At another stage of development, the prospect of breaking a group rule might have been an enticement; at another stage, the members might have focused on other implications of his suggestion (e.g., should members be in a position to lure an unwilling participant back into the group on the basis of highly speculative ideas about the reasons for his departure?). However, at this stage, the reinforcement of the rules gives members a sense of security. Members in this stage make decisions quickly, decisions that they have little interest in following (Brabender & Fallon, 1993; Wheelan, 2005). Notice that the group immediately embraces Lee's suggestion, failing to subject it to critical evaluation. No effort is made to discover whether a minority position exists. In most instances, the group will show little interest in following the decision it has made and will certainly not do so for any significant duration.

The stance toward the therapist in this session is characteristic of this stage. The group treats the therapist as an expert from afar, a remote figure whose pronouncements are to be revered rather than used. Inevitably, the group will invite the therapist either to show her expertise, as in Mort's query, or to take a more controlling stance, as in Henry's request to be told when he was monopolizing the group. These efforts are characteristic of the tendency of members to emphasize their individual rather than collective relationship with the therapist (Caple, 1978). However, when the therapist is not forthcoming, members will not give strong and clear expression of their frustration. Along these lines, members who are neglecting to talk about the role of the therapist in Mark's departure is notable. Although members are likely to have many private doubts about the role the therapist is assuming in the group, they have not yet cultivated the resources to approach the therapist directly.

Yet, as many (e.g., Bennis & Shepard, 1956; Mann, 1966) have pointed out, preliminary subgrouping toward issues related to the therapist's control can be seen. We see some members endorsing the idea that they should be dependent on the therapist for direction and others advocating for greater self-sufficiency. As an example of the former, Henry and Jade join together to support the therapist's active role in interrupting members who are too verbose. The latter subgrouping is seen in the support Lee receives from Zachariah and Cassidy in relation to her countersuggestion that members organize a go-around to deal with the issue of sharing the group's time. However, in general, subgroups are less stable at this time than they will be at later stages (Mann, Gibbard, & Hartman, 1967).

Tasks and Conflicts. Most group members come to the group with some expectation that group participation will benefit them. They may be hopeful that psychological problems will be ameliorated, or they may in the short run anticipate that the pain of these problems will be lessened by the discovery that others share them. Members may also look to the group for interpersonal fulfillment not found elsewhere in their lives. For example, lonely individuals may seek companionship. They, like all human beings, yearn to belong, to be accepted and affirmed by others.[1] Some individuals may simply harbor an anticipation that relationships in the group will be fulfilling because of satisfactions enjoyed in past relationships. All of these factors are ones that compel members in the direction of attachment: They create in members a quality of openness to becoming emotionally connected to the other members of the group.

Yet, the urge to become involved with one another is not the only motivational element operative in the group. Another force driving members is the opposing wish to stay apart from others (MacKenzie & Livesley, 1983), a wish that (like the desire to connect) has multiple roots. Members' fears of involvement, conscious and unconscious, move them in the direction of isolation. For example, members fear being insulted, shamed, or rejected by other members, events that could imperil their self-regard. They fear that they may contract others' psychological problems, somewhat in the same way a person might fear being hospitalized on a unit in which the other patients had various types of contagious illnesses. Some members worry about their own destructive potential vis-à-vis the other members of the group. Beyond these specific fears, many members harbor a more general concern that engagement with others will bring about the loss of identity. All of these forces will press on members to maintain an attitude of mistrust and distance.

In the vignette, both poles of the conflict can be seen. Members' interest in the departing member and attempts to discern the reasons for his decision reveal their connection-seeking motive. Members' collective effort to identify with Henry's loss to assuage his guilt is another manifestation. Members' differentiation of themselves (the strong ones) from those on the outside (the weaklings) is both another way of connecting with each other and establishing themselves as a group. By contrast, members do not explore is-

---

[1]Zimbardo (2007) used the findings from the Stanford prison experiments of the early 1970s to describe how the yearning to belong can be powerful enough to induce individuals to respond in a manner at odds with their own values and strictures. In this experiment, individuals who volunteered to be guards engaged in a series of abusive acts toward their prisoners in violation of their own beliefs about what is right. Although Zimbardo outlined a host of situational factors causing a transformation in the guards, a key factor was their longing to be accepted by the other guards. He wrote about how the same force was operative in the Abu Ghraib prison abuses of the Iraq war.

sues but dispense with them. For example, Henry raises the issue of a given member (in this case, himself) preventing others from deriving benefit from the group. Members respond to this possibility by reassuring him rather than by exploring it thoroughly. Lee's interest in regimenting members' interactions through the go-around and others' support of this proposal is still another way in which members show their avoidance of a full immersion in their mutual relationships.

A major task the group must accomplish during this period for it to progress to later developmental stages is to resolve the conflict between involvement and separation in the direction of involvement (also portrayed by some writers as the conflict between trust and mistrust). Such a resolution does not require that the group disavow the dangers of group involvement and the perils of relationships. In fact, such a resolution, predicated as it would be on a denial of members' experience, would provide a less solid foundation for work in later stages and make the group vulnerable to regressive episodes. However, such episodes create an opportunity for the group to address once again the conflict in a more integrative way.

A product of the group's successful resolution of the involvement and separation conflict is a rudimentary level of cohesion wherein members experience a sense of belonging and commitment to the group. However, as MacKenzie (1990) noted, two other tasks also intensify cohesion, which is the cornerstone of all further group development. These tasks include the delineation of the external and the internal boundaries. This delineation enables the group to be established as a psychological reality in members' awareness, as an entity with a clear identity. The external boundary defines the group in space and time and is achieved as members experience the consistencies of where and when the group is held. For the group to develop an external boundary, the group must perceive itself as separate from the rest of the world. For example, a group that takes place on a noisy inpatient unit in which patients not in the group can look at the group through windows and make comments that are readily heard by the group members may be perceived by its members only as a collectivity rather than a bona fide group. All groups are to some extent porous; however, there is a degree of ingress and egress of information to and from the outside environment beyond which the group will no longer be perceived as having a distinct identity by its members.

The internal boundary of the group is the establishment of the group membership. Members define the group by who is in it. Consequently, it was of utmost importance for the therapist in the vignette to share with the group members Mark's status; members' keen interest in this topic is characteristic of this period in which the group is an emerging psychological reality. Absences and lateness, when established as a focus, can serve as growth opportunities. Arrow and McGrath (1993) found that student work groups with membership disruptions, both spontaneous and experimentally imposed, achieved higher cohesion than groups with membership stability. The less stable groups also performed better on tasks requiring reflection on their own processes. The instability may have catalyzed such reflection.

In addition to the resolution of the involvement–separation conflict and the establishment of the external and internal boundaries of the group, members, with the help of the therapist, must perform a third task—the crafting of a culture that promotes growth. During this period, norms are established that can either promote or hinder the group's progress (Brabender, 2002). Behaviors that are seen as supporting group development are (a) regular attendance and promptness, (b) the open expression of thoughts and feelings, (c) self-reflection, and (d) the giving and receiving of feedback.[2] Depending on the focus of the group, other elements also may be important.

Stage 2: Conflict and Rebellion

When the reader last saw our featured group in the third session, Lee had proposed a means by which the group could have its needs met—the go-around. Groups commonly discover techniques such as a go-around to eliminate the ambiguity of the situation. Such discoveries are met with enthusiasm and relief. Finally, members believe, the group knows how it should proceed. Yet, as is true with our featured group, these techniques never have longevity within the group because of group members' tacit recognition that they are disconnected from the therapist's management of the group; it is the therapist and only the therapist who can provide the ultimate direction to spare members from, as they see it, wandering aimlessly.

The passage of time leads to disappointment and frustration. Members increasingly realize that their expectations of the group are being violated. If the group has accomplished the tasks of Stage 1 (formation and engagement), this disappointment and frustration will become more prominent in members' experience, which will make the experiencing of these emotions available for exploration.

Early Stage 2 Vignette

The group is in its eighth session, and members arrive on time.

    Jade: Thanks everyone for telling me to stick up for myself with Rod. This week I got a restraining order on him and because of that this week has been so peaceful. I didn't feel I needed him either. I went to work. I went to the gym. I went out with my friends. I was fine.

---

[2]At this point, the value of the feedback is in members' beginning recognition of its importance in terms of their group work. Often the content has little usefulness because of members' superficial knowledge of one another.

Henry: Great news, Jade! I can't tell you how angry it made me to think about what he has done to you . . . what all those men did to you.

Cassidy: You're such a dad! I wish I had a father like you. You're nothing like my own father, who was a worthless excuse for a human being. You're a lovely, lovely group dad.

Henry: Makes me feel good to hear you say that—not the part about your father but what you said about me . . . makes me feel like I still have some purpose. After Esther died, it seemed there was no point anymore.

Mort: [peevishly] I'm glad you found a point.

Lee: Mort, now what do you mean by that?

Mort: Never mind, I was just being sarcastic.

Jeffrey: You may have been sarcastic, but you also meant something.

Mort: Henry's a nice guy—who couldn't like him? He's found a reason to live and I'm glad . . . but I just can't say that for myself. I tried antidepressants—made me feel worse. Then, I came here mainly to get my family off my back, I've been here 8 weeks, and nothing's better. I didn't expect anything to get better.

Jeffrey: Has it ever occurred to you that your expectation determines outcome?

Jade: Like a wish-fulfilling prophesy? I studied that in Intro to Psych.

Mort: Is this a group for people who went to college?

Lee: What Jeffrey is merely saying is that maybe you had a negative attitude coming in here, and so you haven't gotten anything out of it.

Henry: Attitude is everything, Mort. We'd all like to see you get something out of coming here.

Mort: You sound like my family now. "Mort, you've got to try." "Mort, you've got to lift yourself up." "Mort, you know you can do better than this deli."

Lee: Okay, now let me ask you just a few questions. Mort, when was the last time you had a girlfriend?

Mort: Maybe about 5 years ago . . . didn't last that long . . . 1 month, maybe 2.

Lee: [wagging her index finger] Mort, when you tell me that, immediately I see a problem. This fact alone tells me that you are not taking enough initiative in your social life. What do you think: Someone is just going to knock on your door? No one can be happy without a close relationship, and you are not even working on one! [*Mort shrugs*]

Jeffrey: That's the point. Mort isn't working on anything. He takes control of nothing in his life. We see it in here every week: Mort doesn't say anything unless we call on him.

Mort: That's not true! I asked if this was a group for college graduates, didn't I?

Jeffrey: That's not what I mean. You don't say anything to help yourself. You're passive. You don't even take control of your own flatulence in here. [*members laugh*]

Zachariah: [*shaking his head*] That was nasty!

Mort: That was an accident!

Jeffrey: No—it was a metaphor.

Lee: Jeffrey, you're getting away from Mort being lonely.

Mort: I'm not lonely; I'm miserable.

Lee: Of course you're lonely. And now that New Year's is coming, I think we should figure how to help you out of your predicament. There must be some nice young woman you can ask out for New Year's.

Jeffrey: How do you know he's into girls? [*Cassidy laughs*]

Zachariah: Yeah, how do you know? Lee, you can't go around just assuming that kind of thing.

Mort: [*sullenly*] I'm not gay.

Lee: So we've established that. Now, if you will be so kind to answer, I will repeat my question, "When was . . ."

Mort: I don't know. It terrifies me to ask a woman out. I try to avoid it whenever possible. [*group laughs; Mort looks bewildered*] I decided I wasn't going to do it anymore, but my relatives are always fixing me up with blind dates. I'd like them to leave me alone.

Lee: So right before you call the woman, what goes through your mind?

Mort: It's sort of hard to remember. I suppose I think, "What if she says no?"

Lee: And what if she does say no? What would that mean?

Mort: That I'm a big fat loser? Yeah, that's about it.

Lee: But don't you draw that conclusion anyway? If you were to get a positive response, then, you'd have some ammunition against that idea that you're a . . . what did you say . . . "a big fat loser"?

Jade: That's a great point, Lee. You're like having an extra therapist in the group.

Jeffrey: If Lee wants to be another therapist I think that's fine, but I refuse to pay her, too. [*Zachariah and Cassidy laugh; Jade frowns*] Anyway, I have a different perspective. Lee, you're great and all, but I think that you're barking up the wrong tree. Mort doesn't need a relationship . . . he needs a willingness to help himself. I haven't heard Mort talking about wanting a girlfriend, a boyfriend, or any kind of friend for that matter. He wants to open a hobby shop. He wants to strike out on his own. That's what we should we be focusing on.

Henry: Come on now, guys. You're both trying to help him. What's wrong with having a girlfriend and having a new occupation?

Therapist: It seems as if group members are keenly interested in fixing Mort—whether it be through his social life or his work life. Perhaps it feels that by being effective in assisting Mort, each member will be repairing whatever it is that makes you unhappy with yourselves.

Lee: Well, I think helping someone else always makes you feel better.

Jeffrey: I think Mort would be better off figuring out how to help himself.

Lee: Then, pray tell, why are we here?

Characteristic Early Stage 2 Behaviors Seen in This Vignette. In this session, members are less polite and formal with one another than they were in the previous vignette. Behaviors that might be offensive to one another (such as Mort's flatulence in a session) are identified by other members not so much with an interest in exploring the behavior's basis but in reprimanding the member for the behavior's occurrence. At this time, members are willing to express opinions that are different from those expressed by other members, and members may form subgroups around these differences. Lee's probing of Mort's social life leads to the formation of a subgroup defined by the valuing of relationships. Reacting to the position of this subgroup is another subgroup, spearheaded by Jeffrey, that values autonomy. This conflict exists at only a nascent level during this stage but will reach full flowering later in the group's life. Such foreshadowing of the tensions of later phases within an earlier phase is common across the group's development. Members will increasingly experience polarized feelings in relation to one another, having warmth and affection for those who share their positions and hostility for members who do not (Gavin, 1987).

Another aspect of the group is the relationship forming between Lee and Mort. Lee clearly adopts the position of authority figure and helper in relation to Mort, exploring his issues in the way a therapist might, as Jade notes. However, Lee is much more directive and forthcoming than the actual therapist is and gratifies members' longings for a different type of therapist. For his part, Mort presents as someone who is wholly helpless to identify his difficulties, prioritize them, and recognize possible ways of approaching and solving them. As Agazarian (1997) noted, this dynamic of therapist and patient within the group is a common one at this time. The group selects the member perceived as most vulnerable, and members' ways of interacting with this person induce him or her to behave in a way that puts in bold relief that individual's weaknesses. It is as if the group is attempting to show the therapist through this one member how needful members are. Through the member assuming the role of therapist, the group is providing the therapist with a model of the more active and giving stance they would like the therapist to take. Yet, the members do not show total satisfaction with the substitute. Although they allow Lee to minister to Mort, they are also quick to state their disagreement with her or denigrate her for her assumption of authority (Jeff sarcastically states that he refuses to pay her). The emergence of a subgroup that takes a counterdependent authority-challenge stance is characteristic of this period (Bennis & Shepard, 1956).

Tasks and Conflicts. Early in Stage 2, the group approaches a set of conflicts pertaining to members' relationships to authority. At the most general level, members grapple with the conflict between longings to depend on authority in the total way an infant relies on the mother and the desire for mature self-sufficiency. However, as noted, the members of different subgroups will experience this conflict in a somewhat different ways. Members possessing greater awareness of their yearning for the therapist to rescue them in their plight will struggle with the urge to express disappointment and fear of what the consequences of such an expression might be. They say to themselves, "I am not getting what I need and my need is desperate. But if I speak up or criticize her [the therapist], I may doom myself to never getting it, and besides, she'll hate me." For them, expressing opposition invites separation and deprivation. The members who are more aware of their longings to act independently tacitly understand that in their expression of opposition to the therapist is also an acknowledgment of a need for the therapist. They fear that the surfacing of this need will place them in an infantile, helpless position. Early in Stage 2, members merely begin to stake out their positions and affiliate with others having similar positions. At this time, the conflict begins to crystallize so that later in Stage 2 it may move toward resolution.

However, the resolution of the authority conflict of Stage 2 requires that members complete certain tasks such as achieving the ability to express disagreement with one another (MacKenzie, 1990). Although some mild intellectualized disagreement can occur in Stage 1, the disagreement in Stage 2 is increasingly immediate and affective. To acquire the confidence to confront the therapist, members must first practice the management of conflict in their relationships with one another. When members express mutual disagreement and nothing traumatic occurs, they move on to more ambitious confrontations. Members also must achieve a modicum of comfort in the overt acknowledgment of dissatisfaction toward authority through their expression of discontent with therapist substitutes such as authority figures outside the group and member helpers within. They must also learn about their resources for handling authority. For instance, certain members typically will show greater ease in expressing discontent with authority. Others will show skill at dissipating tension when it reaches intolerable levels.

Late Stage 2 Vignette

The group is in its 15th session. Zachariah walks into the session 10 minutes late. Cassidy had entered 5 minutes earlier with no explanation for her tardiness. The group had been conversing in a desultory way, possibly because they were expecting the missing members to arrive and knew the group session would then begin anew.

Henry:	So bro, what's happening? [*group laughs at Henry's uncharacteristic use of language*]
Zachariah:	I just broke up with my old lady . . . just this afternoon. I sat in the park with her for 2 hours and tried to get her to lighten up. She was crying and crying, and I couldn't figure out how to get away from there.
Jeffrey:	So what did you do? I'd like to know because I've been in that situation myself. Maybe I can finally get something from one of these sessions that I can actually use.
Zachariah:	I told her that I'm really screwed up, that I can't stay in relationships very long, and that she shouldn't think it's her.
Cassidy:	Did it work?
Zachariah:	I'm here, aren't I?
Lee:	Well, you're here late.
Zachariah:	So what did I miss? Nothing, I bet. I wouldn't have been late if this jerk of a cop hadn't stopped and given me a ticket. [*Mort laughs and makes a crude gesture to convey his support of Zachariah's attitude toward the policeman, and Cassidy laughs in response to Mort's action*]
Jade:	I think the way you treated your girlfriend was very callous. You told her some story about yourself just to make her less upset so you could leave. That's what men do to me.
Zachariah:	It's not a story. I at least half believe it . . . maybe . . . I don't know. [*he shrugs*]

Jade: If you half believed it, you'd be more upset. When I think about myself being screwed up, it really depresses me.

Zachariah: Yeah, well, I'm just relieved to be out of the thing and to have my freedom back . . . and away from that idiot cop.

Lee: [to Zachariah] You've said to us before that you "love them and leave them." It's very clear to me that you are leaving this young woman not because anything was wrong with her but because as you yourself suspect, this is your problem—just like you said to her. Don't just half believe it; believe it and do something about it. The most important step you could take here is to look at your childhood and figure out where this comes from. Can you tell us about your relationship with your mother?

Jeffrey: You are not his therapist! You are exactly like one of us and have as many difficulties as we do, and I get exasperated by how you try to elevate yourself in this room.

Lee: I would be the last one to deny my difficulties. Just because I try to help someone else in the group does not mean that I don't need help . . . that I don't crave help. But my understanding of this group is that we are here to help one another. And if I must say so, if I didn't keep things going in here, I think that we'd waste a whole lot of time.

Jade: She has a point.

Henry: I absolutely, wholeheartedly agree. I appreciate everything Lee does in here. In fact, you've made many comments that have helped me.

Mort: Maybe we could just meet with Lee.

Therapist: So it sounds as though the group is wondering whether I'm needed at all.

Lee: I do think you're needed. In fact, I think we really need you, and I for one would be happy if you would help Jade, and Zach, and Mort, and me, and everyone to figure out how we've gotten to be the way we are. I think it would be better for you to be asking Zach about his relationship with the group, but when that doesn't happen, I just can't stop myself from jumping in to help. Maybe that's part of my problem—I can't just stand sitting here when I see so much suffering.

Jeffrey: You know, Lee, I find myself—and I know this is a rare moment—agreeing with you. I have had the thought, "What is she really doing in here?"

Jade: Maybe she's here to make sure we don't hurt one another.

Jeffrey: You mean physically—I think we're all civilized enough for that not to be a worry.

Zachariah: It's the whole rip-off by the psychiatric profession. We're told we need these people, and like sheep, we believe it. If we weren't here to pay these people, what would they do? Work at a carwash?

Lee: I wouldn't go that far! My individual therapist has helped me greatly. I understand so much more about how my past has affected me. But it's just in here. I think you [*speaking to the therapist*] see us as being able to do far more for ourselves than we can.

Jeffrey: I have to agree on that point! I can't relate to Zach's whole view of the psychiatric profession's corruption. But I do have my doubts about whether my resources are well spent on this group where we talk and she remains silent.

Henry: Whoa! That's not fair: She makes a lot of comments.

Jeffrey: Okay—true. I mean that she doesn't give us any concrete input about our problems.

Jade: You sound really irritated.

Jeffrey: Of course I'm irritated—I don't like wasting my time or my money. [*to therapist*] But I don't like quitting things either. I really think you should be more vigorous in giving us input. [*the members are silent for several seconds*]

Jade: Jeff, how can you talk to her that way? You sound so hateful . . . so disrespectful. She's going to get disgusted with us and walk out.

Henry: She's too professional for that.

Cassidy: There's nothing wrong with Jeff speaking his mind to her. You can't always stop yourself by worrying about what someone is going to do if you let them know how you feel. You'd never say anything and other people would always have their way. [*to the therapist*] I agree with Jeff: You just haven't been doing your job.

Zachariah: Wait a minute . . . let me get something clear. [*speaking to Jade*] You mean to say *you* think she's doing a good job?

Jade: Well . . . I have had some moments of doubt.

Zachariah: What do you mean? Just say what you feel.

Jade: I feel that I don't like how Jeff talks to her . . . his tone, his whole manner . . . but I think he's right about what he's saying. Are you happy now?

Zachariah: As a matter of fact, yes.

Characteristic Late Stage 2 Behaviors Seen in This Vignette. The session opens with two members absent because of tardiness, a type of boundary violation characteristic of this phase. As MacKenzie (1990) noted, the adolescent feel to members' attitudes and behaviors at this stage is characteristic. Although one member reprimands Zachariah, this censure and the tardiness itself are otherwise ignored by the group. An emotional climate of negativity is present and builds over the session. Zach's expression of hostility toward a figure of authority is supported by other members of the group. Such manifestations of negativity toward authority figures other than the therapist usually presage an increasingly direct expression of dissatisfaction with the therapist. In fact, as Lee moves into her familiar role of helper, the group makes a more virulent attack on her than it had at an earlier point in this stage. Were Lee to react in a way that suggested that she had been damaged by members' hostilities, the group would have difficulty continuing in their path toward the therapist. However, Lee responded with a challenge of her own. Both her robustness and the therapist's failure to show retaliation when confronted may have been the conditions enabling the group to continue its progress toward the therapist, albeit with a show of concern from some members, such as Jade.

In many cases, the therapist may need to help the group speak in less symbolic ways toward him or her. In this circumstance, because of the level of functioning of the members and particular relational styles of some (e.g., Jeff was able to express a sentiment strongly without worrying the group that his anger could destructively escalate), members were able to make this movement on their own. Jeff's giving voice to the group's irritation with the therapist and the agreement expressed by other members were the culmination of this movement. As Agazarian (1997) noted, it is not until members can completely abdicate responsibility for their difficulties that they can begin the painful task of owning them.

Tasks and Conflicts. Members continue to complete the tasks and address the conflicts of early Stage 2. Members continue to work to crystallize their understanding of the perils of both dependency and rebelliousness. For example, Jade clarifies that a felt risk of rebelliousness is the loss of the caretaking figure. Her articulation of this worry is important because it enables members to address its congruence with their actual experience. Henry is able to note that the therapist has not demonstrated a tendency to react in the way Jade anticipates she might. The completion of this task enables the pursuit of the formidable task of expressing dissatisfaction with the therapist at a group level. The barometric event described by Bennis and Shepard (1956), a symbolic expression by the group as a whole, does not occur in this group, and that is not unusual. What does occur is an expression of discontent that includes members of the dependency subgroup. This subgroup movement establishes the expression as a group level event and signals that Stage 2 is coming to an end. Yet, it is insufficient: Members must perceive that the therapist survives the attack and, in this way, come to the realization that feelings and their communication are not inherently destructive. At this juncture, it is not enough for the therapist to bear members' reaction to him or her; the therapist's containment must be evident to members.

In sum, then, in early Stage 2, members learn to express disagreement with one another. This achievement establishes the groundwork for later Stage 2 work—taking on the authority figure in the group.

Stage 3: Unity and Intimacy

The group's challenge of the therapist is an event that is exciting, frightening, surprising, and vitalizing. When members see that both they and the therapist survive this event, they feel an immense satisfaction that cements their relationships with one another. The emerging feeling is somewhat like the esprit de corps that results from participation on a successful survival mission with a team; it is laced with a euphoria that temporarily obscures any concomitant negative reactions.

Stage 3 Vignette

The group, now in its 20th week, has not met for 2 weeks because of the therapist's vacation. The group members assemble for the session on time. Cassidy arrives with bleached blond hair in sharp contrast to her former dark brunette color. She is also attired in a rather sexually provocative outfit.

Jade: I missed you all. I mean, I enjoyed having some free time on Thursday evening, but I missed you all, [*to the therapist*] even you. [*members laugh*]

Henry: I thought of all of you on the last two Thursday nights. I said to myself, "I wonder what Lee is doing and Zach and Jade on her trip to Mexico."

Jeffrey: You notice that he doesn't mention me.

Henry: You, I thought about especially.

Jeffrey: [*playful tone*] What exactly were you thinking about in relation to me? I'm quite curious.

Henry: Well, I had a beautiful image of you out on a date with a gorgeous woman . . . fine restaurant, excellent wine . . . and then later . . . let's just say I knew you would use your free Thursdays well.

Jeffrey: Reality can be so disappointing. [*Mort chimes in, "Tell me about it" and the other members laugh*]

Jade: I just feel we should have a celebration now that we're back . . . [*dreamily*] back with our best friends.

Henry: Yeah, I think we should celebrate this young woman's new look [*nodding toward Cassidy*] Hubba, hubba! [*Henry laughs loudly and Cassidy smiles*]

Jeffrey: [*ignoring Henry*] I'm always ready to celebrate, but I don't know if . . . this best friend thing is a bit much.

Lee: It's just a way of speaking, Jeffrey. You don't have to be so . . . precise every moment.

Mort: So we're not one another's best friends? I mean I really don't have any other friends so I guess by default you would be . . .

Lee: Gracious! Could that be true?

Mort: Well, not really. I have some relatives but no friends. I know I told you already that I'm afraid to ask women out, but the real truth is I'm afraid of all people and I just stay away from them. In fact, if I see someone I know, I cross the street so I won't have to interact. I was going to the community college, and I had to drop out because I was panicked that I would be called on in class. [*Henry whistles in amazement*] I even stay away from little kids because I know they'll call me fat, like a little girl did in the supermarket. In fact, it took me 3 years to get the courage to come in here. Geez, I never admitted that stuff to anyone.

Cassidy: I think it's so great that you shared that with us. I knew you had problems with women, but it sounds like it goes a lot farther. Now we can help you better.

Jade: Yeah, Mort. We definitely are best friends. That's why I want to have a party!

Lee: Of course, we can't do that. It really isn't . . . it's not consistent with . . .

Zachariah: C'mon Lee. Don't keep yourself out of the party. Just join in.

Characteristic Stage 3 Behaviors Seen in This Vignette. In this session, the group manifests a very positively toned affective climate. The erotic tinge revealed in Henry's fantasy about Jeffrey's romantic life and the group's evident interest in this topic are also characteristic of this stage. Cassidy's sexualized appearance and Henry's response to it also underscore the heightened sexuality in the group. Indicators are present that cohesion is high. For example, members reveal that they think about one another when separated. Another characteristic feature of this stage is members' increased level of self-disclosure as reflected in Mort's revelation of the high level of social anxiety. As Wheelan (2005) pointed out, the success of Stage 2 diminishes members' fears of rejection, and they feel they can safely risk deepening their disclosures, both in terms of the content and the spontaneity of the process. Still another aspect is a disregard for boundaries. Jade suggests a celebration, and other members appear ready to follow her. Even Lee, who is usually ready to assert the importance of boundaries, provides anemic opposition to the idea of a party. The view toward the therapist is also altered. With the heightening of members' interest in one another, the preoccupation with the therapist of early stages has gone. Yet, the therapist is acknowledged as being a member of the group. Finally, members show impatience with a focus on process and value expression over its understanding. For example, when Jeffrey raises a caution with members' expression of unrealistic sentiments, he is summarily ignored.

Tasks and Conflicts. Members in this period of group life give expression to one side of the conflict that emerges in the pursuit of intimate relationships—the longing of members to establish relationships of such total closeness that the distinction between self and other is obliterated. The clear emergence of this force enables its exploration later when both sides of the conflict are evident.

The tasks in this stage are threefold. First, the cohesion in the group intensifies. This strengthening of members' bonds with one another provides a nurturing web that protects them as they engage in the difficult investigations of the next stage. Second, members deepen their knowledge of one another and their ability to share private material with one another. Implicit in this sharing is some recognition of responsibility for their own psychological difficulties. Members are saying in effect, "I know it is up to me to get somewhere in this group, and so I will take a risk to open myself up to you." Third, members renegotiate their relationship with the therapist. Although shards of the original dependency on the therapist may always remain (Billow, 2006), members nonetheless begin to see the special resources the therapist has to offer to the group. By abandoning their idealized view of the therapist to some extent, they can gain access to the therapist's unique capacities for assisting them. In addition to completing these tasks, members may develop a language to capture the range of positive emotions humans experience.

Stage 4: Integration and Work

The ecstatic feelings of Stage 3 cannot last indefinitely. This stage is predicated on members' denial of their own negative feelings about one another and events in the group as well as on the denial of the differences among them (Agazarian & Peters, 1981). Eventually, members' awareness of those realities that are warded off in Stage 3 intrude and demand integration with those psychological elements holding sway in the prior stage. Furthermore, the extreme level of closeness sought by some members in Stage 3 arouses others' anxiety about the preservation of their own autonomy (Jackson, 1999). Those concerned about their autonomy often take an active role in raising questions of the perils of absolute intimacy and the radical dissolution of interpersonal boundaries. This effort enables the establishment of a balance between closeness and the preservation of individuality. Stage 4 is distinguished from Stage 3 by a marked shift in mood from ecstasy to apprehension and then to a more free-ranging set of affects depending on the specific content of the sessions. Stage 4 is also characterized by a clearer work orientation on the part of members wherein their behaviors are congruent with the goals they established on entering the group.

Stage 4 Vignette

The group is in its 25th session, and Lee comes in looking rather dejected. Obviously concerned and puzzled, Henry stares at her while other members are talking. Cassidy is talking about a situation at work, and others are listening and responding.

Cassidy: I just don't understand what business it is of hers [*referring to her employer*] how I look when I'm doing my job. My attendance has been perfect since she said something to me about it.

Jeffrey: Well . . . [*shrugs*]

Cassidy: Well, what?

Jeffrey: Well . . . look, I'm not the most compliant employee; I have my share of run-ins with my supervisor . . . but . . . it really *is* her business how you look.

Henry: Yeah, but Cassidy looks swell. When I saw her, I said to myself, "Woo hoo!"

Jade: Henry, let me ask you something: Are you being completely honest with Cassidy? Do you truly feel that she looks . . . what did you say, "swell"?

Henry: [*placing his hands in front of his face in mock self-defense*] Hey, let up on me.

Jade: [*frowning*] No, I'm not going to let up on you. Let me put this point another way. Do you think Cassidy looks better now or before she got her hair bleached?

Henry: Mmmm . . . I like her both ways!

Zachariah: What a dodge.

Mort: [*laughs and mutters*] You got him there, Zach.

Cassidy: I feel you're dodging, too. Which way do you like my hair better—before or after?

Henry: Okay, okay, okay. When you ask me that way, I'd be a liar if I didn't say that I liked how you looked before—more natural.

Cassidy: Then why did you make the big fuss? My family says I look like a slut, so I would really appreciate an objective perspective. Why did you act as though you liked it?

Jeffrey: Have you every heard of irony?

Zach: What?

Jade: [ignoring Jeffrey] Henry, you are a very kind person, but you just tell people what they want to hear, and sometimes that turns out not to be the kindest thing. Like Cassidy, here . . . her supervisor feels her appearance isn't professional enough. At the nursing home where I work, we are after the aides all the time for how they have their hair and dress lengths. When you're in a work setting, you need to observe a dress code.

Henry: I know that. Of course I know that.

Jade: I was sure you did. My point is, Henry, you try too hard to be a people pleaser. If I want to know the truth, I'll ask Jeffrey or Lee or someone else. I won't ask you because you will just say what I want to hear . . . not what I need to hear.

Cassidy: I agree with Jade. In fact, Henry, when you were telling me that I look good, I didn't even believe it. Most of the time, I don't know what you really think. I know that you care about us, but beyond that, I'm not sure.

Jeffrey: To be perfectly straight, pal, it can even be a little irritating.

Mort: Henry doesn't irritate me.

Zachariah: Me, either. I wish more people were like Henry.

Jade: Well, I would say more "frustrating" because I really do want to know what you think, Henry. Your true, most heartfelt opinions are hidden from us.

Henry: [with perplexity] I'm not always sure what they are myself.

Jeffrey: I could see how that might be true. You've worked so energetically to accommodate to everyone else that you've lost sight of where you stand.

Jade: But some of the time you do know, Henry . . . like . . . did you really like Cassidy's hair?

Henry: No, not really.

Cassidy: I'm not surprised; I'm not sure how I feel about it. Maybe I'll go back to my old . . .

Jade: [interrupts Cassidy and says to Henry] I think you can do it. Just remember that we want to know what you really think, not what you think we want to hear.

Henry: What I really think right now is that something's wrong with Lee.

Lee: Henry, please, don't use me as your shield.

Henry: Nonsense! I got the point, and I'm going to work on it in here and out there. But right now, I think we all are aware that something is going on with you.

Jade: Lee, you know Henry's right. You're making us worried.

Jeffrey: You look completely dejected. We've never seen you like this.

Lee: I left my husband. I discovered that he, well, has another life. I'm not sure I'll be able to afford the group.

Jade: Oh, Lee, I'm so sorry.

Lee: Right now, if it's all right with all of you, I don't want to go into the sordid details. But I probably should let you know that my financial situation has changed . . . rather drastically . . . and I'm not sure I'll be able to make this financial commitment. I discussed this with her [*referring to the therapist*], and she said she could work with me but I don't know . . . I don't feel it's right for me to get any special allowances.

Jeffrey: Are you out of your mind? You ended your relationship with your husband and you think this is the time you should leave treatment?

Lee: No, I don't think this is the time . . . I know it's exactly the wrong time . . . but, what can I do?

Jeffrey: You can work with the good doctor.

Lee: [*softly*] This isn't a clinic.

Jeffrey: [*looking annoyed and puzzled*] What's that supposed to mean?

Lee: I just would never prevail on the sympathy of someone else . . . I can't accept charity. I simply have too much pride for that.

Jeffrey: Are you saying the doctor offered to let you come to the group for free?

Lee: I didn't get quite that impression, but I didn't really talk to her about it. I just said that I didn't want any special consideration, and she said I should explore the issue in the group.

Zachariah: I feel the same way as Lee. If someone offers me a handout, I wonder what they want from me.

Mort: If I lost my job, I would want special consideration.

Cassidy: I know how you feel, Lee. I turned to alcohol and other things because I didn't want to depend on people.

Henry: Ever since you joined this group, you have been focused on everybody else's difficulties—you wanted to find Mort a social life, help me recover from my wife's death, encourage Zach to hold onto his relationships longer, but what about you?

Jeffrey: He's right, Lee. You exert yourself for others. But it always feels to me that it is a protection—just like you were saying about Henry, a second ago. You thought he turned to you to avoid the input we were giving him. It's exactly what you do, Lee, and we let you do it way too much. Sometimes I wonder what you get out of the group.

Jade: I didn't even remember you had a problem with your husband. I know you mentioned something at the beginning of the group, and maybe you've alluded to it from time to time, but that's about all. Yet you talk a lot in here—maybe more than anyone else—but I don't think that you ever let us say anything to you that might be helpful.

Lee: It's helpful to me just to help all of you. I feel very warmly toward each of you.

Jeffrey: But, Lee, you're not just here to help us or to have people around whom you like. You're here to learn about yourself, and you're so busy controlling your interactions with each of us that you close out any opportunity we might have to say something to you that you can use to get on better in life.

Lee: What do you mean?

Characteristic Stage 4 Behaviors Seen in This Vignette. This session illustrates a more mature working group in which members have shared senses of goals and processes. Members converge around the idea that this group is a place in which they can improve their relationships with one another and use their observations of one another as the means by which this interpersonal change can occur. We see that members are willing to confront one another on those styles that most hinder their achieving fulfillment in relationships, even though doing so entails taking on the risk that they and others may be made uncomfortable by these confrontations. For example, the group takes on Henry's resistance to sharing anything other than what other members will find pleasing despite the possible hurt that such a confrontation might evoke. Within this stage, we see the emergence of authentic concern for one another. Winnicott (1963) noted that the infant's concern for the mother emerges out of the mother's survival of the infant's hatred of her. Within the group, the therapist's and members' survival of the authority crucible enables members to achieve a level of concern that involves accepting discomfort (e.g., the discomfort of having to confront Henry) for the sake of another member's growth.

Although descriptions of this period of group life often emphasize the work aspect, the reader may notice that members regulate their difficult interactions with one another with a measure of lightheartedness. Members during this stage develop not only a capacity for work but also for play, and this play is not unlike the play of children in which difficult issues can be addressed within a framework of safety. The group environment more than at any other time achieves Winnicott's (1953) notion of a transitional space in which the group lies at the intersection of reality and fantasy. Its distance from reality allows members to experiment in their relationships without risking the long-term consequences that attend interactions in their worlds outside the group.

Tasks and Conflicts. Early in Stage 4, the position that danger is created by an insistence on absolute intimacy gains sway. During this early period, an attitude of aloof suspiciousness prevails over other affect states. In large part, this posture corrects for the denial of both the realistic threats (e.g., hurt, rejection, and disappointment) attached to the enterprise of relating to others and members' continuing psychological difficulties. Yet, the yearning for closeness remains in the group, and a subgroup of members will typically persist in asserting the importance of emotional contact among members. The conflict between these two forces dominates much of the activity at the beginning of this stage. The tension between apartness and intimacy can resolve itself through the operation of any number of factors, in isolation or combination. Bennis and Shepard (1956) discussed the role of the *independents*—individuals who are relatively free of conflict in this area—in mediating between the two subgroups. Agazarian (1997) identified subgroup members' acts of differentiating from one another as setting the stage for the burgeoning of their identifications with the psychological positions of members of the opposing subgroup. Conflict resolution is also abetted merely by members' articulation of their different positions. Members have already learned to appreciate one another's subjective experience and are poised to look for facets in others' reactions with which they can identify.

The resolution of the conflict entails that members accept an inherent ambivalence in human relationships, the dialectical tension between the longing for closeness and its perils. Although this integration may give rise to depressive reactions within the group, it also enables members to begin the performance of important tasks. For example, the use of feedback (wherein members become more aware of others' reactions to their ways of being in relationships) emerges as a viable process for change (Brabender, 2006). Members' allegiance to one another and the group allows them to proceed through the difficult tasks of deconstructing their reactions to get to a level of specificity that will be helpful. "You get on my nerves" will, through a slow process of analysis, change to, "When you give me a bland response of assent, it angers me because I mistrust the genuineness of your reaction." This stage makes great demands on members to bear the pain of observing, thinking, and feeling. Members not only deepen their appreciation of others' experience of them and their experiences of others, but also increasingly learn to maintain connection amidst discord, disjunctions, and disappointment in relationships.

Stage 5: Termination

In groups that have a fixed ending date, a separate termination stage will be more evident than in groups in which members leave the group at different times. In the latter circumstance, the phenomena seen in Stage 5 may be mixed with whatever stage work the group had been addressing before the member's departure approached.

Rarely is the initial discussion of termination direct. Typically, members will respond to an impending termination with disguised references as a way of limiting the pain associated with endings. Even in circumstances in which the group has met for a very brief duration, the ending of the group is a significant psychological event because it is associated with other losses and endings that members have experienced (Piper, McCallum, & Azim, 1992).

Stage 5 Vignette

The group met over a 2 1/2-year period during which time each member did intensive work on a wide range of interpersonal and intrapsychic issues. For example, Lee learned a great deal about the apprehensions that had led her to attempt to regulate others' actions and the negative social consequences of these attempts. Over this period, Lee achieved greater confidence in others' genuinely positive feelings for her, and this confidence enabled her to make herself vulnerable in relation to others. The group is approaching termination in a month. Although the group began as an open-ended one, the therapist's decision to retire from practice led the group to plan its own ending. The therapist had given members the option to continue with another therapist. However, because several members would be terminating in the foreseeable future, members decided they would rather have a group ending rather than sequential individual endings. A subset of members will be beginning other groups almost immediately after leaving the current group.

Jade:	So, what did she say? I have been waiting the entire week. What did she say?
Zachariah:	Yeah, I've been wondering too.
Mort:	She said . . . [*smiles sheepishly*] . . . "Yes."
Jade:	That's terrific!
Mort:	I was scared to death.

Lee: But you went through with it—that's the important thing.

Mort: Yeah, well—once the group is over, I don't know if I can do anything without all of the cheerleading.

Cassidy: You're going to be in another group soon, right?

Mort: I am, but who knows whether it will work—if I'll even feel comfortable enough to stay. I remember when I started here. I was in individual therapy, and my therapist wouldn't let me off the hook. He supported me all through that process. And I know I'll be comparing my new group to this group, and it will seem inferior to me and not worth the trouble.

Jeffrey: Don't succumb to that feeling. You've made too much of a start in this group to go in reverse.

Jade: When I think of where you were when you began and where you are now!

Therapist: So, Jade, what do you see as the difference?

Jade: [to Mort] You were positively . . . [Jade struggles for a word]

Cassidy: [with a matter-of-fact tone] Out of it . . .

Jade: [laughing] Yes, out of it!

Therapist: Can you say exactly what you mean by that?

Jade: We would be talking about something and then out of the blue, you would say this completely random thing—it was like, "Where is he coming from? Was he even listening?" Actually, it was cute in a painful way.

Lee: That's amazing . . . I had forgotten that's how you were, Mort. You were sort of like our mascot, tagging along . . . being endearing in your mulishness. Now, I just don't think of you that way anymore. I mean, you're still endearing but not in a mulish way.

Jeffrey: I'm not sure he's quite so endearing.

Henry: [ignoring Jeffrey's comment] And aside from sitting in this room each session, you didn't seem set on helping yourself. You're very different now. Like you wanted to ask that young woman out, you came here and talked about it, and then you followed through.

Mort: [shrugs] I had to do something. But thanks.

Jeffrey: So what about me?

Zachariah: What about you?

Jeffrey: You're telling Mort how he has changed, and I wonder whether you think I've changed.

Cassidy: Hmmm . . . where you're concerned, it's a bit more complex.

Jeffrey: Sounds ominous.

Cassidy: No, I don't mean it that way . . . it's just that there's a more subtle way that you've changed. For—I don't know—half of the time that you've been in group, I just knew that when I made a statement that was different than what you were saying, you wouldn't give it a moment's thought. You still dismiss our points of view very quickly a lot of the time.

Mort: Jeffrey is very intelligent.

Zachariah: We all know that, but being smart doesn't mean you're always right.

Cassidy: Of course, but I feel that Jeffrey is much less arrogant—well, maybe not much less, maybe just a little less arrogant now and more open to other opinions even if he still likes his the best.

Lee: I remember it used to be so important to you Jeffrey to have the therapist speak up more because you felt that she was truly the only person who could help you.

Jeffrey: Well, that each person in here could tell me something valuable about me has been a pleasant surprise. I think what you took for arrogance was partially fear—perhaps I thought that the therapist would not say something to rock my world in the way that all of you could. And I don't quite know how I'll fare without seeing you every week.

Jade: My God! I never thought I'd hear you say something like that.

Henry: And, by golly, I think he means it.

Jeffrey: Of course I mean it.

Jade: I absolutely believe you. Except when you are being sarcastic, which, admittedly, is often, you say what you mean. I know that I feel similarly. I'm sort of glad the group is ending. I've been in it so long, and I'm kind of curious to discover how it will be for me without it. Somehow I think that it will lead me to spread my wings a little, but knowing that whatever happens, I must now do it for myself. Yet, the idea that I won't have each of you to offer your particular way of seeing me is almost unfathomable.

Mort: Are you talking about the therapist, too?

Jade: I am. [*speaking to the therapist*] You don't direct a lot of individual comments to me and early in the group, I felt disappointed in you. But I have come to realize that what you do say to all of us I can apply to myself and somehow, practicing that makes me feel more ready to leave the group.

Therapist:	In what sense?
Jade:	It's the application part. Truths in group need to be applied to different circumstances and different personalities—I'm sure we've all been doing that already—and somehow the fact that you haven't spoken directly to me as much as maybe I would have liked has made it easier to take what I've learned in here into the world. And I'll have to do so even more now.
Therapist:	And yet, still some disappointment may linger.
Jade:	Perhaps. I suppose it does. But it's not like it was.
Zachariah:	Say, I wonder what ever happened to Mark. Man was he a loser.
Lee:	Just a very foolish young man. He missed a great deal.
Zachariah:	Yeah, like all the other people out there who don't bother to help themselves.

Characteristic Stage 5 Behaviors Seen in This Vignette. The taking stock in which members engage is a natural process as the group approaches termination. This group, like others, spontaneously noted changes in one another (e.g., the group's retrospective analysis of Mort's progress in the group) and sought summative impressions (e.g., Jeffrey's request for members' perceptions concerning changes). Yet, the role of the therapist at this point is not incidental. Members of this particular group required some assistance from the therapist to articulate their perceptions to a degree that would be helpful to the member whom these perceptions concern. Other groups may need more encouragement to provide all members with the kind of feedback received by Mort and Jeffrey.

At this time, members grieve different losses associated with their vanishing group experience. That they grieve the loss of their relationship with one another and the therapist is expected. Other sources of grieving may be more subtle and unanticipated. For example, members may experience wistfulness over the loss of the self who entered the group. This reaction is shown in the group's collective nostalgia over Mort's early "mascot" status.

Toward the end of the group, an echoing of earlier themes and a resurfacing of previously addressed conflicts often occurs. Members may revisit their relationship with the therapist and, in this connection, redress authority conflicts. Jade revisits her relationship with the therapist and acknowledges that the disparity between what she wanted from the therapist and what she received may have promoted her growth. Yet, the ache connected with this frustrated hope for the relationship—a hope for a highly personal relationship—pressed for integration with her more mature perspective.

Tasks and Conflicts. At this time, group members must reconcile their colliding views of the group, themselves, each other, and their futures. The collision is one that takes place both within each member and within the group at large. Each member must integrate the group experience as one that is both helpful but also disappointing in its failure to enable members to realize all of their fantasies about the benefits of group participation. This disappointment also encompasses their sorrow over changes that may not have occurred in other members (e.g., the taming of Jeffrey's arrogance). Members must reconcile the delightful and vexing aspects of themselves and the other members. They must recognize a future that is hopeful yet uncertain.

Members are torn between the urge to simplify their conceptions of themselves, the other members, and the group (thereby avoiding the sadness that attends a full experience of loss) and to accept the dichotomies and contradictions in their reactions (thereby enjoying the fruits of their prior group work). Their efforts at simplification entail their discounting some major dimension of their fund of reactions in the group. For example, some members will idealize the group, the members, and themselves; others will devalue the experience. The work members do in subgroups, the contribution of members who have a greater tolerance of polarities, and the therapist's interpretation of the defenses all play a role in enabling members to accept the complexity of their affects and cognitions in relation to the group and its endings. Such work can create in members the capacity to cope with the inevitable loss in their future lives.

A second task is members' appraisal of what has been accomplished in group, what challenges lie ahead for members in their application of learning from the group to their extragroup lives, and what new work remains to be done. The task on which the featured group was embarking in the last vignette, reviewing each member's transformations over the course of the group, is a component of this process. Through it, members cultivate their ability to engage in their own retrospective analysis to effect personal change processes outside of the group. MacKenzie (1990) emphasized the importance of members' reviewing critical incidents in the group to internalizing the group experience, a process that will then enable them to fortify those coping techniques and conflict resolutions that have been achieved over the course of the group.

CONCLUSIONS

This chapter features a long-term group of fairly high-functioning members as they proceed through the stages of group life. In Stage 1, the group approached issues of belonging and norms for participation. In Stage 2, the group addressed their relationship with the authority in the group, the therapist. However, this task involved first accepting and expressing differences among themselves. In Stage 3, members savored their newfound independence from the therapist and their enhanced sense of intimacy with one another. In Stage 4, members participated in in-depth interpersonal exploration, including a focus on conflicts related to the establishment of intimate connections with others. Stage 5 entailed members' investigation of their reactions to the totality of the group experience and their hopes for the future as well as an exploration of conflicts pertaining to loss.

The manner in which this particular group unfolded was crucially linked to membership and context. For example, for most of the members, some adequate resolution of Stage 1 and 2 conflicts had occurred prior to their entrance in the group. For this reason, they could proceed relatively quickly through these stages and focus their energies on the issues of later stages. The context of the group was a private practice situation in which members entered the group with the understanding that they could remain in the group as long as necessary. This temporal feature of indefiniteness allowed members to pursue their work in the same way that any tasks are completed when there is no deadline in sight. On the one hand, members could be thorough and take their time in attending to details. On the other hand, members could lose focus and, lacking a temporal pressure, take old defensive routes to addressing problems rather than pursuing new more threatening options. In later chapters of this volume, we explore the variables that can alter not only the developmental stages themselves but how they are pursued by members given the members' characteristics and the context of the group.

6

DEVELOPMENTALLY FOCUSED LEADERSHIP ACTIVITIES OF THE THERAPIST

In chapter 5 of this volume, we presented a vignette that provides the reader with an opportunity to see a group unfold with minimal intervention from the therapist. The current chapter is devoted to an examination of the role of the therapist in catalyzing the group's development. In chapter 3, we discussed the research findings across a number of studies that the further a group progresses through the developmental stages, the more productive the group is when *productivity* is defined as a group's accomplishing its specified goals. Consequently, members are likely to benefit from group participation to the extent that the therapist can assist the group in moving through the developmental stages.

In introductory texts on group psychotherapy, therapists receive guidelines for how to conduct an effective group. These guidelines are inherently development fostering and should be observed throughout the life of the group. Were the therapist to observe these guidelines reliably, the therapist's stance would promote development even without a consistent, explicit focus on stages. This notion is somewhat akin to the situation of the parent who, without ever thinking in a systematic or explicit way about developmental processes and milestones, provides nurturance that is development fostering. We begin our consideration of the role of the therapist by outlining these guidelines and then proceed to stage-specific considerations for the role of the therapist. We conclude the chapter with a discussion of leadership structure, in particular how practitioners can function most effectively as cotherapists in leading groups.

Although this chapter's primary focus is how the therapist functions in the group to promote group development, the individual members and subgroups of members also play critical roles in whether a group progresses, stagnates, regresses (Agazarian, 1997; A. P. Beck, 1981a; Wheelan, 2005), or configures itself as an antigroup (Nitsun, 1996). As such, the leadership of the group is not owned by the therapist. Individuals and subgroups of members who play a crucial role in helping a group to move through a stage or from one stage to another are emerging or informal leaders (A. P. Beck, 1981a). Their involvement has been shown to be critical to group efficacy, which is the group's confidence in its ability to perform tasks (Pescosolido, 2001). A crucial function of the therapist, the designated or formal leader, is to create an environment in which these emerging leaders can provide the special resources necessary for the group's growth.

COMMON FUNCTIONS OF THE DEVELOPMENTALLY SENSITIVE THERAPIST

Scholarly writing on the therapist's activities in leading psychotherapy groups has yielded a number of systems that catalog the therapist's critical set of interventions. However, few systems are based on an empirical investigation of groups. To date, the most comprehensive study of leadership behaviors and their influences on members occurred not with psychotherapy groups but rather with encounter groups. Lieberman, Yalom, and Miles (1973) studied 18 encounter groups that met over a period of 30 hours distributed in varying ways over a 12-week period. From their factor analysis of an array of variables reflecting different leader behaviors, they identified four factors that accounted for the variability among leaders. Although subsequent research (Tinsely, Roth, & Lease, 1989) has not consistently supported each of these four dimensions, the conceptual scheme has survived over time because of its considerable pedagogical value. The encounter groups' variation in theoretical orientation (10 orientations were represented) ensured that the resulting framework had considerable breadth of application. The four functions are *executive, caring, meaning attribution,* and *emotional stimulation.* Each is described in terms of how the group psychotherapist conducts him- or herself in the sessions and what the group psychotherapist does. However, these four functions are updated in light of post-1970s theory and research. How the therapist performs a given function differently from stage to stage is discussed following the general presentation of the functions.

The Executive Function

Across the developmental stages, the group psychotherapist must perform the executive function, which pertains to those activities by which the structure of the group is established and the safety of members is ensured. The capacity of the group to develop is supported by the therapist's establishing a therapeutic frame that creates predictability in important aspects of members' group experience. Consistency in when meetings begin and end, where the meetings are held, and who attends the meetings all enhance the group's developmental potential. Although some features of predictability are easily within the therapist's immediate control (e.g., the time when the group begins), other features pertain to member behavior. For example, consistency of membership in the sessions entails that members achieve good attendance. The therapist must cultivate the group norm (behavioral patterns that are both common and accepted by members) of good attendance by assisting members in recognizing that missing sessions rarely ensures progress toward members' goals and by treating absences as significant group events (Brabender, 2002).

The executive function also pertains to the creation of physical and psychological safety within the group. The therapist promotes physical safety by helping members understand the criticalness of expressing feelings in words and by selecting members capable of behavioral restraint. Among the many ways in which psychological safety is created is through members' confidence that what they share within the group will be treated as confidential. Confidentiality entails the therapist's unflagging attention to communications both inside and outside the group, creation of consequences for confidentiality violations, and cultivation of members' recognition of the unintended harm from violations of confidentiality (Brabender, 2002). As Cohen, Ettin, and Fidler (1998) noted, safety also requires the therapist's protecting members from narcissistic injuries sufficient in severity to discourage the members' continued active participation in the group. According to Lieberman et al. (1973), leaders who exhibit a moderate level of the executive function conduct groups with more favorable outcomes than leaders who show low or high levels of the executive function. A moderate level provides enough structure to meet members' safety needs but not so much regulation that it unduly curtails members' freedom of expression.

The Caring Function

The function of caring is realized in the therapist's conveyance of warmth, acceptance, respect, and concern for the group members. The therapist exhibits caring throughout the life of the group by his or her dependability; careful listening; and recognition of members' feelings and needs, even when those needs cannot be gratified. The caring therapist shows nondefensiveness in response to the changing but often intense feelings members express toward him or her from stage to stage and willingness to acknowledge his or her behaviors (often inadvertent) that may appear at odds with caring. Lieberman et al. (1973) found that the relationship between caring and outcome is simple and direct: The greater the caring, the better the outcome. This finding is consistent with an extensive empirical literature in individual psychotherapy showing the importance of the therapist's caring, an aspect of the therapeutic alliance, in relation to outcome (e.g., see the meta-analytic review of individual therapy studies by D. J. Martin, Garske, & Davis, 2000). One mechanism by which caring operates is to promote the creation of an environment that has growth-promoting features. For example, Antonuccio, Davis, Lewinsohn, and Breckenridge (1987) found that the therapist's degree of warmth was directly associated with the level of cohesion in depression treatment groups.

The Meaning Attribution Function

Meaning attribution, the third function, is the therapist's activity of helping members recognize the significance of their own and others' experiences in the group. The specific form of the therapist's meaning-making activity and the level of analysis (group, subgroup, individual) are likely to depend on the therapist's theoretical orientation (for further discussion, see Brabender, 2002). Variability among group psychotherapists notwithstanding, what is key is that the therapist invests heavily in efforts to help members make sense out of their reactions. Lieberman et al. (1973) found that the greater the meaning attribution on the part of the group leader, the more favorable the outcomes at the group's conclusion. More recently, meaning attribution has been understood not merely in terms of what the therapist does but a value that the therapist imparts, a value of which the therapist is a symbol. Through his or her unflagging efforts to spur members on to look more closely at and more deeply into their reactions, the therapist creates an ethos by which understanding of oneself and others is seen as having worth (Cohen et al., 1998).

The Emotional Stimulation Function

Emotional stimulation entails the therapist's intervening to increase members' level of arousal or the intensity of feelings within the group. Therapists might accomplish these ends by engaging in confrontation, sharing their own reactions, or directing members to self-disclose. In the 1970s, when Lieberman et al. were writing, some encounter group leaders were notorious for creating an extremely intense level of affect within the group. Leaders would quickly disarm members of their defenses or home in on their areas of most acute vulnerability. Such efforts, Lieberman et al. (1973) demonstrated, were not in the service of members' well-being: Participants in groups with leaders who induced a high level of excitation achieved less favorable outcomes than members of groups whose leaders were only moderately stimulating. However, Lieberman et al. found that members of groups in which emotional stimulation was low also performed relatively poorly, possibly as a result of their lack of engagement with change processes. Writings on group psychotherapy (e.g., Yalom & Leszcz, 2005) have continued to emphasize that affective engagement among group members is important. Therapists use a variety of means of fostering members' emotional engagement with the group, such as assisting members in identifying with one another's affective experiences and directing members to explore their here-and-now reactions.

In addition to identifying some of the critical functions of the therapist, the Lieberman et al. (1973) study demonstrated that what the therapist does within the group will have a determining role in what the members obtain from the group. In the section that follows, the notion is developed that it is not only what the therapist does in the group but also when the therapist does it that bears on outcome.

STAGE-SPECIFIC THERAPIST INTERVENTIONS

Just as a parent's interactive style will typically be different with a preschool child versus an adolescent, so too must the group psychotherapist's bearing vary across the life of the group for the group to be maximally helpful to its members. The concept that to be effective aspects of therapist behavior should vary depending on a variety of circumstances, including the developmental stage of the group, is the *situational leadership model* (Hersey & Blanchard, 1982; Vroom & Jago, 2007). Next we consider how the tasks and conflicts of each stage place differential requirements on the therapist for stage-specific interventions that will enable the therapist to maximize its developmental potential.

Stage 1: Formation and Engagement

As noted in chapter 4 of this volume, the major task of Stage 1 (formation and engagement) is for members to engage with one another and with the therapist. Support for the importance of engagement early in the life of the group has been found in a number of studies including Kivlighan and Lilly's (1997) in which members of a process group showed greater progress on their personal goals when the group members showed a high level of engagement early in the life of the group. Similarly, Ogrodniczuk and Piper

(2003) found that in both a supportive and an interpretive 12-session group for individuals with complicated grief reactions, level of engagement in the earliest phase of group psychotherapy was predictive of outcome. They speculated that engagement enables members to use therapeutic processes and perform the tasks of this stage and ensuing stages.

How does the therapist foster engagement? Typically, members enter the group cognizant of potential detriments and benefits of engagement. The therapist's broad strategy in Stage 1 is to diminish resistance while strengthening attraction to involvement. Members will not engage if they perceive engagement as dangerous. The dangers can be far ranging, from physical assault to confidentiality violations to experiences of hurt or rejection. To lessen members' apprehension over the risks of involvement, the Stage 1 therapist assiduously performs tasks related to Lieberman et al.'s (1973) executive function.

In establishing the group and conducting initial sessions, the therapist maintains the therapeutic frame of the group (Brabender, 2002). That is, the therapist creates salient sources of regularity, such as meeting time and place. The therapist also establishes rules, highlights them in members' awareness, and enforces them. The therapist cultivates members' appreciation of the importance of boundaries so that they will collaborate with the therapist in their maintenance (Cohn, 2005). In performing this executive task, the therapist is acting in accord with a *transcendent* model of leadership (Campbell, 1964/1976), by which, according to Cohen et al. (1998), the leader places him- or herself above the group and operates on the group. As the group develops, the therapist's transcendent leadership style recedes. The executive functions the leader performs for the group (such as enforcement of rules), members will, to a much greater extent, be able to perform for themselves. The therapist's relative emancipation from executive functioning will enable him or her to act in accordance with an *immanent* style of leadership, wherein the therapist functions as a collaborator with members (Campbell, 1964/1976).

In addition to perceiving danger, members also worry that the group may not benefit them, and this concern may limit their investment. Research suggests that when members do have a negative expectancy, their sense of collaboration with the therapist or sense of a therapeutic alliance is diminished, which in turn adversely affects outcome (Abouguendia, Joyce, Piper, & Ogrodniczuk, 2004). This potential obstacle to members is addressed through another executive activity, the provision of structure with respect to goals and processes early in the life of the group (Kaul & Bednar, 1994). When members understand the fit between the goals established for group participation and the processes deployed to achieve those goals, their concerns about the benefit of group work are likely to diminish and their expectancy about deriving benefit from the group increases. Suppose that the goal of a particular group is to alter positively each member's style of relating to others, and feedback is a process integral to pursuing this goal. In this instance, the therapist would help members gain a clear grasp of what feedback is and how it relates to interpersonal change. In some group situations, helping members appreciate the alignment between goals and processes occurs in the orientation and pretraining; in others, it occurs in the sessions themselves.

In addition to diminishing the obstacles to engagement, the Stage 1 therapist also strengthens the forces that motivate members to engage with one another. One method to increase engagement is to support members' identifications with one another. Such identifications, when expressed, have benefit for both the member expressing a want or feeling and the member identifying with that want or feeling. Both members derive relief from the aloneness that so frequently attends psychological suffering. The importance of members' recognizing their common ground early in the life of the group has been found in a number of studies (Kivlighan & Mullison, 1988; MacKenzie, 1987). For example, Kivlighan and Goldfine (1991) used the Critical Incident Questionnaire to assess what types of events were important to participation in an elective class on group process. They found that universality is seen as important by participants in the beginning of the group and diminishes linearly over the course of the group. Dugo and Beck (1984) found that when a member does not identify with any members of the group, that member is at risk for dropping out.

A second means to support engagement is by encouraging the expression of positively toned exchanges. Within the group psychotherapy literature, research repeatedly has shown that members are more open to receiving information from other members if the feedback is positive, or in the case of constructive (i.e., critical) feedback, if it has been preceded by a good deal of positive feedback (Brabender, 2006). In this vein, Levine and Moreland (1990) urged therapists to encourage expressions of warmth and liking among members.

A third means is to avoid such a high level of focus on any single member that members fail to forge a variety of connections with one another (Kivlighan & Tarrant, 2001). The following vignette illustrates this possible consequence of an unduly individual focus.

> Sarah, a member of a newly formed close-ended group, conveyed a high level of fragility. She frequently cried silently, and the precipitant of her crying was not evident to either the supervisor or the relatively new group therapist. The latter felt anxious seeing a member of the group being in such distress and was the first to encourage Sarah to put her feelings into words. Often the therapist would ask a multiplicity of questions about the circumstances surrounding Sarah's well-being. After three sessions, the therapist reported to her supervisor that the typical manifestations of cohesion she had read about in her group psychotherapy text seemed to be missing from her group. Collaboratively, the therapist and her super-

EXHIBIT 6.1
Therapist Behaviors in Stage 1: Formation and Engagement

- Foster identifications among members.
- Encourage positive exchanges among members.
- Avoid a high level of focus on individual members.
- Focus on the here and now.
- Support members' hopefulness about the group.

visor developed a hypothesis that the therapist's solicitude in relation to Sarah interfered with members' bonding to one another.

Yet, the therapist's intensive focus on members' involvement with one another should not lead the therapist to regard his or her individual relationship with each member as inconsequential. An emerging body of research (e.g., Joyce, Piper, & Ogrodniczuk, 2007) reveals the patient–therapist alliance to be a significant predictor of outcomes such as symptom intensity and life satisfaction. The therapist, then, should convey to each member his or her investment in the member's well-being (caring function) and readiness to collaborate with the member to enhance it (see Exhibit 6.1).

Within each stage, pressures on the therapist exist that may interfere with the therapist's making critical developmentally based interventions. However, recognition of these pressures helps the therapist to avoid operating under their sway. Many therapist feelings that are likely to hinder him or her from providing optimal responsiveness to the group are in response to the enormity of members' dependency needs. Members show through their prolonged stares and scrutinizing glances, their reverential silences after the therapist speaks, their beseeching manner, and so on that they see the therapist as the key not merely to their progress but to their survival in the group. Members convey the belief that they can do nothing for themselves. This degree of helplessness easily arouses intense anxiety in the group psychotherapist who recognizes, tacitly or explicitly, the limits of his or her ability to support members and the consequent likelihood of frustrating and disappointing them. To abate anxiety, therapists may engage in a variety of behaviors to diminish members' demonstration of voracious helplessness. Some therapists may provide such a high level of structure (e.g., by directing almost each and every interaction between and among members) that members are deprived of sensing their own dependent longings. Other therapists may be more inclined to demonstrate to members their inability to support members (Brabender, 1987) by mistakes, insensitiveness, or declarations of weakness or incapacity. Dr. Stance manifests all of these problems:

> Dr. Stance was conducting the second session of a group and was struggling with having two members in the group with similar names, Cheryl and Sharon. During the first session, she called Cheryl "Sharon" and vice versa. In the second session, she found herself confused as to which

member had which name (despite having interviewed them both over several sessions). She decided to disclose her difficulty, "If I address you incorrectly, you'll just have to excuse me. I'm hopeless with names. I have this problem all the time." After one lapse (or what she worried may have been a lapse), Dr. Stance reasoned to herself that it was better to reveal her difficulty rather than allowing members to conclude that they were inherently unmemorable.

Dr. Stance's admission, consciously motivated by the desire to protect the two members from their own self-criticism, could also have been rooted in a wish to shed the burden of members' idealization. ("Let's get this over with—I'm not as great as you think.") Whether it is through collusion with or frustration with members' dependency longings, the consequence of these therapist responses is the hindering of members in eventually taking back the power they have projected on the therapist (Cohen et al., 1998).

Stage 2: Conflict and Rebellion

In this stage, members learn to differentiate from one another, achieve an ability to express disagreement, and recognize and express dependency longings for and dissatisfaction with authority figures. The therapist's task is to facilitate the group in all of these endeavors by creating an atmosphere or climate that is welcoming of a range of feelings and impulses, including ones that members are likely to regard as negative or unacceptable. A number of outcome studies show that members' perception of the environment as a safe one mediates the favorableness of the outcomes (Bolman, 1971; Kivlighan & Tarrant, 2001; Phipps & Zastowny, 1988)

The interventions therapists can use to cultivate such an atmosphere are myriad. Most fundamental is the therapist's own robustness or capacity to maintain his or her therapeutic bearing in relation to all types of member communications. Therapists who are perceived as being extremely injured, hurt, angry, or otherwise discomfited will elicit in members apprehension over the perceived dangers of certain affects and impulses. Conversely, therapists who convey sturdiness as members make their fledgling efforts to express oppositionality will be able to continue in these efforts.

Apart from the therapist's all-important emotional stance, he or she can engage in a variety of technical interventions by which the emotional elements of Stage 2, elements that are far more intimidating to members than those of Stage 1, can be invited into the session. The therapist can interpret the nascent manifestations of hostility or dissatisfaction that are likely to appear in a disguised, symbolic form. Members may speak of the shortcomings of other authority figures (e.g., "My mother always made me pack my own lunch for school"). Such interpretations are often best delivered in a manner that is not doctrinaire. Better than, "In speaking of your mother's failings, you are really talking about me," is a statement such as,

"Perhaps in here members feel I make you do for yourselves what I should be doing." Were members to disavow the comparison, they would nonetheless know that from the therapist's vantage, the communication of complaints about him or her is welcome. Moreover, the level of the intervention—a comment to the group as a whole rather than to the individual speaking of her parent—frees an individual member from being the sole repository of a particular feared psychological content.

An alternate method derived from systems-centered psychotherapy (Agazarian, 1997) is to create a functional subgroup of members who are coalescing around a given position on authority-related conflicts of Stage 2. Suppose the comment of the member whose mother refrained from lunch packing was followed by the comment of another member, sympathetic to the first, who described her disappointment in her dad for his tendency to be dilatory, a tendency that resulted in his driving her to school late. The therapist would help these members to identify themselves as a unit and invite other members to join their subgroup. In so doing, the therapist would be affording members a greater degree of safety than they would have individually in exploring a set of affects and impulses related to authority that are often seen as dangerous.

Early in Stage 2, members begin to differentiate from one another and therapist interventions that support this movement may be helpful. MacKenzie (1997) advised the early Stage 2 therapist to assume a slightly more confrontational style to model for members' self–other differentiating behaviors. This alteration should be subtle and slight—otherwise, members will respond not to developmental tensions but rather to the shifts in the therapist's behavior.

The literature is beginning to suggest more specific ways in which the therapist can promote differentiation in Stage 2. Rybak and Brown (1997) studied the kinds of verbalizations leaders made in a master's level group class prior to the flowering of conflict in the group. They coded the leaders' verbalizations using the Sequential Analysis of Verbal Interaction (SAVI) system (Simon & Agazarian, 1967), by which each verbalization is classified as an *avoidance*, *approach*, or *contingent* behavior. Whereas avoidance and approach behaviors limit and increase the transfer of information in a session, respectively, contingency statements are neutral, and whether they transfer information depends on the context. Examples of contingency types of statements are speculating, interpreting, and sharing personal information. Rybak and Brown found that in the period prior to the surfacing of a conflict, the leader's number of contingency statements increased. Although their findings warrant replication, especially in a psychotherapy group, they suggest that the contingency statement may be useful in enabling the group to progress through the stage rather than becoming ensconced in it. These investigators speculated that contingency statements encourage members to identify their individual roles (an act of differentiation) and to explore the meaning of group events. This methodology of looking at the structure of verbal communication by leaders using instruments such as SAVI[1] holds promise for determining developmentally optimal types of responses of therapists across the life of the group.

As Stage 2 progresses, interventions that convey the therapist's robustness and that deemphasize the individual as the exclusive voice of a challenging posture vis-à-vis the therapist are consistent with the research on changes in group climate and outcome. Ogrodniczuk and Piper (2003) found that when conflict is high as is the case for Stage 2, outcomes are more favorable when engagement is low. Kivlighan and Lilly (1997) assessed the perceptions of the qualities of the therapeutic environment in a group of undergraduate and graduate students participating in a group process class. They obtained similar findings showing that a high-low-high engagement pattern when paired with a low-high-low pattern of conflict was optimal. These research studies suggest that members should be afforded mechanisms by which they can regulate their own degree of involvement with the thematic content of Stage 2. Using functional subgroups and group-as-a-whole statements enables members to establish a degree of engagement that is personally manageable.

As in Stage 1, therapist reactions during Stage 2 can interfere with the therapist's provision of a response geared to members' developmental needs. These stage-specific reactions will tend to be rooted in aspects of members' diverse responses to the authority conflict. Like group members, therapists will differ on the stances they take in relation to authority conflicts that may relate to their longstanding ways of dealing with their own relationships with authority.

Some therapists may establish a strong, ego-syntonic identification either with members' dissatisfaction with authority or with their rejection of figures in the group who give voice to strong dependent longings. Either identification will make the therapist vulnerable to departing from neutrality. An over identification with discontent with authority will lead to a tendency to join with members as they take on authority figures. Rarely do members begin their work on the authority conflict with a direct challenge on the therapist; typically, members will select a figure who represents the therapist. As noted by Agazarian (1997), this figure might be a member who takes on a therapeutic role in relation to a member who shows particular vulnerability. Although initially, members often welcome the efforts of the therapist-member, eventually, they see this individual as an imposter and a human obstacle to the therapist's providing critical help. Were the therapist to join the group's criticism (whether in subtle or nonsubtle ways), the therapist would be creating an alliance with members in their campaign. The therapist would thereby stunt the group's capacity to move beyond their displace-

---

[1]An advantage of an instrument such as SAVI is that it was specifically designed to examine group development, as Agazarian and Gantt (2003) noted.

ment object to the therapist him- or herself in their expression of a challenge. Were the member to leave the group because of the therapist's and other members' rejection of him or her, the group would be depriving itself of a member who brings to the group considerable resources in helping the group to accomplish the task of differentiation (Moreno, 2007).

An alternate therapist disposition typically manifests itself as members begin to approach the therapist with their dissatisfaction. A high level of apprehension on the part of the therapist can lead him or her to show fragility, a communication that typically dissuades members from allowing the crystallization of their challenge. Fragility can be betrayed in therapist withdrawal, dejection, or an apologetic manner. Whatever the type of expression, it is likely to evoke in members a worry that if they proceed in this direction, they will incapacitate the figure on whom their hopes continue to be pinned.

Decisions in relation to group composition can affect each of the stages. Progress in Stage 2 is aided by the presence of members who can tolerate the expression of hostility. These members, in making fledgling efforts to model the expression of discontent, provide a model for members more fearful of such communications. Visintini, Ubbiali, Donati, Chiorri, and Maffei (2007) found that group psychotherapists show a disinclination to refer to psychodynamic therapy groups individuals who scored high on measures of hostility. On the one hand, this referral bias may be protective of the group given that highly hostile individuals have been shown to have poorer group psychotherapy outcomes and are more likely to drop out of treatment (MacNair-Semands, 2002). On the other hand, these individuals may provide the group with a psychological commodity to support its progress in Stage 2 (see Exhibit 6.2).

Stage 3: Unity and Intimacy

In this stage, members forge stronger ties with one another and achieve a lessened dependency on the therapist. The therapist must nurture these ties in several ways, the first of which is simply to allow members to pursue their increased interest in one another. Any undue therapist intrusion into members' interactions at this point can undermine the transition from a leader-centered to a member-centered group. Such an intrusion might convey that the therapist is unwilling to brook any lessened focus or reliance on him or her. Although members are ready to give up their assumption that the therapist will be their exclusive source of assistance in the group, they nonetheless continue to see this tie as a valuable one as they will throughout the group (Billow, 2006). On a behavioral level, this shift generally means that the therapist is less active certainly than in Stage 1 in which the therapist fosters engagement and in Stage 2 in which the therapist creates safety for members' grappling with conflict.

EXHIBIT 6.2
Therapist Behaviors in Stage 2: Conflict and Rebellion

- Assume a slightly more confrontational stance.
- Make contingency statements.
- Demonstrate acceptance of challenging behaviors.
- Provide means for members to regulate their levels of involvement with conflict.

Yet, the therapist continues to have crucial specific tasks to perform to support the members in achieving greater independence from the therapist and interdependence on one another in a fashion that will serve the group's long-term development. During this period of group life, which is usually short lived (Agazarian & Peters, 1981), members are vulnerable to acting-out episodes, some of which can have an injurious effect on members' continued progress. The greater cohesion in the group (Wheelan, 2005) and the strong positive affect members feel for one another fuel an urge to abrogate all boundaries between them. Given the climate, one arena in which acting out is especially likely is sexual: Members may succumb to the temptation to form libidinal relationships with one another outside the group. Such liaisons often involve flouting the rule prohibiting members from indulging in extragroup contact. Rutan and Stone (1993) noted, "Sexual relations between members, whatever the specific meaning of the action to the couple, evoke in other members powerful feelings of envy, frustration, rejection, and distrust" (p. 180). When the group or the therapist discovers these violations (often through a change in the behavior of the members that is probed by the group), the therapist must take an active role in encouraging members to talk about the boundary violation in the group. The therapist must also reassert whatever rules were broken and assist members in recognizing the consequence of such violations. The therapist must also respond to lesser violations such as bringing food to the sessions. As the stage progresses, a subgroup of members will gradually emerge who feel uneasy about the total closeness prescribed by other members, and they will aid the therapist in reinforcing the group's boundaries (Brabender, 2002).

During this stage, members' depth of self-disclosure increases, and members report deriving significant relief from this sharing (Kivlighan & Goldfine, 1991). The therapist can support this process by helping more reticent members to recognize opportunities for sharing personal information by articulating their identification with the struggles of more openly expressive members (see Exhibit 6.3)

One of the cardinal features of group psychotherapy, particularly in relation to individual psychotherapy, is the potential for feedback, that is, the communication of observations of individual's interpersonal styles and others' reactions to those styles (Brabender, 2006). A task of the therapist is to support the group's engagement in feedback exchange and to shape the feedback so that it is maximally useful (Barlow & Burlingame, 2006). Over the

EXHIBIT 6.3
Therapist Behaviors in Stage 3: Unity and Intimacy

- Help members to avoid acting out that would undermine the integrity of the group.
- Support broad-based engagement in self-disclosure, including by more reticent members.
- Help members develop a positive attitude toward feedback by facilitating the exchange of positively toned feedback.
- Support members' greater reliance on one another and lessened reliance on the therapist.

group's development, the amount of feedback members offer one another increases (Leichtentritt & Shechtman, 1998; Rothke, 1986; Shechtman & Yanov, 2001), and in this stage in particular, members show heightened attendance to one another's particular qualities relative to earlier stages. Yet, members' perceptions of others are less specific than they will be in later stages and more fully biased toward one another's positive qualities. The therapist can tap these features of members' interpersonal perceptions to nurture their receptiveness to the more particular and balanced feedback that will be offered later in the group. The author W. Somerset Maugham (1915) wrote, "People ask for your criticism but they want only praise" (p. 267). The behavior of group members is consistent with this observation. One of the most robust empirical findings in the group psychotherapy literature is members' greater acceptance of positive than negative or constructive feedback (for a review of this literature, see Brabender, 2006), a phenomenon called the *credibility gap* (Jacobs, Jacobs, Feldman, & Cavior, 1973). Their acceptance may be reflected in their agreement with the feedback or, as Shechtman and Gluk (2005) demonstrated in their study of grade school children, in their ability to remember the feedback at a later point. This differential acceptance rate can pose a challenge to the group psychotherapist in that it is the negative feedback that provides members the grist by which to make potentially useful changes in their ways of interacting with others. However, researchers have also found that negative feedback is more likely to be accepted if it is preceded by positive feedback (e.g., Stockton & Morran, 1981) or sandwiched between positive feedback events (e.g., Morran, Stockton, Cline, & Teed, 1998).

During this stage, the therapist can promote members' exchange of feedback by helping members recognize opportunities for providing feedback and create agendas by which they actively solicit certain types of feedback (Kivlighan, Jauquet, Hardie, Francis, & Hershberger, 1993). For example, if Andrea says, "I admired so much how you expressed yourself so easily to the therapist. I always take a back seat," the therapist could point out that Andrea might establish an agenda of learning whether others perceive her in this way. Because of the climate during this period of group life, the feedback members are likely to receive is almost always positive. Therefore, members are able to have a positive feedback experience that will enhance their receptiveness to more difficult feedback in the next stage. The therapist also can gently guide the members to develop feedback as a multidirectional process. The opportunities for learning from feedback are artificially limited if the focus is only the recipient of the feedback. The therapist can launch a process wherein members come to realize that the feedback provider also gains self-knowledge from the group's examination of the perceptions he or she shared:

Parker: [to Andrea] I think you have much more presence than you realize. Yes, it's true that you didn't speak a great deal when we were expressing our feelings about Dr. Czar, but I felt that you gave us strong backing.

Andrea: That makes me feel great . . . less like a human lump.

Dr. Czar: How do others feel about Parker's perception of Andrea?

Maurice: His observation was astute, and I've noticed his perceptiveness before.

Here the therapist is broadening the scope of what members will see as grist for the mill as they proceed. Also, because perceivers (those offering perceptions), like those perceived (those receiving observations), will tend to obtain positive feedback at this time, members experience an early agreeable process of having their perceptions examined by the group.

Yet, we might notice that Parker's comment to Andrea was vague. Feedback at this point has a global, diffuse quality that reduces its usefulness. The therapist can shape the feedback that will be offered in later stages by urging members to achieve more precision in their observations.

Dr. Czar: You said she gave you "strong backing." What did that look like?

Parker: She had an affirming expression on her face and also seemed very attentive to each exchange.

The level of detail is still likely to be insufficient given that members have a resistance to recognizing differences (Agazarian & Gantt, 2003). Nonetheless, the intervention educates members by establishing specificity as an important feature of their communications with one another.[2]

The pressures on this therapist at this stage concern the response to members' greater independence from him or her. Some therapists experience this transition as a loss and attempt to reassert their importance to the group

---

[2]Further research is needed on the types of feedback that are most likely to be useful to member. Recently, investigators (Davies, Burlingame, Johnson, Gleave, & Barlow, 2008) found that feedback to members about their perceptions of group climate did not favorably affect outcome. However, the type of feedback most commonly described in the literature (e.g., Yalom & Leszcz, 2005) concerns members' behaviors and the reactions they evoke in other members.

members by, for example, conveying that only they can perform certain functions for the group. The therapist may appropriate to him- or herself the delivery of certain types of interventions, such as group-as-a-whole statements, by providing these in abundance and interpreting other members' doing so as resistance. Such therapist behavior, as in the prior stages, will have a chilling effect on group development. Members will understand tacitly that their progression toward greater independence and interdependence is at the cost of the well-being of the therapist and their relationship with him or her. Another stance equally detrimental to the group's growth involves joining members in their quest for utter closeness:

> Dr. Barker announced at the beginning of the session that Miguel would not be attending because he was in the hospital with a broken elbow. Group members were very concerned and said they wanted to use the session time to drive to the hospital to visit and console him. Dr. Barker felt on the one hand that leaving the session would violate the frame of the group that she had worked to establish but, on the other hand, declining their request would sap their initiative, a product of their successful negotiation of the authority conflict. She suggested, instead, that they call Miguel, but after the session had a sense of uneasiness about her intervention. Further, she noticed that in the succeeding session, two members were absent.

Collusion with members' effort to eradicate boundaries is not the exclusive province of those therapists who have a limited appreciation of boundaries. Like Dr. Barker, the Stage 3 therapist may understand the importance of consistency of time, place, and other features that define the group. Yet, an effort to reaffirm boundaries may be experienced by the therapist as a destructive act, particularly because the demands of this stage heighten the sense of all participants that closeness, at all costs, must be preserved. However, the cost of this preservation is to increase the apprehension of those members who will be instrumental in moving the group to the next stage.

Stage 4: Integration and Work

In Stage 4, members are able to function with considerable independence, but three tasks are especially important for the therapist to pursue at this time. The first task involves supporting members who are experiencing discomfort with the absolute intimacy and denial of differences of Stage 3. In this vein, Jackson (1999) wrote, "Group leaders need to maintain an awareness of the unspoken dissent in the room, even at moments when there is a strong pull to merge with the 'in crowd' or more acceptable feelings in the group" (p. 53). Once the therapist recognizes these often subtle negative reactions, the therapist can invite their emergence by aiding members in realizing that they are not alone with them. Rarely is only a single member discomfited by members' fusion of their identities and experiences. Examples of how the therapist might assist the group are posing a question such as "Who else has a glimmering of a feeling that the group seems a bit sticky right now?" or making an observation such as "I have a sense others share Alexei's feeling that the group is running roughshod over each member's unique reaction." Alternatively, if two or more members have articulated apprehension over the pressure to conform, the therapist might assist them in forming a subgroup, which would provide them with a measure of comfort and safety in exploring their currently unpopular reactions.

The second task is to continue to develop members' ability to use feedback productively. Three aspects of the feedback process require the therapist's specific attention. The first is the specificity of the feedback. Rarely will members sufficiently appreciate the necessity of offering comments sufficiently concrete to be useful to the recipient of the feedback. For example, members will tend to more readily make a statement such as "You look angry" than a statement that includes the actual behaviors of the member that suggest anger, such as "You are furrowing your brow and looking away from me." The latter comment requires greater work by the feedback provider to clarify and refine his or her own perceptions. However, research (Jacobs, Jacobs, Cavior, & Burke, 1974) suggests that such behavioral feedback is associated with more favorable outcomes than global-affect-laden feedback. The therapist can encourage members to perform this extra work by helping them see how the feedback receiver is differentially affected by vague versus specific statements. Examining the effects of the feedback also enables the therapist to incorporate another aspect, the exploration of what can be learned about the feedback provider on the basis of the observations he or she offers other members. Further discussion of this point is provided in chapter 8 of this volume. The third aspect of the feedback process to which the therapist should attend is members' openness to offering constructive feedback. Research (Robison & Hardt, 1992)[3] suggests that one way to counteract members' inhibition about providing constructive feedback is to provide them with a rationale for this type of feedback (e.g., "By Chase's knowing how his poor eye contact affects you, he can determine if that is or is not a behavior he'd like to modify"). Additionally, the therapist can help members process their fears and concerns about offering feedback:

Therapist: You seem afraid to respond directly to Allison's question about whether she is too intrusive.

Josh: I just don't want to say anything that will shatter her. Last week, Allison left the group crying.

---

[3]In Robison and Hardt's (1992) study, the rationale for constructive feedback was delivered during pretraining. We argue that this information should be offered again during the developmental stage in which members are most likely to use it.

Allison: Yes I did, but I was fine about an hour later. And I thought a lot about what Stan said and how I can use it. So just go ahead.

In this interaction, Josh, by giving expression to his fear of damaging Allison, is able to obtain data that disconfirm the fear. Even when members find that some basis exists for their worries, they often discover that the reality is not even remotely commensurate with their fantasy about the consequences of potential communications.

During this stage, the group members show a greater capacity to be self-reflective and identify questions concerning facets of their interactional style to which they desire input. For example, Agnes may know that people see her as aloof but have little idea why. By posing this question to the group, Agnes is using a *feed-forward system* (Bogart, 1980) by which she establishes an agenda (obtaining data on her aloofness) and thereby determines the responses she obtains from others. What distinguishes a feed-forward from a feedback system is that whereas the latter is reactive, the former is proactive. Kivlighan et al. (1993) found that members who were trained to activate feed-forward systems by setting here-and-now agendas saw themselves as having more positive outcomes from group participation. The therapist's role in this process is to identify opportunities for members to formulate questions about themselves that can be answered in the context of the group.

Often, these questions will entail deeper levels of self-disclosure than members have engaged in previously. Research (Farber, Berano, & Capobianco, 2006) suggests that prior to making such disclosures, individuals experience significant ambivalence about doing so. This ambivalence can have a sharply inhibiting effect on the member's willingness to communicate aspects of his or her experience. Underpinning the negative pole of the member's ambivalence is the anticipation of shame. By being attuned to the ambivalence that precedes significant disclosures, the therapist can mobilize group resources to create a greater sense of safety for members wishing to be known more fully by the group.

A third task is for the therapist to recognize and use therapeutically opportunities for members to engage in group decision making. In this era of group life, the therapist will witness genuine cooperative activity, an achievement predicated on the recognition of differences and the positive value placed on those differences. Even though in earlier stages members act in concert with one another (as in Stage 2, in which members join forces in challenging the leader), these efforts represent what Rychlak (2003) termed "parallel individualism" (p. 4)—alliances formed out of convenience rather than out of a genuine respect for the other members. This capacity for cooperation and lessened dependency on the therapist provide members with the opportunity to participate in a thoroughgoing decision-making process in which members can assiduously explore diverging positions on a topic. However, in the midphase of therapy, this ability must be nurtured by the therapist by

EXHIBIT 6.4
Therapist's Tasks in Stage 4: Integration and Work

- Provide members with opportunities to refine the types of feedback they provide one another.
- Encourage members to develop a feed-forward system by articulating questions they have about themselves.
- Identify opportunities for group decision making.
- Support members' engagement in self-disclosure by facilitating their awareness of diverse feelings that accompany disclosures.

providing opportunities for members to participate in this process (Rose, 1977). Inevitably, in the course of conducting group psychotherapy, decisions must be made concerning the group: Should a new member enter at this time? Should the time of the group be moved to accommodate a particular member? Should a member who anticipates she will be 30 minutes late to the next session attend that session? Whereas in earlier stages of development, the therapist often makes these decisions for the group in recognition of the group's limited decision-making capacity, at this stage, the therapist's handing over some decision-making power to the group allows the group to further develop this function. Each member's participation in this group level process affords them a model of decision making in their individual lives (see Exhibit 6.4).

For some therapists, members' greater focus on one another and lessened focus on the therapist elicits negative feelings (Brabender, 1987). Unconsciously, the therapist may feel compelled to reestablish his or her conspicuousness by promoting dependency and interfering with members' efforts to engage with one another. Such a move and the frustration it can induce in members are likely to have a number of untoward effects on them. These include regression, premature dropout, or members' formation into an *antigroup* (Nitsun, 1996), in which members' unconscious goal is to dismantle the group.

Stage 5: Termination

Termination most fully and obviously constitutes a developmental stage when the group is ending—when all members are terminating. However, in some sense, when a single member departs, the group does end because, as when a new member arrives, roles must be renegotiated. A departure of a member is the end of the group as members currently know it. Whether the group enters a full-blown termination stage or merely exhibits aspects of this stage, the therapist must assist the group in performing the tasks of separating. These tasks include (a) responding to loss constructively, (b) taking stock of the past, and (c) preparing for the future.

However, the performance of these tasks involves experiencing psychological discomfort. To avoid this discomfort, members are likely to engage in a variety of behaviors that are at odds with their pursuit (Farrell, 1976). An important function of the therapist is to assist members in maintaining the frame of the group, the frame that has supported members' explorations throughout its life, and to help members to recognize behaviors that undermine both the frame and their own growth during this last period of group life. The therapist's anticipation of behaviors likely to be detrimental to the completion of termination tasks facilitates identifying them and responding to them with alacrity. Although the number of ways members are likely to avoid termination tasks is as various as their personalities and backgrounds, four patterns of behavior have been identified with some frequency in the literature: *premature termination, group prolongation, distraction*, and *projective identification*. Each is discussed in turn. Note that because of the need for the therapist's attention to these nonconstructive ways of responding to termination, in many cases, the therapist will be more active than in the prior stage to meet members' developmental needs during this critical period.

One method used by members is to end the group prematurely, perhaps the most radical and effective means to ensure that the member does not confront termination within the group. MacKenzie (1996) recommended that the therapist alert members to the temptation to leave early and ask members if they have contemplated this option. He noted that such a query fosters a rich discussion about the loss associated with such a defensive tact and thereby lowers the probability of its occurrence.

In some groups, rather than leaving early, members conspire to have the group not end at all (for a vignette of such an occurrence in a time-limited group, see Riess, 2005). This prolongation effort may take the form of requesting additional sessions or by hatching plans to meet after the group. Joyce, Duncan, Duncan, Kipnes, and Piper (1996) described a group in which members began to meet for coffee following sessions as the group approached its end date. Such activity can set the stage for postgroup contact. Although different therapists may have different policies on involvement among members after the group ends, the therapist crafting a policy must consider that such contact prevents members from dealing with loss in its fullness. Ethical issues may exist as well. Group members who meet after the group has ended may have great difficulty preserving one another's confidentiality as group members. The therapist's task is to look for manifestations that such efforts are underway and to make them a focus of group discussion. Often, some members of the group who are able to articulate the dangers inherent in plans for contact following termination (typically the members who assisted the group in transitioning from Stage 3 to Stage 4) will come to the fore.

Apart from hastening or retarding the ending of the group, members may attempt to avoid the experience of the group's ending by creating a distraction. A member may, for example, engage in a high level of disclosure about sensitive material that seems to demand the group's attention. Often, the individuals who engage in this behavior at this time are members who have not disclosed greatly in the past. The group is caught between the desire to respond to this individual and the wish to focus on termination. Although the disclosing individual is operating in the service of his or her own resistance, he or she may also be functioning as a voice for the group's longing to avoid a full experience of termination. Tschuschke and Dies (1994) found that individuals who self-disclose late in the life of the group tend to have less favorable outcomes. They observed that the disclosing members received feedback on the disclosures and proceeded to withdraw rather than subjecting both the disclosures and the feedback to thorough exploration. This finding suggests that the disclosure serves more of a defensive function than a bona fide effort at self-understanding. Furthermore, the fact that the disclosure and reactions to it remain unmetabolized by the group creates the potential for the disclosing member to leave the group in a disengaged position, a disengagement that may adversely affect outcome.

Tschuschke and Dies's (1994) findings suggest that the therapist should monitor the level of disclosure and discourage those disclosures that are either too primitive or too removed from the task of termination (MacKenzie, 1996). One means of limiting self-disclosure is to show the member how the content of the self-disclosure relates to a potential goal that can be established for work that will succeed the group experience (work that could be pursued either in an alternate therapy or independently as the individual applies the insights gathered in group). For example, two sessions from termination, the group is discussing their relationships to siblings and how their experiences when older siblings left home were similar to those they are experiencing in the group's termination. Martha discloses to the group that the reason she did not like George, her older brother (something the group had learned earlier), was because he had often physically beaten her (a new revelation). The therapist intervenes,

> That must have been quite difficult as you were growing up. Your cautious reaction to some of the men in our group is now understandable. Just as you have learned to stand up to Jules and Elvis in the group, perhaps when you join the new group in the fall, they will be able to help you tackle this problem both in the group and with George.

Finally, members must be helped to avoid succumbing to projective identification at the end of the group. The ending creates an opportunity par excellence for members to export unwanted psychological elements, elements that have been activated by the regression that termination often precipitates. This opportunity is a particularly enticing one because once a member has left the group with a psychic load attached, like the proverbial scapegoat sent into the wilderness, members imagine that they are rid of that load forever (Schermer & Klein, 1996). The cost of this maneuver is that members fail to achieve a more robust sense of self that is inclusive of all parts of their person, a sense that is less subject to fragmentation of self and dissolution of self-esteem with the appearance of some hitherto warded-off element. Therefore, the therapist should vigorously interpret any effort on the part of the group to coerce a member into serving as the "container" (Bion, 1961) for some psychological content for other members or the group as a whole.

In addition to helping members avoid prolonged and intensive engagement in behaviors to fend off reactions to the group's ending, the therapist must be poised to assist members in doing the actual work of ending. This work has three components. First, the therapist must assist the group members in exploring their responses to loss and separation. Piper, McCallum, and Azim (1992) wrote, "Termination represents a unique opportunity for the patients to explore and reexperience their idiosyncratic reactions to loss that have created so much difficulty for them in the past" (p. 114). Although their comments were offered in relation to individuals who had been referred to their short-term groups specifically because of their struggles with unresolved grief reactions, the potential is present for termination to activate the loss-related conflicts of all members, no matter what the purpose of the group. The risks of not helping members attend sufficiently to loss were seen in a study on clients with borderline personality disorder who dropped out of outpatient group psychotherapy after participating in a day hospital group. The authors (Hummelen, Wilberg, & Karterud, 2007) found that members' attachment to the outpatient group was hindered by their failure to grieve adequately their loss of the day hospital group.

The therapist can assist members in exploring reactions to the loss of the group by unpacking the meaning of loss metaphors that arise at the time of termination (Fieldsteel, 1996). For example, the therapist can help the group investigate what two members' discussion of their anxieties about the health problems of their aging parents might signify about apprehension of the loss of the group and its parental dimension. Members also should be assisted by the therapist in recognizing fantasies they may have about responding to loss in a way that differs from their past ways (Brabender & Fallon, 1996). For example, a member who appears inconsolable at the loss of the group may harbor fear that by not actively grieving intensively, she may lose access to the memories of the others and of the group as a whole. Another member may believe that by expressing a negative sentiment about the group, the therapist or other members may take a negative view of him or her away from the group.

The therapist must also help members take stock of the past as a way of preparing for the future. At this time, members often spontaneously engage in a retrospective appraisal of their experiences and comment on the growth each member has undergone. The task of the therapist is to ensure that the feedback members receive is feedback they are able to metabolize either during the termination sessions or on their own. As discussed earlier, constructive or negative feedback has been found to be more readily accepted if it is both preceded and followed by positive feedback (Morran et al., 1998). Therefore, the therapist should help members have a clear awareness of positive changes and strengths that other members see in them as they depart from the group. The therapist should also ensure that the strong affects that members tend to experience at this time do not interfere with the delivery of feedback on more concrete behavioral changes, given the research finding that operational feedback is more helpful than sweeping statements (Jacobs et al., 1974).

Any constructive feedback that members do receive at this time can be used to enable members to develop goals for and anticipate challenges in the future. The following exchange that occurred at the end of an eight-session group illustrates this point:

Stefan: I just feel I could have gotten more out of this experience. I don't know exactly how, but I do have a sense of incompleteness.

Dorian: That doesn't surprise me. I feel I don't know you as well as others.

June: Yes, I agree: Stefan, you're still a mystery to me.

Added to the sense of failure Stefan has in relation to his group experience, Dorian's and June's comments could be quite deflating. Yet, the therapist can sculpt this exchange into something that could be at once useful and hope inspiring.

Therapist: [to Stefan] In the future, you will be entering new social situations. From your self-observation and Dorian's and June's comments, what is one thing you would like to do differently?

Stefan: I think right off the bat, I'll try to be more active. I sit back in the beginning, and then it's difficult for me to change, even though everyone tried to help me to do so.

As Stefan articulates this insight, he is able to appreciate that he did obtain a psychological commodity from group participation that may enable him to relate more productively in his future life (see Exhibit 6.5).

Group termination can invite the emergence of the therapist's own conflicts in relation to endings. Of course, the group represents a loss for the therapist as well as for the group members. If the therapist's stance toward loss is conflictual, the therapist may collude with any of the defensive behaviors in which members tend to engage during this stage. However, even apart from long-standing difficulties in relation to loss, therapists may have been stimulated by the unfolding group events to respond in a way contrary to members' best interests. For example, therapists who are dissatisfied with the degree of positive change in group members may discourage members from carefully examining their own progress over the course of the sessions lest

EXHIBIT 6.5
Therapist Behaviors in Stage 5: Termination

Challenge defenses associated with avoidance of loss:
- Prevent premature departures.
- Challenge attempts to extend the group.
- Interpret scapegoating.
- Support the group's recognition of members' use of distraction.
- Curtail intensive and raw self-disclosures.

Assist the group in examining responses to loss and separation:
- Interpret derivatives or metaphors.
- Explore fantasies.
- Take stock of the past.
- Prepare for the future by setting goals.

this examination produce a negative evaluation. If self-punitive impulses are stimulated by guilt in relation to the success of the group, the therapist may discourage members from speaking about the group in positive terms. Another example is therapists who feel relieved that the group is ending, who may ward off this recognition by discouraging members from talking about their pleasure in relation to the group's termination.[4] In other words, there can be various linkages between the internal life of the therapist and his or her behavior in the group.

Whatever the specific circumstances, most important is that the therapist make a thoroughgoing effort to engage in self-reflection about his or her full range of responses to the group's endings that may lead the therapist to veer away from what would be developmentally optimal. In addressing termination reactions, therapists may benefit from supplementing their own self-inspection with the counsel of a supervisor or coparticipants in a peer supervision group.

DEVELOPMENTAL IMPLICATIONS OF THE LEADERSHIP STRUCTURE

Throughout this chapter, we have been addressing the circumstance in which a solo therapist is leading the group. Another leadership structure involves the collaboration of two therapists. We have seen that the conflicts and unfinished tasks of the group psychotherapist can be a limiting factor in the group's capacity to mature: If the stage engages a therapist's own areas of psychological concern, that therapist may unwittingly act in a fashion to frustrate the group's developmental needs and thereby contribute to a fixation or regression. When therapists engage in cotherapy, it is not only the

---

[4]In particularly intense groups, such as MacColl's (2007) 9/11 parent support group, this relief may be particularly great but also egodystonic.

psychological status of the individual therapist that is influential but the relationships between the two therapists.

Dugo and Beck (1997) identified nine systems that have been constructed to describe how the cotherapy relationship develops over time. These systems posit a series of stages through which the relationship between the cotherapists progresses. Some of the systems, such as Dugo and Beck's own, see the dynamic changes within the cotherapy relationship as existing in parallel to those through which the psychotherapy group progresses. The parallelism between the group's and cotherapists' developmental stages can be understood from a general systems theory standpoint as an example of the isomorphic relationship among the processes and structures of living systems, especially systems existing within a given array of systems (Dugo & Beck, 1997).

Dugo and Beck (1997) held that a group can progress no further than the maturity level achieved by the cotherapy team. This notion is consistent with the idea advanced in this chapter that the therapist's own conflicts and areas of immaturity can interfere with his or her ability to respond in a developmentally appropriate fashion. Some work within the cotherapy relationship can occur while the therapists are leading the group together. However, particularly useful is the cotherapy team's completion of the first three stages specified by many of the systems prior to beginning to work as a team because without this work, the therapists will be unable to perform the leadership tasks of the initial stages effectively (Wheelan, 1997). One survey providing some indirect support for this notion showed that cotherapists who see their relationship characterized by a high level of competition have dissatisfaction with their work as cotherapists (Lonergan, 1995). The experience of a high level of competition is consistent with a relatively immature cotherapy relationship. Most likely, cotherapists who experience dissatisfaction with their group work are going to have difficulty being effective. However, empirical work on the relationship between cotherapy and group developmental statuses would be extremely useful.

Given the importance of the first three stages to cotherapy work, we discuss each in turn. The first stage (or *phase*, as Dugo & Beck [1997] termed it) entails the creation of a contract in which the cotherapists work out the goals and methods of the group. Each cotherapist clarifies to the other his or her model for how individual and group change occurs. Depending on the model being applied, the therapists may work out different roles in the group. Dugo and Beck (1997) noted, "The degree of explicitness in the initial contract determines the degree of ease and clarity with which the co-therapy team proceeds" (p. 296).

In Stage 2, a period that can have the storminess of Stage 2 in the group at large, cotherapists address thorny issues related to authority, competition, and differences in perspective as they craft their identity as a cotherapy team. Even though the therapists can do substantial work on these issues outside of the group (especially if the therapists have an active, ongoing work relationship), the cotherapists may need to return to these areas of dynamic concern as the group stimulates competition and conflict between the them. It is one thing to discuss competition prior to the commencement of the group and another to experience competitive impulses during a session.

The successful negotiation of these issues leads to Stage 3, which (as in the psychotherapy group) enables cotherapists to move to greater collaboration and interdependency as they learn to capitalize on each other's strengths and rely on one another for perceptions that complement, disconfirm, or affirm their own. Within this stage, the group begins to realize the advantage of cotherapy. Because the group has different developmental needs and because the cotherapists bring different funds of resources to the group, the group is likely to have its needs from the leader fulfilled when a greater array of resources on which to draw is available. The reader is referred to Dugo and Beck (1991) for a discussion of the later developmental stages of their model.

A question unaddressed by the empirical literature is whether the leadership format of the group makes a difference in terms of the group's movement through the developmental stages. That is, does it matter whether the group is conducted by a cotherapy team or a solo leader? Concannon (1995) observed from her own group work that cotherapy, relative to solo therapy, produces an abbreviated and less intense Stage 1. The members seem to be less inspired to attempt to gain a privileged relationship with the therapist vis-à-vis the other members. Possibly, members believe that each therapist already has a special person with whom to relate in the group—the cotherapist. Concannon noted that cotherapy-led groups instead appear to concentrate their efforts on working through the issues of Stage 2 to achieve greater cohesion.

Concannon's (1995) observations serve as useful research hypotheses for future studies. However, in looking at the developmental ramifications of the solo–cotherapy difference, investigators should consider other variables. Dublin (1995) identified a number of variables that could affect the perception of the cotherapy team, such as whether the two therapists begin the group at the same time, whether one member is the group's permanent therapist and the other temporary, the status of the two therapists (e.g., is one member of the pair in a student role?), and the degree of theoretical compatibility. Each of these variables characterizing the cotherapy relationship could have more or less importance depending on the group's developmental stage. Presumably, by knowing what stimulus demands are created by each leadership configuration, the therapists can take advantage of its strengths and compensate for its limitations in planning interventions.

SUMMARY

Zaccaro (2007) wrote that effective leaders need to have an "expansive behavioral repertoire" (p. 9) and be able to apply the skills in this repertoire appropriately as circumstances change. In this chapter we have outlined this behavioral repertoire as it applies to the developmentally attuned group psychotherapist. We have provided a discussion of the stances and activities of the effective group psychotherapist, including those elements that remain constant from stage to stage and those that vary. With respect to the latter, in Stage 1, the therapist focuses on providing structure, so that members have a clear grasp of the goals of the group and the processes that serve those goals, and fostering the engagement of members with one another. In Stage 2, the therapist supports members in the management of conflict in the group, creating safety but also allowing for the expression of difficult feelings and impulses. Stage 3 requires the therapist's attention to potential disruptions in the frame of the group. The therapist also assists members in cultivating processes that will be used fully in the mature group. In Stage 4, the therapist supports the full emergence of processes such as feedback exchange and self-disclosure. The therapist helps members exercise their greater independence from the therapist by providing them with opportunities for decision making. In Stage 5, the therapist assists members in nondefensively approaching the feelings and cognitions associated with the loss of the group, taking stock of experiences in the group, and preparing for the future. Although some research basis exists for developmentally based interventions, particularly in the areas of structure, self-disclosure, and feedback, much additional work needs to be done. Finally, in this chapter we also have considered the effects of the two most common leadership formats—solo therapy and cotherapy.

7

STAGE DEVELOPMENT WITH STRUCTURED GROUP APPROACHES TO PSYCHOTHERAPY: COGNITIVE, COGNITIVE–BEHAVIORAL, AND BEHAVIORAL

A number of approaches to group psychotherapy, such as cognitive, cognitive–behavioral, problem-solving, and postmodern approaches, deviate both theoretically and technically from the long-term unstructured group psychotherapy approach that we have presented thus far in this volume. In this chapter, we first review the evidence for a developmental framework across theoretically diverse groups. We then turn our attention specifically to the structured group approach and describe such groups briefly, focusing on how they differ structurally in terms of content and process from the groups portrayed in chapters 5 and 6 of this volume. Next, we describe the relationship of group structure to stage development and present the research on stage development that is more germane to structured groups. Fourth, we make the argument that structured content does not preclude group development. A structured process may affect development depending on the degree and type of structure in the sessions. We indicate how structured group

161

therapies, cognitive and cognitive–behavioral groups in particular, can benefit from a developmental approach to group therapy. Fifth, we illustrate how our five-stage approach of group development can be beneficially infused into several different kinds of structured group therapies (e.g., a relaxation or an anger management group) and provide clinical vignettes from such groups to exemplify each stage. We demonstrate how the therapist was able to adhere to a particular model for the group while at the same time engaging in responses appropriate to the tasks required for that stage of development.

EVIDENCE FOR DEVELOPMENTAL POTENTIAL ACROSS TYPES OF GROUPS

Group developmental states have been studied most vigorously within the theoretical perspectives from which they were derived. Whether group developmental stages can be observed in groups beyond the theoretical frameworks in which they have traditionally been considered has been studied minimally. However, the applications of different models each lead to the creation of a particular type of session with certain characteristics. For example, some approaches are associated with highly structured sessions or sessions in which the leader has a very prominent role. Does group development occur in a wide range of groups with highly varying characteristics, or is it observable only under a narrow range of conditions? In other words, to what extent is group development better understood as precious or irrepressible?

Group developmental concepts were originally applied to groups that were unstructured, long-term, and characterized by a fair degree of stability in membership. Can group developmental phenomena be seen in groups that are structured, short-term, and changing in membership? Investigations on the occurrence of developmental phenomena on structured therapy groups are few. However, one relevant study was conducted by Stockton, Rohde, and Haughey (1992), who randomly assigned individuals presenting for treatment in a campus community counseling center to conditions in which they either received practice at the beginning of each session in the processes that would help members achieve their goals or did not receive training at the beginning of the session. The investigators used the short version of MacKenzie's (1983) Group Climate Questionnaire (GCQ–S) discussed in chapter 4 of this volume.

The investigations found that the group receiving the structure showed changes in members' engagement and avoidance scores that much more closely approximated the development trends suggested by most progressive stage models. As developmental theory predicts, conflict increased across initial sessions and then diminished, but this trend was similar for both experimental and control conditions. The investigators explained that the structure helped the group to be more consistent and to avoid recycling through earlier stages. For this discussion, the important point is that group development can occur in structured sessions.

Some models of group psychotherapy assume a fairly short-term group experience. For example, groups run according to a cognitive–behavioral approach typically take place in 12 to 16 sessions. Can group development occur in this brief a time frame? Although the variable of time frame is examined in depth in chapter 9 in this volume, here it is sufficient to note that a brief group experience does not preclude group development. MacKenzie (1983) obtained patterns consistent with developmental theory on the GCQ–S for groups meeting across 35 sessions. These patterns were replicated by Brabender (1985, 1988) using the GCQ–S on seven groups meeting for 8 sessions each.

Can group development occur in a situation in which membership changes continuously? Although anecdotal evidence exists on the development of a group with a constantly changing membership (e.g., a description of support groups for terminally ill cancer patients by Kosoff, 2003), two formal studies pertinent to this question have been done. Schopler and Galinsky (1990) investigated 116 outpatient and inpatient groups covering a wide range of types, including skills training, psychoeducational, support, treatment, and assessment. The therapists, all highly experienced, rated the extent to which members of groups completed the formative tasks of the earliest development stage related to goals, bonds, roles, and norms. For example, a formative task with respect to goals was "Group purpose and/or goals are clear to most members" (Schopler & Galinsky, 1990, p. 438). They found that half of the groups were seen by the therapists as having completed the tasks of the early stages. Furthermore, the less the membership changed, the greater the number of tasks they completed. Hence, stable membership is the friend but not the sine qua non of group development. In an investigation of community meetings in a hospital in which new members entered and old members exited on an ongoing basis, McLees, Margo, Waterman, and Beeber (1992), using the GCQ–S, detected the presence of developmental patterns over the course of 12 weeks.

Extant evidence, though limited, suggests that group development is robust. Although it can be hindered by a wide variety of factors, group development appears to occur under highly varying conditions. For this reason, the application of any given theoretical model is unlikely to vitiate the possibility that developmental phenomena will be present. The question then arises what effect group development might have on the delivery of a given theoretical approach.

The phenomena of a given stage may interfere with the pursuit of group goals. For example, if the group is addressing authority issues at the same time in which they are asked to generate solutions to a particular member's problem, members' rebellious urges toward authority may manifest themselves in their proffering solutions that are few in number or poor in quality. Conversely, the phenomena of a given stage may enhance the pursuit of group goals. For example, a group that has reached maturity and is capable of a deliberative decision-making process will be facilitated in performing the step of the interpersonal problem-solving model (for full description, see Brabender & Fallon, 1993) in which members determine among a range of solutions the preferable one.

To show the breadth of application of group developmental concepts, in this chapter and chapter 8 we present approaches that cover considerable theoretical terrain. In this chapter, theoretical approaches such as cognitive–behavioral therapy that have developed independently of developmentally oriented approaches are to be explored. In chapter 8, we focus on recently emerging theoretical frameworks that have a good deal of common ground with theoretical approaches that historically have been most closely associated with group developmental thinking. These more recent frameworks are labeled *postmodern* because, as we explain, they followed the abandonment of the epistemological assumption of modernity that human beings can know an objectively verifiable reality. These approaches may not only be enriched by a developmental perspective but also have a great deal to contribute to the understanding of group development and the therapist's range of interventions for influencing group development. The particular models chosen are intended as illustrations of how group developmental thinking can be integrated beyond its theoretical homes to the benefit of the group members.

STRUCTURED GROUP PSYCHOTHERAPIES

There have been a large number of structured approaches to group psychotherapy, including J. S. Beck's (1995) cognitive model, Ellis's (1992) rational emotive therapy, Goldfried's systematic restructuring (Goldfried, Decenteceo, & Weinberg, 1974), Meichenbaum's self-instructional training (Emmelkamp, Mersch, Vissia, & Van der Halm, 1985; Meichenbaum, 1977), stress inoculation (Meichenbaum & Novaco, 1985; Puder, 1988), Maultsby's (1975, 1991) rational behavior therapy, Lazarus's (1981) multimodal therapy, cognitive appraisal therapy (Wessler & Hankin-Wessler, 1989, 1997), interpersonal problem solving (Brabender, 2002; Spivak, Platt, & Shure, 1976), social skills training (Jones & McColl, 1991; Mueser, Valenti-Hein, & Yarnold, 1987), and psychoeducational training (Brown, 2005; Furr, 2000).

The enormous array of groups can be reduced to five broad categories: (a) cognitive–behavioral groups, which use cognitive and behavioral techniques to change cognition; (b) behavioral groups, which focus primarily on changing particular behaviors that are environmentally maladaptive; (c) interpersonal problem-solving groups, which use a single model rigidly applied to each individual's problem; (d) social skills groups, which concentrate on one social skill at a time, partitioning the skill into its behavioral components and behavioral role-playing and practicing with feedback; and (e) psychoeducational groups, which most often use the topical lecture format to educate a group.

In essence, these models emphasize examining and changing cognition, behavior, or both. They have clearly defined goals, focus on behavioral change, entail low to moderate levels of inference from behavior, and emphasize empirical outcome. Major efforts are focused either on disturbed or maladaptive behavioral patterns or the "mediational processes [which] give rise to maladaptive emotional states and behavior patterns" (Kendall & Bemis, 1983, p. 52).

In terms of technical interventions, this group of models differs from the unstructured group in the level of activity of the therapist, the amount of structure provided, the articulated use of behavioral techniques and strategies to accomplish individual goals, and thus the amount of interest and energy placed in interchanges between members. Each of these dimensions is discussed subsequently. Within each group, the dimensions can vary depending on problems to be tackled, goals to be accomplished, time allotted, and functional level of the participants. For example, in a group of day hospital patients, a small psychoeducational group may focus on the importance of medication compliance, alternating between leaders presenting and members being called on to share their experiences of noncompliance. In contrast, a psychoeducational group of executives learning stress management may use lecture, demonstration, and individual practice of specific techniques with little emphasis on sharing or social interaction. In both types of groups, active therapists, who limit content domain and use specific behavioral strategies, provide high levels of structure. The groups, however, differ on the amount of interpersonal exchange that is encouraged. Although the amount of structure introduced may vary from model to model, almost all models and their variations use considerably more structure than is present in the model presented in the previous chapters.

THE RELATIONSHIP OF GROUP STRUCTURE TO STAGE DEVELOPMENT

Most groups classified under the rubric of the cognitive and behavioral groups are more structured than the types of groups on which progressive stage models are based. Three features that relate to structure are more prevalent among the cognitive and behavioral groups. The first is that these groups are often homogeneous in psychopathology. For example, groups are formed on the basis of presence of anxiety (A. C. Page & Hooke, 2003), social phobia (Edwards & Kannan, 2006; Heimberg et al., 1990), panic (Lang & Craske,

2000), obsessive–compulsive disorder (Jacqueline & Margo, 2005), depression (Oei, Bullbeck, & Campbell, 2006), trauma (Pifalo, 2006), eating disorders (Radomile, 2000), sexual offenses (Beech & Hamilton-Giachritsis, 2005), schizophrenia (Bechdolf, Köhn, Knost, Pukrop, & Klosterkötter, 2005), bipolar disorder (Bauer & McBride, 2003), and substance abuse (Kaminer, Blitz, Burleson, Kadden, & Rounsaville, 1998). Therefore, the content that unfolds in groups is determined by the presence of a shared set of symptoms.

The second characteristic is that the majority of these groups have a high degree of structure. Often patients complete individualized questionnaires related to their symptoms at the beginning and end of each session. Then each patient is engaged in establishing an agenda for the session (or a stylized go-around) and works specifically on that agenda using identified techniques (e.g., mini-lectures, identifying the distorted cognition, identifying and following through on specific steps of problem solving, role-playing, guided imagery). Homework is assigned, and the group ends with session evaluation.

Last, emphasis is almost always on the individual outcome of a particular symptom, which is either internal (e.g., distorted cognitions) or behavioral (e.g., decreased phobic behavior). Because of this last feature, the many empirical studies examining participants in behavioral and cognitive–behavioral groups almost always have focused on symptom attenuation and rarely have included measures of group process. To date, only three studies using the behavioral or cognitive–behavioral group approach have included efforts to understand or measure group development or stages (Castonguay, Pincus, Agras, & Hines, 1998; Nickerson & Coleman, 2006; Tasca, Balfour, Ritchie, & Bissada, 2006).

Content and Process Structure and Group Development: A Review of the Research

Most research on group development has used models that were low in structure. Stages of development were most clearly established and consistent when these groups were also closed ended and time limited; context, task, time, degree of homogeneity, style of leadership, and theoretical model (MacKenzie, 1994a) also influenced developmental phenomena. Most of these factors involve some aspect of the dimension of structure. The unitary term *structure*, however, belies its bidimensional character. Groups can vary in structure for both content and process. The range of these two dimensions of structure needs to be delineated when considering its impact on development of group process.

Level of Structure: Content

Groups can range in content from highly structured to having little structure. Groups that convene to complete a task, discuss a certain topic, or learn how to cope with a specific set of symptoms are likely to be highly structured. Most groups using cognitive, cognitive–behavioral, or behavioral models, being similarly focused on specific goals, are highly structured in terms of content (e.g., for posttraumatic stress disorder [PTSD], see J. G. Beck & Coffey, 2005; for social phobia, see Edwards & Kannan, 2006; for obsessive–compulsive disorder, see Jacqueline & Margo, 2005; for depression, see Oei et al., 2006; for auditory hallucinations, see Pinkham, Gloege, Flanagan, & Penn, 2004). When a group is homogeneous for symptoms, the group is educated in terms of the prevailing and accepted theory, taught methods for symptom reduction, and given specific instructions as to how theory and technique are applied in the group. Task and work groups, often seeking a specific outcome, are usually highly structured in terms of content. Psychotherapy groups with heterogeneous symptomatology have a medium-to-low range of structured content (Gersick, 1988; Yalom, 1995). Sensitivity training, laboratory training groups, and process groups have the lowest designated content structure. Many of these groups do not delimit what can be discussed in the group.

Whether the content of the group is highly structured, the existing empirical evidence suggests that either high or low structure will not necessarily limit developmental phenomena. MacKenzie, Dies, Coché, Rutan, and Stone (1987) studied both process groups (low in structured content) and special interest groups (groups formed around a specific, often academic, topic on group therapy and high in structured content) over the course of 14 hours of working together. They concluded that the two types of groups developed similarly; neither type of group showed a greater propensity for maturity. Wheelan, Murphy, Tsumura, and Kline (1998) have also provided evidence that ongoing groups with specific tasks appear developmentally similar to the MacKenzie et al. groups. In both studies, the more successful groups appear to have traversed the earlier stages of development. In the Wheelan, Murphy, et al. study, higher productivity was associated with reaching more mature phases.

Level of Structure: Process

Independent of content is the level of structure occurring in the process. In a group that is low in structure on this dimension, the leader may not have a set agenda for any of the sessions, although he or she may follow guidelines in the earlier sessions (e.g., introduce members to each other, review contract). The most extreme example of this is the training process groups available for group therapists at national group psychotherapy meetings (as was examined by MacKenzie et al., 1987). At the other extreme might be psychoeducational groups (Burlingame et al., 2007; Furr, 2000), Meichenbaum's (1977) self-instructional training, and social skills training (Mueser et al., 1987). In the psychoeducational groups, lecture is the preferred format, often with some audience participation. In social skills training, almost every aspect of the group is preplanned; with therapist guidance and direct instruction, group members take turns with practice and role-playing, and specific structured feedback is provided by both therapist and group members. In these groups, agendas are set at each session; often, specific skills are taught, applied to the self, and then practiced in the group setting. Homework is assigned. These groups are highly structured in both content and process.

The central question is whether these latter groups also proceed through stages of development. Although the evidence is limited and we have to draw some inferences, we contend that it is the nature and degree of this structure that is likely to determine whether developmental processes will occur or perhaps even be enhanced.

A study by Sexton (1993) suggested developmental processes are not inhibited in groups designed with some explicit process structure. In this study, Norwegian patients and therapists completed symptom scales before each session. This was followed by verbal therapy, light aerobic exercise, group exercises, and brief discussion. Unfortunately, no information about what took place in the verbal part of the session is available. Although the developmental processes as defined by us and others were not measured as such in this study, therapist–patient processes were examined and were found to have differential effects depending on whether it was an early or later session. Patient outcome appeared related to the nature of the early therapist–patient relationship rather than the nature of that relationship later in the group. From this finding, we can infer that different processes are important depending on when they occur in group life and that the structured nature of this group did not inhibit group process from developing.

Type of Structure and Group Development

Several studies have examined where and what kind of structure might be helpful to the process of development. Lee and Bednar (1977) varied levels of structured exercises for self-disclosure, interpersonal feedback, and group confrontation in groups of university students. Groups participating in the highest level of structured exercises benefited the most in terms of producing behaviors most relevant to change (intensity and depth of communication). This trend was particularly evident for participants who were low in risk taking: With structured exercises, these participants were virtually identical to the high risk takers on relevant group behaviors—self-disclosure, interpersonal feedback, and confrontation. From this study, it appears that structuring the process is particularly helpful to those individuals who may be more reluctant to reveal themselves in group initially. These behaviors are relevant to the forwarding of group progression. However, the one caveat to this study is that increasing group structure decreased cohesion, a necessary component to stage development.

Using a similar methodology, Evensen and Bednar (1978) attempted to differentiate types of structure. Their study began with an initial period of behavioral practice, cognitive instruction, behavioral practice, and cognitive instruction or minimal structure. This was followed by a relatively unstructured period in which interpersonal feedback, self-disclosure, and group cohesion were measured. Contrary to the previous study, risk-averse participants did not benefit differentially from any type of initial structure: They still perceived risk to occur. Those with a high-risk disposition, however, benefited most from the behavioral practice, producing the most intense, appropriate, and in-depth interpersonal communication, and reported the highest level of group cohesion. In general an initial cognitive structure, which emphasizes verbal instructions about feedback, disclosure, the importance of it in group and resistance, has no impact on what occurs subsequently in the less structured sessions, and the combination of cognitive structure and behavioral practice has not added benefit over behavioral practice only in producing subsequent appropriate disclosure and feedback. It appears that at least initially, those with low-risk dispositions need to have continued structure to increase their level of self-disclosure and appropriate interpersonal feedback and perceived cohesion.

The previous studies used measurements that occurred in a single session. Results may differ as the group progresses. With these studies as background, Stockton et al. (1992) attempted to promote group progression by providing a structured exercise at the commencement of each of six weekly 2-hour groups designed to facilitate the occurrence of a particular phase of development (universality, differentiation, and individuation). When compared with groups not given these low-risk structured exercises, the exercise groups had increased level of cohesion, more engagement, and less overall avoidance. The most significant finding was that conflict increased more and then significantly decreased compared with groups not using these structured exercises. Stockton et al. maintained that group development was enhanced as a result of increased consistency over the weeks and less revisiting of earlier developmental phenomena. Given that most of the group time was unstructured, it was unclear whether the positive findings were due to the content of the exercises, which primed the group and expedited it into a more productive working phase, or the initial structure.

Whether structuring the process aids the developmental progression may be dependent on the stage of the group. Kivlighan (1997) found that in those groups in which group leaders were judged by the group members to be more task oriented during the early sessions (i.e., more structured) and more relationship oriented during the later sessions (i.e., less structured), group members showed a reduction in their target symptoms at the conclusion of the group therapy. Conversely, leader task orientation late in group life and relationship orientation early in group life was unrelated to group member outcome.

Cognitive–Behavioral Therapy and Stage Development Research

Recent studies have focused more specifically on the question of whether group development can occur within particular structured approaches. Two studies have addressed the existence of group development in cognitive–behavioral group therapy—both studies involved the population of individuals with a binge-eating disorder. Castonguay, Pincus, Agras, and Hines (1998) followed 65 women over the course of 12-week manualized group treatment. Using a group version of the Therapy Session Report (Orlinsky & Howard, 1966), the investigators found that the members' progress through stages of development was associated with symptomatic improvement. Specifically, groups that showed high engagement at the beginning of the group and high conflict during the middle showed greater symptomatic change than groups that were lower on engagement at the beginning and lower on conflict during the midsessions. Specific limitations of this study are cited in chapter 4 of the current volume. However, the study does suggest that progressive stages may emerge in structured groups.

In a second and more recent study, Tasca et al. (2006) randomly assigned women meeting the criteria for binge-eating disorder to either cognitive–behavioral or psychodynamic–interpersonal groups with both groups meeting for 16 sessions. Adherence to treatment manuals was successful, and independent observers could distinguish the treatments from each other. Our interests are in the cognitive–behavioral model, and so the structure of those sessions is discussed in some detail. Goals of treatment included the diminution of dietary restrictions, exposure to a wider food range, reduction of inflexible food rules, improved body image, and fewer cognitive distortions specific to binge-eating disorder.

In the first of three phases of treatment, therapists sought to establish healthy and flexible eating habits by having clients complete a diary focused on eating and cognitions, which highlighted dysfunctional eating patterns and thinking. In the second phase, anxieties associated with control loss and eating were examined, and alternative cognitions and coping skills were introduced. Members focused on problem-solving strategies when situations might trigger a binge. The final stage addressed lifestyle strategies to weight loss and relapse prevention (Tasca et al., 2006).

The GCQ–S ratings provided evidence that a cognitive–behavioral model of group therapy will permit the development of group. However, the course of development may not be the same one that the psychodynamic–interpersonal model elicits. In the cognitive–behavioral group, a linear increase in engagement over the course of the group occurred. Avoidance, initially greater in the cognitive–behavioral model than in the psychodynamic model, decreased linearly over the life of the group, making it comparable to the psychodynamic model by termination. Conflict decreased over the course of the group and was also significantly less than in the psychodynamic model.

Thus, it appears that at least for this particular population, a group following a cognitive–behavioral model may display either a stage progression (as in Castonguay et al., 1998) or continuous change, but unlike a psychodynamic model, it will not occur in clearly demarcated stages and may not follow the same pattern of engagement, avoidance, and conflict.

In this cognitive–behavioral therapy, the therapists structured the early sessions by setting the agenda, teaching cognitive underpinnings of the disorder, and educating clients about healthy habits, which is not untypical for this model and lends itself to the perception that there is high avoidance, little conflict, and perhaps lower engagement than has been discussed in the model presented earlier. However, in this particular model, as therapy progressed, patients were encouraged to become more active with each other by developing problem-solving solutions and relapse prevention ideas, which are likely to result in increased engagement and decreased avoidance. With continued structure and emphasis on problem solving rather than interpersonal issues, conflict is less likely to occur.

Summary

The cognitive–behavioral group model involves a higher level of structure than does the more unstructured group on which group development theory and research have rested historically. Structure can be delineated into the dimensions of content and process. Structured content appears not to affect group development as we have previously delineated. Structured group processes may influence aspects of group development, depending on the degree and nature of the process. In the research reviewed, it is apparent that some structure may actually enhance group progression. Structured exercises placed at the beginning of a group and incorporating behavioral practice rather than didactic presentation seem to enhance group development and outcome for at least some group members. Initial attention to task and later emphasis on the relationship aspects of treatment are likely to result in the best outcomes. Those structured approaches that encourage member participation and responsibility and foster member-to-member interactions for at least some portion of the group time will likely allow for group progression. However, the type of progression may be influenced by the degree of structure imposed; the more structured the process, the less members will experience cohesion and the less they will permit conflict to erupt overtly.

How Cognitive and Behavioral Group Therapists Can Benefit From a Developmental Approach

The cognitive and behavioral approaches to treatment are fundamentally problem oriented and skill based. Symptom relief and amelioration of stress are accomplished by the teaching of individual skills, which enables modification of cognitions, behavior, or both. A perusal of the current literature in the use of the group format for cognitive and behavioral approaches indicates that many applications appear to use primarily an individual emphasis in a group setting and that the group setting is used for practical reasons (e.g., human resource limitations) rather than for the unique advantages that a group setting has to offer. Research studies testing the efficacy of group for a particular disorder rarely look at process variables. Outcome measures are almost exclusively focused on behavioral measurement of symptom amelioration. Manuals address the tasks and agenda of the group with little effort to provide a healthy group climate in which change can occur. With the notable exceptions of Rose (1977; Rose, Tollman, & Tallant, 1985), Gavin (1987), and Burlingame et al. (2007), cognitive and behavioral group therapists do not articulate the importance of norms, the development of cohesion, the usefulness of interpersonal learning and interaction, and the essential role that the therapist plays in fostering the use of these group resources (Brabender, Fallon, & Smolar, 2004).

All therapists have had groups in which members enthusiastically attend and work on their issues and finally leave when they have achieved some level of improvement. Then, in other groups, members never seem to engage, members drop out, group members only reluctantly work on issues that have brought them into treatment, and most do not accomplish their goals. In addition to individual variables, closer scrutiny often reveals that the groups that work well have reached a level of mature development, and the groups that do not are stuck in the earlier phases of group development. The significant difference between these types of groups is related to the process. The most compelling reason for group therapists to be familiar with group development and process is that over the range of types of groups, from work groups in schools, hospitals, and corporations to traditional group therapies, groups that achieve mature development have greater productivity (Wheelan, Murphy, et al., 1998), and members have better outcomes (e.g., MacKenzie et al., 1987; Tschuschke & MacKenzie, 1989).

Fostering initial opportunities for group members to discovery the commonalities of their experiences encourages individual hope, increases cohesion, and helps group members become more invested in the group. Increased connection to the group decreases group dropout rates, the first major impediment to recovery. Establishing the norm of member-to-member exchange, rather than merely therapist–client communications, even in a skill-based group may be necessary for some patients who struggle with anxiety around interpersonal connection (Tasca et al., 2006).

Many goals are more easily accomplished if the therapist enlists the aid of the group's interpersonal resources. Such summoning allows for vicarious learning, permits natural practice of social skills, and fosters generalization of a newly learned skill when practice is done. It is an important thing for a group to learn when socioemotional activity is necessary even when it does not appear on task. Bales (1950) discovered that even task groups find it necessary periodically to engage in socioemotional activity seemingly unrelated to that task at hand to function well.

Although most who have published on structured groups do not mention development in their efficacy and outcome studies, recognition of the importance of group climate among some cognitive and behavioral therapists who run groups has dawned (Gavin, 1987; Rose, 1977). This awareness takes the form of an acknowledgment of the importance of cohesion (J. G. Beck & Coffey, 2005; Beech & Fordham, 1997; Beech & Hamilton-Giachritsis, 2005), instillation of hope (Beech & Hamilton-Giachritsis, 2005), and open expression of feelings (Beech & Hamilton-Giachritsis, 2005). Despite this greater cognizance of group process, little guidance has been offered for how such process can be tapped.

Understanding group development and applying that knowledge to improve the functioning of group members dictates that therapists alter their interventions depending on the group's developmental stage. For example, knowing when to encourage commonality or individuality rests on the maturity of the group. An examination of two different sessions of a cognitive–behavioral outpatient group whose members all have varying degrees of bulimia nervosa illustrates this point.

> In the first session, members quietly await the therapist's entrance. The therapist begins by clarifying the nature of the group and provides information regarding the frame and rules for participation. All members are then invited to introduce themselves by giving their name and a brief introduction about what has brought them to treatment, which may include a little about their background. During this exercise, the therapist invites others to ask questions. As they make their introductions, the therapist frequently comments on the similarities between members and invites other members to notice them also. For instance, the similarity between the hopelessness implicit in one member's declared suicidality and another member's expression of despair over the never-ending cycle of binge–guilt–purge are noticed and explicitly acknowledged. Commonalities salient to the disorder (such as the wish to be thin, the futility of dieting, the inability to control binging, feelings of guilt and shame, body image distortions), similarities in age of onset, family environment, precipitating events, family and friends' lack of understanding, and life circumstances are underscored. As the exercise continues, each member experiences the sense of being heard and a camaraderie with the other group members based on an impression that others possess important similarities to their own plight. The group ends with instructions on how to keep a food diary for the coming week.

In this group, the task of introducing each member is supplemented with the therapist's modeling of listening and underlining similarities between members and encouraging other members to do also. This is done to highlight the universality of the group members' circumstances and therefore the relevancy of this group for each of its members. In doing so, the group becomes ensconced in an atmosphere of "we're all in the same boat," providing for the possibility of hope and strengthening each group member's connection to the group. Individual differences are not emphasized. Members' participation with each other is encouraged, but in a way that promotes similarities and diminishes differences. We contrast this group with this same group eight sessions later.

> Before the session begins, members are animated, discussing tidbits from their intervening week. They are passing around a fashion magazine and joking about who can wear which outfits. In the initial check-in, members report on their week and give an example from their weekly diary of a binging (or almost binging) incident. The therapist records each on a large flip chart with columns for environmental circumstances that surrounded the event, the dysfunctional thought(s), the emotion that followed, and how that then led to the binging. The first two of the eight members were able to provide a sequence. Tina had trouble formulating her sequence. She identified the binge and the precipitating circumstance. She was attending a wedding of a good friend. Although she was prudent in the number of hors d'oeuvres she ate, her last one was a large fried egg roll that she "slathered in" the sweet duck sauce. During the buffet dinner she went back for three large plates of food, several trips to the dessert station, and then two pieces of cake, after which she slipped into the bathroom and vomited. She recognized that she felt horrible and ashamed but was not able to identify the dysfunctional thoughts that preceded her binge. Janice suggested that perhaps Tina was feeling miserable because she was not married. Janice, now 35 and unmarried, believed that most of her binging would stop if she were able to find a male partner who would marry her.
>
> The therapist expressed appreciation that Janice was able to add to the discussion, but she wondered if Janice had any evidence that marriage was an issue for Tina considering the fact Tina had recently extricated herself from an abusive marriage; had gone back to school; and had expressed interest in being on her own, traveling, and not being tied down. The therapist asked Janice and others to think of a question that might clarify how Tina did feel about attending the wedding. Janice then asked how Tina felt about going to this wedding. Tina was able to explain that she was not interested in getting married or having a long-term commitment at this point but felt the bride and "everyone around" was so much thinner than she was. Tina also thought that she would never be able to resist eating those delicious appetizers and therefore was doomed to being overweight. Tina then realized that these thoughts combined with her belief that eating that last appetizer would mean that she could never lose weight, so why bother to try? This dysfunctional thought led to hopelessness and a binge ensued.
>
> After all members worked on their sequences, members were then asked to summarize their own sequence. Time remained for one member

to work on ways to break the particular associative train. Rita volunteered with the anecdote of her binge after a fight with her sickly mother who wanted her to stay home instead of going out with friends; she offered one solution—to go out regardless of what her mother wanted. Two other members suggested other ways for Rita to break her pattern. Each was discussed, with other members being encouraged to give feedback on this solution in terms of the pros and cons of it working for Rita. Attention was paid to Rita's unique circumstances—her mother's real versus manipulated illness and Rita's dependence on her. In a final go-around, members listed a cognitive distortion that they would be on guard for and its impact on them. The therapist commented on the number of different distortions and how each uniquely affects their behaviors around dieting and binging.

In this group, the therapist attempts to differentiate the antecedents and the cognitive distortions that contribute to binging behavior of each member. Similarity has already been previously established, and additional efforts to accentuate this aspect are not likely to augment members' connections to each other. Members now need to focus more on their individual triggers and the sequences that follow, although types of cognitive distortions and ensuing emotions may overlap. Each member's struggle to formulate his or her personal sequence can vicariously inform others of the struggle and despair in dealing with this disorder, but emphasis on the verbal articulation of these painful aspects is likely to disillusion group members and will not aid in the differentiation process. Differences among them should be noted so that each member can appreciate that he or she alone must accept responsibility for his or her symptoms and for finding the unique resolution for his or her behavior. When group members base their questions on their own particular circumstances (e.g., "I know what you mean because when that happens to me . . . "), rather than common ground, the therapist initially may intervene to articulate the differences between each member's situation. With time and appropriate modeling, the therapist can request other members to help a member differentiate her own circumstances from that of others. As group members become competent in differentiating their own issues from others, the therapist should facilitate members in making these observations, rather than attempting to do all the work him- or herself. The latter is likely to stymie the individual members in learning these skills.

In these two group sessions, awareness of the group stage helps the therapist determine whether to encourage members to see the commonalities or the differences between them. When group members begin a group, isolation is high, and strategies to decrease the isolation should be prominent in the therapist's repertoire. When members already experience an esprit de corps, individuating and learning to accept differences become important tasks for group members if they are to resolve their own difficulties. In the latter stages of a group, having group members actively participate in observing and commenting on others' circumstances allows for practice naturalistically and encourages generalization.

INTEGRATING THE FIVE-STAGE MODEL WITH STRUCTURAL GROUP APPROACHES

The wide array of structural approaches makes it impossible to delineate how each kind of group might infuse group development principles into the group structure. We can give a sampling of what, where, and how strategies might be applied at the different stages of a group to several different types of group structure.

Stage 1: Formation and Engagement

The initial sessions of a structured group are often filled with the therapist's providing information about the nature of the group. Frequently, the therapist lectures to the group with little input from the members. When they do participate, the interchange takes the form of therapist–client–therapist–client (Rose, 1977). Although the initial structure may serve to reduce anxiety for those not originally involved in the exchange, if this is not soon replaced by encouragement from the therapist for client–client interactions, cohesiveness is hindered and interpersonal learning, a valuable resource unique to the group setting, is sacrificed. The next vignette shows how a structured six-session closed-ended stress management group might further develop cohesion and use interpersonal learning.

> In the first session of a stress management group, information about the sessions, including what is to be accomplished in each, is discussed by the therapist. After answering questions, the therapist goes on to provide a model for understanding stress, factors affecting it, and the body's response to it. Participants are then asked to lie on the provided mats and are taken through a guided tense–relax pattern of the 16 muscle groups. At the end, a sheet listing the 16 muscle groups is provided for participants, and they are asked to practice this exercise twice a day over the next week.

We contrast this scenario with that of a group therapist who registers and analyzes information about the stages of development.

> The first session begins with the therapist giving a brief introduction about the group and referring members to the handout that provides the same information and lists a brief summary of each of the sessions. She then asks members to introduce themselves and list one or two things that each finds stressful.
> The therapist adds, "It does not have to be the most stressful circumstance in your life, but one that you happen to think about now. Let's

keep it to 20 words or less, as we have so much to cover. If someone else has already said it, you can add to it as they are talking."

The therapist lists each on a flip chart. As each of the first participants introduces his or her stressful experience, the therapist provides a brief supportive comment. When general overlap occurs, the therapist makes the connection (e.g., "So, like John, you find work really stressful," or "Judy, you, like Martha, also find making dinner with the kids clamoring for attention to be particularly stressful"). If the therapist observes nonverbal agreement, she comments, "I see you nodding—you can relate to this also? Did you want to add anything to what she is saying?" Once all have had a chance to speak, the therapist provides a brief introduction to a theory of stress and possible ways that it can affect one's body, life, and relationships.

After entertaining questions, the therapist asks group members to use their mats, and the therapist goes through each of the different 16 muscle groups, with members first tensing then relaxing each group. They are given paper that lists each group and asked to practice this exercise twice a day. In addition, group members are given several 3-inch × 5-inch cards and asked to write for next time the ways in which they react to stress. They are told that these will be collected in the following session, read aloud anonymously, and organized into clusters of general categories.

In the second group described here, the therapist's lecture component is briefer than in the first, and from the beginning, the therapist engages each group member, assisting participation. Members' active involvement increases a connection to the group and fosters investment. The therapist also highlights commonalities among participants, asking each to add to the others' input. The strategy of encouraging members to provide additional input about a particular stress promotes initial member-to-member interchange and permits members see the immediate relevancy of this group to their problems. Leaders who do not support member-to-member interactions often have groups that develop a less effective mode of operation (Karterud, 1988).

In the initial stages of a group, it is not necessary or even beneficial for members to share their lives or problems in great detail. Affiliations can begin to emerge even with superficial similarities. Some "cocktail talk" is necessary for a deeper relationship to ensue. In fact, some anxious individuals who prematurely disclose what they perceive to be highly personal may experience shame when reflecting back on their contributions in the group, creating the potential for premature termination. The group, unprepared for this level of disclosure, can be nonreactive or can respond in a way that is perceived as unhelpful or derogatory to the person who has disclosed. In groups in which a number of individuals have experienced similar traumas, premature disclosure of specific details of such an event may heighten anxiety, particularly in those members listening who had similar experiences. Thus, it is often necessary to carefully craft what will be revealed in the initial sessions. For example, J. G. Beck and Coffey (2005) worked with groups of participants who met criteria for PTSD after a motor vehicle accident. They found that setting norms for what and how information about each individual's accident was shared was important for the successful management of their PTSD groups. These therapists advocate for greater emphasis on feelings and not on the actual circumstances of the accident. Structured groups are often better at adhering to this recommendation because therapists of such groups are accustomed to being in a didactic role and providing highly specific instructions. Moreover, participants come to expect this kind of guidance rather than feeling constrained by it.

Stage 2: Conflict and Rebellion

As mentioned in chapter 5 of this volume, Stage 2 occurs after the initial enthusiasm for the group has waned. Disappointment with the therapist's offerings coincides with the realization of hard work looming ahead. The less directive the therapist is, the more pronounced this stage is likely to be. Thus, in a structured group in which the therapist has provided considerable direction and patients are actively participating and pursuing their assignments, this stage may take a more muted form. Most cognitive and behavioral therapists apply principles of the individual framework to the group setting so that if the conflicts and issues apparent in this stage do not appear as salient individual symptoms, member dissatisfaction will have little place in the therapy and will continue to be largely ignored in the literature. If the therapist does not heed the budding discontent and address it in some manner, it may lead to premature dropouts and often a nonproductive stalemate in work for some members.

This stage is characterized by the challenge of authority. The group therapist may become aware of its existence when a group member or members question norms and values set by the therapist. It can be manifested in the process of the group session, taking the form of acting out, as when group members are late, do not show up for sessions, do not pay their bill, or do not complete homework assignments. It can take a more passive form in the process as group members do not take much initiative with each other, seem satisfied only when the therapist has given an opinion on their issue, and express disappointment and frustration that they are not getting enough from the therapist. It can also be presented in the content as members express difficulties with bosses, parents, teachers, and others in authority.

Sometimes manifestations of this stage are viewed by the therapist as solely an individual's problem. Rather than recognize the universality of the phenomenon, with the individual as a spokesperson for the group, the therapist perceives the problem as resident in the individual member whose challenges and hostility need to be contained, not explored. Viewed as an individual problem, the individual becomes a scapegoat of the group, a repository for all members' negativity toward authority. Handled in this manner, group members perceive the danger in challenging authority.

The example that follows is the fourth session of a six-member traditional outpatient cognitive–behavioral group designed to work with mildly to moderately depressed individuals. In the first session, patients introduced themselves briefly. The therapist presented an overview of the group, had members complete the Beck Depression Inventory (A. T. Beck & Steer, 1987), and then introduced the method of mood monitoring (for a description of this technique, see White, 2000). Members were asked to rate their day thus far once a day for the next week. A brief introduction of the cognitive–behavioral theory of depression ended the first session. In the second session, members presented their findings, and group members collectively worked with observations of each patient. An activity-monitoring technique was introduced (Persons, 1989). Members were asked to continue monitoring their moods and to complete the activity monitoring for 1 day. The session ended with a review of the theory of depression. In the third session, one member, Joan, did not show up. Members again presented summaries of their mood ratings. Members were asked to make observations about the overall trends for each other. Activity monitoring was discussed and fine-tuned for more or less detail, and members were given the assignment to continue monitoring their moods each day and complete the activity log for 5 of the 7 days. The relationship of mood, activity, and depression was discussed and related to each of their situations. As the fourth session begins, Mary, Patrick, and Donna are present. Joan is again missing, as are John and Nancy. None of the absentees has provided an explanation prior to the group meeting. The therapist has a choice as to how to begin. The first vignette is the more typical.

> The therapist waits approximately 7 minutes, allowing group members to chat and hoping that other members will arrive and that they might begin without interruption. As usual, she begins with an initial go-around in which results of the homework establish the agenda for each member. Patrick has not finished his homework and is questioned about the obstacles to its accomplishment. With only three present, this step is completed in less than 10 minutes, and they begin to work on their agendas. Two members arrive approximately 15 minutes late with apologies for traffic and unexpectedly having to work later than usual. The therapist summarizes the work they are currently addressing. The latecomers report on their homework and establish their agendas. The group continues with work on activity logs and mood monitoring.

Without some attention to the burgeoning resistance to the stated task, the therapist will have difficulty maintaining cohesion and preventing scapegoating. The next vignette presents an alternative the previous scenario.

The therapist begins on time even though there is some question as to whether waiting a few minutes might allow those coming late to join without interruption. Beginning on time sets the expectation and therapeutic frame clearly. The therapist opens with a question: "What are members' thoughts about the missing group members?" Doing so addresses the "elephant in the room," allowing the members who are not present to remain a part of the group and their actions to be understood as originating from individual characteristics and common roots.

Mary expresses fear that Joan, the member missing for two sessions, may not be attending because when Joan said that it took her 2 hours to get to group by public transportation, Mary had offered Joan a ride when she discovered that they only lived a few miles from each other. Mary worries that this may have offended her in some way. Mary reasons that if she had not wanted to accept the ride, she would not have been able to say this directly and would have avoided the situation altogether.

Patrick reports that he could never renege on a commitment and so will see this through for the required 12 sessions but also sometimes feels resistance to coming to group. He reveals that he is somewhat disappointed that he is not getting better more quickly, did not complete his homework, and has been feeling more depressed this week. The therapist questions whether this disappointment has also made it difficult for Patrick to complete his homework—has he been questioning whether it is worth doing? He acknowledges that the exercise seems trivial. Donna says that she imagines that the missing members have gone to the beach; given the loveliness of the day, she wishes that she could join them.

When both latecomers enter, they are apologetic with appropriate explanations; John had to work later than he had anticipated, and Nancy complained of the traffic. The therapist thinks that their lateness could have been avoided with proper planning and prioritization, but she chooses not to articulate these thoughts. The therapist summarizes what Donna, Patrick, and Mary have said and asks for the latecomers' thoughts about their lateness and Joan's absence. John says that he finds himself thinking about other things when members review their homework and feels that it is the least important part of the session. John confesses that when he realized he would be late, he thought he would not miss much. Nancy jokes, "I wish I could have found someone to go to the beach with. Donna let's you and me go next week if the weather is good instead of coming to group!"

The therapist summarizes the disappointment and frustration that the group members are feeling, as expressed by John and Patrick. She acknowledges that feeling better will take work and that at least some members were hoping that the therapist could and would do more to help. She also points out that each has his or her own underlying schema that is activated toward helpers and persons in authority such as herself and that each member reacts differently, such as by taking blame, feeling more depressed, or wanting to replace the group with a more enjoyable activity like going to the beach. She suggests that anticipation of attending group today may even have affected their mood ratings for yesterday and today. She also offers that as they review their homework and set the agenda for the day, they may wish to incorporate what they learned about their own mood and actions as they relate to the activity of attending the group. The group reviews their homework.

Although actual group events are seldom this blatant, there is usually more than one indication that the group is struggling with issues of authority; in this case, frustrations and disappointment toward the leader can be discerned. The manifestations presented here are common for depressed individuals, some of whom also may have a proclivity to act out their disappointments by avoidance or a counterdependent stance (e.g., going to the beach). In the first vignette, not completing homework is seen as an individual resistance, and lateness is taken at face value. In the second vignette, lateness, absence, and incomplete homework are considered part of a group phenomenon expressed by one or more members of the group. Although response to authority may be addressed as a group event in unstructured groups, within a cognitive–behavioral framework, it may be conceptualized as individuals' activated schemas, some of which could be dysfunctional. Appraisal of these events within the here-and-now framework of the group setting is likely to further generalization of the understanding of dysfunctional schemas to real-life situations rather than remain a purely intellectual endeavor.

If the group members already have some familiarity with the Automatic Thought Record,[1] reactions can be listed on this record along with concomitant feelings and actions. At least some group members are likely to see these thoughts as dysfunctional and relate them to other current life situations such as reactions to parents, bosses, and other authority figures.

Depressed patients often are reluctant to acknowledge openly their frustration and anger often resulting in helplessness, passivity, and a worsening of depressed feelings. Although the previous example had individuals more likely to act out than to become passive and depressed, this may not be the case in some groups. Expression of anger and disappointment with authority figures such as the therapist may feel too dangerous for particular groups. Use of a structured exercise at the beginning of group may be helpful in bringing these feelings out in the open (Stockton et al., 1992).

Stage 3: Unity and Intimacy

As described in chapter 5 of this volume, this stage is characterized by increased cohesion, greater disclosure, and the pursuit of more intimate rela-

---

[1]The Automatic Thought Record originated with Aaron T. Beck's therapeutic approach (A. T. Beck, Rush, Shaw, & Emery, 1979). It is a written chart kept by patients, initially taught in the session but often used as part of assigned homework, which identifies the situation and the immediate thoughts, feelings, and behaviors that occur. This document and the ensuing discussions of it during group help patients to identify triggering situations and modify dysfunctional thoughts (White, 2000).

tionships in the group. The dependence on and idealization of the therapist gives way to a more realistic view and use of the therapist's skills. The task of the therapist is to continue to foster member-to-member exchanges and to aid group members in achieving greater levels of disclosure; at the same time, she must help maintain the boundaries and assist members in recognizing that complete disclosure is not necessarily required for a deepened level of intimacy to occur.

This next example features a one-semester, time-limited outpatient group composed of male and female college students who have been diagnosed with social phobia. The 16-session group therapy is based on a model refined by Edwards and Kannan (2006) and uses a combination of systematic desensitization, exposure, psychoeducation, strategies for reducing self-focus, identifying and challenging cognitive distortions, and cognitive restructuring, all tools that have been known to be effective in attenuating social phobia (Edwards & Kannan, 2006). Excessive focusing on negative beliefs about the self heightens self-consciousness, which consumes energy and attention needed for accurate perception and responsiveness to social interchange. The idea is to disrupt excessive self-focusing and allow participants to discover and develop natural and spontaneous styles of interaction.

Sessions 1 through 5 were designed to help participants individually analyze their socially phobic behavior in terms of affected situations, assumptions and beliefs that make the individual vulnerable to phobic behavior, specific anxiety symptoms and the resulting self-focus, and behaviors used to protect the individual and mask the problem. During this early period, two of the six members dropped out. Although initially all group members displayed many overt symptoms of anxiety, said little to each other, and had little eye contact, the remaining members continued to attend, were diligent in completing assignments, and gradually appeared to display less overt anxiety. Cohesiveness increased along with acceptance and mutual support as each recognized the similarities of their difficulties. Beginning with Session 6, group members were encouraged to expose themselves to graded, gradually increasing anxiety-provoking situations (predetermined in prior group sessions) and to attempt to act without the safety of defensive behaviors. This was done with role-plays in the group and with homework between groups. These assignments were structured as experiments in which negative predictions are recorded in group prior to the activity.

The following vignette from Session 8 illustrates Stage 3 phenomena:

> All four members arrived on time. Mary began reporting her experience of giving an oral presentation in class. She had predicted that classmates would be bored during her presentation and not pay attention. She thought they would think she was not very smart. As she went to the front of the class, she dropped her notes because she was physically shaking. A classmate helped her pick them up and said something about ev-

eryone being nervous. Mary acknowledged that she was nervous too. Mary reported that she did make it through the presentation but felt miserable afterward. The therapist encouraged the other members to explore Mary's underlying thoughts. Mary reported that even though she knew the classmate was trying to be supportive, she had some trouble shaking the idea that the girl said that to her because she was so pathetic. She also wished that she had not revealed that she was feeling nervous because revealing it may have highlighted it. It was not like "being here where we all know that we suffer from this disorder."

The leader commented on the difficulty of Mary's task, praised her for completing the assignment, and commented that she seemed uncomfortable disclosing what almost everyone in her situation was feeling even after someone else articulated it for her. She seemed to be struggling with what was an acceptable level of disclosure under the circumstances. Mark commented that he also could not tell what could and could not be said. He felt nervous and exposed. Dinah and Juan agreed.

Dinah was next, reporting on meeting with one of her male classmates for coffee. She reported that it had gone well as far as she was able to tell. She had dropped her safety behaviors of preparing questions so that she would never have to reveal anything about herself and did not move her hands around (to avoid the signs of shaking). Dinah was able to concentrate on what he was talking about and noticed things about his demeanor, such as clearing his throat many times, that suggested that he perhaps was also nervous. However, she could not shake the notion in her head that he was humoring her.

When Dinah explored this preoccupation with the group, she said that there were things about herself that she had not revealed to anyone in the group about her past, but she was sure that if the classmate knew and if the group knew, they would not find her acceptable, despite her newfound skills. Mary and Mark assured her that whatever was in her past would not influence the positive way they felt about her. Yet, Dinah was not persuaded, and she reported that delving into this area made her feel more anxious and alone. The therapist commented that Dinah appeared to regard the group as almost mandating her to reveal all, but no such stipulation from the group was evident. Revealing inner secrets and the pain attached to them required a certain comfort level for both her and the group or with whomever she chose to share.

Mark and Juan chose to attend a school function as their homework assignments. In the next session they reported that they had seen each other in the school cafeteria and decided to go to a party together instead. Mark was able to approach two girls and reported feeling great success, which he attributed to their work in group together. He said that he had kept in mind some of the comments that Mary and Dinah had given him the previous week and thanked the members for their support. Mark said knowing that he would have the group to talk this through helped him be willing to risk rejection. Juan had not been as successful. He picked out a girl he wished to approach but watched from a corner of the room. He observed Mark and other guys "picking up" girls and wondered what he was missing. The meeting outside of group was an aberration from previous behavior, and socializing together had been discouraged from the beginning.

Although the therapist wanted to support their spontaneity and encourage group cohesion, this was an attempt to challenge previously established boundaries. The leader questioned what lead to the change in the previously assigned homework. Juan revealed that having Mark there initially alleviated his anxiety. Yet, when his efforts failed, it made Juan feel even worse. Dinah reminded the men of the rule not to socialize outside of the session. After a little more discussion, the leader set up a role-play in which Mary and Dinah gave Juan feedback on his behavior. The feedback was vague and overwhelmingly positive ("That was great!").

The therapist encouraged them to be specific about what was great and include perhaps one specific thing that might be improved. Juan tried again and the second time, received comments about his casual and confident style. He said, "The group knows me in ways no one else ever will, and I know they just can't say what a loser I am." He reiterated the persistent belief mentioned in previous sessions that had they not known him, they too would pity him.

As is characteristic of this stage, members feel warmly toward each other, bonding around their perceived social failures. They desire to increase their closeness with each other yet manifest anxiety and struggle in relation to levels of appropriate disclosure both inside and outside the group, which is particularly true in a group like this one whose members are suffering with social anxieties. This tension was apparent when Mary spoke of her discomfort in sharing that she was nervous but was most poignantly displayed in Dinah's conflict over revealing inner secrets. Part of Dinah's distorted thinking centers around the blackness she feels about her previous traumas. At this stage of the group's development, it is important for her to learn that she can be accepted and liked by the group and others without having to disclose everything.

Consistent with their mutual positive feelings, feedback to each other is both positive and vague—for example, when Mary and Dinah told Juan his role-play was great. The leader facilitates member-to-member exchange and feedback, rather than giving it herself, to increase member interdependence. However, she does intervene to ensure that the feedback will be specific and constructive. The demand on the therapist of structured therapies is to achieve specificity in feedback, and this element can be used to foster increased connection within the group.

A boundary violation (not uncommon in this phase) occurs when the two male members change their assignments and do their homework together. If the therapist does not acknowledge the violation and attempt to understand its place in their behavior, she too has colluded with them. For many cognitive and behavioral groups, outside connections are permitted. It is likely, however, that boundary violations may occur in some other form for these groups, and the nature of legitimate outside interchanges should be spelled out from the beginning of the group so that violations are apparent and can be addressed.

Stage 4: Integration and Work

In this stage, group members struggle with issues around individuation both in terms of group process and the exploration of their individual issues. The push for the deepening of relationships among the members clashes with fears of intimacy. Successful negotiation of this stage helps participants continue their connectedness despite conflict and disappointment. Members also give and are able to receive specific feedback to and from each other, which enables behavior to change. The therapist must facilitate these processes by encouraging members to deal directly with each other.

An example of Stage 4 phenomena is provided by a closed-ended group of older caretaker adults who have been referred to a time-limited, 14-session, problem-solving group to help them deal with spouses or parents who require full-time caretaking because of medical conditions. Although those referred have not been given a diagnosis, many suffer from mild to moderate depression and have been judged by the medical team to be overwhelmed by the caretaking of their family member. The procedure uses the structured approach of identification and clarification of the problem, generating solutions, evaluation and selection of the solutions and methods of implementation, possible role-playing, and practice assignments (Spivack, Platt, & Shure, 1976). After evaluation and assessment of each individual using the Beck Depression Inventory (A. T. Beck & Steer, 1987), Dysfunctional Attitude Scale (Weissman, 1979), and an interview (Thompson et al., 2000), eight members started with the group. Following initial introductions and psychoeducation about the problem-solving model, members presented their chosen problems. This method enabled two to three problems to be discussed each session. Problems concerned managing the sick family member's needs, integrating other family responsibilities into the caretaking of the sick family member, and the conflict around care of the sick one and the member's individual needs. Initial problems were concretely presented and solved. With time, underlying conflicts concerning anger, guilt, anxiety, and responsibility became more apparent. We review a part of the 11th session:

> The therapist announced that Janice and Monica left messages that they could not attend. Monica indicated that she could not get someone to stay with her husband because the person who had helped her in the past was no longer available, and she was requesting a change in the group's meeting time. Sally jumped in, "I second this as the first problem that the group tackles today. I too have difficulty getting someone to stay with my mother at this particular time."

The therapist agreed that this problem could be the first discussed, but before doing so wanted to check in with those who had discussed their problems last week to see if anyone had tried to implement his or her solution. Martha reported to the group that she had applied the work that she had done the previous week in group and was able to enlist the aid of her sister-in-law to stay with her husband for an afternoon while she got her hair done and then had lunch with an old friend. When she returned, she sensed that her sister-in-law was irritated, and Martha worked hard not to feel guilty, using what she has learned about her own dysfunctional thoughts. She expressed her gratefulness to the group and exclaimed that no one else understood her the way the group did and that she has never known such a wonderful group of caring people.

Chris said that she was unable to attempt the solution because she knew before she left that there really was no solution to her problem, even though the group had tried to provide one. The therapist suggested that time permitting, they could look at the failure in more detail because the group seemed unable to offer her a solution that worked for her. The group began discussing the problem of attendance and time. In identifying the parameters of the problem, most members found the time difficult; spouses and children were more available in the early evening.

Gail asked the group leader if it was possible to change the time because there seemed to be no point in discussing this further if time and date change were not possible. The group leader confirmed her willingness to change the time provided that everyone could be accommodated. Martha, Sally, Gail, and Karen generated a dozen solutions, some involving various time and day alternatives. They also included sharing lists of outside caretaker services and sitters and an alternating schedule of taking turns caring for others' family members.

The therapist noticed that Chris had not contributed and encouraged her, but she declined, saying that others had articulated the solutions. The therapist wondered if the entire problem had been identified. Was the availability of helpers the only problem related to attendance? That is, the group members were making certain assumptions about attendance based on their own positive feelings about the importance of the group. Martha, Sally, Gail, and Karen expressed surprise, reiterated their mutual feelings for each other, their sense of closeness based on their similarities, and their feelings of being helped by the group. The therapist cautioned, "But perhaps not everyone feels as if they have been helped. Chris said that we did not help her last week."

Chris responded, "I knew last week when I left it was not going to work but did not want to dampen your enthusiasm that you found a good solution for me. It would have probably worked for others, but I guess my situation is different."

The therapist remarked, "Perhaps we did not pursue the details of your perspective or explore in-depth your underlying schemas to understand how your struggles deviate from others' struggles even when they appear like the same issues. We can pursue this a little later, but perhaps you can comment on your own feelings about coming to group."

Chris commented that she sometimes felt left out. Others seemed to be so similar, and she felt different and wondered if she could be close to others despite this difference. The therapist then said, "Possibly attendance is part of the outcome of the larger problem for the group to tackle. Can differences among us on everything from concrete problems to more elusive issues of closeness be encouraged and accepted without sacrificing the positive feelings we have about each other and the group?"

Apparent in this vignette is the therapist's empowering group members to take responsibility for a possible time or date change, the domain of the therapist in earlier sessions. This structured problem-solving group has progressed from the earlier solving of individual concrete problems (how to get relatives to help) to becoming more comfortable tackling group issues involving relatedness. With this development also comes a willingness to examine underlying resistances (e.g., dysfunctional thoughts and undergirding schemas). The therapist addresses this resistance when she asks the group if time is the entire problem with attendance, alluding to varying levels of enthusiasm and connectedness among group members. She highlights this conflict by contrasting the four enthusiastic members with Chris, who does not feel helped by the group's work with her. The missing members are possibly in this latter subgroup, but without their presence, the therapist is reluctant to include them in this subgroup. Chris confirms her experience of difference and the question of intimacy with this difference. Attendance is then seen as only a small part of the larger issues of learning to accommodate and embrace differences. This more accepting attitude then allows for further individuation, an accomplishment particularly difficult for this group or any homogeneous group.

Related to this exploration and acceptance of difference is the therapist's encouragement of specificity. In the vignette, the therapist requested that the group revisit the identification of the problem to expand their notion that difficult times and lack of caretakers lead to failed attendance. Later in the vignette, the therapist reformulated Chris's perceived lack of help from the group as a failure to appreciate the way in which her problem may be different in spite of its apparent similarity to others' problems. That is, the underlying dysfunctional thoughts and schemas producing her response may be different and need to be understood in specific detail before any adequate solutions might obtained.

Within the problem-solving framework, Chris's presentation at this stage of the group can either be viewed from an individual or group perspective. Viewed individually, Chris's "yes, but" response to the group suggestions can be seen as a problem requiring more specific exploration. Her characteristic stance can be discussed as a problem in isolation or as an interactional style requiring an understanding of the underlying dysfunctional thoughts and schemas that support this behavior. The task of the therapist is to help her distinguish her problem from other members' problems that may appear similar. Her rejection of the solutions may also be an effort to decrease the closeness that the rest of the group appears to be pushing. Within a developmental framework, Chris's problem may be conceptualized as an individual response or challenge to the task at this stage of group development, which includes how to be connected without sacrificing individuality and ignoring difference. Chris's problem is representative of the group and its struggle to be close but respect individuality, which includes members' varying levels of comfort with both closeness and difference.

Stage 5: Termination

This final stage is demarcated by the visible end of the individual's tenure in the group. The three tasks of this stage are acknowledging and responding to the loss of the group and its members, evaluating what has been learned, and preparing for the future with awareness of what is still left to change. Time-limited structured groups are usually well engineered to deal with certain aspects of the termination process, particularly the latter two tasks. Inherent in the structure of the group are efforts to identify new skills learned, ascertain goals still remaining, and ensure a successful future by encouraging the generalization of skills acquired in the group to life outside the group. What is often not given adequate emphasis is the task of attending to the losses associated with group termination.

The following example illustrates some of the Stage 5 issues. In a 12-session anger management group designed for an outpatient mental health setting, the first 10 sessions help clients understand and identify their anger and aggression; identify the events and cues that trigger anger; develop a personal plan to control their anger, including learning progressive relaxation, cognitive restructuring, assertiveness training, and a model for conflict resolution; and learn how past family interactions around anger affect current behavior and emotion. The final 2 sessions involve review and consolidation of concepts of anger management and strategies learned and skills developed to control their aggression (Reilly, Shopshire, Durazzo, & Campbell, 2002). In preparing for termination, the therapist should note in the earlier sessions those clients for whom the events and cues triggering anger may include loss and abandonment. These individuals may have more difficulty as the group reaches its final sessions.

Within the model, it is predominantly in the last two sessions that we encourage the examination of termination. As an overall plan, we advise exploring loss more vigorously in Session 11, whereas efforts at consolidation and future plans should be the focus of Session 12.

In Session 11, basic concepts of anger management are reviewed and summarized. Homework (monitoring the level of anger on the anger meter on a scale of 1 to 10; identifying events that triggered anger and the physical, behavioral, emotional, and cognitive cues associated with the anger-provoking event) is discussed. Strategies used to avoid reaching 10 on the anger meter are elucidated and reinforced as appropriate. However, references to loss may be indirect at best or otherwise avoided, a characteristic common to both structured and unstructured groups. Individual group members' efforts to elude termination by group prolongation, a feature of many unstructured groups in termination, are likely to be suppressed by adherence to the original contract and specified format of the structured group. Likewise, attempts to avoid dealing with termination by distraction are usually limited because of the structured nature of the group session. What is likely to happen when issues of termination as defined in chapter 5 are introduced by group members is that they are seen as irrelevant to the specified task and so are likely to be ignored by the leader.

How might a therapist attuned to developmental stages and interested in addressing the task of dealing with loss intervene in Session 11? We have two suggestions that would not alter the basic structure of the session yet would allow for the acknowledgment of loss—loss of the former self, loss of the group as a support, and loss of individual members' continuing impact on their lives.

First, we recommend that the therapist draw attention to the process of termination by reminding the participants at the beginning of Session 11 of the time left with a straightforward statement such as, "We have two more sessions together." This simple statement calls attention to the time-limited nature of the group and reminds all that ending is near. The set of responses that follow the therapist's remark, particularly if uncharacteristic of the members may signal a reaction to termination. For example, a member might joke, "and it could not happen any too soon." Although this remark may seem irrelevant to the specific tasks at hand, the therapist's response to these extraneous comments will encourage members to acknowledge their reaction to the termination as a reaction to loss and/or a defense against that loss. In Table 7.1, we present termination dialogue: some examples of member responses, their possible meaning in terms of termination, and suggested therapist responses.

Other members should be encouraged to join or disagree with these reactions. It is important that the therapist remember that termination is met usually with a mixture of reactions within each individual, whether he or she can voice both sides of the ambivalence. Even though only one member may give voice to a reaction, if time were available, most may be able to acknowledge each of the reactions.

Second, during the discussion of their homework, members may include loss events that trigger anger. After the triggers and cues are discussed, a parallel can be drawn between loss as a trigger event and the upcoming loss of the group. This brief vignette is informative.

TABLE 7.1
Termination Dialogue

Group member response	Possible meaning related to termination	Possible therapist response
I am a new man. Not that my "me" was such a bad monster. [*laughs*] My old lady thanks you, and I thank you.	Grieving the loss of the old self, taking stock of behavior past and present.	So you can see all the changes that you have made over these last 11 sessions, and your wife notices also. It feels good. Yet I hear a little wistfulness about the old angry you.
Who cares? It's not like we got nothing else to do with our time.	Devaluation of the group experience, denial of the group's importance.	You feel like you will easily be able to find other things to do when group is over. Do others also have that feeling?
I can hardly believe that it's almost over. I don't know if I can keep the anger under wraps.	Denial of group's ending, fear and anxiety that gains will not be able to be maintained.	It sounds like you feel that you will not be able to keep your anger down without us. How do you feel you will be without the group when it ends?
[*in a joking tone*] Yeah, and it will be a relief to be done with this.	Devaluation of the group's value.	You said "relief." It was tough to get through this group—being confronted each week, having to do homework. Yet you came every time and gave it your all and made lots of changes in reducing your anger. What about that?
Yeah, things got much better after Joe left. He was too angry, and he was not gonna reform. [*group nods in agreement*]	Use of projective identification, a rejection of their angry selves, and a scapegoating of a single member.	Joe did have his difficulties. Does anyone remember they once, too, got that angry? Could that have been any one of us on a really bad day?
Girl, [*referring to another participant*] you changed! You ain't never gonna be that angry again. Don't worry.	Idealization of the new self, denial of the fears of the future.	Ellie, you are right, Gina did do well in controlling how she expresses her anger, and the future is looking good. But I bet we all have some doubts about whether we're gonna be able to keep up the good work.
Is there an advanced anger management group we could join together?	Attempts at prolongation of the group as a way to preempt dealing with termination.	If we had another advanced anger management group we would not have to think about ending our work together and all that it means to each of us. What wouldn't we have to face?

Don has just completed telling the group that his anger meter reached 9, higher than in the previous 3 weeks. The event, a fight between him and his girlfriend, began with his sarcastic comment escalating to her threatening to leave the relationship. He explored the behavioral, physical, and emotional cues leading to the incident and reluctantly acknowledged his sensitivity to being abandoned by her but only in the context of it being so much work to replace her.

Therapist: Loss is really an emotional trigger even if it is only because it makes you mad that you have to put so much work into finding a replacement. It really "got to you" even more this week than in a while, despite the fact that you fight at least twice a week, and it most often ends with her threats, which thus far have been empty. Why did her threat to leave you bother you more this time?

Don: Don't know. Now it seems pretty stupid, but I saw red that I hadn't seen in a while. You know you just get used to something or someone, and it is pain in the butt and too much work to deal with the change.

Therapist: Losing your girl is an inconvenience, but it's also a worry for you. But, perhaps you are facing another change that your conscious mind has not been thinking about but was triggered when your girl threatened to leave. You know the group is ending, and you've done a great job in using it to make big changes in the way you control your anger. Maybe you're thinking that the group is really leaving you too.

Don: [*laughs*] These blockheads? I don't know—maybe.

Therapist: Others have any connections to this for themselves?

At the same time that the therapist may want to remark on these references, the therapist is aware that this is a group of individuals who are acutely sensitive to self-image and particularly reactive to issues that may touch on personal shame. To acknowledge the meaning of a loss may be inconsistent with the self-image of being in control of one's emotions and impervious to past and ongoing losses. Thus, the therapist needs to tread lightly, being careful about the language used. For instance, when Don perceived the loss of his girlfriend in terms of the work required to replace her, the therapist acknowledges where he is by using the word *inconvenience* but then goes on to insert *worry* as well.

As designed, the tasks of the final session include reviewing individual anger control plans; rating the usefulness of the various treatment components; and completing a final exercise that discusses topics such as anger management, how the strategies of individuals' anger control plans aid in controlling anger, what areas of improvement are still needed, and how anger control can be strengthened after the group has ended. Finally, a certificate of completion is awarded on completion. The focus is on what has been learned, what can still be acquired, and how can it be acquired.

To enhance the termination process, we suggest adding a question that focuses on the loss of the group—for example, "As you continue to use your anger control plans, what are the things about this group that have helped you, and what you will miss?" Allowing members to recognize the loss of the former self, the group as a whole, the therapist, and the individual members of the group will be a step in accomplishing this third previously ignored task. A second question to follow might be, "How will you make up for these losses?" These two questions will not alter the form and structure of the session but potentially will allow for the acknowledgment of the loss of the group, its members, and the support it provides.

As a final note, the therapist who conducts a structured group but desires to make use of the importance of the developmental approach will struggle to find the appropriate compromise between completing the tasks of the session and responding to members' indirect and direct anxieties over the loss of the group and its support. To the same extent, however, that the therapist heeds the latter, he or she will do justice to the former.

Integrating Group Development Stages Into the Structured Therapy Model

Traditionally, the more structured models of group therapy have focused primarily on understanding and aiding the client by working with the individual in the group setting. Some have acknowledged the importance of cohesion, and a few have considered other group phenomena. However, at this time, only a small number of writers and researchers have taken group process seriously, even though understanding and cultivating group processes are not in conflict with the focus on individual outcome. In each of the vignettes presented in this chapter, the therapist successfully operates within the structured model but summons stage development theory to augment his or her decisions about when, how, and at what level to address particular individual concerns. With each model and with each group of clients, the stage may manifest slightly differently. Each vignette was specifically chosen because that model of group and type of patient would benefit from the infusion of stage theory with conceptualization of the individual's problem. Our thesis is that all groups, structured or unstructured, must proceed through these stages of development if maximum benefit is to be gained from the group for each member.

We acknowledge that specific models and some types of patients may require technique modification. For example, the social phobia group, which illustrated Stage 3, is likely to have considerable difficulty with Stage 2 because any social interaction causes considerable anxiety. Thus, when dealing with group members who have symptoms of social phobia, the work of Stage 2 may be done primarily by the therapist, who may actively titrate attenuated expression of dissension, conflict, and challenge to authority. In contrast, for bulimia sufferers, the work of Stage 2 and in particular the investigation of the negative feelings that typify this stage are absolutely essential for a good outcome (Castonguay et al., 1998).

HOW STRUCTURED GROUP MODELS CAN AUGMENT GROUP DEVELOPMENT

Those trained in the cognitive and behavioral traditions appreciate the importance of structure, which encourages high levels of specificity in articulating a group therapy model. Were these same therapists willing to regularly integrate the theory of development into their model, we would expect the same level of pith and precision in their presentation. There is good reason and empirical support for the efficacy of this incisiveness, and group therapists trained in an unstructured tradition could benefit from integrating some of this specificity into their technical armamentarium.

For example, high levels of structure can lead to fewer casualties at the initial stage of group, when dropout is most likely (Piper, Debbane, Garant, & Bienvenu, 1979). At the beginning of any group, members experience a certain amount of anxiety. This anxiety, as discussed earlier, is precipitated by not knowing what to expect. It is also instigated by the demand on members to forge interpersonal connections. Lack of participation increases the likelihood of dropout (Oei & Kazmierczak, 1997). Carefully constructed structured exercises, sometimes known as *ice breakers*, reduce this anticipatory anxiety; sanction a certain kind of connection; and, properly positioned, can aid in group development (Evensen & Bednar, 1978; Stockton et al., 1992). Having a repertoire of exercises designed to contain strong affects or evoke and increase awareness of unarticulated feelings may actually further group development and individual growth.

Sometimes, however, the anxiety is overwhelming, as is the case for patients with social phobia. The use of relaxation training and mindfulness, often a part of many structured approaches, can aid in the decrease of overwhelming anxiety, allowing members the energy to begin forming bonds. J. G. Beck and Coffey (2005) worked with patients with PTSD resulting from motor vehicle accidents. Patients driving to sessions were agitated and anxious, but mindfulness training at the beginning of each session helped decrease this intense anxiety.

Most structured models involve the formulation of an agenda for each session specifying what each member will accomplish in the session. Research has shown that agendas change over time (Kivlighan & Jauquet, 1990). With time, goals become more focused on the here and now and more interpersonal rather than intrapsychic. Although instituting articulated agendas may disrupt an unstructured group process, the leader's attention toward the implicit goals of the individual with efforts toward moving these in the direction of the interpersonal here and now is likely to help the progression to a mature phase.

Another contribution structured models can make is that their interventions use a language that is closer to accessible experience than more traditional unstructured models. For instance, we have found that patients are more willing to examine "automatic thoughts" than consider what may be in their "unconscious." Similarly, group development might be better fostered were psychotherapists able to talk where members live emotionally and cognitively. Vague interpretations foster distance from psychotherapeutic process (Yalom, 1995). Descriptions of schemas can be more incisive, closer to consciousness, and easier for group members to accept than some of the psychodynamic interpretations of unconscious conflicts or internalized images that therapists make.

Experience with high levels of specificity in feedback, the hallmark of the more structured models of group, is likely to aid the therapist in helping members formulate specific feedback to others, particularly when there is a tendency among members to provide more global and impressionistic comments in Stages 3 and 4. The shaping of the specificity is determined by the particular model used. For example, in social skills training, specific feedback is modeled initially by the therapist. As the group progresses, after a role-play, members are helped to formulate what went well. After this is exhausted, there is usually one person permitted to indicate what would improve the performance. Over time, members hone their observational skills and learn to give very detailed feedback.

SUMMARY

In this chapter, we have shown that the cognitive, cognitive–behavioral, and behavioral group models involve a higher level of structure in both content and process than do the more unstructured groups on which group development theory and research is based. Structured content does not preclude group development. A structured process may affect development, depending on the degree and type of structure in the sessions. In the research presented, some structure may foster group progression. Structured exercises and procedures at the commencement of group may encourage participation, decrease anxiety, and enhance group development. Structured approaches that can accommodate and encourage member-to-member interactions and cultivate responsibility for the group foster its progression. Vignettes for each of the stages of group development using structured models have been presented, and they have demonstrated that a therapist can adhere to the model and at the same time engage in responses that deal with the tasks required for that stage of development. Group therapists conducting unstructured groups could widen their therapeutic repertoire by learning from the techniques used in structural models to provide specificity and incisiveness to their interventions.

8

POSTMODERN APPROACHES AND GROUP PSYCHOTHERAPY: CLINICAL AND DEVELOPMENTAL IMPLICATIONS

Developmental approaches to group psychotherapy have rested so far on a relatively circumscribed group of theories, including psychodynamic approaches (particularly classical and object relations perspectives) and general systems theory. In this chapter, we focus on recently emerging theoretical perspectives that share common ground associated with these theories. We label these emerging perspectives *postmodern* because they abandon the epistemological assumption of relatively modern times that human beings can know an objectively verifiable reality. These approaches may not only be enriched by a group developmental perspective but they may also have a great deal to contribute to the understanding and practical implications of this perspective. The particular postmodern approaches we present here were selected because they best illustrate this mutually beneficial relationship.

We begin by providing an overview and history of constructivism; social constructionism; and the intersubjective approaches, including narrative methods. Next, we consider how these approaches are congruent with a developmental approach to group process and group psychotherapy and how each provides the developmentally focused clinician with tools for understanding group process and for negotiating the stages of development.

CONSTRUCTIVISM, SOCIAL CONSTRUCTIONISM, AND INTERSUBJECTIVE APPROACHES

Although constructivism has its roots in the postmodern, late-20th-century era, it has significant roots in the writings of Immanuel Kant (1791/ 1969) who posited that human beings are knowing agents whose understanding of the world is sculpted and fashioned by them. The vehicle for such crafting is a universal set of concepts or categories, which he called *categories of the mind*. Kant (unlike Hegel, who held that the mind can know only itself) did not see human knowledge as a detached intellectual product but rather the result of the individual's immersion in the world. Similarly, the epistemological assumption underlying modern constructivism is that all knowledge is constructed in that it involves the active shaping and organizing of the knower (Mahoney & Moes, 1997). In other words, individuals are not passive receptacles capable of achieving pure knowledge about the world uncontaminated by the person as knower.

From a social perspective, constructivism (Gergen, 1994), social constructionism, and intersubjective approaches to treatment associated with these frameworks all rest on an epistemological assumption about how human beings come to know one another, which distinguishes these approaches from earlier schools of thought that were based on Western positivist thinking (i.e., objective knowledge as achievable). In application to therapy, positivism would indicate that the therapist *can* know the client in an objective way. That is, with training and careful attention to potential blocks in the therapist's perception of the client, he or she can achieve accuracy in the understanding of, or the "truth" about, the client. To the extent that the therapist allows his or her own subjectivity to color the perception of the client, the therapist's acumen is deficient.

A somewhat revised perspective still within the positivist framework is the more recent idea that the therapist's subjectivity can be used as a tool (Racker, 1972). This viewpoint holds that the client actively influences the therapist to react as he or she does, and by reflecting on his or her own reactions, the therapist can learn something about the client. Because the therapist's observations are understood as referring back to only the client, this framework can be understood as a one-person psychology (Ogden, 1997).

Constructivism is primarily concerned with the social character of the individual's world (i.e., much of what defines an individual's world are other people). Understanding is achieved in the context of a human interaction (such as the therapy situation) and involves at least two knowing agents. Such understanding is coconstructed: Each person is affected by the other in the views they form of themselves, the other person, and the events that proceed between them but also actively organizes (and in that sense "constructs") those views (Neimeyer, 1993, 1995a).

The recognition of the social aspect of experience necessitates the introduction of another meta-theory related to constructivism—*social constructionism,* or *social constructivism,* as it is sometimes called (Franklin, 1995). Both constructivism and social constructionism share the rejection of the possibility of direct contact with some identifiable objective reality in favor of a view of knowledge as inextricably tied and actively fashioned from one's experience in the social world. Yet, whereas constructivism emphasizes the sculpting role of the individual's cognitive structures in organizing experience, social constructionism explores the individual's relationship to his or her context (e.g., cultural and familiar environment) and the meanings he or she finds in experiences (Franklin, 1995).

Both constructivism and social constructionism are relevant to group psychotherapy. For example, suppose the therapist sees the client's questioning of the therapist's credentials as an act of rebellion against the therapist's authority. From a classical psychodynamic perspective, this interpretation would be seen as having potential accuracy and usefulness to the client. From both constructivist and social constructionist standpoints, although the statement may capture some aspect of the therapist–client interaction, it most likely does not do descriptive justice to its complexity.

The constructivist, focusing on cognitive structures, would explore how the therapist sifted through all of his or her experiences with the client and selected this particular behavior as worthy of speculation about client motives. The constructivist would also take great interest in both the client's and the therapist's language. Using the perspective of George Kelly (1955) on the relationship between language and experience, the constructivist might note the client's use of language that may suggest that the client thinks in dichotomous terms about the therapist—as being qualified or not.

For the social constructionist who focuses more on contextual factors, the client may be seen as rebellious because the therapist has adopted a stance of privilege leading to an expectation that expertise should be assumed by clients. In fact, the acknowledgment that privilege or power alters an individual's perspective is a contribution of social constructionism (O'Leary & Wright, 2005). The client may question the therapist's credentials because the therapist manifested a series of misattunements in relation to the client's experiences. In such a case, the rebellion may be "a valid challenge" rather than a resistance to some alternate awareness (Billow, 2006, p. 274).

Still within this framework, we posit that the client may question the therapist because to do so is typical within his or her culture. It may not be typical of individuals within the therapist's culture, and hence, the therapist may see it as something out of the ordinary and in need of explanation. This examination of how culture or context affects human transactions is another major contribution of social constructionism. From this vantage, none, some, or all of the previously mentioned possibilities concerning the therapist–client interaction may have descriptive and practical value.

As the example suggests, the social constructionist perspective is a two-person psychology in that both parties (in the individual therapy setting, both therapist and client) are recognized as contributing to the understanding each has of the other. Within this perspective, not only the client's but also the therapist's internal life is acknowledged as a significant force in shaping the communications between them.

Although constructivism and social constructionism are broad epistemological frameworks, intersubjectivism refers specifically to modes of treatment that embrace the assumptions of social constructionism. That is, the intersubjective perspective embodies the idea that one's experience is inherently and thoroughly subjective, emerging through the interaction with others' subjectivities (Stolorow, 2002). This participation in another's experience, such as when a patient and therapist ascertain each others' feelings, is what is meant by *intersubjectivity*.[1]

In our discussion of the relationship of the group to constructivism and social constructionism, we first examine how the social constructionist perspective provides an understanding of the relationships between interactions among members and members' development of meaning systems related to their group experiences. However, constructivism becomes important as we look at how members' organizing proclivities change over time as a consequence of being in the group.

A Social Constructionist Approach to Psychotherapy Groups

As Brower (1996) noted, the mediums of group psychotherapy, group developmental concepts, and social constructionism are highly compatible. He wrote,

> small groups can provide an ideal arena for the study of the operations of social constructionism, because a group's development of norms, roles, rules, and beliefs can serve as an analogue to the process that society goes through to develop its own norms, roles, rules, and beliefs. (p. 337)

This idea of the relationship between the group and society may have the familiar ring of interpersonal theory's concept of the group qua microcosm (Yalom, 1995). However, important differences are present, the awareness of which reveals the distinctive contributions of social constructionism. Both interpersonal theory and social constructivism plumb the intricacies and deli-

---

[1]The relationship among these theoretical frameworks is complex and characterized in different ways by different writers. However, many writers regard intersubjectivity as an outgrowth of self psychology, and relational psychology as a development of object relations theory (Stern, 2005).

cacies of perceptions and meanings, yet each in a different way. Within interpersonal theory (Sullivan, 1953), the individual is afforded the opportunity to correct parataxic distortions, perceptions based on past (and probably early) experiences. Parataxic distortions lead to social behaviors that are maladaptive because of their lack of fit with contemporary reality. The notion of distortion locates this concept squarely within an objectivist epistemology wherein perceptions can be more or less on target versus off base vis-à-vis current social realities. For social constructionism, perceptions are creative products. In the absence of an objectively discernible reality, they can be neither true nor false. Yet, they may have certain characteristics that either serve the individual's well-being or beget unhappiness.

Social constructionists see the group as a place where members can explore their perceptions and meanings and those of other members. More specifically, members have the opportunity to achieve a clearer and more explicit awareness of what their perceptions of interpersonal events are and the meanings (or set of meanings, which is defined as a narrative) that they assign to those perceptions. However, within constructionism, meaning is not a product resident in an isolated human mind but rather emerges from the interactions individuals have with one another (Gergen, 1994). In this vein, O'Leary and Wright (2005) stated, "To a large extent, mental life is social life" (pp. 262–263). Group psychotherapy naturally provides a medium in which the social embeddedness of narratives can be understood (Laube, 1998). Through members' explorations of their involvements with the other members of the group, they come to appreciate the contextual basis for the meanings assigned to experiences.

Narrative psychotherapy approaches, methods that center on "the storied nature of human knowledge" (Hoshmand, 2000, p. 382), are particularly important within this framework. For those individuals who have in the past encountered malignant cultural and familial contexts, the supportive environment of the group provides an opportunity for the cocreation of an alternate narrative. Even as members revisit past experiences and see them in relation to current social conversations in the group, the organization of those experiences changes (O'Leary & Wright, 2005). The new narrative gains power as the member articulates it in front of an audience—the other group members (Laube & Trefz, 1994).

The following vignette illustrates this process:

> Blythe disclosed to the group that her adoptive mother frequently deprecated her biological mother for giving her up for adoption. She described her own sense of worthlessness in relation to the realization that she was not of sufficient value to her biological mother to keep and raise. Another member of the group had given up a child because of her inability to care for him. She described her own anguish in taking that step but awareness that to do otherwise would be to serve her own needs at the cost of the child's. As other members talked about difficult decisions in

parenting, Blythe expanded her narrative to encompass other possibilities about her biological mother in a way that bolstered her self-regard.

The group did not seek to correct Blythe's narrative as might have been done within an objectivist-based treatment. Rather, this "rebiographing" (Howard, 1990) aims to enhance the effectiveness of the individual's narrative. This example also highlights one way in which social constructionism departs from interpersonal theory, particularly as it has been explicated by Yalom (1995). Within interpersonal theory, the therapist attempts to move group members from a discussion of past events to a focus on here-and-now phenomena. For the social constructionist, an individual's narrative about the past does dwell in the here and now. Blythe's adoption story is carried into current life events, including her time in the group.

This narrative work not only effects changes in the content of the narratives but also in the individual group member's attitude toward meaning. The member becomes a constructivist who understands that "truth" is one's momentary individual truth. It is not, by necessity, another's truth. Nor is it what will be experienced by the member as the truth in the future across all contexts. The cultivation of this sensibility addresses the disconnections that create unhappiness in relationships. For some members, what is critical to the benefit they derive from group participation is its engendering of openness to other viewpoints and acceptance of differences. In the absence of an attitude that is doctrinaire and judgmental, the individual is more likely both to approach dialogue with curiosity—for others' meaning systems necessarily have worth—and to face his or her own meanings with uncertainty—for all seeming truths are temporary (O'Leary & Wright, 2005; Wright, 2005). For others, a move away from objectivism may be helpful in learning to *privilege* (or value over others) one's own narrative, particularly if the individual has had a history of privileging his or her own narratives less than others.

A Social Constructionist Approach to Group Development

How does group development fit into the social constructionism perspective as a setting in which members can explore their multiconstructed narratives? For the social constructionist, narratives are inherently developmental. The account of group development is itself a narrative developed by a community of group psychotherapists. It is a scheme that many group psychotherapists have found to be helpful in conducting groups. The question of whether group development is real lacks standing with the social constructionist because it assumes an objectivist epistemology. Instead, the social constructionist asks, "Does the idea of group development capture aspects of the therapist's and members' experiences?" and "Are developmental ideas helpful in the therapist's work with the group?"

Social constructionism, on the one hand, does not exact from the group psychotherapist the kind of justification for developmental stages that we provide in chapter 3 of this volume. The fact that this narrative has been developed from the shared experiences of a community of group psychotherapists is sufficient. On the other hand, this perspective discourages the therapist from reifying group developmental concepts. To the extent that in any group at any moment these concepts do justice neither to the therapist's nor members' experiences, the concepts should be put aside in favor of constructs that have greater here-and-now congruence. Social constructionism liberates the therapist from the seeming obligation to impose a collective narrative on his or her individual, unique experiences within a particular context.

Early Group Development and Anomie

Social constructionist writers such as Brower (1989, 1996) and Laube (1998) have not only recognized the compatibility between social constructionist ideas and group developmental approaches but also have sought to invigorate the latter by showing how this lens provides a fresh perspective on developmental phenomena. Their ideas incorporate a constructive emphasis on the cognitive scheme of the group member and the shifts in this scheme that occur across a sequence of interactions with other members. We look at the succession of stages as they would be seen from social constructionist and constructivist frameworks. Our description primarily draws on Brower's work (1989, 1996) but incorporates other contributions from the slim literature on social constructionism, constructivism, and group development.

In the beginning of the group, members are overwhelmed by a sense of anomie as it was proposed by the sociologist Emile Durkheim (1893/1984) and described further by Robert K. Merton (1957) to explain social deviance on a group level. *Anomie* is a state in which a breakdown occurs in societal norms and in which individuals no longer know what to expect of one another. Anomie entails a sense of disconnection between goals and means to achieve them, self and others, and self and environment. Members navigate the situation by accessing their schemas or conceptual frames of group situations. For example, the individual's belief may be that

> new groups are precarious because I don't know at a deep level others' values, wishes, needs, or habitual behaviors. The safest course of action is for me to just play it safe until I figure out what is going on.

Kelly (1955) noted that it is in this circumstance that individuals lack constructs or schemes to understand their current situation that they react with anxiety. According to personal construct theory, anxiety motivates the individual to find ways to make his or her present situation more predictable. For the group member, this effort takes the form of attending to cues. In determining whether any given scheme fits, the member will select from the array of potential cues. For example, the member may notice that one member grimaced while another member was speaking and privately say, "Yes, this group is filled with danger; see how that member is evincing disapproval of another member."

Group Development and Schemas

The schemas of members are likely to differ from one another because these members have had diverse group histories from which they have developed varying sensitivity to different cues in social situations. For example, whereas the previously cited member noticed the grimace, another member might see the therapist nodding her head and construe an opposite meaning—that a behavior had been manifested in the group that elicited approval.

As the group proceeds, the differences in members' schemas become increasingly evident to them. Members wonder which schema is correct. Is the group one in which members are likely to be at odds and find fault with one another? Is it a setting in which expressiveness is likely to be valued and rewarded over self-restraint? Brower (1996) referred to this juncture as constituting a "reality crisis" (p. 338) because members see others' definition of the group situation in opposition to their own. These clashing perceptions create apprehension among members who then seek to determine which perceptual frame is accurate. Brower further noted that members have in place a ready means for resolving the question of which schema is the correct one. They merely do what is often done in any ambiguous circumstance in which an authority figure is present: learn which schema the therapist regards as correct. When the therapist accommodates the group, anxiety abates: Members now have a schema that can regulate their interactions. However, the cost is that they submerge their own power in the group by deferring to the therapist's power.

The importance of the leader's schema to the containment of anxiety motivates members to defend that schema if need be. Cohen and Schermer (2002) pointed out that scapegoating emerges as a means of safeguarding the leader's schema or later in the group whatever schema has achieved dominance. Within their perspective, the schema is a kind of moral order that encompasses the collective conscience and ego of the group. The scapegoat is the one who presents to the group psychological elements at odds with that ideal. By repudiating the targeted member, members can both preserve the moral order and see themselves as acting in accord with it.

Externalization: A Different View

Developmental theorists recognize members' tendencies to use externalization during the early periods of group development (e.g., Agazarian & Peters, 1981). Social constructionism provides a different perspective on externalization by seeing this mechanism as a helpful tool in enabling members to establish distance between their identities and their difficulties (White & Epston, 1990). Hence, the goal of the constructionist would be not to dismantle this tool but rather to accept its emergence and flowering in the group for the developmental benefits of this mechanism to be realized. For example, early in the group, members often will adopt the position, "They [individuals outside the group] don't understand us. They are the problem." The social constructionist would respect the legitimacy of this perspective. In his or her context, the member may experience a lack of understanding that is tied to the person's unhappiness. Additionally, however, the therapist would recognize that by members' placing their difficulties outside the group, they have the freedom to relate to one another bereft of difficulties and thereby begin to craft a set of shared meanings that are not symptom based.

Later Group Development: Tolerating Chaos and Achieving Organization

Even with the benefit of scapegoating and externalization, members rarely find the moral order or schema provided by the leader to be serviceable for any length of time. As experiences accrue, members increasingly appreciate that the schema does not provide a blueprint for members' negotiation of the more intricate circumstances that they encounter. For example, if the schema they adopt on the basis of the therapist's communications is "share your reactions as openly as possible," members soon discover that hefty consequences can result from the candid sharing of reactions. Although many observers of group life have noted that members face a crisis at this juncture, Brower (1989) saw the social constructionist's way of describing the crisis as distinctive. Increasingly, the member doubts the value of the therapist's and other members' schemas and attempts to have his or her own schema shape interactions. Stated otherwise, members undergo a shift from an acceptance of the therapist's power to a realization of their own (Brower, 1989).

Brower (1996) made the point that whereas the earliest stage of group life presents members with a common problem, the dilemma in which members find themselves at this time is less familiar and the solutions more variable. Members may drop out, become disorganized (being present in the group without embracing any schema), or begin to negotiate with one another. The alternative of negotiation has several aspects. First, it entails a lessened commitment to the schema borrowed from the therapist, which was so critical in members' early involvement in the group. Second, it incorporates loyalty to important aspects of one's own schema. Third, it encompasses openness to others' schemas. This openness may activate that experience of anomie that was salient in members' early involvement. Yet, although some schematic fluidity occurs that begets anxiety, members, tethered by their beliefs and values, find it more bearable than they did early in the group. In this way, members learn how to approach the experience of anomie, which can arise outside the group when they encounter a changing or unfamiliar environment with ambiguous norms.

The depiction of group life as a shift from anomie to organization is compatible with the notion of chaos–complexity theory described in chapter 1 of this volume: Complex systems moving through periods of chaos from which organization emerges (Masterpasqua & Perna, 1997). This group work enables members to achieve a tolerance of chaos that is supported by a hopefulness of emerging organization (Brabender, 2000). The circumstance of having a solid access to their own schemas while being receptive to others sets the stage for members' movement into the next stage.

The member's own schema serves as a platform for his or her engagement with others' schemas, particularly elements of others' schemas that are also found in the member's schema. The give and take of comparing one another's schemas leads to a very gradual carving out of a common understanding of what will be the rules and norms of the group. Still later, members recognize the characteristic behaviors of each member, the perception of which results in a shared view of one another's roles.

In this period of group life, members rely on the exchange of feedback to further detail their shared understandings. However, feedback is construed somewhat differently than within an interpersonal approach in several respects. Within interpersonal theory, emphasis is given to the informational value of the feedback for the recipient. In social constructionism, feedback is seen as being at least as revealing about the donor as it is about the recipient (Cohen, 2000). The feedback a member gives tells what that member emphasizes in his or her perceptual world. Further, within interpersonal theory, an advantage of the group format is the multiplicity of observations: This feature enables members to receive feedback that is presumed to have some sturdiness, particularly in areas in which observers agree. In social constructionism, consensual observations are not privileged: All points of view, even those that are unique, are seen as having value (Cohen, 2000; Efran & Fauber, 1995). Within interpersonal theory, feedback is typically regarded as sharing of perceptions and reactions to members' experiences of one another within the here and now. In social constructionism, the past dwells within the present, so reactions to a historical event narrated by the member are also part of the feedback process.

For the social constructionist, the concept of feedback must also be supplemented by concepts that capture the anticipatory nature of the individual's experience in the world (Neimeyer, 1993). One such concept is the notion of a feed-forward system wherein the individual structures how and what information he or she obtains from other members on their perspectives (Adams-Webber, 1989). Within this stage, the individual's ability to obtain information pertinent to the reconstruction of a narrative increases. Consider the following example.

> Kateri shared with the group that her family always saw her as the smart person who is incompetent in negotiating life's practical difficulties. She tended to think of herself the same way. She asked members if their perception of her was similar to that of her family. Members responded that they were impressed with Kateri's ability to help the group proceed through an effective decision-making process when the therapist ap-

proached the group about whether a new member should be brought into the group. Two members, however, noted that they were surprised that Kateri was so able because she often had a confused expression on her face. This information helped Kateri to construct a more complex narrative with broader contextual grounding than that derived from her family experiences.

In this example, what is important is not merely the alteration in the content of the Kateri's narrative but also the change in the characteristics of her feed-forward system (Adams-Webber, 1989) in that she achieved a system that involved weaving different narratives lines. At this mature point of the group's development, members' anomie is drastically reduced; their perceptions of the group are substantially shared; and their orientation is group centered rather than self-centered (Brower, 1996).

Mature Group Development: Building Narratives

For Brower (1996), once the group has achieved maturity and has acquired a set of shared understandings, the social constructionist therapist can most productively use the many techniques particular to this theoretical perspective, techniques that will enable members to use maximally the group's resources in the service of their well-being. Preeminent among these is the use of narratives or stories, which on general level helps members find meaning in and continuity among their experiences. Neimeyer (1995b) wrote,

> The function of client-generated narratives is as varied as the clients' writings themselves, which may historicize their struggles, reach into the past, or project into the future, consolidating a sense of oneself over time and suggesting new choices or life directions. (p. 241)

One function the therapist serves is helping members to learn how to build narratives. The narrative, members are told, involves the positing of an endpoint with a series of actions leading to that endpoint (Gergen & Gergen, 1986). Narratives are inherently integrative in that they involve the three realms of temporal experience: the past or historical context, the present or current circumstance, and the future or anticipated endpoint. Members practice developing narratives by maintaining journals in which they routinely write stories about themselves from three standpoints: their lives outside of the group, themselves within the group, and the group as a whole (Brower, 1996). Within the group, time is then allocated for members to share journal material and to help one another to edit and refine their narratives and to recognize new options for their development. Through this journaling, members pull in a greater array of experiences and their meanings than would be possible otherwise, as in the following example:

> Dottie's interactional style in the group was mild. Her customary response was to identify common ground among members who had staked out different positions. When members would commend her for this service,

she would smile wryly and say, in effect, "If only you knew how I am at home." Her journal entries, shared with the group, were studded with vague references to feelings of annoyance with family members for various misdeeds. However, as her journaling progressed, she described incidents in which she would become verbally abusive when her family members did not live up to her expectations. The sharing of these entries was marked by the expression of feelings of shame. In response, members would disclose the painfulness of disappointments they suffered in their relationships with persons in their lives outside the group. As this process proceeded, Dottie was able to broaden her repertoire of behaviors in the group, clinging less tenaciously to the persona of herself as an unwaveringly supportive helpmate. As she did so, her self-narrative became more consolidated and less fragmented. Furthermore, because she experienced herself as more deeply known by members, she was able to assume a less dismissive and more embracing stance to their contributions.

Role-playing is another tool of social constructionist group psychotherapy. *Role-plays* refers to a set of dramatic techniques designed to expose group members to new ways of being in the world and to emancipate themselves from the behaviors associated with encrusted roles. For example, in the case of Kateri described earlier, the therapist might have Kateri experiment with more confident ways of comporting herself during problem solving to emancipate herself from her tendency to communicate more perplexity and less capability than she possesses.

Social Constructionist Views on Termination

Although Brower (1989, 1996) did not posit a separate termination stage, other social constructions' writings have implications for the last period of group life. The social constructionist view recognizes that termination invites a multiplicity of meanings. According to constructionists Epston and White (1995), termination, when addressed in traditional therapy, has been dominated by a loss metaphor in which the transition is portrayed as a movement from a state of support to one of lonely independence. They noted further that this conception of the isolation of the posttermination state is based on a Western culture privileging of the individual above all other social units. Therapy is complete when the individual is able to be alone. According to Epston and White (1995), this perspective for dealing with loss

> subtly reinforces the dependency of the person seeking assistance on the "expert knowledge" of the therapist . . . this dominant metaphor fails to legitimize the person's own role in freeing himself or herself from the problem-saturated identity that brought him or her to therapy in the first place. (pp. 340–341)

Epston and White's (1995) critique of the traditional view of termination has less applicability to group psychotherapy than it does to individual therapy. The entire point of interpersonally oriented group psychotherapy is to enhance an individual's capacity to have satisfying relationships outside of the group. Termination is typically construed as the acknowledgment of the member's readiness to have successful external relationships. Moreover, inattention to loss would devalue the relationships members have formed with one another. Still, group psychotherapists can learn from Epston and White's social constructionist view of termination as a rite of passage. This metaphor, they argue, facilitates members' transition from a view of themselves as a person beset by psychological difficulties to one who has established distance between the self and his or her problems and, therefore, can define the self in other terms. One potentially useful way the individual can define him- or herself, Epston and White held, is as a consultant possessing knowledge that will benefit him- or herself and others, including members of the group, the therapist, and others outside the group. To assist members in cultivating this aspect of their identity, they encourage the therapist to raise with the departing member questions such as the following:

- When reviewing your problem-solving capabilities, which of these do you think you could depend on most in the future? Would it be helpful to keep your knowledge of these capabilities alive and well? How could this be done?
- Just imagine that I was meeting with a person or family experiencing a problem like you used to have. From what you know, what advice do you think I could give that person or family?

Epston and White's (1995) ideas are likely to be more easily implemented in the open-ended group psychotherapy situation than in individual therapy. Because the psychotherapy group offers in the immediacy of the situation a number of individuals who might benefit from this departing member's consultation, the consultative role is more than hypothetical.

POTENTIAL INTEGRATIONS OF DEVELOPMENTAL THEORY AND SOCIAL CONSTRUCTIONISM

Traditional approaches to group development and social constructionism can enrich one another. At a theoretical level, social constructionism helps the group psychotherapist to recognize that theories are constructions based on shared experiences in the community of group psychotherapists (Schermer, 2006). Like any narrative, a theory is subject to continual revision based on new contexts and experiences (O'Leary & Wright, 2005). This view encourages the group psychotherapist not to be so fettered by specific conceptions of stages that he or she fails to recognize the unique and novel in the psychotherapy group and thereby develop alternate narratives of the group process (Brabender, 2000; Elfant, 1997).

A second overarching theoretical notion is the coconstructed meanings assigned by group psychotherapist and group members. For example, in the initial stage of group development, members' dependency on the group psychotherapist is based not only on transference but also on the therapist's placement of members in an unfamiliar situation. Members' disappointment with the therapist is based in part on the therapist's actual demonstration of inability to meet the members' expectations. The acceptance of the coconstructed aspect of experience and the therapist's explicit acknowledgment of his or her contribution to members' experiences help the therapist to convey attunement with members' reactions.

Yet, misattunements to members' experiences by the therapist are inevitable in group life, and social constructionism argues that an important function of the group psychotherapist is to repair such ruptures. At times, the therapist may have a sense that a misattunement has occurred but be unable to identify its locus. Both traditional developmental theory and social constructionism have different contributions to make to the generation of hypotheses to elucidate misattunements. Traditional developmental theory can aid social constructionism by providing the therapist with some hypotheses concerning potential developmentally based obstacles to attunement. For example, in Stage 1, therapists can succumb to finding members' idealism of them so gratifying that they strive unduly to perpetuate it (Brabender, 1987). Alternatively, therapists may respond to it with a sense of shame-laden unworthiness that compels them to challenge the idealism (e.g., by making blatant mistakes such as calling members by the wrong names). Once therapists recognize these obstacles, social constructionism sees not only their removal as important to the reestablishment of reconnection with members but also in many cases their acknowledgment to members.

Social constructionism helps the traditional therapist appreciate that cultural background can make a difference in understanding moments of disconnection in the therapeutic relationship, as in the example that follows:

> Eloise became silent and withdrawn after the therapist interrupted her. In fact, the therapist believed she was finished speaking but the halting quality of her utterances created ambiguity as to whether she had completed her thought. Nonetheless, the therapist recognized that his own cultural background and family environment created a proneness to behavior that might be experienced by others as rude or even aggressive. He commented to Eloise that he noticed her lack of participation and wondered aloud whether he had cut her off. Eloise said she thought he was giving her a message that she should get to the point more readily.
>
> Having little confidence in her ability to speak incisively, she remained silent. The therapist admitted that he struggled with sensitivity in this area and that this challenge was rooted in his own cultural background. A discussion about conversational norms ensued, with different members sharing the messages they had received from their cultural and fa-

milial backgrounds. This discussion seemed to foster greater sensitivity from the more verbally uninhibited members and less reactivity to interruptions on the part of more inhibited members such as Eloise. In other words, members of the latter subgroup could impute a more varied set of meanings to another's interrupting behavior than the notion that interruptions signify a deficiency in the interrupted party. The developmental and cultural perspectives can be considered in an integrative fashion. For example, Eloise's scheme of the meaning of interruptions may exert itself in a more strenuous way before the group has addressed and resolved conflicts related to authority.

Social constructionism and traditional development theory offer each other technological enrichments. Social construction offers the developmental therapist the tool of narratives. The narrative is particularly suited to developmental work because a narrative can be created to tell the story of the group. As Neimeyer and Stewart (2000) noted, a narrative avoids the reductionism that occurs when therapists work with small units of meaning. Narratives capture the multifaceted and textured aspects of experience. Social constructionists provide the therapist with an array of interventions to help members to develop their narratives.

Social constructionist Real (1990) regarded the therapy session as a conversation in which the therapist participates not by "standing apart and acting *upon* a system but, rather, as positioned in potentially useful ways within the system" (p. 259). Real described five positions or stances that the therapist, in his or her role as "participant-facilitator," can assume. All of these stances can assist members in clarifying and revising narratives. For example, the *eliciting* stance entails the therapist's taking a one-down position in relation to group members and conversing with them in such a way to merely abet them in drawing out their positions. Successively, the therapist seeks clarifications of a member's position, progressively asking for greater specificity, and as that process proceeds, the individual's narrative develops by his or her giving attention to what was considered only minimally previously. As Real noted, this stance is most effective with individuals whose narratives have become petrified over time and, therefore, *nondialogic* (closed to the input of others). This method, which members are likely to experience as more supportive than challenging, might have great usefulness in the earliest stage of group development in which members' assertion of fixed schemas hinders them from hearing or identifying with others. Table 8.1 lists all of the stances identified by Real and indicates when they may have particular developmental usefulness.

Thus far, social constructionists have considered extensively the individual narrative and the individual operating in the circumstance of a dyad. Although a few exceptions exist (e.g., Laube & Trefz's [1994] work on the use of narratives in the group treatment of depression), narratives at the subgroup and group-as-a-whole levels of organization are less commonly used by

TABLE 8.1

Real's (1990) Social Constructionist Stances, Description of Stances, and Group Developmental Uses

Stance	Description	Developmental use	Relevant stages
Eliciting	The therapist queries the member in a way to encourage the member to achieve greater specificity.	Helpful early in development or whenever a member or combinations of members show rigidity in their way of narrating some aspect of their experience.	1, 2
Probing	The therapist provides the member an alternative perspective without conveying that that perspective has greater privilege.	Useful when the developmental demand requires members to tolerate differences in the group.	2, 3, 4
Contextualizing	The therapist shifts the focus away from the internal reactions of the individual to their embeddedness (especially political) in the broader social system.	Enables the undoing of a projective identification that may be unhelpful to both the group and to the individual who is the target of the identification (e.g., removing a group member from the position of scapegoat).	2, 4
Matching	The therapist reflects back to individuals or the system as a whole what has been manifested.	Fosters a group's movement through the early period of any stage in which the psychological elements relevant to that stage are appearing nascently.	1, 2, 3, 4, 5
Amplifying	The therapist facilitates the emergence of an element already in evidence in the system that may serve as a resource in the group's work.	Helpful when one side of a conflict is privileged over the other (e.g., when members can attest to their dependency on the therapist but give only minimal expression to longings to rebel).	1, 2, 3, 4, 5

social constructionists. In fact, O'Leary and Wright (2005) saw social constructionism as providing an antidote to the theoretical neglect of the individual group member and his or her internal functioning in deference to the broader social units. Yet as these same authors admit, social context is important to consider in understanding the individual. Traditional developmental theories provide techniques for helping therapists to illumine those narratives existing at different levels of group organization. For example, Agazarian (1997) described a variety of therapist interventions for facilitating members in recognizing elements of their narratives that are shared, first by helping members to coalesce into subgroups and then by fostering their identification with the positions of members of alternate subgroups. Agazarian's technology could help the social constructionist assist members in seeing opportunities for new narratives. The developmental stages are another means of helping members to expand on narratives. Laube and Trefz (1994) suggested the therapist's explicit use of the concepts of group development and group dynamics would enable members to develop their group narrative in as full a way possible.

AN INTERSUBJECTIVE APPROACH TO GROUP DEVELOPMENT AND GROUP PSYCHOTHERAPY

Recall that intersubjectivism embraces the assumptions of social constructionism and clinically refers to such experiences as when a patient and therapist ascertain and perhaps clarify each other's thoughts and feelings. The focus on intersubjectivity, Stern (2005) held, has permeated a number of contemporary psychoanalytic approaches including self psychology, relational therapy, and social constructionism. Although this section focuses on the intersubjectivist application, much of the material has relevance for the other applications.

Creating an Intersubjective Field in Individual and Group Psychotherapy

According to Stern (2005), one of the leaders in the intersubjectivist movement, the capacity to achieve intersubjectivity is of critical importance to human beings because it enables them to function in groups, and it is through group functioning that problems are solved and survival needs are met. Evidence exists that babies have a core intersubjective capacity or readiness to become involved in another's subjectivity. However, this ability develops over time and is influenced by the various interpersonal contexts in which the person resides. For example, a child who received attunement from important figures in her life is likely to have nurtured both her confidence in the validity of her own subjectivity and her capacity for engaging in others' subjective lives. Conversely, when a child's cognitive–affective states are routinely ignored, misunderstood, or rejected, that child's own sense of self and ability to participate meaningfully in others' subjective lives will be compromised (Stolorow & Atwood, 1992; Stolorow, Brandchaft, & Atwood, 1987).

Within therapy, an intersubjective field is created in which the subjective experiences of patient and therapist are codetermined. Inevitably, the patient's symptoms will emerge out of the subjectivity that the patient brings to the relationship but also the therapist's lapses in grasping, understanding, and affirming the patient's psychological states. For example, the splitting that is often discussed in relation to borderline pathology is seen within an intersubjective perspective as responses to oscillations in the therapist's responsiveness. When the therapist achieves attunement, the patient responds with intense pleasure; failures of attunement lead to extremely negative responses (anger, disillusionment, etc.). When moments of disjunction occur between patient and therapist, both parties are given the opportunity to appreciate the truth (or validity) of the patient's reaction to the therapist and the conscious and unconscious meanings of the event. In this way, disjunctions are repaired enabling the development process, which had been thwarted by these disjunctions, to move forward (Stolorow, 2002; Stolorow et al., 1987). The therapist's and patient's careful attention to and immersion in the microevents occurring within the therapeutic process, particularly the affect associated with those events, enables the self to become more robust, vitalized, and available for full and rich engagement in the intersubjective field.

Group psychotherapy is an intersubjective field that invites the interplay of multiple subjectivities. Within the sessions, the therapist and members can forge relationships in which all participants can grow through the exploration of their codetermined subjectivities. The multiplicities of subjectivities create many occasions for conjunctions and disjunctions, both of which constitute the therapeutic resources of the group work. Intersubjective group psychotherapists create safety in the group by their stance of affirming the subjective reality of each member's experience and by monitoring and responding with empathy to the affect and emerging vulnerabilities in the group, with the latter being defined as "the subjective sense of newness and risk, and in the sense of being exposed and seen; it is the subjective experience of relinquishing habitual patterns of self-protectiveness" (Livingston & Livingston, 2006, p. 74). As group members have the ongoing experience of having their affects and subjective states recognized and understood, they are increasingly able to perform these functions for other members.

Stages Versus Themes in Group Development

Given that the intersubjective approach entails the therapist's full immersion in the moment, to what extent might developmental concepts have usefulness? As Schermer (2005) pointed out, the intersubjectivists do not affirm the existence of group-as-a-whole phenomena but rather see them as constructions of the community of group psychotherapists.[2] Traditional de-

---

[2]To the extent that the observations of group psychotherapy writers are dismissed as being mere constructions, intersubjectivist writers are adopting a nonintersubjectivist view in that they are

velopmental stage theories illumine the functioning of the group as a whole rather than the individual. For the intersubjectivist, the primary focus is the individual and his or her subjectivity. At first blush, then, it would seem that developmental stages have little relevance to an intersubjective perspective. Yet, if the group psychotherapist regards stages not as a set of group dynamics that inexorably unfold over time but rather as a grouping of themes capturing the shared conscious and unconscious aspects of the subjectivities of all members of the group over its history, then a developmental view would be pertinent.

Meanings and Affect States

The intersubjectivist group psychotherapist's knowledge of the common themes that emerge during different periods of group life may enhance the therapist's sensitivity to the affects and vulnerabilities associated with these themes. This sensitivity is especially likely to be enhanced when affects are nascent and vulnerabilities hidden. For example, anxiety that members experience early in their group participation is often masked by an adherence to social protocol. The early manifestations of hostility or disappointment in relation to the therapist are diffuse and mild, often appearing as crankiness or lethargy. Members' fear of the emerging closeness in the group often initially shows itself as remoteness. By the therapist's awareness of the feelings that may reside latently in members' reactions, the therapist can strive to create an environment hospitable to their full flowering. Part of that work may be achieving an understanding of what aspect of the therapist's relating to the group that might hinder members from allowing certain affects to come forth.

Just as developmental theory can help the intersubjectivist attune him- or herself to members' reactions, so too can this theory facilitate intersubjectivists in coming to an appreciation of the meanings associated with affect states. In exploring the complex meanings associated with affects, the intersubjective group psychotherapist might be helped to clarify meanings by thinking developmentally about such situations as the following:

> Enrico walks into the group and says to another member who typically sits adjacent to him, "In the last session, you kept bumping your chair into mine. I didn't want to say anything because the session was under way, but it got annoying. Could you move your chair over so it doesn't happen again?"

Most experienced group psychotherapists will recognize that there may be more to this confrontation than initially evident and see it as worthy of

---

denying the influence of the group members with whom these group psychotherapy authors have interacted as influencing these depictions of group life. Intersubjectives do acknowledge the importance of context (see Miller, 2008). Stages of group development can be seen as an aspect of temporal context.

exploration in the group. Additional meaning may be found if the therapist keeps in mind developmental stages. Suppose, for instance, Enrico's statement was made after the group members partook of a high level of self-disclosure following expressions of hostility toward the therapist. His reaction could be not merely to his neighbor but also to the culture of the group. Enrico may be saying to the group as well as his neighbor, "I do not like the cloying and invasive quality of members' interactions and want my own psychological space."

Like the constructivist, the intersubjectivist would insist that the group psychotherapist's use of theory should never interfere with his or her attendance to what is occurring in the moment. Were developmental thinking to remove the therapist from the moment, to have reduced sensitivity to the individual member's subjectivity, to deliver experience-remote interventions, or to obscure what is unique in the present interaction, then its influence would be more negative than otherwise.

Intersubjectivism and Traditional Stage Approaches

What usefulness might the intersubjective approach have within a more traditional developmental approach? Group developmental writers have given scant attention to the broader contextual aspect of the developmental phenomena commonly observed. The unfolding of developmental stages is seen as residing in the inherent properties of group life. The intersubjective approach calls attention to the cocreated aspect of developmental phenomena (Eig, 2005). The intersubjective lens helps the group psychotherapist to recognize that many of the commonly documented reactions that members show over time can be traced back to the activity of the therapist within the group. The anxieties that members evince early in their participation in the group are a consequence of the therapist's creation of an ambiguous environment in which processes and norms are unfamiliar if not unknown. As the therapist conveys appreciation of the subjective reality of these reactions, members' sense of being understood provides containment of the anxiety and safety. Yet, members' experiences early in the life of the group are cocreated with the therapist, not created by the therapist. The group members' own organizing principles, which include their expectations and apprehensions about group involvement, shape their early group experience. The therapist's responsiveness to members' anxiety may allow a sense of safety that enables members to explore how the current situation triggers expectations and apprehensions that are rooted in what Stolorow et al. (1987) called "developmentally preformed themes" (p. 12). Members' yearning for some direction from the therapist is also highly reasonable given that it is the therapist to whom members have come for relief of their suffering. Furthermore, in the unstructured group, the therapist's lack of directiveness enhances the members' longings for the therapist's provisions.

As the group progresses, the frustration and challenges that can be observed have in part been created by the therapist's continued failure to provide members the direction they seek. In groups in which the therapist is directive, members' subjectivities are less likely to contain frustration, disappointment, and anger. Were the therapist to react negatively to members' challenges, the members' subjective experience would be modified accordingly. As writers on group development have noted, members will differ on how they respond to violated expectations of the therapist. This variation highlights the different organizing principles that members bring to their group interactions, organizing principles that become available for exploration.

Once the therapist's behavior shows acceptance of members' rebellious strivings, intimacy and yearnings for closeness follow. The intensity of members' feelings of triumph and closeness naturally elicits worries of the perils of extreme intimacy, especially from those members who have directly experienced those perils. Each of members' reactions in the session is determined by each member's own organizing principles and the organizing principles of the other members. Here again the notion of feedback is modified from the traditional interpersonal perspective. If Member A provides feedback to Member B, the feedback reflects on both the lived experience and organizing principles of Member A. Although Member B earlier in the group's development may construe the feedback as merely an objective appraisal of his or her person (particularly if other members resonate to Member A's perceptions), Cohen (2000) believed that with the group's development, members increasingly appreciate one another's subjectivities. They recognize that other members' comments and how they behave is a result of those members' world views (in addition to their own behavior). The function of the group psychotherapist is to illumine the multiconstructed character of the intersubjective field, a field that includes members' and therapist's experiences, with the goal of assisting members to participate fully and richly this field.

Thus far, the therapist's activity and authority have been considered to grasp how these realms are instrumental in the creation of the developmental stages. Billow (2003) has described a set of therapist anxieties and emotional states characteristic of each of Bion's basic assumptions and resistances to the analysis of these anxieties and states.[3] How intense the resistance is and how the therapist manifests the resistance is determined by the therapist's present and historical intrapsychic and interpersonal life as well as by the intersubjective pressures placed by the group members. For them, the dismantling of the therapist's resistance sets the stage for the analysis of their

---

[3]Schermer (2006) in a review of Billow's text, *Relational Group Psychotherapy: From Basic Assumptions to Passion*, argued that the postulation of basic assumptions, particularly when they are seen as endemic to group life, is not wholly intersubjective; he also argued that objectivism and intersubjectivity can each provide a useful perspective on group life.

own. Unless the therapist's resistance is overcome, he noted, it leads to therapist–member enactments that produce stagnation, locking the group in the current basic assumption pattern. The therapist must be passionate, he observed, in his or her willingness to grapple with personal resistance in the search for emotional truth. As discussed in chapter 3 of this volume, the basic assumptions are the conceptual ancestors of the developmental stages. Consequently, Billow's insights about what psychological contents are activated in the therapist during the basic assumptions have relevance for the therapist's subjectivity during the developmental stages.

Billow (2003) gave a number of examples of ways therapists, given their personality proclivities, engage with the basic assumptions. For example, operating within a pairing basic assumption culture, the therapist may support members in a turn-taking pattern wherein individual members are targeted as being the patient and are cured by other members playing the role of therapist. In a dependency basic assumption group, the therapist may succumb to members' longings for individual ministrations and provide individual therapy within the group. Billow averred that in some cases, the therapist's disclosure of some part of his or her reaction may be useful; yet, what is always needed is the therapist's analysis of the elements underlying his or her resistance specific to each basic assumption mode.

The Role of Therapist Self-Disclosure

The intersubjectivist, in underscoring the coconstructed aspect of members' group experiences, may provide group developmentalists with an opportunity to work in a way that creates safety and allows for a greater depth of exploration of members' intrapsychic lives than would be so were the group psychotherapist to disavow his or her own subjectivity and its influence. The intersubjectivist point that validation of members' subjective experience, which comes through the acknowledgment that the members' reactions are in part determined by the therapist's activity, fortifies members' commitment to and courage in self-exploration bears further consideration. This notion also invites a revisiting of the psychodynamic therapist's stance on self-disclosure. The therapist's sharing of reactions and associations catalyzes the treatment by affirming members' subjectivities:

> Monica began the session saying that she had felt irritated with the therapist off and on all week because she noticed that the therapist had seemed uninterested while Cecil, a typically reticent group member, was giving a rather lengthy account of an argument he had had with his spouse. The therapist immediately acknowledged to herself that she had been preoccupied by what she experienced as this member's rant against his wife. She asked herself why it might be that the member had behaved in a way to induce her to have this feeling. However, she detected within herself some element of defensiveness and on exploring it further, realized that

some of his criticisms of his wife could also pertain to his reaction to her. She shared this thought with Cecil, and he acknowledged that in prior sessions, the therapist had manifested some of the same tendencies that he disliked in his spouse. His mood appeared to lighten, and he said it was a relief to be able to have a direct discussion about his feelings—something he had not managed to do with his wife.

The content of this session is characteristic of Stage 2 within our approach. At this time, members have achieved comfort with negatively toned feelings, and this comfort would support the members' capacities to assimilate the self-disclosure. Within Stage 1 of our model, this same self-disclosure would likely be more threatening to a member. Consequently, whether and how the therapist's shares his or her subjectivity is always a matter of judgment.

The Role of Enactments

Like the constructivist approach, intersubjectivism provides the traditional psychodynamic group psychotherapist with a set of potentially helpful concepts and tools that can enable the group to continue its development. One means by which members and therapist explore their interacting subjectivities is through investigation of enactments. Wright (2004) indicated that within the relational school, the *enactment* is defined as

> an automatic, unformulated, nonreflective moment involving all participants in the therapeutic interaction. It can be deleterious or beneficial, repeating old traumas or advancing new experiences of growth. It differs from acting out in that it is mainly an interactive concept reflecting what occurs in the relationship between patient(s) and therapist. (p. 239)

The enactment provides a medium par excellence for members to develop new organizing principles for their experiences. Each period of the group's development invites the emergence of a number of enactments. It is through the enactment that the therapist and member can explore the coconstructed aspects of their experience and, thereby, in a more subjectively vibrant and immediate way than would be otherwise possible, grapple with the fulcrum points of development. For example, the enactment that follows occurred between the therapist and a member after the group:

> The therapist had noticed that when members complained about the temperature in the group room, she began to focus on the heat controls. Every few minutes, she would get up and manipulate the dial. After her third effort, Chase said with irritation, "I think it's okay now," and the therapist acknowledged the tone of his communication. He said, "Well, it was annoying how you kept popping up. It seemed excessive, but I felt bad being annoyed with you. You were trying so hard to make us comfortable." The therapist pondered Chase's reaction and realized that she

had been sensing members' growing hostility toward her. Her excessive reaction to the complaint, she recognized, was an effort to stave off hostility, if only temporarily. She revealed to the group that she thought she had been unwittingly appeasing them to avoid the unpleasantness of having the group express anger. She also acknowledged how important it was for members to explore these feelings and speculated that this awareness drove her to placate members in such a clumsy way. Chase went on to talk about his mother's tendency to become extremely sad whenever he would show anger as he was growing up, the guilt he felt in relation to her sadness, and his heightened sensitivity to others' reactions to his negative feelings.

In this instance, the group was facing a set of emotional reactions typical of Stage 2. These reactions could have been dealt with in a variety of ways, such as interpreting derivatives (Brabender & Fallon, 1993) or assisting the group in forming subgroups (Agazarian, 1997). However, what the analysis of the enactment does is to enable members to experience in vivo disconnections and ruptures in a way that is potentially healing and validating of members' subjective reactions. Whether the exploration of enactments provides the group psychotherapist with a more powerful and effective way to enable members to move forward is an empirical question. Given the promising case studies on this tool (e.g., Wright, 2005), it is a question worthy of investigation.

SUMMARY

Group development can occur under a variety of structural conditions. Whether the group psychotherapist allows developmental considerations to inform his or her thinking about the group and behavior in it potentially affects the extent to which developmental phenomena operate in the service of members' treatment goals. This chapter and chapter 7 of this volume form a couplet in showing how group development can be used with a wide range of theoretical approaches. This chapter has focused on postmodern approaches that do not embrace the epistemological assumption of modernity that an external reality is knowable. Rather, these approaches see knowledge as inherently subjective. Both approaches, social constructionism or constructivism and intersubjectivity, entail seeing developmental theory itself as a constructive act rather than a description lying outside of the therapist's perspective. However, even with this reformulation, developmental theory provides the therapist with the potential for heightened awareness of common affects, yearnings, cognitions, and vulnerabilities that are associated with the history of members' relationships with one another. Reciprocally, postmodern psychodynamic perspectives offer a more comprehensive understanding of members' experiences, including their rootedness in the therapist's reactions and activities and the structure the therapist has created. By embracing the codetermination of members' and therapist's subjectivity, the therapist is more favorably situated to respond affirmingly to members' reactions and to repair the inevitable disconnections that inevitably occur when human beings interact.

III

THE FUTURE OF DEVELOPMENTALLY RELEVANT THEORY, RESEARCH, AND PRACTICE

9

CONTEXTUAL VARIABLES
REQUIRING FURTHER EXAMINATION

Although progressive stages can be observed in all types of psychotherapy groups, therapists can observe variability among groups in how long a group spends in each stage; whether a group progresses, remains fixated, or regresses; and how a group exhibits and resolves conflicts and performs the task of each stage. Furthermore, as Elfant (1997) noted, groups appear to possess unique, idiosyncratic ways that are simply not captured by developmental theory. In this chapter, we examine some categories of variables that account for the differences among groups. The group will be understood in terms of its context. By *context*, we mean all of the characteristics that define a particular psychotherapy group and distinguish it from some others. We argue that to the extent the group psychotherapist takes into account these contextual variables, he or she can intervene more effectively.

We include member characteristics, comprehending three categories: identity variables, personality and interpersonal style, and diagnostic variables. Identity variables include gender and status, ethnicity, and age. A discussion of future research on the examination of these variables is provided as well as a model, optimal theory, that holds promise of advancing thinking on group development and identity. Following a presentation of member

225

characteristics is a consideration of time frame. What are the developmental ramifications of the group's having only a brief period of time in which to develop in which to develop versus an extended or even unlimited period? We address the group environment itself: What features of the setting influence a group's movement through the stages? We discuss the effects of preexisting relationships among members, the group's degree of embeddedness in a broader treatment environment, and whether the group is face to face or on line. Finally, we address how the size of the group affects group development.

MEMBER CHARACTERISTICS

Many anecdotal accounts exist concerning how member characteristics relate to the stages of group development. However, because researchers have placed emphasis on the search for a universal pattern of group development, the study of participant characteristics has been fairly minimal. Findings from the small amount of research that has been done, however, suggest that a consideration of composition may be especially helpful in learning more about how individual members engage with the developmental issues at hand. This information is important given that in a psychotherapy group, the therapist's obligation is to ensure that every member derives maximum benefit from group participation. The pool of potential variables that can be investigated in terms of member characteristics is enormous. To give order to the variety, these features can be broadly classified into three categories: identity, interpersonal, and diagnostic variables.

Identity Variables

According to Hays (2007), a person's identity is fashioned from multiple influences. Some of these features are captured in her ADDRESSING framework, which is an acronym corresponding to Age and generation, Developmental and acquired Disabilities, Religion, Ethnicity, Socioeconomic status, Sexual orientation, Indigenous heritage, National origin, and Gender. These variables are by no means comprehensive of all aspects of a person's identity. However, consideration of them usually leads the clinician to expand his or her awareness of the facets of a client's identity beyond what it typically would be. Unfortunately, only a few of them have been subjected to empirical study in terms of their ramifications for stages of development.[1]

Three questions are important in considering member characteristics in relation to group development. First, in isolation and in combination, do these variables affect the course of group development when group members

[1]In Brabender, Fallon, and Smolar's (2004) *Essentials of Group Therapy*, a much more extensive account is given of the applicability of the Hays model to group psychotherapy.

deviate little from one another in their position on a given variable? It is critical that these variables be considered together because a difference between two groups varying on one dimension could be driven by a second dimension that was unexamined. Second, in isolation and in combination, do these variables affect the course of group development when the group is heterogeneous for these variables? The third question looks at group development not as an effect but as a cause. Do the stages of group development create special therapeutic opportunities for individuals with particular identities as defined by these variables?

Gender and Status

The variable receiving the most substantial attention in the empirical literature is gender. As Wheelan (1996a) noted, past research efforts on the distinctiveness of male versus female contributions to the group suggest that group development may be affected by gender composition. For example, Wheelan cited the large number of studies (e.g., Aries, 1976) showing that women are more active than men in performing *maintenance functions*, which are activities that contribute to a safe and positive affective climate. As we have discussed elsewhere in this volume (see chaps. 4 and 5), these aspects of climate are particularly important in the earliest stage of development.

To determine the contribution of gender composition, Verdi and Wheelan (1992) studied developmental patterns in all-male, all-female, and mixed-gender groups conducted in the context of a human relations conference. Using the Group Developmental Observation System, which captures dependency, counterdependency, fight, flight, pairing, and work statements, they found that the patterns were the same for both groups. Although gender was not influential, the size of the group was. In the larger groups (27 participants), flight was more pronounced and work was less intensive as time progressed. Although this finding does not have relevance for most psychotherapy groups, it is pertinent to community meeting groups conducted on inpatient units and partial and day hospitals. As MacKenzie (1994a) noted, a limitation of Verdi and Wheelan's design was that the participants studied went from one group configuration to another. Consequently, they may have been affected by their prior group experiences in the conference.

Wheelan (1996a) pointed out that past studies on gender as it affects group behavior have not taken into account other factors that may covary with gender and account for the variance produced by gender. One variable that is potentially important is status because, she noted, women tend to occupy lower status positions in groups than men. Wheelan conducted a field study in which she compared all-female or female-dominated, all-male or male-dominated, and mixed-sex groups. These groups also varied by status. In a high-status group, the members had titles suggesting positions of authority, the possession of a college degree, or both, features that members of the low-status group lacked. A total of 171 work groups were studied. At the end of one of the work sessions, measures of productivity and effectiveness as well as the Group Development Questionnaire (GDQ; for a description of this instrument, see chap. 3, this volume) were administered.

From this study, Wheelan (1996a) obtained a complex pattern of results. In comparing all-female or female-dominated groups with all-male or male-dominated groups, Wheelan obtained no significant differences, with one exception. The female or female-dominated groups had higher scores on the Dependency and Inclusion scales of the GDQ. To determine whether this difference might be attributable to differential perceptions of status, Wheelan contrasted high- and low-status groups. She found that when groups are of low status, male groups are seen as less dependent and inclusive than female groups. A comparison of the high-status and low-status female and female-dominated groups also showed that in the latter, members were perceived as more dependent and inclusive. In a comparison of the mixed-gender groups, the lower status groups had higher counterdependency and fight scores and lower trust, work, and effectiveness scores than the higher status mixed-gender groups.

Wheelan (1996a) interpreted her findings as suggesting that differences in status lead to differences in perceptions of the group. Generally, higher status groups are perceived as establishing trust more readily, showing a stronger tendency to work, and achieving a higher level of effectiveness. Lower status groups are more inclined to exhibit dependency and to engage in counterdependent and fight behaviors. Wheelan posited that when status is evident, gender does not substantially influence members' perceptions. When status is unclear, members use gender as a factor in determining status.

Wheelan's (1996a) interpretation of her data is consistent with an emerging body of social psychological research and thought pointing to the role of status in mediating gender effects (Lively & Powell, 2006; Martin & Fuller, 2004). Further, research (Huberman, Loch, & Onculer, 2004) shows that across cultures, the desire to obtain status is a powerful motivating factor apart from any gains associated with status such as monetary rewards. However, some research also suggests (Huberman et al., 2004) that culture and gender may affect the intensity by which individuals pursue status. Women may be less disposed to pursue status then men.

The ramifications of gender and status for group development in the context of group psychotherapy have not been considered. Except in cases in which members of a group have been together in a larger treatment context, such as a day hospital, members of psychotherapy groups have little access to external status information compared with the participants in Wheelan's (1996a) study. Her findings suggest, then, that gender composition may influence members' perception of developmentally relevant aspects of the group. Members are likely to have status information concerning the therapist, and this knowledge may have an effect on their perceptions of the group. However, after the group is underway, members acquire progressively more information about one another and also develop internal mechanisms for determining status. For example, individuals who occupy certain emerging leadership roles (see A. P. Beck, 1974) accrue status. The research, then, should address the roles of status and gender as they affect perceptions of developmental processes. Account should be taken for the status of the members and the therapist as well as members' status inside and outside of the group.

Two additional considerations apply related to gender. First, as noted by Ogrodniczuk (2006), the design of future studies should incorporate the recognition that gender is a multifaceted phenomenon. He wrote,

> Such a paradigm should consider the different ways that gender is constructed, including gender role identity (the degree to which a person identifies with socially defined masculine or feminine behaviors), gender role attitudes (the degree to which a person endorses socially defined roles for men and women), and gender role salience (how important gender roles are in a person's life). (p. 459)

Second, extant models offer a descriptive account of group development. Prescriptions are limited to expediting the group through the developmental stages and facilitating the individual members in taking advantage of the growth opportunities within each stage. Schiller (2007), writing within the framework of a relational model of group development, suggested that therapists must be attuned to the possibly unique developmental pathways of women and the implications of this uniqueness for the conduct of women's groups. Her model sees the creation and maintenance of relational ties as of paramount importance in a women's group. In each of the initial stages, members seek to hold their ties as they perform the other tasks of the stage. For instance, when members approach the task of recognizing differences, they attempt to do so while at the same time maintain their ties to one another. Schiller argued that the therapist should work with group development stages prescriptively taking into account the unique trajectory of the members in the group. In the case of women's groups, the therapist must respond to women's need to maintain connection, even when the group is dealing with challenges, by providing increased safety for members and containment of conflict so that it will not destroy connection. Schiller's contention that women's groups have a unique trajectory, based on her own observational data, warrants further study.

Ethnicity

This important aspect of group and individual identity has been the topic of a great deal of multicultural research; however, in the group psychotherapy literature, its treatment has been minimal. A groundbreaking study on ethnicity and group development was conducted by Shechtman and Halevi (2006), who contrasted two of the ethnic groups living in Israel—Jews and Arabs—in their group performance over time in a 14-session group counseling experience. The investigators hypothesized that the social behaviors of the two groups might be different given that the Arabs were drawn from a more collectivist culture and might approach certain common group behaviors such as self-disclosure (particularly with respect to family issues) with more resistance. Across four stages, which were defined by the session number (e.g., Sessions 1 to 3 were considered to be Stage 1), the investigators examined a set of variables. Different types of self-disclosure, such as expression of feelings and disclosures about friends, family, and self, were measured using Jourard's (1979) Self-Disclosure Questionnaire. The investigators used the Client Behavior System (Hill & O'Brien, 1999) to look at an array of group behaviors reflected in the scales: Resistance, Simple Response, Cognitive Exploration, Emotional Exploration, Insight, and Therapeutic Change.

Consistent with developmental theory, the pooled results showed highest resistance in Stage 2 and greatest emotional exploration at the end of the group. However, Arab and Jewish members showed somewhat different patterns with respect to resistance. For the Arab participants, resistance was lower than for Jewish participants in Stage 2, and the latter group showed a steeper decline in resistance in ensuing stages than the former group. For both groups, self-disclosure appeared to increase in linear fashion as the group progressed. However, the Arab members peaked in their disclosures about their families in Stage 1; the Jewish members did so in Stage 3. These findings did not support the investigators' hypothesis that a more collectivist orientation leads to a slower rate or lower level participation in the group, resulting in less efficient passage through the stages of development.

This study demonstrates the importance of exploring ethnicity because it shows that assumptions about how a cultural group may respond in a group setting may not be borne out in practice. Moreover, the Shechtman and Halevi (2006) study, if replicated, would show that variation in ethnic composition may be associated with subtle developmental differences. What is useful about this study is that the investigators generated hypotheses about group behavior based on knowledge of culture. Although their hypotheses were largely disconfirmed, such an approach over time is likely to make a greater contribution to understanding of the role of culture than studies that contrast groups in the absence of a theoretical rationale. This study, however, has a significant methodological weakness. The stages were psychologically arbitrary, established on the basis of session number (objective time) rather than on a study of the group process itself (psychological time).

Future ethnicity and culture studies should not only contrast individuals from different ethnic groups but also examine the developmental consequences of placing individuals from different ethnic groups in the same group. As Jung, Sosik, and Baik (2002) noted, globalization ensures that individuals will frequently find themselves in groups with individuals with diverse backgrounds, but little understanding currently exists for how this type of heterogeneity affects group process. Moreover, research tools must be developed to enable the conduct of cross-cultural group research (Wheelan, Buzaglo, & Tsumura, 1998). Finally, research should be directed toward identifying ways in which cultural diversity within a group can be used to enhance members' growth. As Anderson (2007) noted, group psychotherapists must have the means of ensuring that group processes do not replicate the victimization that some members may have experienced outside of the group.

Age

A small research base is forming of studies that focus on children's groups as they develop over time. Shechtman and Gluk (2005) hypothesized that the differences between the developmental needs of children and adults may be associated with variations in the types of processes that are activated in the psychotherapy group. In an effort to look at how group processes unfold over time, Leichtentritt and Shechtman (1998) contrasted the verbal response modes of boys and girls across three stages of development (developmental stage was defined by session number, as in the study by Shechtman & Halevi, 2006). The investigators studied 101 children between 9 and 12 years of age who were participating in school-based counseling groups conducted over sixteen sessions held during an 8-month period. Their group behaviors were classified using six out of eight categories of the Hill Verbal Response Modes System (Hill, 1986).

The investigators found that gender differences were minimal with one exception: Girls began the group exhibiting a higher level of self-disclosure. Their level of self-disclosure decreased to the boys' level, which remained relatively stable over the three stages. Overall, all types of verbal communications, including self-disclosures, feedback, questions, paraphrases, and statements of encouragement, increased across the stages.

Shechtman (2007b) interpreted the results from this and other studies as suggesting that the developmental stages for children and adolescents are different from those of adults. Specifically, she held that a two-stage sequence characterizes the developmental life of children's groups. The first stage is characterized by a high level of self-disclosure (especially in relation to adult groups) and a readiness to work. A second transitional stage is one in which children and adolescents become more aggressive, verbally and physically. Refusing to participate and engaging in distracting behaviors were relatively common. Over the course of this stage, manifestations of aggression diminish (Shechtman, 2007a). Shechtman (2007b) also noted that the process research on children and adolescent groups lags far behind that on adults; her work represents a substantial beginning.

Future Research on Gender, Status, and Identity

Future research should be directed not only toward variables that have been studied in a preliminary way, such as gender, ethnicity, status, and age, but also toward the variables in Hays's acronym (ADDRESSING) that have been neglected altogether. Studies should explore whether these variables interact in their influence on various aspects of group development and the practical implications of these variables' effects on how the therapist might compose a group and intervene at various points in the group's life. Ideally, models would be developed that would help the group psychotherapist approach areas of diversity that may be unfamiliar. The unfamiliarity could be due either to a shift in the context in which the therapist is working or a societal shift.

Optimal Theory and Stage of Development

An example of a developmental model that deals with the issue of diversity is Haley-Banez and Walden's (1999) application of optimal theory to a psychotherapy group. *Optimal theory* describes a non-Western Afrocentric system (Myers, 1993) that is designed to engender harmony among individuals. Another more specific therapy model has been derived from optimal theory to provide a means by which individuals can achieve a holistic sense of identity, which entails a synthesis of all aspects of one's person including gender, class, culture, and so on. This model is referred to as "optimal theory applied to identity development" (OTAID). The OTAID model postulates a series of stages through which individuals proceed on the road to identity development. The individual begins the identity odyssey as an infant with no awareness of self or sense of separateness from others; proceeds through phases of recognizing differences, constantly asking "Who am I?"; joins with those similar to him- or herself; achieves self-worth on the basis of aspects of the self that are important to him or her; and develops a deeper understanding of self (a depth that allows for a depth of connection with others). Finally, the individual redefines the self in a way that incorporates the individual's history and place in the totality of human experience—both elements boost the individual's capacity for agape and sense of rapport with humankind.

One important distinction that Haley-Banez and Walden (1999) made is between apparent and inapparent diversity. *Apparent diversity* is a set of differences that are evident to members when they enter a group. *Inapparent diversity* is the set of differences that members do not recognize at the outset that may become evident in the course of the group. For example, after 6 months of group psychotherapy, members may learn that Rachel is the great-granddaughter of a Holocaust survivor and that this fact is a key element of her identity. Haley-Banez and Walden's point is that the therapist must attend to both types of diversity. They reasoned that both types are likely to affect the group dynamics that unfold over the life of the group and the exploration of each type in the group will be a valuable opportunity for members to focus on different aspects of their own identity.

Haley-Banez and Walden (1999) interfaced Trotzer's (1989) model of group development (which has a good deal of overlap with stage models of development reviewed in chap. 2, this volume) with OTAID from screening through termination. In the screening process, Haley-Banez and Walden emphasized the need for the therapist's garnering of information concerning the multidimensional aspects of group members' identities, either through questionnaires, interviewing, or other means. The rituals and practices of members are critical to learn about for the therapist to appreciate the client's worldview. The therapist can catalyze the members' work in this area by querying the incoming member on his or her likely reactions to differences between therapist and group member. For example, the therapist might say, "How are you likely to react to having a Muslim therapist given that you have told me you are a Hindu?" This questioning begins to nurture members' reflectiveness about identity and conveys that speaking about aspects of identity is not merely acceptable but valuable.

In the first stage of development, the *security* stage, the therapist both affirms and assuages members' anxieties by acknowledging that on the basis of members' backgrounds and cultures, a sense of safety in the group may come only with lived experience in the group (e.g., "One of the exciting things about this group is the spectrum of different perspectives based on different backgrounds. Over the course of the group, we will have a chance to explore others' perspectives and, in that way, enrich our own."). An exploratory opportunity within this stage is for members to understand how their own and others' worldviews influence their different experiences of safety in early sessions. During the subsequent *acceptance* stage, members approach aspects of their identity that may be connected with problem areas. The optimal theory therapist works to ensure that as members proceed through this process, they include in their investigation the recognition of culture-based aspects of their identity. A tool that is tapped in fostering this recognition is subgrouping. The therapist encourages fluid subgrouping that corresponds to different aspects of members' identities. For example, the therapist may foster subgrouping based on gender, and as this subgrouping leads members to an expanded awareness of this source of identity, the therapist may move to encourage identifications based on ethnicity. It is interesting that Haley-Banez and Walden (1999) did not consider the importance of the authority conflict in member's movement toward self-acceptance.

In the third stage, *responsibility*, the group's deepened knowledge of one another allows the group to begin to approach differences in values and worldviews. The group approaches those views and values in terms of their influence on members' capacities to take responsibility for esteem-related behaviors and attitudes. For example, a group member may learn that her cultural background's emphasis on containment creates a challenge in her quest to communicate her wishes to others more directly. Once the group identifies these worldviews and values, therapists can use the knowledge of culture-behavior connections to intervene in a manner to move members toward their identity and relational goals (Haley-Banez & Walden, 1999).

For instance, an optimal theory therapist might use *blocking*, wherein more dominating members are urged to give way to more reticent members. However, such an intervention, Haley-Banez and Walden (1999) warned, is only likely to be effective once a climate of respect for different worldviews has been established.

The *work* stage is much like the work stage of most developmental models in that members delve into the here and now and provide feedback to one another as they try out new interpersonal behaviors. The therapist uses optimal theory to help members build bridges across their differences. For example, two members who may be experiencing friction because of differences in gender orientation may be facilitated in recognizing their common ground in another area of identity, such as spirituality or ethnicity. The therapist can also use members' different positions on the identity development continuum as a framework for understanding the connections and disconnections that occur. Generally, members who are positioned in proximity to one another on this continuum will relate to one another more readily than individuals who are situated more remotely. Hence, the therapist with knowledge of the person's developmental status may forge connections that are likely to be successful.

In the *closing* stage, the therapist assists members in moving successfully into a multicultural world. The group work prior to this stage presumably has enabled members to have a more expansive view of self, one that embraces many facets of the person's identity. However, continuing work may be needed in helping individuals to cope with the oppression that they may encounter outside the group. Here, the group therapist can tap into other members' experiences of oppression to find different coping methods. Some members may have had minority status in the group along some identity dimension, and these experiences might be explored to see whether they are associated with experiences of oppression. Also, during this ending of the group, the therapist should assist members in respecting that members may terminate from the group in diverse ways based on their backgrounds. For instance, for some members, the approach may be more cognitive; for others, more emotive.

Optimal theory is one conceptual scheme that enables the group psychotherapist to take into account the diversity in the group as the development of the group is fostered. Although empirical efforts have been made to examine various aspects of optimal theory (e.g., Haggins, 1995), such an inquiry has yet to be extended to group psychotherapy applications. Empirical work on whether groups conducted using the principles and methods of optimal theory show a similar developmental course and what effects a group's advancement across the stages have on outcome would be very useful.

As investigators consider types of diversity, attention must be given not simply to the ways in which one type of diversity may mediate another but also the effects of the covariation of different types of diversity. A potentially useful methodology can be seen in the investigation conducted by Homan, van Knippenberg, Van Kleef, and De Dreu (2007) on work groups. These researchers contrasted the group climate and performance of groups in which types of diversity were and were not correlated. For those groups in which diversity in variables that define members such as gender covary, the subgroups in the group are likely to be highly salient, a configuration that the investigators see as a *fault line*, a divide that makes working together as a group difficult. Agazarian (1997) has referred to these types of subgroups as *stereotypic* subgroups, structures that must be dismantled so that members can develop functional subgroups that capture differences vis-à-vis developmental issues in the Homan et al. study. In the Homan et al. study, groups with a fault line[2] (i.e., with salient subgroups) had less satisfaction, relationship conflict, and task conflict than groups without a fault line. They also had a more negative group climate than the no fault line group. However, investigators found that the effects of a fault line can be ameliorated when members are diverse with respect to the information that they bring to the group.

The hypotheses advanced by Homan et al. (2007) should be tested in psychotherapy groups. However, they suggest that when a group is composed of individuals who can easily be organized into distinct subgroups that share two or more characteristics that differentiate them from the other subgroup, the group is going to have greater difficulty achieving the kind of engagement critical to Stage 1 for progression to occur.

Personality and Interactional Styles

Particularly promising in terms of their effects on group development are variables that pertain to individuals' personalities and interactional styles. Such styles constitute the warp and woof of group treatment: Their manifestation in the group and eventual alteration in a more adaptive direction is a key notion in most contemporary approaches to group psychotherapy. These variables reflect the concept of valence as put forth by Bion (1961) to explain why different individuals respond to the basic assumption patterns differently. Stock and Thelen (1958) provided some preliminary empirical support for the validity of the notion of valency for the basic assumption states within the individual.

Recently, the investigation of interpersonal behaviors has centered on Leary's (1957) two-dimensional theory of interpersonal dysfunctioning. According to Leary, individuals who have difficulties with others do so because they occupy extreme positions on the two critical dimensions of affiliation

---

[2]The investigators created a fault line by having gender, seating arrangement, and bogus personality feedback covary. In other words, individuals with the same gender and bogus personality profile would sit together in the group.

and control. *Affiliation* refers to the emotional tone of the individual's connection to others, a tone that exists on a continuum from warm (or nurturing) to cold. Individuals on the cold end of the affiliation continuum perceive coldness on the part of others, respond to the perception with coldness, and elicit the coldness they perceive. The *control* dimension ranges from a high level of submissiveness to others to a high level of dominance over others. Individuals who are at the dominant end of the control condition see others as exhibiting a submissiveness that justifies their engagement in dominant behaviors. Hence, on the affiliation dimension, behaviors match, and on the control dimension, behaviors contrast.

Kivlighan and Angelone (1992) considered the implications of Leary's model for group process. They followed the members of personal growth groups conducted as part of the requirements of a course on group process over the course of 20 sessions. To categorize members according to their interpersonal styles and difficulties, they used the Inventory of Interpersonal Problems (Horowitz, Rosenberg, Baer, Ureño, & Villaseñor, 1988). Individual variation in Leary's (1957) dimensions of Dominance (ranging from *too dominant* to *too nonassertive*) and Affiliation (ranging from *too cold* to *too nurturant*) was examined for its relationship to the group climate, measured by three dimensions (Engaged, Avoidance, Conflict) of the Group Climate Questionnaire (GCQ–S; see MacKenzie, Dies, Coché, Rutan, & Stone, 1987). The GCQ–S also contains an item reflecting degree of anxiety.

Consistent with their hypothesis, the investigators found that dominant members perceive the group at odds with their personal disposition—that is, they see the group as providing a culture of submissiveness. Their attitude is "I need to step in here if anything worthwhile is going to happen." Also consonant with their expectations was the finding that cold members perceive others as cold (or unengaged). However, contrary to the investigators' anticipation, dominant members did not see the other members as anxious or partaking in conflict.

Although these investigators did not look at changes over time, their findings have ramifications for developmental theory in that the aspects of the group climate that the investigators explored relate to the group's developmental status. In the earliest stage of group development, members must achieve a high level of engagement. To the extent that members occupy positions at the low end of the affiliation dimension, this task will be difficult. The therapist's knowledge of this difficulty could enable him or her to plan interventions accordingly or to prepare members for the group in a way that catalyzes engagement processes. Likewise, in Stage 2, members high in dominance are likely to concentrate their efforts in gaining dominion or controlling the other members. If these dominating members have sway, members may have difficulty coming together in their expression of a challenge to the therapist's authority. Again, the therapist's expectation of this dynamic could enable him or her to have at the ready interventions designed to address this dynamic. For example, fostering subgrouping among those who see themselves as powerful can provide the safety to enable them to recognize gradually their own vulnerability, the element they project on the others whom they seek to control.

Kivlighan, Marsh-Angelone, and Angelone (1994) examined how members' interactional styles affected their perceptions of the group over time. Group participants, students enrolled in an elective group process class, rated the therapist on seven dimensions of behavior by completing the Trainer Behavior Scale (Bolman, 1971). Interpersonal styles were again measured by the Inventory of Interpersonal Problems. The investigators obtained evidence that members did project their own interpersonal issues on the group leader. For example, a member who is highly controlling is likely to see the leader as highly controlling. It is interesting that the manifestations of projection changed across the life of the 20-session group: As the group progressed, members projected both affiliation- and control-based contents less.

This finding is consistent with developmental theory in that over time, members are expected to become less preoccupied with the leader, and this diminished focus should enable the members to see the therapist more accurately. The investigators also found that in Sessions 11 through 20, the correlation between members' scores on the affiliation and their perceptions of the leader's degree of affiliation was greater than the correlation between members' scores on the control scale and their perceptions of the leader's degree of control. This is also congruent with developmental theory, which predicts that control concerns exert a greater influence earlier in the life of the group and that affiliation concerns are present in a more constant way. The practical implication of this study is that by knowing the interpersonal style of a group member, the therapist can make some anticipation of when members' areas of concern are likely to surface.

Piper, Ogrodniczuk, Joyce, Weideman, and Rosie (2007) suggested that group psychotherapists should attend to the overall composition in terms of members' quality of object relations in selecting members for a group. *Quality of object relations* refers to the level of maturity that typifies an individual's relationships. Piper et al. found that when the members were homogeneously low with respect to the quality of object relations, outcomes were relatively poor. Lower functioning members' appeared to require the resources of higher functioning members to take advantage of the group.[3] On the other hand, when members were high in the quality of object relations, homogeneity did not appear to work to the group's detriment. This study suggests that quality

---

[3]Pines and Hutchinson (1993) made the important point that the number of lower functioning members a group can accommodate may be low. They suggested that when a group is composed of predominantly neurotic members, one or two borderline members can meaningfully participate. This aspect of heterogeneity, that is, the relative number of members operating at a given level of functioning, is one that should be studied along with the heterogeneity–homogeneity contrast.

of object relations may be an especially promising variable to investigate in terms of its influence on group development.

Studies that look both at interpersonal and personality variables as well as the identity variables described in the prior section have great potential to increase understanding of compositional context. For example, how does a member's degree of personality compatibility with his or her own culture affect group participation?

Diagnostic Variables

In some settings, members are grouped together on the basis of their sharing a set of symptoms or problems. The question that this raises with regard to developmental stage theory is how this homogeneity affects the group's ability to progress through each stage of the group. Yet, little research exists to address this question. A relevant design would be one in which members who are heterogeneous versus homogeneous in terms of their symptom profile and group goals would be contrasted in terms of developmentally relevant perceptions and behaviors. However, the few studies that do exist involve tracking a group that is either homogeneous or heterogeneous for identified problems but not directly contrasting these compositional conditions. Yet, these studies are valuable in providing suggestions as to whether the patterns of group development that have been observed generally with a group of members in a mixed group can be observed with a homogeneous group.

A spate of studies has been done on homogeneous groupings of members with eating disorders. In chapter 7 of this volume, we describe a study (Tasca, Balfour, Ritchie, & Bissada, 2006) that contrasted groups in which members with binge-eating disorders participated either in group psychodynamic interpersonal psychotherapy or group cognitive–behavioral therapy. For our purposes in this chapter, it is important to note that over the course of the 16-session group in Tasca et al.'s (2006) study, individuals in group psychodynamic interpersonal psychotherapy exhibited a GCQ pattern that was partially consistent with the pattern generally observed in the literature in groups that were heterogeneous for type of problem or symptom. On the basis of an analysis of the growth curve for the engaged dimension, the investigators found the following trend: Group level of engagement increased over the initial sessions, reached a plateau in the middle sessions, and then increased again. This trend bears similarity to MacKenzie's (1997) and others' stage models, wherein engagement builds until Stage 2, when members deal with the authority issue, and then increases again after the authority conflict has been resolved. The avoidance scores in Tasca et al.'s study remained flat over the sessions; MacKenzie's model suggests a decline over the life of the group. However, the avoidance scores were very low throughout the group's life, and this may have created a floor effect. Conflict scores declined linearly over the sessions. This finding is in contrast to MacKenzie's model, which predicted that conflict would rise, reach a peak in Stage 2, and then fall again. Whether the departures from the usual developmental pattern are to any extent due to the homogeneous grouping can be determined only through additional research.

In a separate analysis of this same sample, Tasca et al. (2006) found that the behavior of the group members over time was linked to attachment style. Such a finding reveals the importance of examining diagnoses together with the kinds of interpersonal variables discussed in the preceding section.

Another study considering a homogeneous grouping of members involved the study of schizophrenic individuals. Kanas, Stewart, Deri, Ketter, and Haney (1989) examined shifts in GCQ–S ratings over 12 sessions in three psychotherapy groups composed of schizophrenic individuals. The ratings failed to reveal a stage shift. Instead, Kanas et al. observed that engagement scores increased, and conflict and avoidance scores decreased. This finding could be interpreted either as negative evidence for the existence of developmental stages in general or in the context of a diagnostically homogeneous grouping. However, Kanas et al. suggested that the findings also could be specific to this diagnostic: "Perhaps the social skills deficits and poor tolerance for anxiety experienced by many schizophrenics did not allow these groups to progress to later stages over a short period of time" (p. 72). The findings from this study might suggest, as Tschuschke, MacKenzie, Haaser, and Janke (1996) have argued, that therapists should try to include in their groups at least some individuals who have a ready capacity to engage with one another—a resource the Kanas et al. group may have lacked.

In conclusion, then, diagnostic status does have implications for group development. However, as McWilliams (1994) argued, the same diagnostic pattern in two individuals may be undergirded by differences personality processes, conflicts, and other psychological elements that are likely to have significance for group behavior. Therefore, although diagnosis is worth considering, it may not be worth considering independently of personality (predated by the notion of valency proposed by Bion, 1961).

TIME FRAME

Development always implies time because time is the medium in which development occurs. The two concepts are inextricably connected. The pianist who has the opportunity to practice over a period of years is likely to achieve a level of maturity as a musician and a height of virtuosity to which the fledgling piano student can only aspire.

Although it is widely recognized that time is a resource in development, little clarity exists on how much time is needed to complete the developmental tasks associated with each stage. As Wheelan (1997) noted, research on the minimal duration of each of the developmental stages is needed. This information has practical import in that the time frame allocated for a group must be predicated on what minimal time is required for the group to achieve its goals. For example, if a therapist has established for members a goal of learning about and changing their interpersonal styles, the therapist must allow sufficient time for the group to both complete the tasks of Stages 1 to 3 and to do the interpersonal work of Stage 4 during which the most useful feedback is obtained.

Even without this essential information concerning the minimum duration of stages, we can safely claim that some groups complete the work of a given stage much more efficiently than others. The hypothesis, originated in the individual therapy literature (Mann, 1981) and extended to the group psychotherapy literature (e.g., Piper, McCallum, & Azim, 1992), is that just as time can be a resource, it also can be a limit. As Mann (1981) averred, when a limit is articulated, members are confronted continually with the success of their efforts in relation to the remaining time at hand. Members partake in the sensibilities of the pianist for whom the date of an upcoming recital looms: The shortcomings, the imperfections, the departures from the desirable are painfully evident, and the desire to remedy them is acute. As it does for the pianist, the deadline has a motivating effect for psychotherapy participants. The time limit, as Mann also observed, provides an antidote to the denial human beings mount against the awareness of the finitude of all aspects of human experience and, ultimately, of life itself.

If a time limit potentially has a catalyzing effect on group development, given such a limit, what is the minimum number of sessions in which development can be seen? MacKenzie (1997) suggested that his four-stage model (engagement, differentiation, individuation, intimacy) is suitable for application in a group of 3 to 6 months' duration. Some evidence exists that supports his suggestion. MacKenzie's (1983) initial study in which he demonstrated the group climate patterns suggestive of a stage progression took place over 14 sessions. Brossart, Patton, and Wood (1998) studied four groups held in conjunction with a group counseling course over 28 sessions. They generally obtained the patterns associated with MacKenzie and Livesley's (1983) theory of development. Specifically, the group atmosphere, as measured by the GCQ–S, revealed patterns consistent with the emergence of the engagement, differentiation, individual, and intimacy stages. Brossart et al. found that groups were quite variable in terms of the number of sessions that preceded the group's movement into the differentiation stage. However, groups tended to peak in conflict as early as the first 9 sessions and gradually and rapidly entered into a much lower period of conflict characteristic of the intimacy stage. Their alacrity in proceeding through the first two stages of development gave them a protracted period in which to address the tasks of the later stages.

Working in an even narrower time frame, MacKenzie et al. (1987) observed group climate changes in 53 training groups composed of group psychotherapists conducted over a 14-hour period (over 2 days). They found that many of the groups followed the progression predicted by a stage model, and furthermore, those groups that did so most closely had the best outcomes. Unlike in the Brossart et al. (1998) study, however, sufficient information was not gathered to ascertain when stage transitions may have occurred. Both Brossart et al. and MacKenzie et al. were working with group participants who most likely had knowledge of group development. This factor may have contributed to the groups' efficient movement through the stages. Note that in an earlier study by Brabender (1990, as reported in Brabender & Fallon, 1993), the GCQ used on seven inpatient closed-ended groups that met over eight sessions yielded patterns consistent with MacKenzie and Livesley's (1983) model of group development.

Thus far, the evidence suggests that in short-term group situations, groups are able to progress beyond the formative stages as described by most progressive models. This finding is important in that many of the critical therapeutic processes that entail peer-to-peer contact reach their full flowering once the group has dealt with authority issues. To facilitate a group's progression through the stages, the therapist should, if possible, develop a format in which all members begin and end the group at the same time and keep the ending of the group in the forefront of members' awareness.

Even though groups are able to advance developmentally within a short time frame, it cannot be assumed that the group accomplishes the same depth of work as a long-term group in which the group can have a more protracted stay in each stage. Agazarian (1997), by way of example, pointed out how a group's incomplete work in one stage can make their pursuit of the issues of a subsequent stage more difficult. She said that when the group incompletely addresses members' flight tendencies in the earliest stage of development and fails to accomplish the work of modifying the defenses associated with flight, their work in a fight mode (with one another or the therapist) tends to be less effective. The readiness of flight defenses will hinder members from having a full experience of the sensations, feelings, and cognitions associated with an immersion in the stage (or *phase* as Agazarian labeled it) of fight.

Group Environment

Groups are held in diverse treatment settings—outpatient, inpatient, residential treatment center, day hospitals, prisons, and even over the Internet. The question that arises for the group developmentalist is whether these differences in venue create variation in aspects of the group's work in each stage. Two factors may potentially differentiate these groups from one another. The first factor is whether group members knew one another prior to entering the group. In the outpatient group, members are typically strangers to one another. In an inpatient or prison setting, members may have considerable experience with and knowledge of one another before entering the group. Does this prior experience matter developmentally?

The second factor is the extent to which events in the immediate environment outside of the group are likely to enter the group and affect its processes. In the inpatient environment, a group held in the unit is likely to be influenced by events on the unit and the broader unit dynamics (Cohn, 2005; R. H. Klein & Kugel, 1981). For example, if members of the group were to learn at a community meeting prior to a group session that all weekend passes were suspended because of the misdeeds of certain residents, that event, it might be expected, would have an influence on what members discussed in the session and how they related to one another. On the other hand, the outpatient group typically lacks the same kind of immediate dynamic context to which the group is likely to be responsive. Again, is group development influenced by the immediate context of the group?

Preexisting Relationships

The research provides limited help in answering questions about how preexisting relationships affect group therapy. With respect to the presence, absence, or degree of relationship among the group members, the literature can be summoned to address the most extreme possibility—that the existence of prior relationships prevents the emergence of developmental stages. That the existence of prior relationships does not preclude the unfolding of developmental stages is seen in the fact that training groups such as those led by Bennis and Shepard (1956) in which developmental stages were originally observed were composed of individuals who knew each other within the broader work setting.

Still, the fact that developmental stages do emerge is not incompatible with their being influenced by members' prior relationships. In the Brabender (1990, as reported in Brabender & Fallon, 1993) study discussed in the prior section, groups varied considerably in their level of engagement at the end of the first session. This finding has developmental significance in that a key Stage 1 task is for members to engage with one another; members who begin the group at a high level of engagement are positioned to move through Stage 1 more efficiently than a group in which members exhibit low engagement at outset. Perhaps one factor determining early engagement in the Brabender study was the degree to which members knew and accepted one another prior to beginning the group, which was variable across the seven groups. This feature of members' prior relationships should be examined systematically in future studies. For example, members could rate their levels of familiarity with, closeness to, and attraction to one another prior to the beginning of the group to determine the predictive value of these ratings to rate of progress through the developmental stages.

Degree of Embeddedness of the Group

With respect to the embeddedness of the group in an immediate therapeutic context, a research base does exist that demonstrates that the dynamics of the group are influenced by the dynamics of the broader treatment context. A series of studies by Astrachan and colleagues (e.g., Astrachan, Harrow, & Flynn, 1968) demonstrated that elements of the atmosphere of the unit such as its emotional tenor and staff attitudes appear to affect the climate of the psychotherapy group on the unit. Karterud's (1988) research demonstrated a link between aspects of the treatment environment and specific psychotherapy group behaviors such as the group's engagement in here-and-now exchanges. Ghuman and Sarles (1989) demonstrated that when a psychotherapy group was held on an adolescent unit, the themes that emerged reflected the unit concerns; when members were combined from different units, the psychotherapy group's themes appeared to be group driven rather than unit driven.

Although none of these studies examined group development per se, as a set they have implications for group development. If the broader treatment context can affect the themes of the psychotherapy group and the particular behaviors in which members of the group engage, then this influence can potentially foster growth, regression, or fixation. For example, Karterud (1989) studied six inpatient psychotherapy groups, each of which took place on the unit. He found that the group on a unit emphasizing the maintenance of a consistently positive emotional tone among patients and between patients and staff had greater difficulty allowing anger to be expressed in the group than on units in which the emotional tone was more varied on the unit as a whole. Staff members' cultivation of sanguinity over hostility would be likely to support members' engagement with one another in the first stage of development. However, the unit group studies suggest that in Stage 2, when members must approach their differences, they would be stymied.

The practical implication of the unit group relationship is that the group therapist who is conducting a group in a broader treatment context must attend to the dynamics of that context (Karterud & Urnes, 2004). In some cases, the broader dynamics may have detrimental effects on the capacity of the group to progress through the developmental stages. The group psychotherapist might design the group with a consideration of the impediments to promoting a progroup climate and strive to eliminate them (Rice & Rutan, 1981). That is, through the education of the staff, the therapist might contribute to the cultivation of the atmosphere that supports the group and possibly other therapeutic activities taking place on the unit. Because the exchange of information moves from both the unit to the group and the group to the unit, the psychotherapy group itself, as it progresses, is also likely to affect the climate of the unit.

Online Environment

Until recently, the only type of group event that was studied was one in which members could relate to one another in a face-to-face situation. With advances in technology, online groups are becoming more prevalent. Yet, the process implications of formats other than the conventional face-to-face one have yet to be determined (Haug, Sedway, & Kordy, 2008; B. J. Page, 2004). However, the literature suggests that group psychotherapists are beginning to make a foray into this realm. For example, Chang and Yeh (2003) created an online group for Asian American men. The authors acknowledged the importance of culture and gender as well as technology in thinking about the special issues emerging in a group in which these variables intersect. They saw the closed online group (a group in which members are screened in advance) as providing an antidote to the shame and stigma that this population is especially likely to experience in a high-exposure situation.

Like Haley-Banez and Walden's (1999) OTAID group, Chang and Yeh (2003) specifically structured the group to address identity issues. They saw the earliest stage of development as one in which members have the opportunity to begin to explore aspects of their self-representations. The vehicle for this exploration was having members share the bases for the aliases they are asked to develop as part of joining the group. Although aliases are used to preserve members' anonymity, they also provide rich information about members' real and aspirational selves. Members were encouraged to talk about their backgrounds and their reasons for entering the groups. As in any early group, engagement is a key element to members' deriving benefit. Consequently, Chang and Yeh recommended that the therapist individually e-mail members who had not joined the discussion and commend those who had.

What Chang and Yeh (2003) described as the intermediate stage has elements of Stages 2, 3, and 4 in classical stage models constructed in relation to face-to-face groups. Chang and Yeh aimed to deepen members' engagement with identity themes by posing questions related to the areas of race, culture, and masculinity. They reported that members during this period disclosed reactions to such phenomena as cultural stereotypes, racism, and establishing relationships within and outside of their culture. Members' sense of connection to a broad cultural community became a salient theme in part because the achievement of community can be difficult when one's group is not populous. The group explored how community can be understood in ways more abstract than one's locality of operation; it may derive from, for example, a sense of philosophical or political affiliation. The intermediate stage is also the era in group life in which conflict emerges. Conflicts can occur among participants, they acknowledged, and need to be normalized. However, Chang and Yeh's greater emphasis was on the negative feelings members expressed toward external groups that were experienced as oppressive.

The termination stage requires that members be given plenty of warning of its imminence lest a member who is away for a period miss this stage altogether. Chang and Yeh (2003) counseled that the bulletin board format is particularly helpful relative to other formats such as the chat room because the time demands for participation are less specific. Chang and Yeh observed that members attempted to bypass the process by failing to sign in, similar to the rebelliousness common in the termination stage. To lessen this possibility, Chang and Yeh suggested that the therapist might provide a clear date for posting messages, provide a structure members can use in delivering their good-bye messages to one another, and encourage them to continue to check in with the bulletin board contents after the last posting date.

Although Chang and Yeh (2003) spoke of developmental stages, their primary emphasis seemed to be to help practitioners recognize the feasibility of online groups and their particular usefulness in assisting Asian American men to address aspects of their identity. This emphasis led them to provide a number of recommendations for what the therapist can do at various points in the life of the group to enhance its effectiveness. Chang and Yeh did not concentrate their efforts on documenting developmental phenomena or linking their observations to others who write from a group developmental perspective. Given that online groups, already abundant (B. J. Page, 2004), are likely to occupy an increasing portion of the group psychotherapy landscape, the investigations of the processes characterizing them and their developmental differences from face-to-face groups are important. Researchers will need to consider the various formats in which online groups occur, such as synchronous versus asynchronous, open versus closed, and video versus nonvideo based.

SIZE OF THE GROUP

Although we have addressed major variables that define a context, certainly many others exert an influence in their own right on group development and interact with other variables. An example of such a variable is the size of the group, a feature that has been subjected to some empirical scrutiny. Research has demonstrated that group size variability is associated with variability in the perceptions and behaviors of members, and these perceptions and behaviors are pertinent to group development. For example, group size appears to influence the attractiveness a group has for its members, an aspect that is pertinent to the members' engaging with one another in Stage 1. Marshall and Heslin (1975) had undergraduate student groups of 4 versus 16 members reconstruct paragraphs from a set of phrases. The participants expressed a higher level of satisfaction with the smaller group than the larger group. Were members of a psychotherapy group to experience the same kind of satisfaction, in a larger group they might fail to achieve the level of cohesion necessary in the earliest stage of development to move to later stages. Consequently, the general recommendation of groups not having more than 10 members probably is sound.

However, a group should be sufficiently large that the members have confidence in its robustness (Rutan & Stone, 2001). A group that is tiny (3 or 4 members) may seem to members to be at risk for dissolution. Members may fail to move to Stage 2 out of an apprehension over the consequences that might ensue if conflict were to arise. As Pasternak (2005) noted, though, this apprehension can be assuaged if members know that it is in the therapist's long-term plan to add members. For the mature group, having a rich array of perspectives is important for the feedback process (Brabender, 2002).

Although therapists should establish the size of the group with a mindfulness of what number is likely to be optimal to encourage group development, one piece of research suggests that large groups do not preclude development. McLees, Margo, Waterman, and Beeber (1992) used the GCQ over 12 sessions in a community meeting on an inpatient unit attended by 22 to 33 members (staff and patients). The agreement between patient and staff observations of the group climate was very high. Despite the size of the group and the variability in membership, the investigators obtained GCQ patterns that suggested that the group proceeded through the first two stages of the MacKenzie (1997) model from engagement and differentiation on to individuation. McLees et al. suggested that groups are able to advance despite a changing membership because of "culture bearers" (p. 28) who enable the group to retain developmental achievements from one session to the next. In the context of a group relations conference, Wheelan and McKeage (1993) also found evidence for a common developmental pattern in small (8 to 10 participants) and large (31 participants) groups.

SUMMARY AND CONCLUSIONS

In this chapter, we have looked at four categories of contextual factors that may influence the development of any psychotherapy group: member characteristics, time, group context or environment, and group size. Member characteristics include gender and status, ethnicity, age, personality, and interaction styles and diagnoses. Time variables focus on time limits in different group contexts. Contexts, in turn, focus on treatment settings, such as outpatient, inpatient, and computer-mediated groups. Size concerns the optimal number of members in any given context.

Each category of variable has the potential to enable members' engagement in psychological work and to influence the development of stages throughout the group's life. Thus, within any group, the therapist should attend to all these variables from both an individual member and a group-as-a-whole framework.

Throughout this chapter, we have seen that although research on these variables exists, it is insufficient to answer the practical questions the clinician may have. However, by examining extant research, we can better identify what these questions are. In chapter 10, we consider how these and other important questions with regard to group development might be pursued.

10

GROUP DEVELOPMENT: INTEGRATING THEORY, RESEARCH, AND PRACTICE

In this final chapter, we take stock of the status of our knowledge theoretically, empirically, and practically on group development as it unfolds in the psychotherapy group. Woven into this analysis is an identification of the many questions that need to be addressed in future research. Finally, we integrate the information in prior chapters by illustrating how segments of two sessions can be understood more fully by applying not only a developmental perspective but also the theoretical perspectives that can be integrated with development theory, such as constructivist and intersubjective frameworks and cognitive–behavioral therapy. We show how an enriched understanding of the group's developmental work through consideration of subject, setting, and temporal characteristics of the group may aid the therapist in planning interventions.

THE STATE OF KNOWLEDGE OF GROUP DEVELOPMENT

The three realms of exploration of group development—the construction of theory, research on group development, and the extraction of the implications of theory and research for how the therapist conducts the group—interpenetrate. Theories provide the hypotheses that empirical research seeks to assess. Emerging findings must be accounted for in developing new theories or modifying old ones. The implications for practice of both theoretical views and empirical findings must be developed. Successes and difficulties in practice provide fodder for new theoretical and empirical work. The degree of development of each of these realms, which we now consider, will thereby hinder or facilitate advancements in other realms.

Theory Development

Psychodynamic and systems perspectives have contributed richly to theoretical conceptualizations of group development. These frameworks have largely examined development from a group-as-a-whole and subgroup perspectives. The questions of how the group changes globally and how subgroups change have been well addressed in existing models. However, further theory development should be directed toward the achievement of a fuller understanding of the individual's change process given the ways in which he or she organizes and engages with the world. The individual's relationship to the subgroup and to the group as a whole warrants deeper understanding. The theoretical approaches presented in chapters 7 and 8 of this volume hold promise for expanding group developmental models to provide a stronger and more specific understanding of the individual in relation to these larger subsystems and systems.

The constructivist model presented in chapter 8 of this volume emphasizes the importance of recognizing the context from which understanding generated within that context emerges. The developmental approaches described in this book are rooted in a Euro-American worldview. Furthermore, certain theoretical achievements have been made in conjunction with major historical events. For example, Bion's (1959, 1962) work on basic assumption groups occurred during World War II. Certainly Bion's direct exposure to the horrors of war catalyzed his writings on primitive group functioning, and in fact, Bion frequently used the phenomena of war to illustrate his basic assumption groups, especially fight and flight. Yet, a full understanding of how groups evolve requires a consideration of other cultural contexts. Do group scholars from Eastern cultures perceive the conflicts and tasks of each stage in the same way? Would these scholars direct the researcher to collect the same type of data?

Another area of theoretical pursuit concerns those change models that have been proposed over the past few decades to account for the vicissitudes of complex adaptive systems over time other than the progressive stage or life cycle models. Examples of such approaches are punctuated equilibrium, complexity, and adaptive contingency models. Researchers do not yet know to what extent these approaches can be usefully combined with the progressive stage or life cycle models to account more comprehensively for the changes that occur in groups. Is it the case, as Arrow, Poole, Henry, Wheelan, and Moreland (2004) suggested, for example, that with the right set of contextual conditions, a group may jump from one change pattern (e.g., progressive stages) to another (e.g., punctuated equilibrium)? That the integration of such approaches is promising has been suggested by a spate of studies in which the progressive stage model accounted for certain aspects of changes and an alternate model such as complexity theory accounted for others.

Research on Group Psychotherapy

In this section we address what general conclusions can be drawn from extant research, what major questions require further research and attention, and how such investigations should be conducted.

What Researchers Have Learned

Three broad conclusions can be drawn from existing studies. The first is that the progressive stage model accurately describes the process that unfolds in psychotherapy groups. This conclusion is rooted in findings from group climate, therapeutic factor, and leadership studies, all of which were reviewed in chapter 3 of this volume. Evidence is most substantial for an engagement stage in which members build trust and interest in one another; an authority or differentiation stage in which members deal with oppositional feelings toward one another and the therapist; and a stage in which oppositionality diminishes, attachment grows, self-disclosure increases, and members engage in a more intensive feedback process than had occurred previously.

The second conclusion is that developmental progress affects the extent to which members are able to achieve their goals in the group. This evidence was supported by findings from training groups, work groups, and psychotherapy groups. Nonetheless, research is needed to provide more robust support for the association between developmental progress and outcomes. Specific questions beg empirical consideration. Must a group get to a particular developmental stage for the group to reap the benefits of group development? MacKenzie (1997) and Wheelan (1997) averred that the group must progress to the work stage for members to benefit from the group experience. This hypothesis has credibility given that many important processes that are commonly understood as defining group psychotherapy come into play in those stages that follow Stages 1 and 2. At the same time, one may reasonably suppose that Stage 1 opportunities may be significant for members struggling with trust issues and Stage 2 opportunities may be significant for those reactive to authority issues.

The third conclusion is that groups vary in terms of how long it takes a group to complete developmental stages and whether a group progresses, regresses, or becomes fixated. As Wheelan (2005) noted, the fact that stage development has been shown to occur does not establish that it occurs invariably in all circumstances with all populations. As chapter 9 revealed in relation to contextual variables, investigators have yet to research adequately all of the variables that may influence whether and how rapidly a group proceeds through stages.

Questions for Future Research

Past research on group development in psychotherapy groups has been directed in large part toward examining the question of whether group development occurs, especially development understood as a set of progressive stages. Investigators have considered—albeit to a lesser extent—the relationship between group work and members' success in meeting their treatment goals. Although both of these areas could benefit from further study, their pursuit should be accompanied by the investigation of other questions, the answers to which could have implications for how a group is composed and structured and how the therapist intervenes over the course of the group's life.

The developmental implications of group composition are largely unexplored. How the multiple aspects of members' identity, such as gender and ethnicity, collide or complement one another across the developmental stages has been studied in only a handful of investigations. Those studies suggest that researchers must be careful both to recognize ways in which variables that capture the identity of the person may covary and to design studies to determine which variable is responsible for mediating change. Particularly promising are personality and interpersonal variables that affect how members are likely to react to other members and behave in the group. For example, the dimensions of Affiliation and Control associated with Kiesler's (1983) circumplex model (one of a number of models associated with the interpersonal theory proposed by Leary, 1957) have been demonstrated to have a bearing on developmental processes.

Such information on personality–developmental stage connections is useful in at least two ways. First, it may affect the group psychotherapist's decision about how to constitute a group. For example, MacKenzie, Livesley, Coleman, Harper, and Park (1986) found that members of a group designed for individuals with bulimia established an instant cohesion in relation to their eating-related symptoms but avoided other, deeper types of identification. The therapist may strategically introduce different types of symptom heterogeneity (even if only to include other types of eating disorder) to enhance the members' capacity to forge the kinds of deep connections that will facilitate their movement onto later stages. Yet, in many clinical situations, the group psychotherapist has limited control over composition. A second way such information could be used is in the planning of interventions at various points in the life of the group. In the case of the group of eating-disordered individuals, the therapist may intervene to facilitate members in differentiating themselves from one another (e.g., "Shelita and Anastasia are both talking about anger, but Shelita's emphasis is different in that . . . "). Ultimately, patterns of members' characteristics and types of interventions must be linked with outcomes.

Another potentially important area of investigation is the preparation of members to participate in a developmental experience. As Wheelan (1997) noted, members' prior exposure to developmental concepts may facilitate their participating in an exploratory group. Among the ideas that members may usefully assimilate are the notions that times in the life of the group may be fraught with pain, may contrast greatly with earlier periods, and may be experienced as confusing and chaotic (Brabender, 2000). The benefit of cultivating such ideas is that doing so inoculates the individual against the intensity of disappointment that might lead him or her to leave the group. Preparation might stimulate members' curiosity about changes, a curiosity that will allow elements to emerge with sufficient prominence that they can exert influence on the overall group dynamic. One concern that may arise in relation to such developmental preparation is that it could deprive members of the emotional immediacy of experiencing the developmental issues from a fresh and innocent perspective. However, even if training alters a member's perspective (after all, that is its purpose), it is unlikely to do so in a way that precludes members' intensively experiencing the unfolding of the stages. Evidence for members' capacity to participate in the stages even with knowledge of them appears in the set of studies that have been done on experiential groups, composed largely of group psychotherapists (e.g., MacKenzie, Dies, Coché, Rutan, & Stone, 1987). Although it is unlikely that most members go into these group experiences without any prior knowledge of group therapy, experiential or training groups yield evidence of the existence of the developmental stages.

Methodological Issues

For group developmental research to provide more comprehensive descriptions of how a psychotherapy group matures, the following methodological points must be taken into consideration in designing studies: (a) the need to comparatively assess models, (b) the conduct of multisite studies, (c) the use of common measures across studies, (d) selection of an appropriate unit of analysis, and (e) a strategic selection of a point of view.

Comparative Assessment of Models. Although research studies exist showing that developmental stage concepts have some descriptive value for the changes over time that occur in psychotherapy groups, researchers have given scant attention to whether a progressive developmental stage model provides a better description of changes than alternate models. Studies should be conducted in which investigators make alternate predictions of change patterns based on competing models. Such studies occur much more commonly with work groups in an organizational psychology context. Fortunately, these studies can provide the group psychotherapy researcher with methodological strategies to compare competing models.

An example of such a methodology is that used by Arrow (1997), who tested the predictions of three models of group change—robust equilibrium, punctuated equilibrium (see chap. 2, this volume), and adaptive contingency—concerning the continuity of and change in structural patterns over 13 weeks. The robust equilibrium model predicts a brief period of instability followed by a steady state. The punctuated equilibrium model predicts an initial steady state that would remain until major external or internal events precipitate the emergence of a new structure. The adaptive contingency model predicts that changes will occur on the basis of external and internal contingencies.

Arrow (1997) identified structural patterns by having all members rate other members and themselves in terms of influence on decision making in the group. Unfortunately, her data did not permit a comparison of these models with the model that has been emphasized most in this text, the progressive stage model. Arrow also looked at two different formats of groups—face to face and computer mediated. She found that whereas the punctuated equilibrium model best described the face-to-face group, the robust equilibrium model accounted most precisely for changes in a computer-mediated group. She hypothesized that in the face-to-face group, members may have had a greater wealth of cues by which to develop an initial schema compared with participants in the computer-mediated group.

Arrow's (1997) methodology and findings yielded information that would enable group psychotherapists to learn whether different group formats (in her study, face-to-face vs. computer-mediated groups) launch different types of change processes. Her use of a computer-mediated format is especially noteworthy given the burgeoning literature on the delivery of group psychotherapy over the Internet (see B. J. Page, 2004; Shields, 2000). An evaluation of the descriptiveness of any proposed model of group change would also be facilitated by the conduct of research programs that are larger in scope than those from which the major empirical findings on group development have been drawn. Much of the research contributed to the literature has been scattered and has been provided by a team allied to a given theoretical approach. The importance of these research efforts should not be minimized: They have been invaluable in establishing group development as a phenomenon and in pointing to key features of group process that should be taken into account in a comprehensive study of group. A. P. Beck and colleagues' (A. P. Beck, 1974; A. P. Beck, Dugo, Eng, Lewis, & Peters, 1983) work on emergent leadership is an example of an important research program identifying such a critical aspect of group process.

Multisite Studies. At this juncture, the field would benefit greatly from the establishment of a consortium of research settings that collaborate on the careful examination of changes in psychotherapy groups over time. This collaboration would enable a determination of whether the proposed models for accounting for these changes have breadth of application. As Arrow et al. (2004) wrote, "For large-scale temporal studies of groups to be feasible, we need to conduct theory-driven research with multiple groups operating under different task and contextual conditions, which suggests a shift from the individual-researcher model to more multi-site, multischolar large-scale studies" (p. 99). Such collaborations need not require the availability of multiple groups within a single setting. The use of methods such as the case-based time-series analysis with multiple observations before, during, and after treatment (Borckardt et al., 2008) will allow the individual practitioner who is running only a single group to contribute to the data pool on process–outcome relationships.

Common Measures Across Studies. As part of this collaboration, the selection of common measures for reflecting changes in groups should occur. In 1994, MacKenzie (1994a) pointed out that the field is characterized by a hodgepodge of different ways of investigating stage development with the consequence that the results of different studies cannot directly be compared with one another. Differences in findings may be due merely to differences in measures. With common measures, investigators could obtain findings that build on rather than exist in parallel to prior investigations. This building process enables cumulative knowledge rather than the fragmented and scattered set of findings currently characterizing the empirical landscape of group development research.

What measures should researchers use to capture group development? Within the group psychotherapy literature, the Group Climate Questionnaire (short version; GCQ–S) is well established and has been selected for inclusion in the Core Battery–R of the American Group Psychotherapy Association (MacKenzie & Dies, 1981). This measure asks group members to make observations about the group, not about their own position or level of satisfaction in the sessions. As Brossart, Patton, and Wood (1998) noted, "From a research perspective, having nearly every stage delineated in terms of the GCQ is a boon. It gives the researcher an advantage in interpreting results based on theory and assists with hypothesis development and testing" (p. 6). The GCQ, as Johnson et al. (2006) pointed out, has the advantage of a high level of familiarity and use among group psychotherapists—as seen in its being featured in at least 46 studies, 15 of which have linked GCQ scores to outcome. In Johnson et al.'s own study, the factor structure of the GCQ received partial support, and further research to determine the correct factor structure is needed. Work is also needed on the extension of the GCQ–S to adolescent groups (Kivlighan & Tarrant, 2001). When using the GCQ–S to determine the stages of group development, the therapist should administer it at the end of every session because a stage shift could occur within any session.

Two additional instruments, which have been cited repeatedly in this volume, have been applied primarily in the organizational psychology realm.

The Group Developmental Observation System (GDOS; Wheelan, Verdi, & McKeage, 1994), which entails the analysis of audiotapes of sessions using a group developmental system of eight categories. This system is focused on the process of members' interaction rather than the content of verbalizations. Across a number of studies (e.g., Wheelan & McKeage, 1993; Wheelan & Verdi, 1992; Wheelan & Williams, 2003), the agreement among coders ranges from 85% to 95%. The Group Development Questionnaire (GDQ; Wheelan & Hochberger, 1996) is an instrument that taps members' perceptions of the group and yields scores on four scales: Dependency/Inclusion, Counterdependency/Fight, Trust/Structure, and Work/Productivity. The psychometric properties of this instrument recommend its use. Test–retest and intraitem correlations for each of the scales are high, and evidence has been obtained for the GDQ's concurrent validity with other instruments measuring similar constructs. Construct validity has been supported through a study showing that groups that meet for longer durations perceive the group to have the characteristics associated with the more mature stages of development than groups that have met for briefer durations.

The GCQ, GDOS, and GDQ all can play a useful role in future developmental research. The GDOS and GDQ are tied somewhat more closely to developmental theory than the GCQ–S and closely capture the first four developmental stages as they have been described by Bion (1961), Stock and Thelen (1958), Tuckman (1965) and others. Given that the GCQ–S reflects the building blocks of the developmental stages rather than the stages themselves, this instrument is more suitable for considering stages beyond the standard four. The GCQ–S was designed specifically with psychotherapy groups in mind, and as such, the items easily conform to members' impressions of the group. The study of group development would be facilitated by investigations that directly compare the GCQ–S, GDOS, and GDQ to determine in which situations each is best used.

Complementing the aforementioned instruments is a tool that has great potential for expanding our awareness of developmental stages. *Conversation analysis* (CA; Sacks, 1992), a technique that was developed in the 1960s, has been used in a variety of social sciences, and has taken varied forms. Specifically, CA provides a way of studying the group that is distinct from either self-report or reports of group observers. Lepper and Mergenthaler (2005) demonstrated the promise of this technique by using a particular application of CA, computer-assisted text analysis, for a session of a psychodynamic psychotherapy group. Using this tool, they studied group cohesion as it was reflected in topic density (the proportion of a topic in a word group). Within the confines of a single session, they were able to demonstrate movement from question-and-answer responses that occur on a two-party basis to multiparty talk that involves greater reflection. From developmental models, predictions can be made across sessions concerning how conversation is likely to change. This method should help to determine whether groups show a stage progression and the particular segments when the shift from stage to stage occurs.

Sequential Analysis of Verbal Interaction (Simon & Agazarian, 1967), which is described in chapter 6 of this volume, is another tool for capturing group process across the developmental stages. This instrument was used in a process comparison of cognitive–behavioral therapy (CBT) and analytical therapy across the stages of the group by Sandahl, Lindgren, and Herlitz (2000). Methodological problems precluded the use of this study to learn about developmental stages. For example, the investigators did not analyze data from the beginning and end of the 15-session groups. Nonetheless, the investigators did show that interesting differences between the two approaches can be discerned through use of Sequential Analysis of Verbal Interaction. For example, they found that in the middle of the group's life, members of an analytic group exhibited greater empathy than CBT members whereas CBT members experienced greater competition.

Another new frontier in studying group process is the mapping of non-linear dynamic interactions using methods derived from chaos–complexity theory as seen in the research of Wheelan and Williams (2003). Also seen in their work is the use of wavelet transform images and the analysis of such features of the images as visual clarity, color, and overall tone. These methods enable the researcher to discern both what is unique about psychotherapy groups as distinct from other systems and what is unique about each group, and they will be especially useful in the pursuit of the goal identified in the "Theory Development" section of this chapter: the comparison and integration of different models of change patterns in groups.

Use of any of the aforementioned measures is preferable to another practice in the literature of basing developmental stages on the time a group has met. For example, some current investigators declare that Sessions 1 and 2 correspond to Stage 1. Throughout this text, we have discussed the fact that groups are variable in terms of the efficiency with which they proceed through a developmental stage. We have also noted that groups are capable of fixating or regressing. Hence, in the absence of any evidence that the interactional patterns, themes, or emotional reactions manifested in a session correspond to a stage, the assignment of a stage to a session is arbitrary. Given the arbitrariness of the assignment of particular stages to sessions, the continuous measurement of group processes across the life of the group is appropriate (Fuhriman & Barlow, 1994).

Attention to outcome measures is also important as investigators design studies to determine possible group development outcome links. Burlingame, Fuhriman, and Johnson (2004) saw outcome management methods as having great promise for helping researchers to determine the outcome pattern in any group. Such a method involves the creation of a database from a variety of systems, the development of norms, and the comparison of the results of any given study with those norms.

Unit of Analysis. Another methodological issue in group developmental research concerns the appropriate unit of analysis in group studies. Within the literature, arguments have been made that the fundamental unit of analysis should be the summated group reactions at any point in time on the basis of the notion that group development concerns the group as a whole. Although this point has some theoretical reasonableness, the individual's performance is critical to looking at connections between participation in the developmental stages and outcomes. An example of such a methodology is Brossart et al.'s (1998) Tuckerized growth curve analysis, which entails a longitudinal data-sampling technique that retains information about the performance of the individual; it is an ideographic approach to the study of the group. As Burlingame et al. (2004) pointed out, the key disadvantage of this technique is the complexity of the statistical analysis.

Strategic Selection of a Point of View. Future research should be designed with a careful consideration of the range of possible perspectives that can be garnered on the development of any particular group. Whose observations concerning group development are most useful—those of trained observers, naive observers, therapists, or group members—and in what circumstances? This research is useful for two reasons. First, it provides information on what type of perspective may be most useful given the research question. Second, it enables researchers to know the generalizability of findings based on one perspective to group observations from other perspectives. A burgeoning literature base addresses this question. For example, Hurley and Brooks (1988) contrasted members' and observers' observations using the GCQ–S and found a substantial level of agreement. Kacen and Rozovski (1988) studied an actual treatment group, constituted of individuals recovering from myocardial infarctions. They contrasted direct observers who attended the sessions, indirect observers who viewed taped group sessions, and the observations of the group members themselves. Observations were made at three points over the life of the 10-session group. The investigators found a high level of agreement among these three perspectives. Only 1 of 12 group processes showed a difference among the three perspectives. Both direct observers and indirect observers saw growth in self-discovery over time; participants saw greater stability in their level of self-discovery. Although this study suggests that the investigator may enjoy some flexibility in which perspective to adopt, the dimensions being assessed may suggest the desirability of one perspective over another.

Practice Implications

The theoretical and empirical work that has been generated over the last 6 decades of group work has led insufficiently to developmentally based practice guidelines. The emphasis in both theory and research has been on understanding the natural unfolding of a group—a descriptive rather than prescriptive endeavor. Psychotherapy groups are conducted to lessen members' suffering and enhance their adaptation. However, findings of work groups, psychotherapy groups, and training groups point to an association between the maturity of the group and the group's capacity to meet its stated goals. Given this association, group psychotherapists' interventions should be designed, at least in part, to facilitate the group's development. Such interventions require sets of knowledge and related skills. As noted in chapter 5 of this volume, a set of core skills must be in place that the therapist will draw on across stages. Such skills include those related to providing for members' safety, showing members' caring, fostering attention to the cognitive and emotional elements of members' immediate experience, and enabling the creation and discovery of meaning from members' experiences. The therapist must possess the ability to discern the stage of the group and to ascertain when the group is transitioning from one stage to another.

Another area that developmentally informed practice guidelines might address is composition. In the prior section on research questions, we argue that more information is needed on how participant variables influence group development. Such information may help the therapist intervene in a more sensitive and effective way as the group is underway. Yet, at times, the therapist may have greater latitude to direct the composition of the group. Developmental writers have outlined the interpersonal and leadership resources needed in the group (A. P. Beck, 1981a, 1981b; Piper, McCallum, & Azim, 1992). These writers assure us that the group will cultivate the talent needed to perform critical functions. Nonetheless, as these writers might agree, it defies credulity to imagine that some potential members might not perform these tasks as ably as others. When the therapist has the luxury of attending to composition in more than a gross way, what might be the therapist's composition strategy?

Practice guidelines should also provide direction concerning a group's desirable structural features. What is the optimal size, session length, and interval before which a new member is introduced from a developmental standpoint? What considerations should be made concerning the stages in which new members are introduced? What developmental consequences follow from having a particular leadership structure? Does it matter whether there is solo leadership, cotherapy, or a *nequipos* situation (in which a senior therapist is accompanied by a student; see Roller & Nelson, 1991)? Do the monetary practices of the therapist affect group psychotherapy? For instance, does the therapist's having a sliding scale versus fixed fee affect members' readiness to engage with one another (Stage 1) or acknowledge negative feelings toward one another and authority (Stage 2)?

Practice guidelines should also include information concerning the pedagogy of training group psychotherapists to work with developmental stages. In chapter 1 of this volume, we assert that an advantage of attention to a group developmental model is the assistance it provides the neophyte therapist in synthesizing the diverse information from different sources on the group's dynamics. Yet little is known about learning processes by which trainees can increase their ability to discern developmental cues both in the group and in their own person, to integrate disparate pieces of information, and to develop a formulation from which interventions may be devised.

INTEGRATING DEVELOPMENTAL PERSPECTIVES: A RETURN TO THE TRADITIONAL PSYCHOTHERAPY GROUP

This text, through its theoretical, empirical, and practice foci, has attempted to pull together a vast and often fragmented literature on psychotherapy group development. The purpose of this effort is to help the group psychotherapist intervene more effectively, thereby enabling the group members to realize more favorable outcomes from group treatment. Although the chapters have addressed varied aspects of group development, we hope that the group psychotherapist will access all of the areas addressed in formulating a conceptualization and developing an intervention strategy at any moment in the life of the group. To aid the reader in this task, we end with a vignette that integrates much of the material we have addressed in the earlier chapters.

Context

A group composed of five women and three men had been meeting for 9 months on a weekly basis. The group had begun with nine members, but one man left after two sessions. The therapist was unable to explore with this member his reasons for leaving. She suspected that he left because of his extreme social anxiety, the anxiety for which he sought treatment in entering the group.

Each member is characterized in terms of his or her characteristic interactional behaviors.

Bonnie is a confident White woman in her early 40s. This member often confronts others and provokes in different ways. Bonnie is frequently a focus of the group. Bonnie is a customer service representative and has been for many years.

Candy is a 20-year-old White woman who is frequently described by other members as "shooting from the hip." She exhibits a capacity to be highly empathic with other members but also has episodes of rageful outbursts. She is a college student.

Clara is a reticent White woman who emigrated from Germany 3 years ago. Although her command of English is excellent, she speaks self-consciously. She is a sensitive member who resonates to other members' expressions of loneliness and alienation. She is married with three children and does not work outside the home.

Paul is a middle-aged White man who was silent in the beginning of the group except to respond with apprehension over the departure of a member early in the group. Paul reliably expresses concern about the dangers of trusting others.

Rob is a White man in his 30s who has been active in identifying with other members in relation to a great range of psychological experiences. Earlier in his life, he pursued training to become a Franciscan monk. Currently, he is a high school teacher.

Vic is an Asian man who generally attempts to mediate differences between members of the group. His point of view is especially respected, and members actively call on him to intervene when a stalemate occurs.

Yvette is a distractible White woman whose wanderings are tolerated by the group in part because she conveys a sense of fragility and in part because the distractions are at times welcomed by members. Yvette is on disability for a physical ailment.

Sessions 37 and 38

In Session 37, the session before the one we focus on here, several members had spoken of their sexual lives. Only Rob's descriptions, however, were accompanied by the comment, "I have never told this to anyone except a close friend." Paul expressed distress at the end of the session over his perception that Rob's disclosures were too aggressively sought by two other group members, Candy and Bonnie. He stated that Rob was coerced into sharing what he termed "classified information." Paul believed that Rob would regret the disclosures. In response to Paul's concern, Rob expressed himself ambiguously as to whether he saw Paul's worry as having some substance. Candy and Bonnie responded to Paul's assertion with indignation and incredulity. Clara and Vic were perplexed and expressed some sympathy for both positions. The session ended on a tense note.

In the session, group members noted that Rob had not arrived at the time the session began.

> Paul looked irritated and murmured, "I'm not saying anything," Bonnie anxiously pointed out to the group that Rob had been late in prior sessions and "nothing was wrong—just traffic." The therapist wondered aloud what fantasies members had about Rob's absence. As if she hadn't heard the therapist's comment, Yvette, a member who routinely diverted members from difficult issues by sharing her self-preoccupations, began to talk about an argument she had had with her boyfriend. As she was narrating that conversation, Rob walked in. The group members immediately switched attention to him. Paul asked, "How are you doing?" Rob said, "It was difficult for me to come here. I thought about not coming back,

but I also wanted to return." Bonnie said she felt guilty; perhaps Paul was right that she asked Rob too many questions. She told Rob her intent was not to pressure him but merely to help him. She explained, "I remember from the orientation that in the group, you would share what you had not shared before and get relief. I wanted you to get relief." Paul wondered why group members could not see that Rob broke into a sweat somewhere in the middle of the session, a manifestation that group members were being too intrusive.

Rob then said that he believed he was giving the group a misimpression. He stated that he appreciated Paul's concern about him but he felt the caring of other group members as well. He acknowledged that he was somewhat embarrassed by what he had shared but went on to reveal that his greater sensitivity concerned his own religious doubts about his lifestyle. His description of his lifestyle reawakened these doubts. He further stated that at one time he had contemplated pursuing a religious life, and his current lifestyle was at odds with all of the values of his former self, values that were dormant but present.

Clara haltingly said that even though she was sorry that Rob was in torment over what he had shared, she was experiencing a conflict within herself as well. She said that over her time in the group, she had developed a particular fondness for Rob. At the same time, she felt herself somewhat repelled by the sexual practices he described. She perceived group members as exerting pressure on one another to say they accepted Rob's sexual behaviors. At the same time, she did not feel that she liked or respected Rob any less. Reacting to Clara's comments, Bonnie remonstrated with members to accept one another for who they were. Clara argued that accepting a member does not entail the obligation to accept all aspects of that person. The group members then formed coalitions according to their sympathy for Bonnie's ("Why should I share anything if what I reveal may be rejected?") or Clara's ("If we have to accept everything in one another, we will be forced to be inauthentic") positions.

Rob, who had been sitting quietly through these exchanges, noted that he detected a kind of split in himself. On the one hand, he saw himself as needing to accept that he had a longing to engage in certain behaviors and that he had engaged in those behaviors. On the other hand, he believed that he could separately accept or reject those behaviors as part of his future. Other members found the distinction intriguing. Some resonated to it immediately and others found it perplexing. Nonetheless, it seemed that Rob's framing led the group to realize and be willing to explore further the complexity of the enterprise of accepting oneself and others.

Subsequent Sessions

In later sessions, members continued to make significant self-disclosures. However, they appeared to be given more voluntarily rather than in response to other members' persistent questioning. Also, members evinced greater sensitivity to the disclosing member's vulnerability and generated means to support that member (e.g., by asking whether an exploration had gone far enough for a given session).

Analysis of the Vignette

This session can be considered in terms of the stage of development in which the group is residing, the demands on the therapist at this juncture in group life, the membership and contextual variables affecting group process, and the potential contribution of theories other than those typically applied to understanding group development.

Stage Development

The reader may recognize many of the features of the end of Stage 3 of our model described in chapter 4 of this volume. The level of disclosure is high, and the types of disclosures are different from those typically made in Stage 1 in that the latter are well rehearsed. In Stage 3, members feel greater safety in making disclosures that may be associated with shame. The fact that many in the group had talked about their sexual lives and that Bonnie and Candy were so insistent on Rob's sharing is typical of the disregard for boundaries shown by a Stage 3 group.

The group's capacity to work in relative independence of the therapist is another hallmark of the group's residency in a stage subsequent to the first two stages of development. For example, Paul, in taking issue with Bonnie and Candy's level of aggression in eliciting sensitive information from Rob, is performing a safety function that early in the group would be provided primarily by the therapist. However, Paul's willingness to come up against the rest of the group is an indication that another wind is blowing in the group. His assertion of an opinion that is at odds with the expressed group sentiment ("expressed" because one does not know what views are privately held) is in itself a statement of the existence of differences, an existence that is disavowed by the group in Stage 3. Within A. P. Beck and colleagues' system (A. P. Beck, 1981a; Beck, Eng, & Brusa, 1989), Paul is a cautionary leader articulating for the group the perils of absolute intimacy. Because Paul gives voice to a worry that others have held privately, he launches the formation of a new subgroup (Agazarian, 1997), the crystallization of which moves the group into the next developmental stage.

We now turn to the analysis of the session from the enriching perspectives of the leadership, member characteristics, time frame, structure, and theoretical orientations considered in chapters 6 and 7 of this volume.

Leadership

The first demand placed on the therapist was to perform a developmental assessment of the session as was done in the preceding paragraphs. In addition to the pieces of evidence identified in those paragraphs, the therapist would access his or her own internal reactions to mine their diagnostic significance. As was noted in chapter 5 of this volume, therapists within this stage may share in the dominant affect impulse constellation of the group by wishing to eradicate the boundaries that in prior stages had been so critical to the group's ability to progress. As in chapter 6 of this volume, in which Dr. Barker allowed the group to call a hospitalized member who had broken his elbow, the therapist here must participate in the group's urge to pressure members to self-disclose beyond what may be optimal for individual members. Influenced by this element, the therapist could interfere with Paul's effort to raise an objection to the doggedness and intensity of Bonnie and Marianne's questioning of Rob. If the therapist were attentive to impatience with Paul, then this information could be used to recognize both the group's residency in Stage 3 and the presence of a force in the group moving the group forward. Rather than interfering with Paul's efforts, the therapist may support him by facilitating those who agreed with Paul's position to express that fact.

Aside from monitoring his or her feelings, the therapist at this developmental juncture must be vigilant to members' proclivity to defy the boundaries that had been established for the group in the interest of establishing greater closeness among members. Readers might imagine members considering contacting Paul. The fact that this possibility did not occur to members may have been another piece of evidence suggesting that the members were moving toward Stage 4. Had the members considered contacting Paul, the therapist's assisting members in recognizing the possible motives underlying the action (e.g., the wish to deny differences) and the consequences (paradoxically, the increase in mistrust among members) might prevent members from engaging in interactional patterns that would not only hinder the group's progress but also potentially create the conditions for a regression to an earlier stage of functioning. At the same time, the therapist must be mindful of the progress the group has made in addressing past challenges and be chary of assuming a directive stance that could undermine the group's newly won independence.

Membership and Contextual Variables

An understanding of the dynamics of the session is enriched by a consideration of who is in the group and the structured features defining the group situation.

Composition. Features that contribute to each member's identity (Hays, 2007) could influence his or her cognitions, affects, and modes of relating in the group. Moreover, the respects in which members are similar to and different from one another also have a bearing on how the member negotiates this developmental juncture. For example, how members regard the sharing of a secret, particularly concerning sexual material, may have foundation in their cultural contexts. For example, Paul's cultural context may be one in which the prohibition against sharing private information, especially matters of a sexual nature, is great. He would then have a low threshold for experiencing invitations to disclosure of such material as a significant boundary violation. The therapist's appreciation of the role of culture may increase his or her attunement to disparities in members' experiences to the same event, which can enable the therapist to encourage the expression of alternate and more developmentally progressive voices than those currently having sway in the group. Variables that capture interpersonal style also have significance. For example, were the therapist to know that Bonnie has an interpersonal style characterized by a high level of dominance (see chap. 8, this volume), she might anticipate that Bonnie may perceive other members as more passive and weak and in need of her direction. The possession of this information could enable the therapist to direct Bonnie's attention to data in the group at odds with this perceptual bias.

Temporal Considerations. The temporal aspects of the group are also important. The time-unlimited nature of the group may have contributed to a more luxurious unfolding of the developmental stages. In some stage models, the phenomena of Stages 3 and 4 described in chapter 3 of this volume are not depicted as occurring sequentially. Indeed, in a short-term time frame, members may take stock of progress more aggressively, leading them to "get down to business" and enjoy the playfulness of Stage 3 fleetingly. The group in the present vignette immersed itself in a full-fledged Stage 3 that created opportunities for a heightened conflict between closeness and separateness.

Size. Structurally, the group was midsized. This feature created a circumstance in which competition for air time was not excessive. However, a sufficient number of members were present for ease of formation of subgroups. Relative membership stability characterized this group, and this stability may have contributed to the steadiness of the group's progress through the developmental stages.

The Group Through the Lens of Alternate Theories

In this book, we have presented a number of theoretical and practice perspectives on group psychotherapy. Although these in large measure have developed apart from stage models of group development, they nonetheless enrich this perspective. In this section, we focus on three of these: constructivism and social constructionism, intersubjective approaches, and cognitive and behavioral therapists.

Constructivism

Constructivism or social constructionism, as was noted in chapter 8 of this volume, provides recognition of the creative aspect of the schemes that members develop for each of the developmental stages and how these schemes play a role in modifying each member's personal narrative. Using this intellectual motif, the therapist could see Rob's act of sharing aspects of his past as a revisiting and reworking of his personal narrative, an activity for which Stage 3 provides especially rich opportunities. Paul modified his narrative in a way that allowed him to both accept himself and his past while making an independent decision about his future.

Intersubjective Approach

The intersubjective approach directs attention to the cocreated aspect of group members' experiences. Readers can see in Bonnie's statement that she understood the group to involve sharing what had not been shared with others previously as one of the workings of the group. Her encouragement of Rob was an effort to act in accordance with this notion: By helping him to open up in this obviously sensitive area, she believed that she was assisting him in realizing the purpose for his participation in the group. In a more traditional theoretical vein, Bonnie's manner of interacting with Rob can be understood in terms of her history and the construction of self and others that she developed as a consequence of this history. However, the intersubjective standpoint demands an acknowledgment that the frame the therapist created, emerging out of his or her own subjectivity, informed the struggles members experienced in their ongoing interactions. The disclosure prescription without further instruction, direction, or explanation invited the emergence of personal boundary crossings that may have been experienced by some other members as insensitive. Furthermore, the therapist's silence during the exchanges was understandably seen by Bonnie and some others as a condoning of their work with Rob. Had the therapist admitted the way in which her own subjectivity affected Bonnie, she would have cultivated Bonnie's sensitivity to seeing the effects of the expression of her own subjectivity on others.

Another aspect of the intersubjective analysis might have been the exploration of enactments. From the intersubjective perspective, enactments are inevitable, and in this group, a possible enactive sequence was Rob's unaddressed tardiness. What was contained in members' single-minded focus on his discomfort? One interpretation may be that this behavior is merely consistent with a Stage 3 repudiation of boundaries. Another interpretation is that through his lateness, Rob was at once expressing anxiety at being "fed" by the group and restoring an external empty space to match a familiar sense of emptiness inside (Bledin, 2006). A third interpretation, as Meissner (2006) noted, is that tardiness can be an expression of independence and autonomy. The group's fantasy seemed to be that through their disregard for Rob's personal boundaries, they had destroyed him as a member. Possibly the acceptance of his late arrival was an act of restitution: Members were giving back to Rob his ability to determine his own behavior in the group. Such an interpretation might be consistent with a developmental move toward separation—a transition often precipitated by an adverse experience with efforts to achieve total closeness. From an intervention standpoint, by refraining from confronting Rob on his tardiness and allowing the group's reaction to the boundary transgression to unfold in the form of an enactment, the group's pastiche of psychological contents becomes available for exploration.

Cognitive and Behavioral Therapies

The structural perspective would have been especially useful in supporting members' transfer of insights gleaned in the group to the world outside. Cognitive and behavioral models help members acquire skills in recognizing cognitive–affective connections, be they momentary automatic thoughts and their accompanying affects or broad schema providing the substrate of thinking and the affective constellations these schema stimulate when activated. Within a cognitive–behavioral model, the therapist would sculpt a process wherein Clara could identify the automatic thoughts she had that led her to accede to the group's pressure to respond inauthentically. Such a thought may have been, "If these members don't approve of every belief I express in this group, I must be bad," a thought that she learns is associated with depressive affect. By helping her articulate this thought in a precise way and spot its presence whenever it arises in response to group events, the therapist is supporting Clara's skill in engaging in this process in her extragroup life. Such a technique would be especially important were this group to be conducted within a short-term time frame. Additionally, the structured approaches would attune the therapist to encourage members to offer more specific feedback to one another and to recognize the achievement of microsteps toward goals.

CONCLUSION

In this chapter, our survey of the status of theory, research, and practical applications has led to an integrative focus on a single session in one particular group. We have seen how analysis of the group can be enriched by a focus on stages, member characteristics, leadership, group composition and size, and time frame. We have also seen how alternate theories can enrich any therapist's understanding of group process.

Historically, the study of group development has been focused on the question of whether progressive stages exist. We believe, in light of extant research, our own clinical observations, and those of other group psychotherapists, that the statement that progressive models of group development, including our own, possess at least descriptive value and can be applied to the current practice of group psychotherapy, regardless of therapists' theoretical orientations.

GLOSSARY

activity monitoring: Predominantly practiced by cognitive and behavioral therapists, involving a record in which clients record their activities for a specified period of time.

adaptive contingency model: A model of group change that predicts that changes occur on the basis of external and internal contingencies with the superordinate goal of enhancing a system's capacity to adjust to the environment.

anomie: A psychological state in which a collapse in societal norms occurs, placing the individual in a circumstance of not knowing what is expected of him or her (Merton, 1957).

antigroup: A term coined by Nitsun (1996), who described a group process wherein members act to ensure the dismantling of the group.

apparent diversity: A set of differences that are evident to group members (Haley-Banez & Walden, 1999).

Automatic Thought Record: A formatted written diary that clients keep to help them identify thoughts, feelings, and behaviors at the time when they are distressed, used in cognitive–behavioral therapy.

automatic thoughts: Cognitions, usually negative, initially outside of awareness that affect the way individuals feel and behave.

barometric event: An event identified by Bennis and Shepard (1956) by which the members are unified in a symbolic expression of revolt against the leader (see chap. 3, this volume, p. 38).

basic assumption group: A form of group dynamics in which members exhibit primitive interactional, cognitive, emotional, and motivational patterns (see chap. 3, this volume, pp. 33–34).

chi-square (χ^2): A statistic used to determine whether two or more groups of categorical variables or responses are significantly different in counts of categorical responses between two (or more) independent groups.

cognitive distortions: Thoughts, usually negative, that are distorted from reality and/or functionally maladaptive.

cognitive restructuring: A technique originally examined by Meichenbaum (1977) that helps clients identify maladaptive or distorted cognitions; challenge their underlying assumptions; and correct, change, and replace those assumptions and eventually cognitions with more adaptive ones.

consensual validation: A final subphase of a group in which members evaluate their progress and their relationships with one another (see chap. 3, this volume, p. 39).

constructivism: A postmodern philosophical and psychological orientation that investigates how an individual's cognitive structures affect how experience is organized and meaning is found in experience (Franklin, 1995).

contagion: A group phenomenon in which members show a hypnotic level of submissiveness to the direction of others and place a premium on the group welfare over their own (see chap. 3, this volume, p. 29).

counterdependence subphase: In the counterdependence–fight subphase, members communicate their dissatisfaction with the leader, which leads to the **resolution–catharsis subphase**. *See also* **dependence phase**.

credibility gap: The phenomenon wherein members see positive feedback about themselves as having greater accuracy than negative feedback.

cyclic models: A theoretical account of group life such as Schutz's (1958) description of a group proceeding through recursive loops of phases with the absence of any progression. An invariant order through the phases is not necessarily assumed.

defiant leader: Identified by A. P. Beck (1974) and colleagues as a type of leader who expresses caution over the dangers inherent in intimacy and conformity.

dependence phase: A period of group life posited by Bennis and Shepard (1956) to involve members' grappling with their stance toward authority. In the dependence–flight subphase, members flee from the ambiguity of the group situation and their feelings of helplessness while operating under the conviction that any assistance to be had in the group will come from the leader. *See also* **counterdependence subphase, resolution–catharsis subphase**.

discriminant function analysis: A statistic similar to analysis of variance but computed when no experimental manipulation has been performed. It is used to predict which of several variables measured will discriminate between naturally occurring groups.

dissipativeness: An aspect of a system that pertains to the constant exchange of information in which a system and the broader environment in which it is embedded engage.

emotional leader: Identified by A. P. Beck (1974) as the type of leader who provides others with emotional support and fosters cohesion among members.

enchantment–flight: According to Bennis and Shepard (1956), the first subphase of the interdependence phase in which members exhibit positive affects and deny the differences among them (see chap. 3, this volume, p. 38).

feed-forward system: A structure that determines what information a group or a member obtains from other members as the group progresses.

group efficacy: The group's confidence in its ability to perform tasks.

group-level phenomena: Thematic and interactional patterns that are seen within the group as a whole that are not necessarily seen within the subunits of the group (subgroups, dyads, or individual members).

growth curve analysis: A statistic used when an analysis of multiple data points is needed. It is a multilevel analysis that can analyze individual differences and group pattern differences.

immanent leadership: A style of leadership in which the therapist works collaboratively with members (Campbell, 1964/1976).

inapparent diversity: A set of differences among members that may not be evident at the outset but may become evident over the course of the group.

independence: Postulated by Bennis and Shepard (1956) to be a phase of group life in which members recognize their reliance on one another for any progress they are to make in the group.

intersubjectivism: A theoretical orientation to treatment that embraces a postmodern epistemology, sees the therapist's and patient's experiences as cocreated, and relies on the mingling of patient and therapist subjectivities as the medium through which therapeutic goals are accomplished.

irreversibility: A feature of complex systems that refers to the notion that the present status of a system is a result of the entirety of its history.

life cycle model: A type of developmental model that describes the group as proceeding through a series of phases leading to the group's demise (akin to the individual's trajectory from birth to death).

mindfulness: Turning one's attention to one's immediate state. The practice encourages nonjudgmental observation of whatever thought or feeling is experienced in the moment.

mood monitoring: A technique used by both cognitive and behavioral therapists in which clients regularly, typically daily, rate their moods usually on a scale of 1 to 100.

narrative: An individual's or group's story that provides meaning and continuity to experience.

nequipos: A situation in which the senior therapist is accompanied by a student (Roller & Nelson, 1991).

nonlinearity: A characteristic of dynamical systems in which a direct relationship does not exist between a perturbation to a living system and its effect within the system.

parataxic distortions: Perceptions based on past and typically early experiences that are not aligned with present circumstances.

positive psychology: An orientation that seeks to enhance psychological functioning and facilitate an individual's movement toward his or her goals. The emphasis is on health and well-being rather than symptoms.

postmodernism: A contemporary movement that rejects the epistemological assumption of modernity that objective truth can be known.

pregroup phase: A period of group life that predates Stage 1 as it has been characterized in most models. It occurs in groups composed of members who are distinguished by their difficulty in trusting others. Members in a pregroup phase show behaviors suggestive of alienation and difficulty identifying with one another.

punctuated equilibrium model: A model proposed by Gersick (1988) and others by which groups develop patterns early in their histories and continue with that pattern until a major force alters the pattern. The group stabilizes in that pattern until the next force influences the group. This model is an alternative to the progressive developmental model featured extensively in this text.

rebiographing: A process of revising an individual's life narrative so that it contributes to the individual's well-being (Howard, 1990).

resolution–catharsis subphase: Postulated by Bennis and Shepard (1956) to be a subphase of the dependence phase in which members who are relatively unconflicted in relation to dependency needs. This subphase helps the group to approach their feelings toward the leader in a more direct way than they have done thus far in the group's life.

scapegoat: A member who is rejected by other members of the group following their projecting on him or her their unwanted psychological contents.

scapegoat leader: Identified by A. P. Beck (1974) and colleagues to be the type of leader who provides members with examples and support for members' acknowledgment of conflict and differences.

schemas: Underlying maladaptive recurrent patterns that are brought into awareness during the course of cognitive therapy.

self-organization: A property of living systems enabling individuals to move from chaos to order without external influence.

sensitivity group movement: A social development emerging in the 1960s involving the use of groups to foster individual growth, improvement in interpersonal relations, and greater understanding of group dynamics, typically through a focus on here-and-now experiences (see chap. 3, this volume, p. 27).

sensitivity to initial conditions: A property of living systems by which systems are highly and disproportionately affected by events occurring early in the life of a system or group.

social constructionism: A postmodern philosophical and psychological orientation that explores the individual's relationship to his or her context and the meanings he or she attributes to experiences (Franklin, 1995).

social entrainment model: A model (Kelly & McGrath, 1988) that sees living systems as functioning in rhythm with one another.

social skills training: A behavioral approach to the acquisition of specific social skills (e.g., beginning a conversation) that uses a group format. It involves presenting the specific steps, demonstrating the steps, role-playing, and providing feedback.

systematic desensitization: A procedure for reducing anxiety by identifying and rank ordering stimuli that create anxiety in the client. The client is exposed to each identified stimulus in order beginning with the least anxiety provoking stimuli. When the client's anxiety has dissipated in the presence of the first and least anxious event, the therapist proceeds to the next stimulus, continuing through the list until they have dealt with all anxiety-producing stimuli.

systems-centered psychotherapy: A theory of living systems developed by Agazarian (1997) and colleagues , based on general systems theory (von Bertalanffy, 1968). This theory comprehends a group developmental model that elaborates on the model of Bennis and Shepard (1956) and accounts for how the various levels of the systems of the group interrelate.

task leader: Identified by A. P. Beck (1974) and colleagues to be the leader who performs the function of ensuring that members engage in the behaviors and observe the rules that will lead to the accomplishment of the goals of the group.

transcendent leadership: A leadership style in which the therapist places him- or herself above the group and fosters the assumption that the therapist knows best how members should function in the group (Campbell, 1964/1976).

work groups: A term used in two ways. The first is theoretical: The work group, posited by Bion (1961) to contrast with basic assumption groups, is a type of group that engages in activities (or work) to fulfill the articulated goals of the group. The second use refers to groups that occur in organizational settings. The context of use makes clear which meaning of *work group* is intended.

REFERENCES

Abouguendia, M., Joyce, A. S., Piper, W. E., & Ogrodniczuk, J. S. (2004). Alliance as a mediator of expectancy effects in short-term group psychotherapy. *Group Dynamics: Theory, Research, and Practice, 8*, 3–12.

Adams-Webber, J. (1989). Kelly's pragmatic constructivism. *Canadian Psychology, 30*, 190–193.

Agazarian, Y. M. (1997). *Systems-centered therapy for groups*. New York: Guilford Press.

Agazarian, Y. M. (2004). *Systems-centered approach to inpatient group psychotherapy*. London: Kingsley.

Agazarian, Y., & Gantt, S. (2003). Phases of group development: Systems-centered hypotheses and their implications for research and practice. *Group Dynamics: Theory, Research, and Practice, 7*, 238–252.

Agazarian, Y., & Gantt, S. (2005). The systems-centered approach to the group-as-a-whole. *Group, 29*, 163–185.

Agazarian, Y., & Peters, R. (1981). *The visible and invisible group: Two perspectives on group psychotherapy and group process*. London: Routledge & Kegan Paul.

Allport, F. H. (1924). The group fallacy in relation to social science. *Journal of Abnormal and Social Psychology, 19*, 60–73.

Allport, F. H. (1961). *The contemporary appraisal of an old problem*. PsycCRITIQUES (0010-7549). Previously published in *Contemporary Psychology: A Journal of Reviews*, June 1961, Vol. 6, No. 6, 195–196. Retrieved May 30, 2008, from http://psycnet.apa.org/index.cfm?fa=main.showContent&id=2006-06023-002&view=fulltext&format=html

Alonso, A., & Rutan, S. (1984). The impact of object relations theory on psychodynamic group therapy. *American Journal of Psychiatry, 141*, 1376–1380.

Anderson, D. (2007). Multicultural group work: A force for developing and healing. *Journal for Specialists in Group Work, 32*, 224–244.

Anthony, J. (1972). The history of group psychotherapy. In H. J. Kaplan & B. J. Sadock (Eds.), *The evolution of group therapy* (pp. 1–26). New York: Dutton.

Antonuccio, D. O., Davis, C., Lewinsohn, P. M., & Breckenridge, J. S. (1987). Therapist variables related to cohesiveness in a group treatment for depression. *Small Group Behavior, 18*, 557–564.

Aries, E. (1976). Interaction patterns and themes of male, female, and mixed groups. *Small Group Behavior, 7*, 7–18.

Arrow, H. (1997). Stability, bistability, and instability in small group influence patterns. *Journal of Personality and Social Psychology, 72*, 75–85.

Arrow, H., & McGrath, J. E. (1993). Membership matters: How member change and continuity affects small group structure, process and performance. *Small Group Research, 24*, 334–361.

Arrow, H., Poole, M. S., Henry, K. B., Wheelan, S., & Moreland, R. (2004). Time, change, and development: The temporal perspective on groups. *Small Group Research, 35,* 73–105.

Astrachan, B. M., Harrow, M., & Flynn, H. (1968). Influence of the value system of a psychiatric setting on behavior in group therapy meetings. *Social Psychiatry, 3,* 165–172.

Bales, R. F. (1950). *Interaction process analysis: A method for the study of small groups.* Cambridge, MA: Addison-Wesley.

Bales, R. F., & Cohen, S. P. (1979). *SYMLOG: A manual for the case study of groups.* New York: Free Press.

Bales, R. F., & Strodtbeck, F. L. (1951). Phases in group problem solving. *Journal of Abnormal and Social Psychology, 46,* 485–495.

Barlow, S. H., & Burlingame, G. M. (2006). Essential theory, processes, and procedures for successful group psychotherapy: Group cohesion as exemplar. *Journal of Contemporary Psychotherapy, 36*(3), 107–112.

Bauer, M. S., & McBride, L. (2003). *Structured group psychotherapy for bipolar disorder: The life goals program* (2nd ed.). New York: Springer Publishing Company.

Bechdolf, A., Köhn, D., Knost, B., Pukrop, R., & Klosterkötter, J. (2005). A randomized comparison of group cognitive–behavioural therapy and group psychoeducation in acute patients with schizophrenia: Outcome at 24 months. *Acta Psychiatrica Scandinavica, 112,* 173–179.

Beck, A. P. (1974). Phases in the development of structure in therapy and encounter groups. In D. Wexsler & L. N. Rice (Eds.), *Innovations in client centered therapy* (pp. 421–462). New York: Wiley InterScience.

Beck, A. P. (1981a). Developmental characteristics of the system-forming process. In J. Durkin (Ed.), *Living groups: Group psychotherapy and general system theory* (pp. 316–332). New York: Brunner/Mazel.

Beck, A. P. (1981b). A study of phase development and emergent leadership. *Group, 5,* 48–54.

Beck, A. P. (1983). A process analysis of group development. *Group, 7,* 19–26.

Beck, A. P., Dugo, J. M., Eng, A. M., Lewis, C. M., & Peters, L. N. (1983). The participation of leaders in the structural development of therapy groups. In R. Dies & K. R. MacKenzie (Eds.), *Advances in group psychotherapy: Integrating research and practice* (pp. 137–158). New York: International Universities Press.

Beck, A. P., Eng, A. M., & Brusa, J. (1989). The evolution of leadership during group development. *Group, 13,* 155–164.

Beck, A. P., & Lewis, C. M. (2000a). Comparison of the systems of analysis: Concepts and theory. In A. P. Beck & C. M. Lewis (Eds.), *The process of group psychotherapy: Systems of analyzing change* (pp. 415–441). Washington, DC: American Psychological Association.

Beck, A. P., & Lewis, C. M. (2000b). Group A: The first five sessions. In A. P. Beck & C. M. Lewis (Eds.), *The process of group psychotherapy: Systems of analyzing change* (pp. 87–110). Washington, DC: American Psychological Association.

Beck, A. P., & Lewis, C. M. (2000c). Introduction. In A. P. Beck & C. M. Lewis (Eds.), *The process of group psychotherapy: Systems of analyzing change* (pp. 3–19). Washington, DC: American Psychological Association.

Beck, A. P., & Lewis, C. M. (2000d). *The process of group psychotherapy: Systems of analyzing change.* Washington, DC: American Psychological Association.

Beck, A. P., & Peters, L. (1981). The research evidence for distributed leadership in therapy groups. *International Journal of Group Psychotherapy, 31,* 43–71.

Beck, A. T., Rush, A. J., Shaw, B. F., & Emery, G. (1979). *Cognitive therapy of depression.* New York: Guilford Press.

Beck, A. T., & Steer, R. A. (1987). *Manual for the Revised Beck Depression Inventory.* San Antonio, TX: Psychological Corporation.

Beck, J. G., & Coffey, S. F. (2005). Group cognitive behavioral treatment for PTSD: Treatment of motor vehicle accident survivors. *Cognitive and Behavioral Practice, 12,* 267–277.

Beck, J. S. (1995). *Cognitive therapy: Basics and beyond.* New York: Guilford Press.

Beech, A. R., & Fordham, A. S. (1997). Therapeutic climate of sex offender treatment programmes. *Sexual Abuse: A Journal of Research and Treatment, 9,* 219–327.

Beech, A. R., & Hamilton-Giachritsis, C. E. (2005). Relationship between therapeutic climate and treatment outcome in group-based sexual offender treatment programs. *Sexual Abuse: A Journal of Research and Treatment, 17,* 127–140.

Bennis, W. G., & Shepard, H. A. (1956). A theory of group development. *Human Relations, 9,* 415–438.

Billow, R. M. (2003). *Relational group psychotherapy: From basic assumptions to passion.* New York: Jessica Kingsley.

Billow, R. M. (2006). The three R's of group: Resistance, rebellion, and refusal. *International Journal of Group Psychotherapy, 56,* 259–284.

Bion, W. R. (1959). *Experience in groups.* New York: Basic Books.

Bion, W. R. (1961). *Experience in groups* (2nd ed.). New York: Basic Books.

Bion, W. R. (1962). *Learning from experience.* New York: Basic Books.

Bledin, K. (2006). Empty spaces in group-analytic psychotherapy groups. *Group Analysis, 39,* 203–213.

Bloch, S., Reibstein, J., Crouch, E., Holroyd, P., & Themen, J. (1979). A method for the study of therapeutic factors in group psychotherapy. *British Journal of Psychiatry, 134,* 257–263.

Bogart, D. H. (1980). Feedback, feedforward, and feedwithin: Strategic information in systems. *Behavioral Science, 25,* 237–249.

Bolman, L. (1971). Some effects of trainers on their T groups. *Journal of Applied Behavioral Science, 7,* 309–325.

Borckardt, J. J., Nash, M. R., Murphy, M. D., Moore, M., Shaw, D., & O'Neil, P. (2008). Clinical practice as a natural laboratory for psychotherapy research: A guide to case-based time-series analysis. *American Psychologist, 63,* 77–95.

Brabender, V. (1987). Vicissitudes of countertransference in inpatient group psychotherapy. *International Journal of Group Psychotherapy, 37,* 549–567.

Brabender, V. (1988). A closed model of short-term inpatient group psychotherapy. *Hospital & Community Psychiatry, 39,* 542–545.

Brabender, V. (1997). Chaos and order in the psychotherapy group. In F. Masterpasqua & P. A. Perna (Eds.), *The psychological meaning of chaos: Translating theory into practice* (pp. 225–252). Washington, DC: American Psychological Association.

Brabender, V. (2000). Chaos, group psychotherapy, and the future of uncertainty and uniqueness. *Group, 24,* 23–32.

Brabender, V. (2002). *Introduction to group therapy.* New York: Wiley.

Brabender, V. (2006). On the mechanisms and effects of feedback in group psychotherapy. *Journal of Contemporary Psychotherapy, 36,* 121–128.

Brabender, V., & Fallon, A. (1993). *Models of inpatient group psychotherapy.* Washington, DC: American Psychological Association.

Brabender, V., & Fallon, A. (1996). Termination in inpatient groups. *International Journal of Group Psychotherapy, 46,* 81–98.

Brabender, V. A., Fallon, A. E., & Smolar, A. I. (2004). *Essentials of group therapy.* Hoboken, NJ: Wiley.

Brabender, V. M. (1985). Time-limited inpatient group therapy: A developmental model. *International Journal of Group Psychotherapy, 35,* 373–390.

Brossart, D. F., Patton, M. J., & Wood, P. K. (1998). Assessing group process: An illustration using Tuckerized growth curves. *Group Dynamics: Theory, Research, and Practice, 2,* 3–17.

Brower, A. M. (1989). Group development as constructed social reality: A social–cognitive understanding of group formation. *Social Work With Groups, 12*(2), 23–41.

Brower, A. M. (1996). Group development as constructed social reality revisited: The constructivism of small groups. *Families in Society: The Journal of Contemporary Human Services, 77,* 336–344.

Brown, N. W. (2005). Psychoeducational groups. In S. Wheelan (Ed.), *The handbook of group research and practice* (pp. 511–529). Thousand Oaks, CA: Sage.

Brusa, J., Stone, M. H., Beck, A. P., Dugo, J. M., & Peters, L. N. (1994). A sociometric test to identify emergent leader and member roles: Phase I. *International Journal of Group Psychotherapy, 44,* 79–100.

Burlingame, G. M., Earnshaw, D., Ridge, N. W., Matsmo, J., Bulkley, C., Lee, J., & Hwang, A. D. (2007). Psycho-educational group treatment for the severely and persistently mentally ill: How much leader training is necessary? *International Journal of Group Psychotherapy, 57,* 187–218.

Burlingame, G. M., Fuhriman, A. J., & Johnson, J. (2004). Current status and future directions of group therapy research. In J. L. Delucia-Waack, D. A. Gerrity, C. R. Kalodner, & M. T. Riva (Eds.), *Handbook of group counseling and psychotherapy* (pp. 651–660). Thousand Oaks, CA: Sage.

Burrow, T. (1927). The group method of analysis. *Psychoanalytic Review, 14,* 268–280.

Butler, T., & Fuhriman, A. (1983). Level of functioning and length of time in treatment: Variables influencing patients' therapeutic experience in group psychotherapy. *International Journal of Group Psychotherapy, 33*, 489–505.

Butler, T., & Fuhriman, A. (1986). Professional psychologists as group treatment providers: Utilization, training, and trends. *Professional Psychology: Research and Practice, 17*, 273–275.

Campbell, J. (1976). *The masks of God: Occidental mythology.* New York: Penguin Books. (Original work published 1964)

Caple, R. B. (1978). The sequential stages of group development. *Small Group Behavior, 9*, 470–476.

Cartwright, D., & Zander, A. (1968). *Group dynamics* (3rd ed.). Oxford, England: Harper & Row.

Castonguay, L. G., Pincus, A. L., Agras, W. S., & Hines, C. E. (1998). The role of emotion in group cognitive–behavioral therapy for binge eating disorder: When things have to feel worse before they get better. *Psychotherapy Research, 8*, 225–238.

Chang, A., Bordia, P., & Duck, J. (2003). Punctuated equilibrium and linear progression: Toward a new understanding of group development. *Academy of Management Journal, 46*, 106–118.

Chang, T., & Yeh, C. J. (2003). Using online groups to provide support to Asian American men: Racial, cultural, gender, and treatment issues. *Professional Psychology: Research and Practice, 34*, 634–643.

Chidambaram, L., & Bostrom, R. P. (1996). Group development (I): A review and synthesis of developmental models. *Group Decision and Negotiation, 6*, 159–187.

Cissna, K. (1984). Phases in group development. *Small Group Behavior, 15*, 3–32.

Cohen, B. D. (2000). Intersubjectivity and narcissism in group psychotherapy: How feedback works. *International Journal of Group Psychotherapy, 50*, 163–179.

Cohen, B. D., Ettin, M., & Fidler, J. W. (1998). Conceptions of leadership: The "analytic stance" of the group psychotherapist. *Group Dynamics: Theory, Research, and Practice, 2*, 118–131.

Cohen, B. D., & Schermer, V. L. (2002). On scapegoating in therapy groups: A social constructivist and intersubjective outlook. *International Journal of Group Psychotherapy, 52*, 89–109.

Cohn, B. R. (2005). Creating the group envelope. In L. Motherwell & J. J. Shay (Eds.), *Complex dilemmas in group therapy: Pathways to resolution* (pp. 3–12). New York: Brunner-Routledge.

Concannon, C. (1995). The senior–senior team. *Group, 19*, 71–78.

Corder, B. F., Whiteside, R., Koehne, P., & Hortman, R. (1981). Structured techniques for handling loss and addition of members in adolescent psychotherapy groups. *Journal of Early Adolescence, 1*, 413–421.

Corsini, R., & Rosenberg, B. (1955). Mechanisms of group psychotherapy. *Journal of Abnormal and Social Psychology, 51*, 406–411.

Daniell, E. (2006). *Every other Thursday: Stories and strategies from successful women scientists*. New Haven, CT: Yale University Press.

Davies, D. R., Burlingame, G. M., Johnson, J., Gleave, R. L., & Barlow, S. H. (2008). The effects of a feedback intervention on group process and outcome. *Group Dynamics: Theory, Research, and Practice, 12*, 141–154.

DeLucia-Waack, J. L., & Bridbord, K. H. (2004). Measures of group process, dynamics, climate, leadership behaviors, and therapeutic factors: A review. In J. L. DeLucia-Waack, D. A. Gerrity, C. R. Kalodner, & M. T. Riva (Eds.), *Handbook of group counseling and psychotherapy* (pp. 120–135). Thousand Oaks, CA: Sage.

Dublin, R. A. (1995). The junior–senior team. *Group, 19*, 79–86.

Dugo, J. M., & Beck, A. P. (1984). A therapist's guide to issues of intimacy and hostility viewed as group-level phenomena. *International Journal of Group Psychotherapy, 34*, 25–45.

Dugo, J. M., & Beck, A. P. (1991). Phases of co-therapy team development. In W. Roller & V. Nelson (Eds.), *The art of co-therapy: How therapists work together* (pp. 155–188). New York: Guilford Press.

Dugo, J. M., & Beck, A. P. (1997). Significance and complexity of early phases in the development of the co-therapy relationship. *Group Dynamics: Theory, Research, and Practice, 1*, 294–305.

Dunphy, D. C. (1968). Phases, roles, and myths in self-analytic groups. *Journal of Applied Behavioral Science, 4*, 195–225.

Durant, W. (1939). *The life of Greece*. New York: Simon & Schuster.

Durkheim, E. (1984). *The division of labor in society* (W. D. Hall, Trans.). New York: Free Press. (Original work published 1893)

Durkin, H. E. (1964). *The group in depth*. Oxford, England: International Universities Press.

Durkin, H. E. (1982). Change in group psychotherapy: Theory and practice: A systems perspective. *International Journal of Group Psychotherapy, 32*, 431–439.

Durkin, J. E. (Ed.). (1981). *Living groups: Group psychotherapy and general systems theory*. New York: Brunner/Mazel.

Edwards, D. J., & Kannan, S. (2006). Identifying and targeting idiosyncratic cognitive processes in group therapy for social phobia: The case of Vumile. *Pragmatic Case Studies in Psychotherapy, 2*, 1–30.

Efran, J. S., & Fauber, R. L. (1995). Radical constructivism: Questions and answers. In R. A. Neimeyer & M. J. Mahoney (Eds.), *Constructivism in psychotherapy* (pp. 275–304). Washington, DC: American Psychological Association.

Eig, A. M. (2005). The group analyst gets married: A relational perspective on working in the transference and countertransference. *Group, 29*, 407–419.

Elfant, A. B. (1997). Submergence of the personal and unique in developmental models of psychotherapy groups and their leaders. *Group Dynamics: Theory, Research, and Practice, 1*, 311–315.

Ellis, A. (1992). Group rational–emotive and cognitive–behavioral therapy. *International Journal of Group Psychotherapy, 42*, 63–80.

Emmelkamp, P. M., Mersch, P. P., Vissia, E., & Van der Halm, M. (1985). Social phobia: A comparative evaluation of cognitive and behavioral interventions. *Behaviour Research and Therapy, 23*, 365–369.

Epston, D., & White, M. (1995). Termination as a rite of passage: Questioning strategies for a therapy of inclusion. In R. A. Neimeyer & M. J. Mahoney (Eds.). *Constructivism in psychotherapy* (pp. 275–304). Washington, DC: American Psychological Association.

Evensen, E. P., & Bednar, R. L. (1978). Effects of specific cognitive and behavioral structure on early group behavior and atmosphere. *Journal of Counseling Psychology, 25*, 66–75.

Ezriel, H. (1952). Notes on psychoanalytic therapy: II, Interpretation and research. *Psychiatry, 15*, 119–126.

Farber, B. A., Berano, K. C., & Capobianco, J. A. (2006). A temporal model of patient disclosure in psychotherapy. *Psychotherapy Research, 16*, 463–469.

Farrell, M. (1976). Patterns in the development of self-analytic groups. *The Journal of Applied Behavioral Science, 12*, 523–542.

Fieldsteel, N. D. (1996). The process of termination in long-term psychoanalytic group therapy. *International Journal of Group Psychotherapy, 46*, 25–39.

Flowers, J. V., & Booraem, C. D. (1990). The effects of different t ypes of interpretations on outcome in group psychotherapy. *Group, 14*, 81–88.

Forsyth, D. R., & Burnette, J. L. (2005). The history of group research. In S. A. Wheelan (Ed.), *The handbook of group research and practice* (pp. 3–18). Thousand Oaks, CA: Sage.

Foulkes, S. H. (1964). *Therapeutic group analysis.* New York: International Universities Press.

Foulkes, S. H. (1986). *Group analytic psychotherapy: Method and principles.* London: Maresfield Library.

Franklin, C. (1995). Expanding the vision of the social constructionist debates: Creating relevance for practitioners. *Families in Society: The Journal of Contemporary Human Services, 76*, 395–406.

Freedman, S., & Hurley, J. (1980) Perceptions of helpfulness and behavior in groups. *Group, 4*, 51–58.

Freud, S. (1955). Group psychology and the analysis of the ego. In J. Strachey (Ed. & Trans.), *The standard edition of the complete psychological works of Sigmund Freud* (Vol. 14, pp. 243–258). London: Hogarth Press. (Original work published 1921)

Fuhriman, A., & Barlow, S. H. (1994). Interaction analysis: Instrumentation and issues. In A. Fuhriman & G. M. Burlingame (Eds.), *Handbook of group psychotherapy: An empirical and clinical synthesis* (pp. 191–222). New York: Wiley.

Fuhriman, A., & Burlingame, G. M. (1994). Group psychotherapy: Research and practice. In A. Fuhriman & G. M. Burlingame (Eds.). *Handbook of group psychotherapy: An empirical and clinical synthesis* (pp. 3–40). New York: Wiley.

Furr, S. (2000). Structuring the group experience: A format for designing psychoeducational groups. *Journal for Specialists in Group Work, 25*, 29–49.

Gantt, S. P., & Agazarian, Y. M. (2004). Systems-centered emotional intelligence: Beyond individual systems to organizational systems. *Organizational Analysis, 12,* 147–169.

Garland, J. (1992). The establishment of individual and collective competency in children's groups as a prelude to entry into intimacy, disclosure, and bonding. *International Journal of Group Psychotherapy, 42,* 395–405.

Garland, J., Jones, H., & Kolodny, R. (1965). A model for stages of development in social work groups. In S. Bernstein (Ed.), *Explorations in group work: Essays in theory and practice* (pp. 17–71). Boston: Milford House.

Gavin, C. (1987). *Contemporary group work* (2nd ed.). Upper Saddle River, NJ: Prentice Hall.

Gendlin, E. T. (1967). A scale for rating the manner of relating. In C. R. Rogers (Ed.), *The therapeutic relationship and its impact: A study of psychotherapy with schizophrenics* (pp. 603–611). Madison: University of Wisconsin Press.

Gergen, K. (1994). *Realities and relationships.* Cambridge, MA: Harvard University Press.

Gergen, K., & Gergen, M. (1986). Narrative form and the construction of psychological theory. In T. R. Sarbin (Ed.), *Narrative psychology: The storied nature of human conduct* (pp. 22–44). New York: Praeger Publishers.

Gersick, C. J. G. (1988). Time and transition in work teams: Toward a new model of group development. *Academy of Management Journal, 31,* 9–41.

Gersick, C. J. G. (1989). Marking time: Predictable transitions in task groups. *Academy of Management Journal, 32,* 274–309.

Gersick, C. J. G. (1991). Revolutionary change theories: A multilevel exploration of the punctuated equilibrium paradigm. *Academy of Management Review, 16,* 10–36.

Ghuman, H. S., & Sarles, R. M. (1989). Three group psychotherapy settings with long-term adolescent inpatients: Advantages and disadvantages. *Psychiatric Hospital, 19,* 161–164.

Goldfried, M. R., Decenteceo, E. T., & Weinberg, L. (1974). Systematic rational restructuring as a self-control technique. *Behavior Therapy, 5,* 247–254.

Gould, S. J. (1991). The horn of Triton. In S. J. Gould (Ed.), *Bully for brontosaurus: Reflections in natural history* (pp. 499–511). New York: Norton.

Greene, L. R., Rosenkrantz, J., & Muth, D. (1985). Borderline defenses and counter-transference: Research findings and implications. *Psychiatry, 9,* 253–264.

Haggins, K. L. (1995). An investigation of optimal theory applied to identity development. *Dissertation Abstracts International, 55,* 5553B.

Haley-Banez, L., & Walden, S. L. (1999). Diversity in group work: Using optimal theory to understand group process and dynamics. *Journal for specialists in group work, 24,* 405–422.

Haug, S., Sedway, J., & Kordy, H. (2008). Group processes and process evaluations in a new treatment setting: Inpatient group psychotherapy followed by Internet-chat aftercare groups. *International Journal of Group Psychotherapy, 58,* 35–53.

Hays, P. A. (2007). *Addressing cultural complexities in practice: A framework for clinicians and counselors* (2nd ed.). Washington, DC: American Psychological Association.

Heckel, R. V., Holmes, G. R., & Rosecrans, C. J. (1971). A factor analytic study of process variables in group therapy. *Journal of Clinical Psychology, 27,* 146–150.

Heckel, R., Holmes, G. R., & Salzberg, H. (1967). Emergence of distinct verbal phases in group therapy. *Psychological Reports, 21,* 630–632.

Heimberg, R. G., Dodge, C. S., Hope, D. A., Kennedy, C. R., Zollo, L. J., & Becker, R. E. (1990) Cognitive–behavioral group treatment for social phobia: Comparison with a credible placebo control. *Cognitive Therapy and Research, 14,* 1–23.

Hersey, P., & Blanchard, K. (1982). *Management of organizational behavior: Utilizing human resources* (4th ed.). Englewood Cliffs, NJ: Prentice Hall.

Hill, C. E. (1986). An overview of the Hill counselor and client verbal response modes category systems. In L. S. Greenberg & W. M. Pinof (Eds.), *The psychotherapeutic process: A research handbook* (pp. 131–160). New York: Guilford Press.

Hill, C. E., & O'Brien, K. (1999). *Helping skills: Facilitating exploration, insight, and action.* Washington, DC: American Psychological Association.

Homan, A. C., van Knippenberg, D., Van Kleef, G. A., & De Dreu, C. K. W. (2007). Interaction dimensions of diversity: Cross-categorization and the function of diverse work groups. *Group Dynamics: Theory, Research, and Practice, 11,* 79–94.

Horowitz, L. M., Rosenberg, S. E., Baer, B. A., Ureño, G., & Villaseñor, V. S. (1988). Inventory of interpersonal problems: Psychometric properties and clinical applications. *Journal of Consulting and Clinical Psychology, 56,* 885–892.

Horwitz, L. (1993). Group-centered models of group psychotherapy. In H. I. Kaplan & B. J. Sadock (Eds.), *Comprehensive group psychotherapy* (3rd ed., pp. 156–176). Baltimore: Williams & Wilkins.

Hoshmand, L. T. (2000). Narrative psychology. In A. E. Kazdin (Ed.), *Encyclopedia of psychology* (Vol. 5, pp. 382–387). Washington, DC: American Psychological Association.

Howard, G. S. (1990). Narrative psychotherapy. In J. K. Zeig & W. M. Munion (Eds.), *What is psychotherapy?* (pp. 199–201). San Francisco: Jossey-Bass.

Huberman, B. A., Loch, C. H., & Onculer, A. (2004). Status as a valued resource. *Social Psychology Quarterly, 67,* 103–114.

Hummelen, B., Wilberg, T., & Karterud, S. (2007). Interviews of female patients with borderline personality disorder who dropped out of group psychotherapy. *International Journal of Group Psychotherapy, 57,* 67–91.

Hurley, J. R., & Brooks, L. A. (1988). Primacy of affiliativeness in ratings of group climate. *Psychological Reports, 62,* 123–133.

Jackson, D. A. (1999). The team meeting on a rapid turnover psychiatric ward: Clinical illustration of a model for stages of group development. *International Journal of Group Psychotherapy, 49,* 41–59.

Jacobs, M., Jacobs, A., Cavior, N., & Burke, J. (1974). Anonymous feedback: Credibility and desirability of structured emotional and behavioral feedback delivered in groups. *Journal of Counseling Psychology, 21,* 106–111.

Jacobs, M., Jacobs, A., Feldman, G., & Cavior, N. (1973). Feedback: II. The "credibility gap": Delivery of positive and negative and emotional and behavioral feedback in groups. *Journal of Consulting and Clinical Psychology, 41,* 215–233.

Jacqueline, L., & Margo, T. (2005). Group cognitive–behavior therapy with family involvement for middle-school-age children with obsessive–compulsive disorder: A pilot study. *Child Psychiatry and Human Development, 36,* 113–127.

Johnson, J. E., Pulsipher, D., Ferrin, S. L., Burlingame, G. M., Davies, D. R., & Gleave, R. (2006). Measuring group processes: A comparison of the GCQ and CCI. *Group Dynamics: Theory, Research, and Practice, 10,* 136–145.

Jones, E. J., & McColl, M. A. (1991). Development and evaluation of an interactional life skills group for offenders. *Occupational Therapy Journal of Research, 11,* 80–92.

Josselson, R., & Lieblich, A. (2003). A framework for narrative research proposals in psychology. In R. Josselson, A. Lieblich, & D. P. McAdams (Eds.), *Up close and personal: The teaching and learning of narrative research* (pp. 259–274). Washington, DC: American Psychological Association.

Jourard, S. M. (1979). *Self-disclosure.* New York: Robert Krieger.

Joyce, A. S., Duncan, S. C., Duncan, A., Kipnes, D., & Piper, W. E. (1996). Limiting time-unlimited group psychotherapy. *International Journal of Group Psychotherapy, 6,* 61–79.

Joyce, A. S., Piper, W. E., & Ogrodniczuk, J. S. (2007). Therapeutic alliance and cohesion variables as predictors of outcome in short-term group psychotherapy. *International Journal of Group Psychotherapy, 57,* 269–296.

Jung, D. I., Sosik, J. J., & Baik, K. B. (2002). Investigating work group characteristics and performance over time: A replication and cross-cultural extension. *Group Dynamics: Theory, Research, and Practice, 6,* 153–171.

Kacen, L., & Rozovski, U. (1988). Assessing group processes: A comparison among group participants: Direct observers' and indirect observers' assessment. *Small Group Research, 29,* 179–197.

Kaminer, Y., Blitz, C., Burleson, J. A., Kadden, R. M., & Rounsaville, B. J. (1998). Measuring treatment process in cognitive–behavioral and interactional group therapies for adolescent substance abusers. *Journal of Nervous and Mental Disease, 186,* 407–413.

Kanas, N., Stewart, P., Deri, J., Ketter, T., & Haney, K. (1989). Group process in short-term outpatient therapy groups for schizophrenics. *Group, 13,* 67–73.

Kant, I. (1969). *Critique of pure reason.* New York: St. Martin's Press. (Original work published 1791)

Karterud, S. (1988). The influence of task definition, leadership and therapeutic style on inpatient group cultures. *International Journal of Therapeutic Communities, 9,* 231–247.

Karterud, S. (1989). A comparative study of six different inpatient groups with respect to their basic assumptions functioning. *International Journal of Group Psychotherapy, 39*, 355–376.

Katerud, S., & Urnes, O. (2004). Short-term day treatment programmes for patients with personality disorders. What is the optimal composition? *Nordic Journal of Psychiatry, 58*, 243–249.

Kaul, T. J., & Bednar, R. L. (1994). Pretraining and structure: Parallel lines yet to meet. In A. Fuhriman & G. M. Burlingame (Eds.), *Handbook of group psychotherapy: An empirical and clinical synthesis* (pp. 155–188). New York: Wiley

Kelly, G. A. (1955). *The psychology of personal constructs.* New York: Norton.

Kelly, J. R., & McGrath, J. E. (1988). *On time and method.* Newbury Park, CA: Sage.

Kendall, P. C., & Bemis, K. M. (1983). Thought and action in psychotherapy: The cognitive–behavioral approaches. In M. Herser, A. Kazdin, & A. Bellack (Eds.), *The clinical psychology handbook* (pp. 565–592). New York: Pergamon Press.

Kibel, H. D. (1987). Contributions of the group psychotherapist to education on the psychiatric unit: Teaching through group dynamics. *International Journal of Group Psychotherapy, 36*, 3–29.

Kibel, H. D. (2005). The evolution of group-as-a-whole and object relations theory: From projection to introjection. *Group, 29*, 139–161.

Kieffer, C. C. (2001). Phases of group development: A view from self psychology. *Group, 25*, 91–105.

Kiesler, D. J. (1983). The 1982 interpersonal circle: A taxonomy for complementarity in human transactions. *Psychological Review, 90*, 185–214.

Kivlighan, D. M. (1990). Quality of group member agendas and group session climate. *Small Group Research, 21*, 205–219.

Kivlighan, D. M. (1997). Leader behavior and therapeutic gain: An application of situational leadership theory. *Group Dynamics: Theory, Research, and Practice, 1*, 32–38.

Kivlighan, D. M., & Angelone, E. O. (1992). Interpersonal problems: Variables influencing participants' perception of group climate. *Journal of Counseling Psychology, 39*, 468–472.

Kivlighan, D. M., & Goldfine, D. C. (1991). Endorsement of therapeutic factors as a function of stage of group development and participant interpersonal attitudes. *Journal of Counseling Psychology, 38*, 150–158.

Kivlighan, D. M., & Jauquet, C. (1990). Quality of group member agendas and group session climate. *Small Group Research, 21*, 205–219.

Kivlighan, D. M., Jauquet, C. A., Hardie, A. W., Francis, A. M., & Hershberger, B. (1993). Training group members to set session agendas: Effects on in-session behavior and member outcome. *Journal of Counseling Psychology, 40*, 182–187.

Kivlighan, D. M., & Lilly, R. L. (1997). Developmental changes in group climate as they relate to therapeutic gain. *Group Dynamics: Theory, Research, and Practice, 1*, 208–221.

Kivlighan, D. M., Marsh-Angelone, M., & Angelone, E. O. (1994). Projection in group counseling: The relationship between members' interpersonal problems and their perception of the group leader. *Journal of Counseling Psychology, 41,* 99–104.

Kivlighan, D. M., McGovern, T. V., & Corazzini, J. G. (1984). Effects of content and timing of structuring interventions on group therapy process and outcome. *Journal of Counseling Psychology, 31,* 363–370.

Kivlighan, D. M., & Mullison, D. (1988). Participants' perception of therapeutic factors in group counseling: The role of interpersonal style and stage of group development. *Small Group Behavior, 19,* 452–468.

Kivlighan, D. M., Multon, K. D., & Patton, M. J. (2000). Insight and symptom reduction in time-limited psychoanalytic counseling. *Journal of Counseling Psychology, 47,* 50–58.

Kivlighan, D. M., & Tarrant, J. M. (2001). Does group climate mediate the group leadership-group member outcome relationship? A test of Yalom's hypotheses about leadership priorities. *Group Dynamics: Theory, Research, and Practice, 5,* 220–234.

Klein, M. (1948). *Contributions to psycho-analysis, 1921–45.* London: Hogarth.

Klein, R. H., & Kugel, B. (1981). Inpatient group psychotherapy from a systems perspective: Reflections through a glass darkly. *International Journal of Group Psychotherapy, 31,* 311–328.

Kosoff, S. (2003). Single-session groups: Applications and areas of expertise. *Social Work With Groups, 26*(1), 29–45.

Kutter, P. (1995). Levels and phases in group process. *Group Analysis, 28,* 191–205.

Kuypers, B., Davies, D., & Hazewinkel, A. (1986). Developmental patterns in self-analytic groups. *Human Relations, 39,* 793–815.

La Coursiere, R. (1980). *The life cycle of groups: Group developmental stage theory.* New York: Herman Sciences Press.

Lang, A. J., & Craske, M. G. (2000). Panic and phobia. In J. R. White & A. S. Freeman (Eds.), *Cognitive–behavioral group therapy for specific problems and populations* (pp. 63–97). Washington, DC: American Psychological Association.

Laube, J. J. (1998). Therapist role of narrative group psychotherapy. *Group, 22,* 227–243.

Laube, J. J., & Trefz, S. (1994). Group therapy using a narrative theory framework: Application to the treatment of depression. *Journal of Systemic Therapies, 13,* 29–37.

Lazarus, A. A. (1981). *The practice of multimodal therapy.* New York: McGraw-Hill.

Leary, J. (1957). *Interpersonal diagnosis of personality.* New York: Ronald Press.

Le Bon, G. (1960). *The crowd.* New York: Viking. (Original work published 1895)

Lee, F., & Bednar, R. L. (1977). Effects of group structure and risk taking disposition on group behavior, attitudes, and atmosphere. *Journaling of Counseling Psychology, 24,* 191–199.

Leichtentritt, J., & Shechtman, Z. (1998). Therapist, trainee, and child verbal response modes in child group therapy. *Group Dynamics: Theory, Research, and Practice, 2,* 36–47.

Lepper, G., & Mergenthaler, E. (2005). Exploring group process. *Psychotherapy Research, 15,* 433–444.

Lese, K., & MacNair-Semands, R. (2000). The Therapeutic Factors Inventory: Development of a scale. *Group, 24,* 303–317.

Levine, J. M., & Moreland, R. L. (1990). Progress in small group research. *Annual Review of Psychology, 41,* 585–634.

Lewin, K. (1948). *Resolving social conflicts: Selected papers on group dynamics.* New York: Harper & Row.

Lewin, K. (1951). *Field theory in social science: Selected theoretical papers* (D. Cartwright, Ed.). New York: Harper & Row.

Lewin, R. (1992). *Complexity: Life at the edge of chaos.* New York: Macmillan.

Lewis, C. M., & Beck, A. P. (1983). Experiencing level in the process of group development. *Group, 7,* 18–26.

Lewis, C. M., & Beck, A. P. (2000). A summary of the application of the systems of analysis to Group A, Session 3. In A. P. Beck & C. M. Lewis (Eds.), *The process of group psychotherapy: Systems for analyzing change* (pp. 443–467). Washington, DC: American Psychological Association.

Lewis, C. M., Beck, A. P., Dugo, J. M., & Eng, A. M. (2000). The group development process analysis measures. In A. P. Beck & C. M. Lewis (Eds.), *The process of group psychotherapy: Systems for analyzing change* (pp. 221–261). Washington, DC: American Psychological Association.

Lewis, M. D., & Junyk, N. (1997). The self-organization of psychological defenses. In F. Masterpasqua & P. A. Perna (Eds.), *The psychological meaning of chaos: Translating theory into practice* (pp. 41–73). Washington, DC: American Psychological Association.

Lieberman, M. A., Yalom, I., & Miles, M. B. (1973). *Encounter groups: First facts.* New York: Basic Books.

Lively, K. J., & Powell, B. (2006). Emotional expression at work and at home: Domain, status, or individual characteristics? *Social Psychology Quarterly, 69,* 17–38.

Livingston, M. S., & Livingston, L. R. (2006). Sustained empathic focus and the clinical application of self-psychology theory in group psychotherapy. *International Journal of Group Psychotherapy, 56,* 67–92.

Lonergan, E. C. (1995). Discussion. *Group, 19,* 100–107.

MacColl, G. J. (2007). A 9-11 parent support group. *International Journal of Group Psychotherapy, 57,* 347–366.

MacKenzie, K. R. (1983). The clinical application of the group climate measure. In R. R. Dies & K. R. MacKenzie (Eds.), *Advances in group psychotherapy: Integrating research and practice* (pp. 159–170). Madison, CT: International Universities Press.

MacKenzie, K. R. (1987). Therapeutic factors in group psychotherapy: A contemporary view. *Group, 11*, 26–34.

MacKenzie, K. R. (1990). *Introduction to time-limited group psychotherapy.* Washington, DC: American Psychiatric Press.

MacKenzie, K. R. (1994a). Group development. In A. Fuhriman & G. M. Burlingame (Eds.), *Handbook of group psychotherapy: An empirical and clinical synthesis* (pp. 223–268). New York: Wiley.

MacKenzie, K. R. (1994b). Where is here and when is now? The adaptational challenge of mental health reform for group psychotherapy. *International Journal of Group Psychotherapy, 44*, 407–428.

MacKenzie, K. R. (1996). Time-limited group psychotherapy. *International Journal of Group Psychotherapy, 46*, 41–60.

MacKenzie, K. R. (1997). Clinical application of group development ideas. *Group Dynamics: Theory, Research, and Practice, 1*, 275–287.

MacKenzie, K. R., & Dies, R. R. (1981). *Core battery (clinical outcome results).* New York: American Group Psychotherapy Association.

MacKenzie, K. R., Dies, R. R., Coché, E., Rutan, S. J., & Stone, W. N. (1987). An analysis of AGPA Institute groups. *International Journal of Group Psychotherapy, 37*, 55–74.

MacKenzie, K. R., & Livesley, W. J. (1983). A developmental model for brief group therapy. In R. R. Dies & K. R. MacKenzie (Eds.), *Advances in group psychotherapy: Integrating research and practice* (pp. 101–116). New York: International Universities Press.

MacKenzie, K. R., & Livesley, W. J. (1984). Developmental stages: An integrating theory of group psychotherapy. *Canadian Journal of Psychiatry, 29*, 247–251

MacKenzie, K. R., Livesley, W. J., Coleman, M., Harper, H., & Park, J. (1986). Short-term therapy for bulimia nervosa. *Psychiatric Annals, 16*, 699–708.

MacKenzie, K. R., & Tschuschke, V. (1993). Relatedness, group work, and outcome in long-term inpatient psychotherapy groups. *Journal of Psychotherapy Practice and Research, 2*, 147–156.

MacNair-Semands, R. R. (2002). Predicting attendance and expectations for group therapy. *Group Dynamics: Theory, Research, and Practice, 6*, 219–228.

MacNair-Semands, R., & Lese, K. (2000). Interpersonal problems and the perception of therapeutic factors in group therapy. *Small Group Research, 31*, 158–174.

Mahoney, M. J., & Moes, A. J. (1997). Complexity and psychotherapy: Promising dialogues and practical issues. In F. Masterpasqua & P. A. Perna (Eds.), *The psychological meaning of chaos: Translating theory into practice* (pp. 177–198). Washington, DC: American Psychological Association.

Malan, D. H., Balfour, F. H. G., Hood, V. G., & Shooter, A. (1976). Group psychotherapy: A long-term follow-up study. *Archives of General Psychiatry, 33*, 1303–1315.

Mann, J. (1981). The core of time-limited psychotherapy: Time and the central issue. In S. H. Budman (Ed.), *Forms of brief psychotherapy* (pp. 25–43). New York: Guilford Press.

Mann, R. D. (1966). The development of the member–trainer relationship in self-analytic groups. *Human Relations, 19*, 84–117.

Mann, R. D., Gibbard, G. S., & Hartman, J. J. (1967). *Interpersonal styles and group development: An analysis of the member–leader relationship.* New York: Wiley.

Marshall, J. E., & Heslin, R. (1975). Boys and girls together: Sexual composition and the effect of density and group size on cohesiveness. *Journal of Personality and Social Psychology, 31*, 952–961.

Martin, D. J., Garske, J. P., & Davis, M. K. (2000). Relation of the therapeutic alliance with outcome and other variables: A meta-analytic review. *Journal of Consulting and Clinical Psychology, 68*, 438–450.

Martin, E. A., Jr., & Hill, W. F. (1957). Toward a theory of group development: Six phases of therapy group development. *International Journal of Group Psychotherapy, 7*, 20–30.

Martin, J. L., & Fuller, S. (2004). Gendered power dynamics in intentional communities. *Social Psychology Quarterly, 67*, 369–384.

Masterpasqua, F., & Perna, P. (Eds.). (1997). *The psychological meaning of chaos: Translating theory into practice.* Washington, DC: American Psychological Association.

Maugham, W. S. (1915). *Of human bondage.* New York: Modern Library.

Maultsby, M. C., Jr. (1975). *Help yourself to happiness.* New York: Institute for Rational Emotive Therapy.

Maultsby, M. C., Jr. (1991). Prescribed therapeutic self-help for the elderly: The rational behavioral approach. In P. K. H. Kim (Ed.), *Serving the elderly: Skills for practice* (pp. 137–166). New York: Aldine De Gruyter.

McDougall, W. (1920). *The group mind: A sketch of the principles of collective psychology with some attempt to apply them to the interpretation of national life and character.* New York: Putnam.

McDougall, W. (1923). *Outline of psychology.* London: Methuen.

McGrath, J. E. (1991). Time, interaction, and performance (TIP): A theory of groups. *Small Group Behavior, 22*, 147–174.

McGrath, J. E., Arrow, H., & Berdahl, J. L. (2000). The study of groups: Past, present, and future. *Personality and Social Psychology Review, 4*, 95–105.

McLees, E., Margo, G., Waterman, S., & Beeber, A. (1992). Group climate and group development in a community meeting on a short-term inpatient psychiatric unit. *Group, 16*, 18–30.

McLeod, P. L., & Kettner-Polley, R. B. (2004). Contributions of psychodynamic theories to understanding small groups. *Small Group Research, 35*, 333–361.

McRoberts, C., Burlingame, G. M., & Hoag, M. J. (1998). Comparative efficacy of individual and group psychotherapy: A meta-analytic perspective. *Group Dynamics: Theory, Research, and Practice, 2*, 101–117.

McWilliams, N. (1994). *Psychoanalytic diagnosis: Understanding personality structure in the clinical process.* New York: Guilford Press.

Meichenbaum, D. (1977). *Cognitive–behavior modification: An integrated approach.* New York: Plenum Press.

Meichenbaum, D., & Novaco, R. (1985). Stress inoculation: A preventative approach. *Issues in Mental Health Nursing, 7,* 419–435.

Meissner, W. W. (2006). Time on my hands: The dilemma of the chronically late patient. *Psychoanalytic Psychology, 23,* 619–643.

Merton, R. K. (1957). *Social theory and social structure.* Glencoe, IL: Free Press.

Miller, M. (2008). The emotionally engaged analyst I: Theories of affect and their influence on therapeutic action. *Psychoanalytic Psychology, 25,* 3–25.

Moreno, J. K. (2007). Scapegoating in group psychotherapy. *International Journal of Group Psychotherapy, 57,* 93–104.

Morran, D. K., Stockton, R., Cline, R. J., & Teed, C. (1998). Facilitating feedback exchange in groups: Leader interventions. *Journal for Specialists in Group Work, 23,* 257–268.

Mueser, K. T., Valenti-Hein, D., & Yarnold, P. R. (1987). Dating-skills groups for the developmentally disabled: Social skills and problem solving versus relaxation training. *Behavior Modification, 11,* 200–228.

Munich, R. L. (1993). Group dynamics. In H. I. Kaplan & B. J. Sadock (Eds.), *Comprehensive group psychotherapy* (3rd ed., pp. 21–32). Baltimore: Williams & Wilkins.

Myers, L. J. (1993). *Understanding an Afrocentric worldview: Introduction to an optimal psychology* (2nd ed.). Dubuque, IA: Kendall/Hunt.

Neimeyer, R. A. (1993). An appraisal of constructivist psychotherapies. *Journal of Consulting and Clinical Psychology, 61,* 221–234.

Neimeyer, R. A. (1995a). The challenge of change. In R. A. Neimeyer & M. J. Mahoney (Eds.), *Constructivism in psychotherapy* (pp. 111–126). Washington, DC: American Psychological Association.

Neimeyer, R. A. (1995b). Client-generated narratives in psychotherapy. In R. A. Neimeyer & M. J. Mahoney (Eds.), *Constructivism in psychotherapy* (pp. 231–246). Washington, DC: American Psychological Association.

Neimeyer, R. A., & Stewart, A. E. (2000). Constructive and narrative psychotherapies. In C. R. Snyder & R. E. Ingram (Eds.), *Handbook of psychological change* (pp. 337–357). New York: Wiley.

Nickerson, A. B., & Coleman, M. N. (2006). An exploratory study of member attraction, climate, and behavioral outcomes of anger-coping group therapy for children with emotional disturbance. *Small Group Research, 37,* 115–139.

Nitsun, M. (1996). *The anti-group: Destructive forces in the group and their creative potential.* London: Routledge.

Oei, T. P., Bullbeck, K., & Campbell, J. M. (2006). Cognitive change process during group cognitive behaviour therapy for depression. *Journal of Affective Disorders, 92,* 231–241.

Oei, T. P., & Kazmierczak, T. (1997) Shorter communications: Factors associated with dropout in a group cognitive behaviour therapy for mood disorders. *Behaviour Research and Therapy, 35,* 1025–1030.

Ogden, T. (1997). *Reverie and interpretation.* Northvale, NJ: Jason Aronson.

Ogrodniczuk, J. S. (2006). Men, women, and their outcome in psychotherapy. *Psychotherapy Research, 16*, 453–462.

Ogrodniczuk, J. S., & Piper, W. E. (2003). The effect of group climate on outcome in two forms of short-term group therapy. *Group Dynamics: Theory, Research, and Practice, 7*, 64–76.

O'Leary, J. V., & Wright, F. (2005). Social constructivism and the group as a whole. *Group, 29*, 257–276.

Orlinsky, D. E., & Howard, K. I. (1966). *Therapy Session Report (Form T)*. Chicago: Institute of Juvenile Research.

Page, A. C., & Hooke, G. R. (2003). Outcomes for depressed and anxious inpatients discharged before or after group cognitive behavior therapy: A naturalistic comparison. *Journal of Nervous and Mental Disease, 191*, 653–659.

Page, B. J. (2004). Online group counseling. In J. L. DeLucia-Waack, D. A. Gerrity, C. R. Kalodner, & M. T. Riva (Eds.), *Handbook of group counseling and psychotherapy* (pp. 609–620). Thousand Oaks, CA: Sage.

Pasternak, J. (2005). Sizing up the group. In L. Motherwell & J. J. Shay (Eds.), *Complex dilemmas in group therapy: Pathways to resolution* (pp. 17–20). New York: Brunner-Routledge.

Perna, P. A., & Masterpasqua, F. (1997). Introduction: The history, meaning, and implications of chaos and complexity. In F. Masterpasqua & P. A. Perna (Eds.), *The psychological meaning of chaos: Translating theory into practice* (pp. 1–19). Washington, DC: American Psychological Association.

Persons, J. B. (1989). *Cognitive therapy in practice: A case formulation approach*. New York: Norton.

Pescosolido, A. T. (2001). Informal leaders and the development of group efficacy. *Small Group Research, 32*, 74–93.

Peters, L. N., & Beck, A. P. (1982). Identifying emergent leaders in psychotherapy groups. *Group, 6*, 35–40.

Phipps, L. B., & Zastowny, T. R. (1988). Leadership behavior, group climate and outcome in group psychotherapy: A study of outpatient psychotherapy groups. *Group, 12*, 157–171.

Piaget, J. (1960). *The child's conception of the world*. Oxford, England: Littlefield, Adams.

Pifalo, T. (2006). Art therapy with sexually abused children and adolescents: Extended research study. *Art Therapy, 23*(4), 181–185.

Pines, M., & Hutchinson, S. (1993). Group analysis. In A. Alonso & H. I. Swiller (Eds.), *Group therapy in clinical practice* (pp. 29–47). Washington, DC: American Psychiatric Press.

Pinkham, A. E., Gloege, A. T., Flanagan, S., & Penn, D. L. (2004). Group cognitive–behavioral therapy for auditory hallucinations: A pilot study. *Cognitive and Behavioral Practice, 11*, 93–98.

Piper, W. E., Debbane, E. G., Garant, J., & Bienvenu, J. P. (1979). Pretraining for group psychotherapy. *International Journal of Group Psychotherapy, 32*, 309–325.

Piper, W. E., McCallum, M., & Azim, H. F. A. (1992). *Adaptation to loss through short-term group psychotherapy*. New York: Guilford Press.

Piper, W. E., Ogrodniczuk, J. S., Joyce, A. S., Weideman, R., & Rosie, J. S. (2007). Group composition and group therapy for complicated grief. *Journal of Consulting and Clinical Psychology, 75*, 116–125.

Piper, W. E., Rosie, J. S., Joyce, A. S., & Azim, H. F. A. (1996). *Time-limited day treatment for personality disorders: Integration of research and practice in a group program*. Washington, DC: American Psychological Association.

Prigogine, I., & Stengers, I. (1984). *Order out of chaos*. New York: Bantam Books.

Puder, R. S. (1988). Age analysis of cognitive–behavioral group therapy for chronic pain outpatients. *Psychology and the Aging, 3*, 204–207.

Racker, H. (1972). The meanings and uses of countertransference. *Psychoanalytic Quarterly, 41*, 481–506.

Radomile, R. R. (2000). Obesity. In J. R. White & A. S. Freeman (Eds.), *Cognitive–behavioral group therapy for specific problems and populations* (pp. 99–126). Washington, DC: American Psychological Association.

Real, T. (1990). The therapeutic use of self in constructionist/systemic therapy. *Family Process, 29*, 255–272.

Reilly, P. M., Shopshire, M. S., Durazzo, T. C., & Campbell, T. A. (2002). *Anger management for substance abuse and mental health clients: Participant workbook* (DHHS Pub. No. SMA 02-3662). Rockville, MD: Center for Substance Abuse Treatment, Substance Abuse and Mental Health Services Administration. Retrieved February 1, 2008, from http://www.kap.samhsa.gov/products/manuals/pdfs/anger2.pdf

Rice, C., & Rutan, J. (1981). Boundary maintenance in inpatient therapy groups. *International Journal of Group Psychotherapy, 31*, 297–309.

Riess, H. (2005). Containing contagion. In L. Motherwell & J. J. Shay (Eds.), *Complex dilemmas in group therapy: Pathways to resolution* (pp. 258–261). New York: Brunner-Routledge.

Roback, H. B., Ochoa, E., Bock, F., & Purdon, S. (1992). Guarding confidentiality in clinical groups: The therapist's dilemma. *International Journal of Group Psychotherapy, 42*, 81–103.

Robison, F. F., & Hardt, D. A. (1992). Effects of cognitive and behavioral structure and discussion of corrective feedback outcomes on counseling group development. *Journal of Counseling Psychology, 39*, 473–481.

Rogers, C. (1970). *On encounter groups*. New York: Harper & Row.

Roller, B., & Nelson, V. (1991). *The art of co-therapy: How therapists work together*. New York: Guilford Press.

Rose S. (1977). *Group therapy: A behavioral approach*. Paramus, NJ: Prentice Hall.

Rose, S. D., Tollman, R. M., & Tallant, S. (1985). Group process in cognitive–behavioral therapy. *Behavior Therapist, 8*(4), 71–75.

Rothke, S. (1986). The role of interpersonal feedback in group psychotherapy. *International Journal of Group Psychotherapy, 36*, 225–240.

Runkel, P. J., Lawrence, M., Oldfield, S., Rider, M., & Clark, C. (1971) Stages of group development: An empirical test of Tuckman's hypothesis. *Journal of Applied Behavioral Science, 7,* 180–193.

Rutan, S., & Stone, W. (1993). *Psychodynamic psychotherapy* (2nd ed.). New York: Guilford Press.

Rutan, S., & Stone, W. (2001). *Psychodynamic psychotherapy* (3rd ed.). New York: Guilford Press.

Rybak, C. J., & Brown, B. M. (1997). Group conflict: Communication patterns and group development. *Journal for Specialists in Group, 22,* 31–42.

Rychlak, J. F. (2003). *The human image in postmodern American.* Washington, DC: American Psychological Association.

Sacks, H. (1992). *Lectures in conversation* (Vols. 1–2). Oxford, England: Blackwell.

Sandahl, C., Lindgren, A., & Herlitz, K. (2000). Does the group conductor make a difference? Communication patterns in group-analytically and cognitive-behaviorally oriented therapy groups. *Group Analysis, 33,* 333–351.

Scheidlinger, S. (1982). On the concept of the "Mother-group." In S. Scheidlinger (Ed.), *Focus on group psychotherapy: Clinical essays* (pp. 75–87). New York: International Universities Press.

Scheidlinger, S. (2006). A historical addendum to Billow's (2005) review of Lipgar and Pines' edited volumes on W. R. Bion. *International Journal of Group Psychotherapy, 56,* 495–500.

Schermer, V. L. (2005). An orientation to the two-volume special edition: The group-as-a-whole: An update. Can open-ended group move beyond beginnings? *Group, 29,* 109–137.

Schermer, V. L. (2006). Book review of *Relational group psychotherapy: From basic assumptions to passion. Group, 30,* 71–74.

Schermer, V., & Klein, R. H. (1996). Termination in group psychotherapy from the perspectives of contemporary object relations theory and self psychology. *International Journal of Group Psychotherapy, 46,* 99–115.

Schiller, L. Y. (2007). Not for women only: Applying the relational model of group development with vulnerable populations. *Social Work With Groups, 30*(2), 11–26.

Schopler, J. H., & Galinsky, M. J. (1990). Can open-ended groups move beyond beginnings? *Small Group Research, 21,* 435–449.

Schutz, W. C. (1958). *FIRO: A three-dimensional theory of interpersonal behavior.* New York: Holt, Rinehart, & Winston.

Seeger, J. A. (1983). No innate phases in group problem solving. *Academy of Management Review, 8,* 683–689.

Seers, A., & Woodruff, S. (1997). Temporal pacing in task forces: Group development or deadline pressure. *Journal of Management, 23,* 169–187.

Sexton, H. (1993). Exploring a psychotherapeutic change sequence: Relating process to intersessional and posttreatment outcome. *Journal of Consulting and Clinical Psychology, 61,* 128–136.

Shechtman, Z. (2007a). *Group counseling and psychotherapy with children and adolescents*. Mahwah, NJ: Erlbaum.

Shechtman, Z. (2007b). How does group process research inform leaders of counseling and psychotherapy groups? *Group Dynamics: Theory, Research, and Practice, 11*, 293–304.

Shechtman, Z., & Gluk, O. (2005). An investigation of therapeutic factors in children's groups. *Group Dynamics: Theory, Research, and Practice, 9*, 127–134.

Shechtman, Z., & Halevi, H. (2006). Does ethnicity explain functioning in group counseling? The case of Arab and Jewish counseling trainees in Israel. *Group Dynamics: Theory, Research, and Practice, 10*(3), 181–193.

Shechtman, Z., & Yanov, H. (2001). Interpretives (confrontation, interpretation, and feedback) in preadolescent counseling groups. *Group Dynamics: Theory, Research, and Practice, 5*, 124–135.

Shields, W. (2000). The virtual universe, the open large group, and maturational processes in the future. *Group, 24*, 33–48.

Simon, A., & Agazarian, Y. (1967). *SAVI: Sequential Analysis of Verbal Interaction*. Philadelphia: Research for Better Schools.

Slater, P. (1966). *Microcosm: Structural, psychological, and religious evolution in group*. New York: Wiley.

Spivak, G., Platt, J. J., & Shure, M. B. (1976). *The problem-solving approach to adjustment*. San Francisco: Jossey-Bass.

Stacey, R. (2005). Social selves and the notion of the group-as-a-whole. *Group, 29*, 187–209.

Stern, D. (2005). Intersubjectivity. In E. S. Person, A. M. Cooper, & G. O. Gabbard (Eds.), *Textbook of psychoanalysis* (pp. 77–92). Washington, DC: American Psychiatric Association.

Stock, D., & Thelen, H. A. (1958). *Emotional dynamics and group culture*. New York: New York University Press.

Stockton, R., & Morran, D. K. (1981). Feedback exchange in personal growth groups: Receiver acceptance as a function of valence, session, and order of delivery. *Journal of Counseling Psychology, 28*, 490–497.

Stockton, R., Rohde, R. I., & Haughey, J. (1992). The effects of structured group exercises on cohesion, engagement, avoidance, and conflict. *Small Group Research, 23*, 155–168.

Stolorow, R. D. (2002). Impasse, affectivity, and intersubjective systems. *Psychoanalytic Review, 89*(3), 18–20.

Stolorow, R. D., & Atwood, G. (1992). *Contexts of being*. Hillsdale, NJ: Analytic Press.

Stolorow, R., Brandchaft, B., & Atwood, F. (1987) *Psychoanalytic treatment: An intersubjective approach*. Hillsdale, NJ: Analytic Press.

Sullivan, H. S. (1953) *Conceptions of modern psychiatry: The first William Alanson White memorial lectures* (2nd ed.). New York: Norton.

Tasca, G. A., Balfour, L., Ritchie, K., & Bissada, H. (2006). Developmental changes in group climate in two types of group therapy for binge-eating disorder: A growth curve analysis. *Psychotherapy Research, 16,* 499–514.

Thompson, L. W., Powers, D. V., Coon, D. W., Takagi, K., McKibbin, C., & Gallagher-Thompson, D. (2000). Older adults. In J. R. White & A. S. Freemand (Eds.), *Cognitive–behavioral group therapy for specific problems and populations* (pp. 235–261). Washington, DC: American Psychological Association.

Thorpe, J. J., & Smith, B. (1953). Phases in group development in treatment of drug addicts. *International Journal of Group Psychotherapy, 3,* 66–78.

Tinsely, H. E., Roth, J. A., & Lease, S. H. (1989). Dimensions of leadership and leadership style among group intervention specialists. *Journal of Counseling Psychology, 36,* 48–53.

Toseland, R., & Siporin, M. (1986). When to recommend group treatment. *International Journal of Group Psychotherapy, 36,* 172–201.

Trotzer, J. P. (1989). *The counselor and the group: Integrating theory, training and practice* (2nd ed.). Muncie, IN: Accelerated Development.

Tschuschke, V., & Dies, R. R. (1994). Intensive analysis of therapeutic factors and outcome in long-tem inpatient groups. *International Journal of Group Psychotherapy, 44,* 185–208.

Tschuschke, V., & MacKenzie, K. R. (1989). Empirical analysis of group development: A methodological report. *Small Group Behavior, 20,* 419–426.

Tschuschke, V., MacKenzie, K. R., Haaser, B., & Janke, G. (1996). Self-disclosure, feedback, and outcome in long-term inpatient psychotherapy groups. *Journal of Psychotherapy Practice and Research, 5,* 35–44.

Tuckman, B. W. (1965). Developmental sequence in small groups. *Psychological Bulletin, 63,* 384–399.

Tuckman, B. W., & Jensen, M. A. C. (1977). Stages of small-group development revisited. *Group and Organization Studies, 2,* 419–427.

Turquet, P. (1975). Threats to identity in the large group. In L. Kreeger (Ed.), *The large group: Dynamics and therapy* (pp. 87–144). Itasca, IL: Peacock.

Verdi, A. F., & Wheelan, S. (1992). Developmental patterns in same-sex and mixed-sex groups. *Small Group Research, 23,* 356–378.

Visintini, R., Ubbiali, A., Donati, D., Chiorri, C., & Maffei, C. (2007). Referral to group psychotherapy: A retrospective study on patients' personality features associated with clinicians' judgments. *International Journal of Group Psychotherapy, 57,* 515–524.

von Bertalanffy, L. (1950, January 13). The theory of open systems in physics and biology. *Science, 111,* 23–29.

von Bertalanffy, L. (1968). *General systems theory.* New York: Braziller.

Vroom, V. H., & Jago, A. G. (2007). The role of the situation in leadership. *American Psychologist, 62,* 17–24.

Weinberg, H. (2006). Regression in the group revisited. *Group, 30,* 37–53.

Weissman, A. N. (1979). The Dysfunctional Attitude Scale: A validation study (Doctoral dissertation, University of Pennsylvania, 1979). *Dissertation Abstracts International, 40,* 1389B–1390B.

Wessler, R. L., & Hankin-Wessler, S. (1989). Cognitive group therapy. In A. Freeman, K. Simon, L. Beutler, & H. Arkowitz (Eds.), *Comprehensive handbook of cognitive therapy* (pp. 559–582). New York: Plenum Press.

Wessler, R. L., & Hankin-Wessler, S. (1997). Counselling and society. In S. Palmer & V. P. Varma (Eds.), *The future of counselling and psychotherapy* (pp. 167–190). Thousand Oaks, CA: Sage.

Wheelan, S. A. (1996a). Effects of gender composition and group status differences on member perceptions of group developmental patterns, effectiveness, and productivity. *Sex Roles, 34,* 665–686.

Wheelan, S. A. (1996b). An initial exploration of the relevance of complexity theory to group research and practice. *Systems Practice, 9,* 49–70.

Wheelan, S. A. (1997). Group development and the practice of group psychotherapy. *Group Dynamics: Theory, Research, and Practice, 1,* 288–293.

Wheelan, S. A. (1999). Introduction to this special issue on group development. *Small Group Research, 30,* 3–7.

Wheelan, S. A. (2005). *Group processes: A developmental perspective* (2nd ed.). New York: Allyn & Bacon.

Wheelan, S., Burchill, C., & Tilin, F. (2003). The link between teamwork and patient outcomes in intensive care units. *American Journal of Critical Care, 12,* 527–534.

Wheelan, S. A., Buzaglo, G., & Tsumura, E. (1998). Developing assessment tools for cross-cultural group research. *Small Group Research, 29,* 359–370.

Wheelan, S. A., Davidson, B., & Tilin, F. (2003). Group development across time: Reality or illusion? *Small Group Research, 34,* 223–245.

Wheelan, S. A., & Hochberger, J. M. (1996). Validation studies of the group development questionnaire. *Small Group Research, 27,* 143–170.

Wheelan, S. A., & Kesselring, J. (2005). Link between faculty group development and elementary student performance on standardized tests. *Journal of Educational Research, 98,* 323–330.

Wheelan, S. A., & Lisk, A. (2000). Cohort group effectiveness and the educational achievement of adult undergraduate achievement. *Small Group Research, 31,* 724–738.

Wheelan, S., & McKeage, R. (1993). Developmental patterns in small and large groups. *Small Group Research, 24,* 60–83.

Wheelan, S., Murphy, D., Tsumura, E., & Kline, S. F. (1998). Member perceptions of internal group dynamics and productivity. *Small Group Research, 30,* 59–81.

Wheelan, S. A., & Tilin, F. (1999). The relationship between faculty group development and school productivity. *Small Group Research, 30,* 59–81.

Wheelan, S. A., & Verdi, A. F. (1992). Differences in male and female patterns of communication in groups: A methodological artifact? *Sex Roles, 27,* 1–15.

Wheelan, S. A., Verdi, A. F., & McKeage, R. (1994). The group development observation system (HaPI Record) [Computer software]. Pittsburgh, PA: Behavioral Measurement Database Services.

Wheelan, S. A., & Williams, T. (2003). Mapping dynamic interaction patterns in work groups. *Small Group Research, 34*, 443–467.

Whitaker, C. A. (1958). Psychotherapy with couples. *American Journal of Psychotherapy, 12*, 18–23.

White, J. R. (2000). Depression. In J. R. White & A. S. Freeman (Eds.), *Cognitive–behavioral group therapy for specific problems and populations* (pp. 29–61). Washington, DC: American Psychological Association.

White, M., & Epston, D. (1990). *Narrative means to therapeutic ends.* New York: Norton.

Winnicott, D. W. (1953). Transitional objects and transitional phenomena. *International Journal of Psychoanalysis, 34*, 89–97.

Winnicott, D. (1963). The development of the capacity for concern. *Bulletin of the Menninger Clinic, 27*, 167–176.

Wright, F. (2004). Being seen, moved, disrupted, and reconfigured: Group leadership from a relational perspective. *International Journal of Group Psychotherapy, 54*, 235–250.

Wright, F. (2005). Valuing enactments in group therapy. *Group, 29*, 399–406.

Wollin, A. (1999). Punctuated equilibrium: Reconciling theory of revolutionary and incremental change. *Systems Research and Behavioral Science, 16*, 359–367.

Yalom, I. (1970). *The theory and practice of group psychotherapy.* New York: Basic Books.

Yalom, I. (1983). *Inpatient group psychotherapy.* New York: Basic Books.

Yalom, I. (1995). *The theory and practice of group psychotherapy* (4th ed.). New York: Basic Books.

Yalom, I., & Leszcz, M. (2005). *The theory and practice of group psychotherapy* (5th ed.). New York: Basic Books.

Zaccaro, S. J. (2007). Trait-based perspectives of leadership. *American Psychologist, 62*, 6–16.

Zimbardo, P. (2007). *The Lucifer effect: Understanding how good people turn to evil.* New York: Random House.

AUTHOR INDEX

Abouguendia, M., 138
Adams-Webber, J., 206, 207
Agazarian, Y. M., 20, 32, 44–47, 51, 52, 55, 57, 58, 59, 99, 113, 117, 120, 125, 134, 142, 143, 145, 147, 204, 213, 220, 235, 257, 263
Agras, W. S., 88, 91, 166, 170
Allport, F. H., 31, 63
Alonso, A., 51
Anderson, D., 231
Angelone, E. O., 236, 237
Anthony, J., 29
Antonuccio, D. O., 136
Aries, E., 227
Arrow, H., 14, 84, 108, 251, 254, 255
Astrachan, B. M., 61, 243
Atwood, F., 213
Atwood, G., 213
Azim, H. F. A., 125, 154, 240, 259

Baer, B. A., 236
Baik, K. B., 230
Bales, R. F., 33, 41, 64, 65, 67–69, 85, 90, 172
Balfour, F. H. G., 31n2
Balfour, L., 166, 238
Barlow, S. H., 145, 147n2, 257
Bauer, M. S., 166
Beck, A. P., 34, 48, 49, 53, 66, 71, 76–79, 134, 139, 157, 158, 229, 254, 259, 263
Beck, A. T., 179, 181n1, 185
Beck, J. G., 167, 173, 177, 193
Beck, J. S., 164
Bednar, R. L., 138, 168, 169, 193
Beeber, A., 163, 246
Beech, A. R., 166, 173
Bemis, K. M., 165
Bennis, W. G., 28, 36–39, 41, 50–52, 64, 66, 69, 70, 106, 113, 117, 125, 242
Berano, K. C., 150
Berdahl, J. L., 84
Bienvenu, J. P., 193
Billow, R. M., 120, 144, 199, 217, 218
Bion, W. R., 5, 33, 36, 64–66, 69, 70, 154, 235, 239, 250, 256

Bissada, H., 166, 238
Blanchard, K., 137
Bledin, K., 266
Blitz, C., 166
Bloch, S., 72, 74
Bock, F., 43
Bogart, D. H., 150
Bolman, L., 141, 237
Booraem, C. D., 21
Borckardt, J. J., 255
Bordia, P., 60
Bostrom, R. P., 44
Brabender, V., 21, 23, 43, 51, 58, 106, 109, 125, 135, 136, 138–140, 145, 146, 151, 154, 163, 164, 206, 209, 210, 220, 241, 242, 246, 253
Brabender, V. A., 172, 226n1
Brabender, V. M., 163
Brandchaft, B., 213
Breckenbridge, J. S., 136
Bridbord, K. H., 72
Brooks, L. A., 258
Brossart, D. F., 12, 80, 240, 241, 255, 258
Brower, A. M., 56, 200, 203–205, 207, 208
Brown, B. M., 142
Brown, N. W., 164
Brusa, J., 76, 77, 263
Bullbeck, K., 166
Burchill, C., 67, 94
Burke, J., 149
Burleson, J. A., 166
Burlingame, G. M., 12, 21, 56, 67, 145, 147n2, 167, 172, 257, 258
Burnette, J. L., 63
Burrow, T., 30
Butler, T., 5, 73, 74
Buzaglo, G., 231

Campbell, J., 138
Campbell, J. M., 166
Campbell, T. A., 188
Caple, R. B., 41, 43, 106
Capobianco, J. A., 150
Cartwright, D., 63
Castonguay, L. G., 88, 91, 166, 170, 171, 193
Cavior, N., 146, 149

SUBJECT INDEX

and types of groups, 22
Diagnostic variables, 238–239
Differentiating behavior, 142
Differentiation stage, 47, 174–175
Direct approach, 72
Disagreement, 113–114
Disclosure, 177. *See also* Self-disclosure
Discriminant function analysis, 270
Disenchantment–fight subphase, 38–39
Dissipativeness, 57, 270
Distraction, 152–153
Distributed leadership, 33
Distrust, 79
Diversity, 232–235
Dominance, 236

Eating disorders, 170, 173–175, 238
"Edge of chaos," 57, 58
Education, 27
Eliciting stance, 211, 212
Embeddedness, degree of, 243
Emerging intellectual paradigms
    complexity–chaos theory, 56–59
    and group development theory, 22–23
    punctuated equilibrium approach, 59–60
    social entrainment, 60–62
Emotional leader, 48–50, 76, 77, 270
Emotional stimulation function, 136–137
Emotional ties, 30
Empathy, 30
Empirical methodology, 66
Enactments, 219–220
Enchantment–flight, 38, 270
Encounter groups, 136–137
Engagement, 47. *See also* Formation and engagement (Stage 1)
    and feedback, 21–22
    increasing, 79, 80
    in-patient, 89
    of online groups, 244
    and outcome, 92, 93
Entrainment, social. *See* Social entrainment model
Environment
    group, 241–243
    online, 244–245
Epston, D., 208
Ethnicity, 229–231
Evaluation statements, 69
Executive function, 135
External boundaries, 108

External factors, 43–44, 242
Externalization, 204–205
Ezriel, H., 34–35

Fallon, April, 5
Fantasies, 34, 35
Fault line, 235
Feedback
    and change process, 125
    and engagement, 21–22
    openness to offering, 149–150
    preparation for receiving, 139
    in social constructionism, 206
    specificity/examination of, 149
    during termination, 154–155
    therapist's role regarding, 145–147
Feed-forward system, 150, 206–207, 271
Fight–flight assumption group, 6–7
Fight–flight group, 34
Fight statements, 81, 82, 84
Five-stage model, 5–7, 176–193
Flight statements, 81, 83, 84
Force fields, 46
Formal leaders, 134
Formation and engagement (Stage 1)
    illustration of, 101–109
    in structured group therapies, 176–178
    therapist interventions in, 137–141
Forming stage, 41–42, 70
Foulkes, S. H., 35–36, 50
Four-stage model, 47–48
French Revolution, 29, 30
Freud, Sigmund, 30
Fulfillment, of treatment goals, 44–45
Functional subgrouping, 45–47

Gender, 227–229
General systems theory (GST), 32, 55, 56, 58
Gersick, C. J. G., 59–60, 85–86
Gifts, 16–17
Goals, group, 163–164
Greece, ancient, 28
Group
    as concept, 28–32
    as construct, 28
    size of, 245–246
Group as a whole
    concept of, 28
    conflict in, 34–35
    criticism of, 31
    as term, 31

Group change model, 59–60
Group climate, 78–85
    in adolescent groups, 94
    Beck's model studies on, 78–79
    MacKenzie and Livesley model studies
        on, 79–81
    Wheelan's model studies on, 81–84
Group Climate Questionnaire (GCQ), 74,
    79, 255
Group Climate Questionnaire—short ver-
        sion (GCQ–S), 79, 80, 255, 256
Group decision making, 150–151
Group development. *See also* Hypothetical
        illustration of group development
    contemporary testing of progressive-
        stage, 71–85
    contributions of research to, 64–68
    early study of, 68–71
    emerging paradigms for, 56–62
    integrating perspectives on, 260–267
    knowledge about, 249–260
    practice implications for, 258–260
    preparation session for, 162–163, 253
    structured-group-model benefits for,
        193–194
    theoretical conceptualizations of, 250–
        251
    theoretical contributions to, 55–56
    and types of structured therapies, 168–
        169
Group developmental models
    Bennis and Shepard model, 36–40
    comparative assessment of, 253–254
    early, 36–40
    Mann model, 40
    Schutz model, 40
Group Developmental Observation System
        (GDOS), 81, 84, 227, 256
Group Development Questionnaire (GDQ),
        81, 228, 256
Group efficacy, 271
Group environment, 241–243
Group-level phenomenon, 18–20, 271
Group life, 32–36
Group matrix, 35
Group membership, 163
Group mind, 29
Group prolongation, 152
Group Psychology and the Analysis of Ego (S.
        Freud), 30
Group psychotherapy
    alternate theories of, 265–267

progressive stage models applied to, 41–
    42
research on, 251–258
Group rules, 106
Group tension, 33, 35
Growth curve analysis, 67, 271
Guidance, importance of, 74

Hays, P. A., 226
Hegel, G. W. F., 198
Helplessness, sense of, 140
Heraclitus, 28
Homogeneous groupings, 238–239
Hopefulness, 74
Hostility, 144
Human annihilation, 29
Hypothetical illustration of group develop-
        ment, 99–131
    conflict/rebellion (Stage 2), 109–118
    formation/engagement (Stage 1), 101–
        109
    group-members description, 100–101
    integration/work (Stage 4), 120–126
    termination (Stage 5), 126–130
    unity/intimacy (Stage 3), 118–120

Identification
    process of, 30
    projective, 153–154
    therapist's support for, 139
Identity
    of cotherapy relationship, 157–158
    of online groups, 244
Identity variables, 226–235
    age, 231
    ethnicity, 229–231
    future research on, 231–232
    gender/status, 227–229
    and optimal theory/stage of develop-
        ment, 232–235
Immanent leadership, 138, 271
Inapparent diversity, 232, 271
Inclusion, 40, 81
Independence
    defined, 271
    from therapist, 147–148
Individual focus, 19–20
Informal leaders, 134
Inpatient groups, 87, 89–90, 243
Insight, 73
Integration and work (Stage 4)
    illustration of, 120–126

in structured group therapies, 185–188
therapist interventions in, 148–151
Intensive care units, 94–95
Interactional agenda model, 51
Interactional process analysis, 68
Interactional styles
confrontation over, 124
and personality, 235–238
Interdependence, 32, 38–40
Internal boundaries, 108–109
Internal events, 43
Internationalization stage, 40
Interpersonal approach, 18–19, 45
Interpersonal aspect, task vs., 70–71
Interpersonal conflict, 79
Interpersonal dysfunctioning, 235–236
Interpersonal learning, 55, 73–75
Interpersonal problem-solving groups, 164–165
Interpersonal-work stage, 47–48
Interpretation of findings, research contributions to, 68
Intersubjectivism, 213–220
defined, 200, 271
enactments in, 219–220
in individual/group psychotherapy, 213–214
integrating group development with, 266–267
and meanings/affect states, 215–216
and stages vs. themes in group development, 214–215
and therapist self-disclosure, 218–219
and traditional stage approaches, 216–220
Intimacy. *See also* Unity and intimacy (Stage 3)
and apartness, 125
in cotherapy relationship, 158
in interdependence phase, 38
pursuit of, 120
Invincible power, sentiment of, 29
Involvement, 108
Irreversibility, 57, 271
Isomorphic systems, 45
Isomorphism, 32
Israel, 229–230

Journaling, 207–208

Kant, Immanuel, 198
Klein, Melanie, 33, 55

Knowledge state, of group development, 249–260
practice implications, 258–260
research on group psychotherapy, 251–258
theory development, 250–251

Language, 194, 199
Lateness, 14–15, 19, 117
Leader
confronting feelings toward, 38
dissatisfaction with, 37
as parental figure, 30
uncertainty about, 37, 48
Leadership
adolescent attitudes toward, 94
in basic-assumption vs. work modes, 34
distributed, 33
functions of, 76–77
patterns of, 92–93
reorganization of, 49
sociometric measure of roles of, 66
structures of, 77
Leadership patterns, 75–78
Le Bon, Gustave, 29
Lewin, Kurt, 31–32
Life cycle model, 40, 47, 271
Lightheartedness, 125
Living human systems, 32, 45
Loss, and termination, 188–192, 208–209

MacKenzie, K. R., 69
MacKenzie and Livesley model, 79–81
MacKenzie model, 47–48, 53
Maintenance functions, 227
Mann model, 40
Matching stance, 212
Maturity, 44–45, 157, 172, 259
McDougall, W., 29–30
Meaning attribution function, 136
Meanings
and affect states, 215–216
coconstructed, 210
Measures, common, 255–257
Member characteristics, 226–239
diagnostic variables as, 238–239
identity variables as, 226–235
personality/interactional styles as, 235–238
Methodology, research contributions to, 66–67
Micropatterns, 69

and primary organizational levels, 45–47

and punctuated equilibrium approach, 59–60

and social entrainment, 60–62

and task vs. conflict emphasis, 51–54

and theoretical thinking, 55–56

therapeutic factors in, 72–75

therapy group application of, 41–42

Projective identification, 153–154

Prolongation, group, 152

Psychoeducational groups, 165, 167

Psychological work, 73

Psychotherapy group outcomes, 87–92

    inpatients, 87, 89–90

    outpatients, 90–92

Punctuated equilibrium model, 59–61, 85–86, 254, 272

Quality, of object relations, 237–238

Questions (behavior category), 68

Reactions to Group Situations Test, 69

Rebellion. *See* Conflict and rebellion (Stage 2)

Rebelliousness, 117

Rebiographing, 202, 272

Reconciliation, 129–130

Regression, 43, 44

Relationships

    forming, 112–113

    preexisting, 242

Repression, of group tension, 35

Research, on group development, 63–96

    conceptual issues in, 65–66

    contemporary, 71–85

    contributions of, 64–68

    early, 68–71

    on group climate, 78–85

    with inpatient studies, 87, 89–90

    interpretation of findings in, 68

    on leadership patterns, 75–78

    methodology problems in, 66–67

    negative findings in, 85–86

    on outcomes, 86–95

    with outpatient studies, 90–92

    with psychotherapy groups, 87–92

    statistical advances in, 67

    on therapeutic factors, 72–75

    with training groups, 92–94

    with work-settings groups, 94–95

Research, on group psychotherapy, 251–258

    developmental progress and goal achievement, 251

    in future, 252–253

    progressive stage model effectiveness, 251

    time factor, 251–252

Resolution–catharsis, 37–38, 272

Responsibility stage, 233–234

Robust equilibrium model, 61, 254

Role-playing, 208

Rome, ancient, 28

Scapegoat, 48, 272

Scapegoat leader, 49, 76, 77, 272

Scheidlinger, S., 31n2, 36

Schemas, 204, 272

Schizophrenia, 239

Schutz, W. C., 40

Schutz model, 40, 55

Security, sense of, 106, 135

Security stage, 233

Self-confrontation, 49

Self-disclosure

    and age, 231

    ambivalence toward, 150

    and cultural background, 230

    in termination stage, 152–153

    by therapist, 218–219

    therapist support for, 145

    in unity/intimacy stage, 119

Self-exploration, 77n2

Self-organization, 57–58, 272

Self psychological model, 47

Self-revelation, 73–74

Sensitivity group movement, 27, 272

Sensitivity to initial conditions, 272

Separation, 40, 108

Sequential Analysis of Verbal Interaction (SAVI), 142, 143, 257

Sexuality, 119, 145

Shepard, H. A., 36–40, 69, 70

Simultaneity, 46–47

Situational leadership model, 137

Small groups, cyclical patterns in, 68–69

Social constructionism, 199–213

    anomie in, 203–204

    constructivism vs., 199

    defined, 272

    externalization in, 204–205

    in group development, 202–209

    integration of developmental theory and, 209–213

in psychotherapy groups, 200–202
schemas in, 204
termination in, 208–209
therapist stances in, 211–213
Social entrainment model, 60–62, 272
Social phobia, 182–184, 193
Social psychology, 27
Social skills training, 165, 167–168, 272
Socioemotional functions, 33, 172–173
Sociometric measure of leadership roles, 66
Solo therapy, 158
Specificity, 193–194
Splitting, 214
Stage(s)
    as concept, 65
    number of, 47–50
    phases vs., 7, 99
    themes vs., 214–215
Stage development in group psychotherapy, 3–7
    benefits for therapists in, 4–5
    origins of, 5–7
Stage sequencing, 70
Standardization, of data collection, 66
Stanford prison experiments, 107n1
Statistical analysis, research contributions to, 67
Status, 227–229
Stereotypic subgroups, 235
Stock, D., 70
Storming stage, 42, 70
Stress-management group, 176–177
Strodtbeck, F. L., 69
Structure, degree of, 166–168
Structured group therapies, 161–195
    characteristics of, 165–166
    cognitive–behavioral, 170–176
    conflict/rebellion (Stage 2) integration with, 178–181
    content in, 166–167
    evidence for developmental potential in, 162–164
    formation/engagement (Stage 1) integration with, 176–178
    group development and types of, 168–169
    group development augmented with, 193–194
    integrating five-stage model with, 176–193
    integration/work (Stage 4) integration with, 185–188

process in, 167–168
termination (Stage 5) with, 188–192
types of, 164–165
unity/intimacy (Stage 3) integration with, 181–185
Student groups, 24, 95
Subgrouping, 45–46, 106–107
Subgroups
    in complexity theory, 59
    in disenchantment–fight subphase, 38–39
    formation of, 18–20
    in Stage 2, 112–113
Subsystems, interrelationships among, 32
Supportive statements, 83
Symptoms, shared set of, 166, 167, 238–239
Systematic desensitization, 273
Systems, interrelationships among, 32
Systems-centered psychotherapy, 44, 273
Systems centered therapy (SCT), 45–47

Taking stock, 39
Task
    emphasis on conflict vs., 51–54
    interpersonal aspect vs., 70–71
Task accomplishment, 39–40
Task functions, 33
Task groups, 22
Task leader, 48–50, 76, 273
Tavistock Clinic, 33
Technological advances, 67
Tension, regulation of group, 33
Termination stage
    illustration of, 126–130
    in life cycle models, 47
    of MacKenzie model, 48
    of online groups, 245
    social constructionism views on, 208–209
    in structured group therapies, 188–192
    therapist interventions in, 151–156
Terrorist events, 29n1
Testiness, 6
T-groups, 41
Thelen, H. A., 69–70
Themes, stages vs., 214–215
Theoretical history of group development, 27–42. *See also* Progressive stage models
    Robert Bales's contributions to, 33
    Bennis and Shepard model, 36–40
    Wilfred Bion's contributions to, 33–34

ABOUT THE AUTHORS

Virginia Brabender, PhD, ABPP (Cl), is the associate dean and director of the Institute for Graduate Clinical Psychology of Widener University, Chester, Pennsylvania, where she also directs a concentration on group psychotherapy in the doctoral psychology program. She has run outpatient and inpatient groups, the latter at Friends Hospital in Philadelphia, Pennsylvania, where she conducted research on time-limited groups. Dr. Brabender has authored or coauthored three prior books on group psychotherapy, including *Models of Inpatient Group Psychotherapy* with April Fallon, and she is on the editorial board of the *International Journal of Group Psychotherapy*, for which she serves as editor of the video review section. Dr. Brabender is a fellow of the American Psychological Association's Division 49 (Group Psychology and Group Psychotherapy).

April Fallon, PhD, is a member of the psychology faculty at Fielding Graduate University, Santa Barbara, California, and an associate professor in the Department of Psychiatry at Drexel University College of Medicine, Philadelphia, Pennsylvania. Dr. Fallon received her PhD from the University of Pennsylvania in 1981. She has collaborated with Virginia Brabender on several other books, including *Models of Inpatient Group Psychotherapy* and *Awaiting the Therapist's Baby: A Guide for Expectant Parents and Essentials in Group Psychotherapy*. She has also taught and written on topics such as psychological assessment, women's issues, body image, and aggression.